THE SHI'ITE RELIGION

AMS PRESS
NEW YORK

The Golden Dome in Mashhad after the Russian Bombardment of 1912

Frontispiece]

THE SHI' ITE RELIGION

A HISTORY OF ISLAM IN PERSIA AND IRAK

BY

DWIGHT M. DONALDSON, D.D., Ph.D.

MASHHAD, PERSIA

LONDON

LUZAC & COMPANY

46 GREAT RUSSELL STREET, W.C. 1

1933

Library of Congress Cataloging in Publication Data

Donaldson, Dwight M.
The Shi'ite religion.

Reprint. Originally published: London: Luzac, 1933. (Luzac's Oriental religions series; vol. 6)
Bibliography: p.
Includes index.
1. Shi'ah. I. Title.
BP193.5.D66 1984 297'.82 84-45104
ISBN 0-404-18959-8

AMS PRESS, INC.
56 East 13th Street, New York, N.Y. 10003

Reprinted from the edition of 1933, London. Trim size has been slightly altered. Original trim: 14.5 x 23.7 cm.

MANUFACTURED IN THE UNITED STATES OF AMERICA

TO MY WIFE

Companion in Study and Travel

PREFACE

In 1924 Professor Browne wrote that "we still possess no comprehensive and authoritative statement of Shi'a doctrine in any European language" (*Persian Literature in Modern Times*, p. 418). While this book was not undertaken with such an inclusive ambition, yet it would be gratifying if it would in some measure further the study of Shi'ite Islam. An effort has been made to interest readers who are not already conversant with the subject, for numerous stories have been included from the lives of the Imams and their companions; and the pilgrimage cities, where the shrines with the golden domes are located, have been recently visited. The western traveller is seriously limited, however, in his personal observations, for he is not permitted to enter these shrines; but after sixteen years' residence in Mashhad, it has been possible to study at close range the largest of the pilgrimage cities, and to therefore undertake to describe them by giving an outline of their history, and by showing in a concrete way the hope and faith of the thousands of Muhammadans in India, Persia, Mesopotamia, Syria and Egypt who make these long journeys for the forgiveness of their sins.

The primary sources for the study of both the Sunnite and the Shi'ite traditions are in Arabic, and while extensive use has also been made of Persian books, and of the works of European and American authors, yet the patience and friendship of several "Arabic" professors has been frequently recalled with gratitude—Professor Jewett of Harvard, and Professors Macdonald and Shellabear of the Kennedy School of Missions in Hartford, where part of the book was written in the first place as a thesis on *The Twelve Imams*, in partial fulfilment of the requirements for the degree of Ph.D. Professor Nicholson of Cambridge University graciously gave the first manuscript his valuable criticism, and when Professor Jackson of Columbia University was in Mashhad several years ago, he read the original outline and gave the kind advice "not to give it up." Personal thanks are due to Dr. Samuel M. Zwemer, the editor of *The Moslem World*, and to Dr. Robert E. Speer of the Presbyterian Board of Foreign Missions, for their part in stimulating interest in further research in regard to the Shi'ites of Persia. Opportunity is taken to also mention affectionately my mother and sister, whose encouragement has made them partners in my work in this distant land.

That the Persian and Arabic names may appear less formidable in transliteration, " j " has been used for the Arabic " jim " in preference to the " *dj* " that is employed in the Encyclopædia of Islam ; and the initial " ain," as distinguished from the " alif," is indicated by a dot under its appropriate vowel. In the text, long vowels are marked with the accent only occasionally, whereas in the index an effort has been made to have the pronunciation of all names and Arabic terms fully shown. The references that have been utilized are shown in the footnotes, but the Classified Bibliography includes the works of additional authorities that are of special value for more detailed investigation of particular aspects of the subject.

DWIGHT M. DONALDSON.

Mashhad, Persia.

January 2nd, 1933.

CONTENTS

CHAPTER V

CHAPTER VI

CHAPTER VII

CHAPTER VIII

CHAPTER IX

CHAPTER X

CHAPTER XI

CHAPTER XII

CHAPTER XIII

CHAPTER XIV

CHAPTER XV

CHAPTER XVI

CHAPTER XVII

CHAPTER XVIII

CHAPTER XIX

CHAPTER XXIII

CHAPTER XXIV

CHAPTER XXV

CHAPTER XXVI

CHAPTER XXVII

PAGE

THE EARLIEST COLLECTIONS OF SHI'ITE TRADITIONS - 281

No collections of Muslim traditions from the Umayyad period.—The conflict of Malik ibn Anas with political authorities.—How traditions favourable to Ạli survived.—The variety of traditions collected by Ahmad ibn Ḥanbal.—The influence of the Ạbbasids on the canonical collections.—The fate of an-Nasá'í for reading Ạlíd traditions in Damascus.—Accepted without protest in other parts of the empire.—Tirmidhi on the "Virtues of the Household of the Prophet."—Impetus to collectors of Shi'ite *ḥadith* under the Buwaihids.—Biographical information concerning Shi'ite traditionists.—Kulaini, and the *Káfi fi Ilm ad-Dín*.—Ṣaduḳ (Ibn Babuwaihi) and the *Man la yahḍuruhu'l-Faḳíh*.—Ṭusí, and the *Tahdhíb* and the *Istibsár*.—Shi'ite collections influenced by doctrine of infallibility of the Imams. Contents of the *Usulu'l-Káfi*.—A brief Harmony of "the four books" of Shi'ite traditions.

CHAPTER XXVIII

LATER SHI'ITE SCHOLARS AND THEOLOGIANS - - - 291

Tendency of conquering peoples to prefer opposite sect of Islam.—Shi'ite theologians suppressed during periods of Sunnite supremacy. The fall of the Buwaihids ended preferential treatment for Shi'ites.—Shaikh Ṭabarsi the only Shi'ite theologian under the Seljuks.—Extent of Shi'ite participation in the Crusades.—Great Shi'ite scholars under the Mongols.—The works of the "Sage of Hilla."—For 150 years the Shi'ites were again suppressed.—The Rise of the Safavids.—Theologians of the Safavid period.

CHAPTER XXIX

THE DOCTRINE OF THE IMAMATE - - - - - - 305

The question as to whether an Imam was necessary.—Opinion of orthodox Shi'ite scholars.—Discussion of the meaning of the word *imám*.—Argument from the kindness of God.—An Imam required as the guardian of the Law.—Advantages from the Imam in concealment.—Analogy from the mind, "the *imám* of the senses."—"Man a little universe."—The Imamate on the authority of God and the Apostle.—The Faith has no other need so real as that for an Imam.

CHAPTER XXX

THE "SINLESSNESS" OF THE PROPHETS AND THE IMAMS - 320

Statement of the doctrine.—Majlisi's nine proofs for the necessity of the belief.—No limitation to the sinlessness of the Imams.—On the authority of the Ḳoran (Surah ii, 118).—The doctrine explained and confirmed by traditions.—Psychological explanations.—The prophets and apostles are of "four degrees."—Purity of "those of the Household" (Surah xxxiii, 33).—Majlisi undertakes to reply to objections.

CHAPTER XXXI

CHAPTER XXXII

CHAPTER XXXIII

LIST OF ILLUSTRATIONS

INTRODUCTION

NATIONAL unity has never been achieved quickly. The apparent rapidity with which Muḥammad succeeded in uniting the free tribes of Arabia must not be understood to be as complete and thorough going as it was spectacular. The isolated desert homes of the Arab tribes lay between the Romans and the Persians. The protection of the desert was effective, and neither of the two great empires had been able to deprive them of their tribal independence. When however a "prophet" arose among them who interpreted for them things they had begun to hear about from other tribes and peoples, this brought them something of a world vision. He called them to monotheism and gave them an intelligible relationship between themselves and other monotheistic peoples. The stories of Abraham and Joseph and Moses fit into their own environment so well that they looked with contempt upon the changed life of the dwellers in cities, and they readily came to regard themselves, with a conscious sense of their superiority, as the true representatives of the religion of Abraham.

Once the Arab tribes had come together, under the leadership of Muḥammad, they felt the influence of their numbers and recognized also that it was Islam that had brought an inspiring unity of purpose to tribes accustomed to war upon one another. It is doubtful indeed whether their proselytizing zeal would have been sufficient, of itself, to have carried them over the long marches against the neighbouring countries. That larger assertion of their place in the world occurred after the death of Muḥammad, and that because of a great economic necessity that kept pressing them forward. "A vigorous and energetic people, driven by hunger and want," were "to leave their inhospitable deserts and overrun the richer lands of their more fortunate neighbours." (Arnold, *Preaching of Islam*, p. 46.)

A modern instance of what happened in Arabia through the influence of a great leader was worked out during the World War. With British encouragement the Arab tribes united under King Faisal in revolt against Turkey. The unique position of the leader in this movement, holding the tribes together, was not unlike that of Muḥammad among the forebears of those same tribes some fourteen hundred years ago. Perhaps a picture of King Faisal carrying on his delicate work may help the reader imagine the extremely difficult political problems that faced Muḥammad.

" Faisal swore new adherents solemnly on the Koran between his hands, ' to wait while he waited, march when he marched, to yield obedience to no Turk, to deal kindly with all who spoke Arabic (whether Baghdadi, Aleppine, Syrian, or pure blooded), and to put independence above life, family, and goods.' He also began to confront them at once, in his presence, with their tribal enemies, and to compose their feuds. An account of profit and loss would be struck between the parties, with Faisal modulating and interceding between them, and often paying the balance, or contributing towards it from his own funds, to hurry on the pact During two years Faisal so laboured daily, putting together and arranging in their natural order the innumerable tiny pieces which made up Arabian society, and combining them into his own design of war against the Turks. There was no blood feud left active in any of the districts through which he had passed, and he was Court of Appeal, ultimate and unchallenged, for western Arabia. He showed himself worthy of this achievement. He never gave a partial decision, nor a decision so impracticably just that it must lead to disorder. No Arab ever impugned his judgments, or questioned his wisdom and competence in tribal business. By patiently sifting out right and wrong, by his tact, his wonderful memory, he gained authority over the nomads from Medina to Damascus and beyond. He was recognized as a force transcending tribe, superseding blood-chiefs, greater than jealousies. The Arab movement became in the best sense national, since within it all Arabs were at one, and for it private interests must be set aside ; and in this movement chief place, by right of application and by right of ability, had been properly earned by the man who filled it for those few weeks of triumph and longer months of disillusion after Damascus had been set free." (Lawrence, *Revolt in the Desert,* p. 61.)

Muḥammad's task had however been still more difficult. With a group of outcasts from his own tribe he had taken refuge with the despised tradesmen of Medina, and eight years elapsed before he acquired authority in Mecca. After two more years he made a pilgrimage to the Ka'ba, a pilgrimage that was a veritable procession of triumph, and in his company there was a magnificent representation of the tribes. But it was on his return from this journey to Mecca that he fell ill, and in a few days after he reached his home in Medina he died. Of necessity the immediate question was, "Who will take his place?" Any one of several men of strong character, who would have made determined leaders, could have been chosen from among those who had been his close companions. But they were not prophets, and strictly in this capacity there was no one who could take his place, for he had expressly declared himself to be the "seal," or the last, of the prophets. And he had no son to succeed him as a general chief of the united tribes. Yet there was no hope that the Arab tribes would hold together without some virtual successor to Muḥammad, someone to be their leader in interpreting the system of religion that he had taught them and to exercise his judicia and political authority.

The vital question of a successor for Muḥammad quickly revived the old inter-tribal jealousies and revealed the temporary nature of the merely war-time unity that had been achieved. The rise of this question of succession marks the beginning of the most radical and long continued division in Islam. Who was to be the vicegerent of Muḥammad? Had he so "designated" Ạli, his son-in-law, the father of his two grandsons? Or did he expect his successor to be chosen by the leaders of the people in an assembly of some kind? Did his request that his father-in-law, Abu Bakr, should act in his place as leader in the prayers at the mosque indicate that he intended by this to show his wish that Abu Bakr should succeed him? These were questions that rent

Islam in twain, that led eventually to civil war, and that furnished the historical setting for the development of the doctrine of the Imamate.

The party who maintained that Muḥammad had definitely " designated " Ạli, his son-in-law, to be the *imám* or " leader " of his people were known as the *Shi'at Ạli*, the followers or partisans of Ạli. In their vast literature they have elaborately and repeatedly described what they consider to be the divinely ordered institution of the *Imámate*, which is the order of *what ought to be*, by the expressed intention of God and the command of the Prophet. The functions of the Caliph, according to the Shi'ites, belonged rightfully to the Imam, but owing to the vanity, perversity and disloyalty of particular men from among the Companions of the Prophet, the rightful Imam was displaced. It is true that Ạli did secure a belated tenure of office in the Caliphate, after three of these usurpers had preceded him, but Ạli was soon murdered, and from that time until the present no true Imam has ever been Caliph. The terms *Cáliphate* and *Imámate* are sometimes used as though they were interchangeable by Arabian writers who have believed in the Caliphate and have looked with disdain upon the alleged institution of the Imamate, but it will save confusion to restrict the term Imamate to the divinely designated succession of leaders who have been acknowledged by the Shi'ites.

According to " orthodox " Shi'ite belief there have been twelve of these Imams. They were not a group of contemporaries, like the Twelve Apostles of Jesus, but Muḥammad designated the first one, and after that each one designated his successor. The " historic Imamate," or the period of this series of Twelve Imams, lasted through the two hundred and twenty-eight years following the death of Muḥammad. It is the central institution of Shi'ite Islam, and the fact that the Imams failed to retain the actual political supremacy in the empire that went with the Caliphate does not weaken the Shi'ite belief in their inherent right to it, or in their intellectual and moral infallibility. Thus we shall see that in order to establish any particular teaching by authority from the Prophet, the Shi'ite theologian needs only to show confirming traditions that can be traced to one or more of the Imams, for it was their function to continue to exercise the prerogatives of Muḥammad and to guide the believers in the interpretation of the Ḳoran and the traditions.

To compare the two principal divisions in Islam with the Catholics and the Protestants in the Christian Church would be misleading, for both the Sunnites and the Shi'ites are essentially Catholic in theory, in that they both call for a vicegerent of the Prophet on earth. It may be remarked, however, that if the theoretical Imamate of the Shi'ites had ever come to its own in secular and spiritual authority, it would have outstripped the Papacy in its most golden age. As has been observed by a discerning orientalist who is himself a Catholic (H. Lammens, *Islam, Beliefs and Institutions*, p. 147):

"Unlike the Sunni Caliph, a temporal leader deprived of all authority in the matter of dogma, guardian merely of the *Sharī'a* and civil defender of Islam, the Shi'a Imam becomes its Pontiff and infallible teacher. He is not only Muḥammad's temporal successor, but also the inheritor of his dignity, from which he has received the super-eminent prerogatives of witness and interpreter of the revelation. He is in very sooth a religious and spiritual leader, with an even stronger title than that of the Pope in the Catholic Church, since to the privilege of infallibility, *ịṣma,* he adds the divine gift of impeccability. Thus he is the sole and permanent channel of all sanctifying prerogatives and illuminative inspirations."

In further explanation of the character of the Imams, authoritative statements of the doctrine of their sinlessness, *ịṣma*, as set forth by Shi'ite theologians, will be shown to have preceded by several centuries the final acceptance of the dogma of the *sinlessness of the prophets* in the *ịjma*, or consensus of opinion, of the orthodox scholars of the Sunnites. Explicit illustrations will be given also from forms of prayer that are used at the present day to show the practical side of the Shi'ite belief in *the Imams as Mediators*. Many of these prayers, and the description of the rites of pilgrimage, have been taken directly from Arabic and

Persian books that have been prepared for the special instruction of pilgrims.

The belief that the last Imam did not die, but that he disappeared miraculously over a thousand years ago, and that he is expected to return in order to bring about the complete victory of the Muslim theocratic state throughout all the world, is a doctrine that has had most important influence in Persian history. Frequently this expectation has been regarded as politically dangerous, and there have been periods when those who cherished the Shi'ite faith were subjected to severe tests and persecutions. The hope of the return of the twelfth Imam persisted, however, and was reasserted in desperation when the lands of the Shi'ites suffered from the ravages of the Mongols, the Tartars, the Turks, and the Afghans; and when the shrines of their sainted Imams were repeatedly desecrated, and those who refused to take refuge in the doctrine of *takiyya* (dissimulation) were ruthlessly massacred. But in the beginning of the sixteenth century, this belief in the authority of the hidden Imam made such headway that under the Safavid dynasty Shi'ite Islam became the official religion of Persia. This continued waiting for the Imam to reappear has given rise to heretical sects, for in addition to the various schools of Shi'ites that arose from factions that occurred at the death of an Imam, always over the question of succession, there have been other sects, such as the Sháikhís, Bábís, and Baháies, that owe their origin rather to the recurring centuries of disappointment that the hidden Imam does not return.

CHAPTER I

THE QUESTION OF SUCCESSION

THE study of the Imamate requires an examination of traditions that have been woven into the history and theology of Islam. In the first place, the Shi'ites lay great emphasis on the tradition that when Muḥammad was returning from his farewell pilgrimage to Mecca, he stopped at a place known as Ghadir Khum, and there he announced to those who were with him that it was his desire that Ạli should be his successor. The most important one of the classical Arabian historians, in his sympathetic use of traditions favourable to the house of Ạli, is Ibn Wadih al-Yaḳubi (d. after A.D.891), who gives the least embellished account of what is believed to have been said by the Prophet at Ghadir Khúm.[1]

" Muḥammad set out at night, straight for Medina. When he came to a place in the vicinity of al-Juhfa which was called Ghadir Khum, on the eighteenth of the month Dhu'l-Hijja, he stood up to deliver an inspired utterance. Taking the hand of Ali ibn Abu Ṭalib, he said, ' Am I not dearer to the believers than their own lives ? ' They replied, ' Yes, O Apostle of God.' He then declared ' Whoever recognises me as his master, *mawlá*, will know Ạli as his master.[2] He went on to say, ' O ye people, I will now go ahead of you, and you will meet me at the drinking fountain in Paradise. And I will ask you when you arrive concerning two treasures, so

[1] " Ibn Wadih al-Yaḳubi," writes Professor Nicholson (*L.H.A.*, p. 349), " a contemporary of Dinawari, produced an excellent compendium of universal history, which is especially valuable because its author, being a follower of the house of 'Ali, has preserved the ancient and unfalsified Shi'ite tradition." This *History*, edited in two volumes by Professor Houtsma (Leyden, 1883), is one of the earliest and most important works of the Shi'ites.

[2] This tradition is given repeatedly by Ahmad ibn Hanbal, *Musnad*, I, 84, 118, 119, 152, 330. Further references are given by Wensinck, *H.E.M.T.*, p. 15.

be careful how you look after them.' They inquired, 'What treasures, O Apostle of God?' He answered, 'The greatest treasure is the Book of God, because it is from him, given as it were by the hand of God, and entrusted to your hands. Hold fast to it and do not lose it and do not change it. The other treasure is the line of my descendants, the People of the Household.'"[1]

Fully four years before the stop at Ghadir Khum, but also on the eighteenth of Dhu'l-Hijja, when Muḥammad was on his way back from the expedition to al-Hudáibiya, he is said to have made this statement, "He whose master I am has also Ạli for his master."[2] The expedition to al-Hudaibiya was spoken of as the "farewell to the infidels,"[3] and the last pilgrimage to Mecca was called the "farewell pilgrimage."[4] As the essential utterance of the Prophet was the same on both occasions, there is an evident possibility of the one tradition being a repetition of the other. Against this suggestion, however, there is a noteworthy sequence of events that would point rather to the probability that the same utterance was delivered on the two occasions. When in the year 6 A.H. Muḥammad made the expedition to al-Hudaibiya, he had no living son, and his two grandsons, Hasán and Husáin, the sons of Ạli and Fatima, were at that time little boys of three and four years of age. It could only be by the recognition of Ạli as his successor that his grandsons would be able to succeed him for it was not in accord with the genealogical theory or practice of the Arabs for the line of descent to pass through his daughter Fatima.[5]

Bearing in mind that Ạli was not only Muḥammad's cousin and son-in-law, but Ạli's father, Abu Ṭalib, was Muḥammad's

[1] Yaḳubi, *History*, ii, p. 125, edit. Houtsma.

[2] The reference in Mas'udi (*Tanbih wa'l-Ishraf*, p. 255, 1, 18, edit. de Goeje) is, "And on his return from al-Hudaibiya he said in regard to the Amiru'l-Muminín, Ali ibn Abu Ṭalib, at Ghadir Khum, 'Whoever has me for his master, then Ạli is his master.' This was on the eighteenth day of Dhu'l-Hijja. Ghadir Khum is close to the water known as al-Kharrár, in the district of al-Juḥfa. The descendants of Ạli and his party celebrate this day." See also Goldziher, *Muh. Stud.*, ii, p. 118.

[3] Mas'udi, Muruj al-Dhahab, iv, p. 158.

[4] Ibid., iv. p. 160.

[5] Sn. Hurgronje, *Lectures on Muhammadanism*, p. 28.

foster-father and protector, it would not have been unnatural for the Prophet to have desired to have Ạli regarded as second in authority only to himself. It is possible, therefore, that at the time of the expedition to al-Hudaibiya, Muhammad did make this statement, "He whose master I am also has Ạli for his master."

During that same year, and in the year following, Muḥammad married three new wives and took two new concubines. This might suggest that he was not altogether satisfied with the probability of the succession of his immediate family through Ạli and that he was exceedingly anxious for a son of his own. And the next year, 8 A.H., one of his concubines, Mary the Copt, who had been sent to him by the Governor of Egypt, bore him a son. The boy was called Ibrahim. Muḥammad was delighted at the birth of his son, and the seventh day afterwards he observed the ceremony of the *Akika*, or the cutting of the hair with which the child came into the world. It is related that on this occasion he sacrificed a sheep, as is still customary, and when the baby's head had been shaved, he gave the equal weight of the hair in silver as alms to the poor, and commanded that the hair should be buried. The ceremony of the *Akika* had to do with the shaving of the hair of the child,[1] not that of the father, as has been stated by mistake in Muir's *Life of Muhammad* (edit. 1912, p. 426). The mother, Mary the Copt, received so much of the Prophet's special attention after the birth of her son that she aroused the jealousy and active opposition of the wives in the household (cf. Koran, Surah lxvi). Whether Muḥammad ever contemplated the succession of princely office in his own family is a matter of course that is hard to determine with reference to Ibrahim, for the child lived less than two years. But in the same measure that the Prophet scandalized his wives by his disproportionate attention to Mary, the mother of Ibrahim, so when the child died, his grief was likewise so excessive that his followers were constrained to remind him of his counsel to others to be more moderate.

Here, however, the question is pertinent as to whether the

[1] Thompson, R. C., *Semitic Magic*, p. 229-231.

alleged investiture of Ạli at Ghadir Khum may not have been brought about by the Prophet's recent disappointment in the death of Ibrahim, together with the fact that his other new wives had borne him no sons. The date of the death of Ibrahim is given with hesitation as to its accuracy in Masudi's *Muruj al-Dhahab* (iv, p. 160), but in his later work, the *Kitab al-Tanbih wa'l-Ishraf* (p. 274), he states very definitely that Ibrahim died in the month Rabiü'l-Awwal, in the year 10 A.H., and that "the time from his birth until his death was a year and ten months and ten days." It was in the ninth month after this event, on the eighteenth of Dhu'l-Hijja, that the Shi'ites claim that Muḥammad repeated the statement, "He whose master I am has also Ạli for his master."

"I may here observe," in the words of Ibn Khallikan,[1] "that the eighteenth of Dhu'l-Hijja is the anniversary of the Festival of Ghadir, which is the same as that of Ghadir Khum. Khum, situated between Makka and Medina, is a place where there is a pond of water, or, by another account, a morass. When the Prophet returned from Makka, the year of the Farewell (10 A.H.), he halted at Khum and adopted Ạli ibn Abu Ṭalib as his brother, saying, 'Ạli is to me what Aaron was to Moses.' Almighty God be a friend to his friends and a foe to his foes; help those who help him and frustrate the hopes of those who betray him.[2] The Shi'ites attach great importance to this tradition."

An interesting feature in the observation of the festival of Ghadir is mentioned in Hughes' *Dictionary of Islam*, p. 138: "A festival of the Shi'ites on the eighteenth of Dhu'l-Hijja, when three images of dough, filled with honey, are made to represent Abu Bakr, Ụmar, and Ụthman, are struck with knives, and the honey is sipped as typical of the blood of the usurping caliphs. The festival is named *Ghadir*, 'a pool,' and the festival commemorates, it is said, Muḥammad's having declared Ạli his successor at Ghadir-Khum, a watering place midway between Mecca and al-Medina."

[1] Ibn Khallikan, De Slane Trans., iii, p. 383.
[2] Wensinck, *H.E.M.T.*, numerous references, p. 15.

The highly esteemed Shi'ite theologian, Mulla Muḥammad Baḳír, al-Majlísí (d. 1700 A.D.), has given a summary of the traditions that relate what happened at Ghadir-Khum:

" When the ceremonies of the pilgrimage were completed, the Prophet, attended by Ạli and the Musulmans, left Mecca for Medina. On reaching Ghadir-Khum he halted, although that place had never before been a halting place for caravans. The reason for the halt was that verses of the Ḳoran had come upon him, commanding him to establish Ạli in the Caliphate. Before this he had received similar messages, but had not been instructed explicitly as to the time for Ạli's appointment. He had delayed because of opposition that might occur. But if the crowd of pilgrims had gone beyond Ghadir-Khum they would have separated and the different tribes would have gone in various directions. This is why Muḥammad ordered them to assemble here, for he had things to say to Ạli which he wanted all to hear. The message that came from the Most High was this: 'O Apostle, declare all that has been sent down to thee from thy Lord. No part of it is to be withheld. God will protect you against men, for he does not guide the unbelievers' (Ḳoran, v. 71). Because of this positive command to appoint Ạli as his successor, and perceiving that God would not countenance further delay, he and his company dismounted in this unusual stopping place.

" The day was hot and he told them to stand under the shelter of some thorn trees. He then commanded that they should make a pulpit platform out of the pack-saddles about which the people were assembled. Many had fastened their cloaks about their feet to protect them from the heat of the sun. And when the crowd had all gathered, Muḥammad walked up on to the platform of saddles and called Ạli to stand at his right. After a prayer of thanks he spoke to the people, informing them that he had been forewarned of his death, and saying, 'I have been summoned to the Gate of God, and I shall soon depart to God, to be concealed from you, and bidding farewell to this world. I am leaving you the Book of God, and if you follow this you will not go astray. And I am leaving you also the members of my household, who are not to be separated from the Book of God until they meet me at the drinking fountain of Kawthar.' He then called out, 'Am I not more precious to you than your own lives?' They said, 'Yes.' Then it was that he took Ạli's hands and raised them so high that he showed the whites of his armpits, and said, 'Whoever has me as his master has Ạli as his master. Be a friend to his friends, O Lord, and be an enemy to his enemies. Help those who assist him and frustrate those who oppose him.'

"When the Prophet descended from the pulpit it was time for the noon prayers, after which he went to his tent. Near his own tent he had another tent pitched for the *Amiru'l-Mu'minín*, the Commander of the Faithful. When Ạli was seated in this tent, Muḥammad ordered the Musulmans, group by group, to go and congratulate him on his succession to the *imamate* and to salute him as *Amiru'l-Mu'minín*. Both men and women did this, and Ụmar was as much pleased as anybody."[1]

It is important to remember that the historian al-Yaḳúbi (d. about A.D. 891) was contemporary with "the six" most authoritative compilers of Sunnite traditions, i.e., al-Bukhári, Muslim, Abu Ḍá'úd, al-Tirmidhi, al-Nasá'í and Ibn Mája. He was in sympathy with the cause of the house of Ạli and his "History" was written, not only some eight hundred years before the time of Majlisi, but it is at least twenty-five years earlier than the earliest compilation of Shi'ite traditions that is now extant. He gives the following account of the death of Muḥammad:

"When Muḥammad reached Medina he halted several days and determined to place Ụsama ibn Zayd in superior command to the chiefs of the Muhajirín and the Ansár. He gave him as his objective a raid on the place where his father was killed in the land of Syria. It is related the Ụsama said, 'He commanded me to go first to Ụghzu Yubná, in the land of Palestine, and then to go to Iraḳ.'[2]

"The Prophet died at sixty-three years of age.[3] He was bathed by Ạli ibn Abu Ṭalib and al-Faḍl ibn al-Ạbbas ibn al-Muttalib. Ụsama ibn Zayd brought the water. While they were in the room they heard a voice but did not see any person who spoke. The voice said, 'Peace, and God's mercy and blessing be upon you, ye people of the House. Verily he is to be praised and glorified' (Ḳoran xi, 76, Palmer), 'for God only desireth to put away uncleanness from you, as his household, and with cleansing to cleanse you' (Ḳoran xxxiii, 33, Rodwell). 'Every soul shall taste of death: and ye shall assuredly be tried in your

[1] Majlisi, *Hayatu'l-Kulub*, vol. iii, p. 339. Cf. Merrick's Trans., entitled *Life and Religion of Muhammad*. A full account in Persian of the designation of Ạli at Ghadir Khum may be found in the Muṭaruḥu'l-Anthar, by Agha Muhammad Sahih, Mazandarání, edit. Bombay, 1287 A.H., p. 92 ff.

[2] The reading in Mas'udi (*Tanbih wa'l-Ishraf*, p. 273) is: "Then the division under Ụsama ibn Zayd went to Yubná and Azdud, in the land of Palestine, in the province of Syria."

[3] Mas'udi agrees with this statement and discusses differences of opinion (*Muruj al-Dhahab*, iv, p. 145).

possessions and in yourselves. Many hurtful things shall ye hear from those to whom the Scriptures were given before you and from those who join other gods with God. But if ye be steadfast and fear God—this verily is needed in the affairs of life' (Koran iii, 182-183, Rodwell), 'for in God there is an escape from all destruction and there is endurance for all affliction. May God increase your recompenses, and may the peace and mercy of God be upon you.'

"Jaạfar ibn Muḥammad asked the voice, 'Who are you seeing?' and the answer was, 'Gabriel.'

"The Prophet was wrapped for burial in two red garments and a *burda* (or outdoor garment of silk). Those who entered his grave were Ạli ibn Abu Ṭalib and Ạbbas ibn Abu Muttalib; or according to another account al-Faḍl ibn al-Ạbbas and Shukran the 'freedman' of the Apostle of God. It is said that the Ansár exclaimed, 'Let our portion in reference to the Prophet be the same in his death as it was in his lifetime,' and Ạli said, 'One of you may enter.' So they had Aws ibn Khawalá, one of the sons of Hibla, enter the tomb. His grave was dug by Abu Talha ibn Sahl, the Ansár, with the help of Abu Ụbaida ibn al-Jarrah, as there was no one else in al-Medina to dig it. Abu Ụbaida grew tired when he had dug the central part so Abu Talha dug the niche on the side. It has been said that they vied with one another in the digging and that Abu Ụbaida dug more than Abu Talha.

"Prayer was made for the Prophet for a whole day and the people came and sacrificed camels. He was buried on Wednesday night and a fragment of his purple saddle was thrown under him. His grave was in the shape of a rectangle and was not elevated.

"At first when the Prophet died the people said, 'We did not think the Apostle of God would die before he had subdued the world.' In fact Ụmar went out among the people and declared, 'Before God I swear the Apostle of God is not dead and will not die, but he is only *in concealment*, as Moses ibn Imrán was concealed for forty nights and then returned, and God cut off the hands and the feet of the people.' But Abu Bakr said, 'Surely God himself is the announcer of his death to us, for he said, Thou truly shalt die and they too shall die (Ḳoran xxxix, 31, Rodwell). To this Ụmar replied, 'By God I had never read it.' Afterwards he told Abu Bakr that he realized that the Apostle of God had died and that only the violence of his grief had caused him to say what he did.

"Muḥammad left no offspring except his daughter Faṭima, and it was only forty nights later that she died too. Some say it was seventy nights, and still others say it was six months."[1]

[1] Yaḳubi, *History*, ii. p. 125, edit. Houtsma; Bukhárí, Ch. 63, No. 11; Ibn Sa'd, Tabaḳat, II, ii, 42.

There is a tradition, which is given by both Muslim and al-Bukhári,[1] "that when the Apostle of God was approached by death, there were several men in the house, and among them was Ụmar ibn al-Khattab. The Prophet said, 'Come and I will write for you a writing after which ye will never go astray.' But Ụmar said, 'The pain has overcome him, and ye have the Ḳoran, the word of God is sufficient for you.' The people of the house differed about the matter and disputed with one another. Some of them said, 'Bring writing materials so that the Apostle of God may write for you.' And some of them agreed with Ụmar. As the noise and dissension increased, the Apostle of God said, 'Get up from me.' Ụbaidulla related that Ibn Ạbbas used to say, 'Verily the misfortunes, all the misfortunes that have come to us, between the Apostle and his writing for them that writing, have come on account of their disagreement and clamour.'"[2]

Another tradition that is especially noteworthy on account of its bearing on later Shi'ite beliefs about the imams is that A'isha related, "When the Apostle of God was well, I heard him say that before his departure every prophet was allowed the option between this and the next world. When the disease had weakened him he occasionally exclaimed, 'I am with those prophets, saints, and martyrs whom thou hast favoured, and they are the best companions for me.' And he repeated, 'With the highest companions.' Then I knew that he *had been left the option*, and that he had chosen the eternal world."[3]

It is generally considered that Muḥammad died in the arms of A'isha, his favourite wife. This is on the strength of a tradition that is ascribed to her and which is included in the collection of traditions in the Mishkatu'l-Maṣabih.[4] A twig was ordinarily

[1] Wensinck, *H.E.M.T.*, p. 161, with references to Bukhari, Ch. 3, No. 39; Ch. 58, No. 6; Ch. 64, No. 83; Ch. 75, No. 17; Ch. 96, No. 26. See also Muslim, Ch. 25, No. 22; Ibn Sa'd, II, ii, 36 sqq.; and Ahmad ibn Hanbal, I, 232, 293, and 324.

[2] *Selections from Muhammadan Tradition*, Goldsack, 1923, p. 303.

[3] Bukhari, Ch. 64, No. 84; Tirmidhi, Ch. 46, No. 15; Ibn Sa'd, II, ii, 9, 25, 60; Ahmad ibn Handal, I, 267. See also Mirkhond, *Rauzat as-Safa*, ii. p. 173, and Eng. Trans. by Rehatsek, Pt. II, p. 704 sqq.

[4] *Selections from Muhammadan Traditions*, Goldsack, p. 302, and Wensinck, *H.E.M.T.*, p. 14.

used for cleaning the teeth, and it was such a twig that A'isha softened for Muḥammad in her own mouth, and he rubbed it over his teeth and declared, "There is no God but Allah, and verily in death there are agonies." After that he raised his hand and started to pray, "Give me a place with the highest companions," but as he uttered these words his hand fell down and he was dead.

It is not unnatural that the Shi'ites should have another tradition concerning the last moments of Muḥammad's life which gives prominence, not to A'isha, but rather to Ạli and Faṭima. This tradition is ascribed to Ạli and is recorded by several Shi'ite authorities.[1] It is related that during his last illness the Prophet issued various commands, and the one hundred and tenth *Sura* was revealed, which begins, "When the aid of Allah shall come." Ạli asked if these were his last words, and he replied, "Yes, O Ạli, for my heart is distressed in this world." After a few seconds he said, "O Gabriel, aid me and fulfil thy promise." He then called Ạli to come near him and he put his head on Ạli's lap, and his countenance had changed and his forehead perspired. Faṭima was near by, and when she saw this she jumped up in distress. She took the hands of Hasan and Husain and pleaded with her father most tenderly. Again he rallied and opened his eyes, and placed his head on her bosom and prayed, "O God Most High, give patience to Faṭima." And he said to her, "Faṭima, I congratulate you, for you will join me before any other person." He told her that he was in the agony of death, and she broke down completely, so that Ạli commanded her to be quiet. But the Prophet said, "Allow her to shed tears for her father." And after that he closed his eyes for the last time.

One is inclined to think that this tradition represents more what the Shi'ites considered an appropriate death for the Prophet than what actually happened, but at any rate it is what they prefer to believe rather than the story of A'isha.

As soon as the Moslem community faced the question of choosing a successor to the religious and political authority of

[1] Mirkhond, *Rauzat as-Safa*, Eng. Trans., p. 726.

Muḥammad, disagreement arose between the two parties of the Prophet's most intimate associates, the Ansár and the Muhajirín. The Ansár, who were the Medina "helpers," had welcomed and assisted Muḥammad when he took refuge in their city after his flight from Mecca. The other party were his fellow "refugees," who had shared his persecution and had accompanied him to al-Medina. Even before the death of the Prophet an element of disaffection had sprung up between the two parties, for the Muhajirín had begun to show a decided preference for the newly converted Ḳuraish, who were their own tribesmen, and this had aroused the jealousy of the Ansár. Muḥammad had sensed this situation and had apprehended that there might be trouble between the Ansár and the Ḳuraish. The last time he ascended the pulpit it is reported that he declared to the assembled believers[1]:

"A charge is given you concerning the Ansár, for behold they have been my sustenance and my depository of secrets. They have fulfilled what was committed to them and have endured what was necessary. So follow after those of them who do good and overlook their evil-doers."

When the Prophet died the Ansár acted quickly in their own interests and made an immediate bid for supremacy of influence. As related by at-Tabari,[2] "they assembled at the *saḳifa* (a high bench that stood in the hallway) of the Beni Sa'dát to swear fealty to Sa'd ibn Ụbada. Knowledge of this reached Abu Bakr, who went at once with Ụmar and Abu Ụbaida ibn al-Jarrah and demanded, 'What is this?' Their answer was, 'Let us have an Amír.' But Abu Bakr replied, 'The Amirs are to be chosen from us and the Wazirs from you.' He then went on to say, 'As for myself, I am ready to agree on one of two men, either Ụmar or Abu Ụbaida.' But it was at this point that Ụmar arose and exclaimed, 'The one whom the Prophet was pleased to have as his successor in leading the prayers, he is the man to whom the Prophet has granted precedence.' And on saying this, Ụmar

[1] Bukhari, Ch. 63, No. 11; Ibn Sa'd, II, ii, 42.
[2] Tabarí, Series I, p. 1,817. Cf. Ibn Athir, *Tarikh al-Kámil*, Vol. II, p. 156.

swore fealty to Abu Bakr, and the people also did him homage. But there were some of the Ansár who said, 'We will not give our allegiance to anyone but Ạli.' "

Why the Ansár should have been willing to give up their own candidate, Sa'd ibn Ụbada, and to suggest a compromise in favour of Ạli, who was himself of the Ḳuraish, is not explained. In addition, however, to this brief reference to the dissatisfaction of the Ansár, recorded by at-Tabari and Ibn al-Athir, Ya'ḳúbi has left a report of the speeches that were made and of spectacular things that happened in this first political convention of Islam.[1]

The Ansár had already named their candidate, Sa'd ibn Ụbada, of the tribe of the Khazraj. They made him sit on a cushion and wound a turban about his head. When Abu Bakr and Ụmar and others of the Muhajirín came upon the scene they immediately protested that the Ansár were going beyond their rights. In answer, one of their skilful orators set forth their claims and virtues, and to this statement Abu Bakr replied: "We do not deny the Ansár their merits, the virtues in fact that you have related. You belonged to Muḥammad, we admit that, but the Ḳuraish take precedence over you. For example, here is Ụmar ibn al-Khattab, for whom the Apostle prayed 'O God confirm his faith.' And here also is Abu Ụbaida ibn al-Jarrah, who the Apostle said was a leader of this people. Choose one of these, whichever one you wish, and pay homage to him." But both the men named objected at once to Abu Bakr's nominating them, saying, "Indeed we will not take advantage of you, for you yourself were second only to the Apostle of God." Then Abu Ụbaida seized the hand of Abu Bakr, showing his readiness to give his allegiance to him. Ụmar followed his example. There was then a pause in the proceedings, while conciliatory remarks were made to the Ansár. They were asked to concede that they did not have any men who were so well fitted for this responsibility as Abu Bakr and Ụmar and Ạli. In reply, one of the Ansár, al-

[1] Yaḳubi, *History*, ii, p. 136 ff., edit. Houtsma. The account of the assembly at the Saḳifa that is given by Jalalu'd-Din as-Suyuti in his *History of the Caliphs*, Eng. Trans., Jarret, Calcutta, 1881, pp. 67-70, is strikingly similar to that of Yaḳubi. In fact they both have depended on Ibn Sa'd, III, ii, 110, 2.

Manzar ibn Arkám, rose and said, " We certainly do not fail to appreciate the excellence of the men you mention, and in fact there is one of them whose right no one would dispute if he should seek this authority. That man is Ạli ibn Abu Ṭalib."

At this point, however, Bashír, the son of Sa'd, the Ansár nominee, stampeded the assembly by dashing forward to be the first of the Ansár to pay homage to Abu Bakr. Others of the tribe of Khasraj followed and they were joined by the crowd in general. In the excitement, as the foot soldiers rushed forward, leaping over the cushions that had been piled up for Sa'd, this unfortunate first nominee was literally trampled under foot. Ụmar exclaimed, " They will kill Sa'd ! " but Ya'ḳúbi observes, whether in sheer casuistry or with Shi'ite resentment that Saạd should ever have been nominated, " But it was God who killed Sa'd."[1]

The Beni Hashim also made it clear that they were not pleased with the course events had taken. And along with them were several, both of the Muhajirín and of the Ansár, who delayed paying homage to Abu Bakr because they insisted that Ạli should have been chosen. Khálid ibn Sa'íd was away at the time, but when he returned to Medina he desired to swear allegiance to Ạli. It appears that Ạli seriously considered whether he ought not to venture to assert his rights, but he decided finally against such a course, for, as he pointed out to his friends, most of the chiefs were supporting his opponents.

When the news reached Abu Bakr and Ụmar that a number of the Muhajirín and the Ansár had gathered about Ạli in the house of Faṭima, who was the daughter of the Prophet and the wife of Ạli, they took it upon themselves to go in person and see what it was all about. One compensation in the study of these traditions is that they are so delightfully direct and personal. They make good stories, for the most important matters of statecraft were often settled with little official formality. Thus on

[1] Sa'd ibn Ubáda was a native of Medina and the standard-bearer of the Ansár in their expeditions. He died in Hawrán, 16 A.H., and was buried at Mizzah, near Damascus. Cf. as-Suyuti, p. 67, note, and reference to Weil, Leben, *Muham.*, Vol. II, pp. 351, 352.

this occasion, when Abu Bakr and Ụmar arrived at the house of Faṭima they pushed through the assembled crowd until they reached the gate, when behold Ạli himself came out to meet them with a sword. First Ụmar struck Ạli and then they came to grips, when Ụmar threw Ạli down and broke his sword. Abu Bakr and Ụmar passed on through the gate, but suddenly Faṭima appeared before them in a great temper and exclaimed, "Before God, I say, either you get out of here at once, or with my hair dishevelled, and exposed to the public gaze, I will make my appeal to God!" With this rebuff they left the house and the crowd at the gate dispersed.

There were a number of the people who delayed for several days, but gradually, one after another, they all paid homage to Abu Bakr. Ạli, however, did not declare his allegiance until after six months, but according to other authorities it was after only four days.

The few important traditions cited in this chapter show how dissension arose in the Moslem community on account of the question of succession. The task remains to show how the minority party in Islam organized their opposition and developed the doctrine of the Imamate, with all its subsequent requirements.

CHAPTER II

THE THREE USURPERS

WHAT the Shi'ites have believed as to Ạli's immediate right to the Caliphate after the death of the Prophet is expressed briefly in a Persian manual that is much studied at the present day. It is the *'Aḳa' idu'sh-Shi'a,* or The Beliefs of the Shi'ites, which Dr. Browne has taken pains to outline in his *Persian Literature in Modern Times,* p. 381 ff. " Ạli was the true *Amiru'l-Muminín,* or Commander of the Faithful,[1] and as such he should have been recognized as the immediate successor of the Apostle of God. After Muḥammad, it was his function to interpret the commands of God to men. He was born on Friday morning and was thirty years younger than the Apostle. The place of his birth was in the very centre of the Ka'aba. He lived to be sixty-three years of age, thirty-two years during the lifetime of the Apostle, and thirty-one years afterwards. This latter period represents the time of his caliphate but he was forced from this his rightful position for almost twenty-five years. These years he spent in private life.

" The first of the usurpers was Abu Bakr, who was in office

[1] Dr. Goldziher has pointed out that the famous collector of Shi'ite traditions, Abu Ja'far Muhammad al-Kulaini (d. 328 A.H., A.D. 969), has made the positive statement in the Uṣul min al-Jami al-Kafi, Bombay, 1302 A.H., p. 261, that " Ạli alone may lay claim to the title of Amiru' l-Mu'minín," *Vorlesungen,* p. 208. According to Ibn Sa'd (*Tabaḳat,* III, i, p. 202) Ụmar was the first to receive this title: " When the Apostle of God died and Abu Bakr aṣ-Ṣiddiḳ was appointed Caliph, he was called ' the Caliph of the Apostle of God.' When Abu Bakr died and Ụmar ibn Khattab was made Caliph, he was called ' the Caliph of the Caliph of the Apostle of God.' The Muslims were saying that whoever would come after Ụmar would be called ' the Caliph of the Caliph of the Caliph of the Apostle of God,' and this would be too long. They undertook therefore to find a name by which a Caliph could be called who followed after another Caliph. Some of the Companions of the Apostle of God said, ' We are the Faithful (al-Mu'minín) and Ụmar is our Commander (Amir).' Accordingly Ụmar was called the Commander of the Faithful, and he was the first to receive this title."

for two years and three months. Then came Ụmar ibn al-Khaṭṭab, for ten years and six months. He was followed by Ụthman, who held sway for twelve years.[1] And after Ụthman, Ạli was himself recognized as Caliph and continued in that office for four years and six months.

"During this period he carried on three wars. One of them was with the Ḳasiṭín, those who acted unjustly, or the Separatists, i.e., Mu'awiya and his supporters. The second conflict was at Basra with the Nakiṣín, or those who withdrew, meaning A'isha and Ṭalḥa and Zubair. This was called the Battle of the Camel, because A'isha was mounted on a camel. The third struggle was with the Mariḳín, the heretics, who were the Khawarij, or rebels. This battle was fought in the valley of Nahraván.

"Ạli is said to have had seventeen sons and nineteen daughters. After Faṭima (the daughter of the Prophet) died, he married twelve other wives. The total number of his 'mates,' *azwáj*, was three hundred and ninety-five. His mother's name was also Faṭima, and she was a daughter of Asad ibn Háshim ibn Abdu'l-Manáf. His father's name was Ạmr, and he was sometimes called Ịmran, or Ạbdu'l-Manáf the Less. Usually, however, he was known as Abu Ṭalib and he was said to have been a believer and to have acknowledged the oneness of God."[2]

It is important to notice that at the time when the Prophet died Ạli was only in his thirty-third year. He was therefore an extremely young man for the Arab tribes to have entrusted with the chief administrative responsibility. It was not unnatural that prominent and influential men of "the Companions" who were much older should be chosen in preference to him for a period of almost twenty-five years. In fact there appears to

[1] The substantial accuracy of these statements of time each of the first three Caliphs reigned is confirmed by Mas'udi, Muruj al-Dhahab, Vol. IV, pp. 175, 190 and 250; and there is a slight variation of months in as-Suyuti, Trans. Jarret, p. 87. Yaḳubi (ii, pp. 156, 183 and 205) gives the reign of Abu Bakr as two years and four months; of Ụmar as ten years and eight months; and of Ụthman as twelve years.

[2] *Aḳa'idu'sh-Shi'a*, by Hajji Mirza Aḳasí, Bk. IV, ch. 2. Ahmad ibn Hanbal (*Musnad*, i, p. 79) shows that Ạli's father, Abu Ṭalib, refused to say the Muslim prayers; and that he would not recognise the unity of God in confession on his deathbed is pointed out by Bukhari (Ch. 23, No. 81; Ch. 63, No. 40; and Ch. 65, Sura 9, b. 16, and sura 28, b. 1). Cf. Wensinck, *H.E.M.T.*, p. 9.

have been a consistent recognition of seniority in the choice of the first four Caliphs, for when Abu Bakr was given this responsibility he was past sixty, Ụmar was almost fifty-three, Ụthman was about seventy, and Ạli was either fifty-nine or sixty-four, according as we reckon that he was ten years old or fifteen years old at the time when he first accepted Islam

Very soon after the death of the Prophet, Ạli went with Faṭima to Abu Bakr to ask for her inheritance from her father. But Abu Bakr said to them, " I call you to witness before God, do you not know, or did you not hear, that the Apostle of God declared that all his property, except the living expenses of his family, should be for charity; and that there are to be no heirs?" They answered, " Yes, but the Apostle of God always spent his money for his family and was true to them."[1] When she was asked just what property it was that she wanted, Faṭima replied, " Fadak and Khaibar, and the tithe lands of Medina—my portion therein, even as thy daughters will inherit of thee when thou diest." But the Caliph answered, " Truly thy father was better than I, and thou art better than my daughters, but the Prophet hath said, ' No one shall be my heir, but that which I leave shall be for alms.' "[2]

It is said that Faṭima was much displeased at Abu Bakr's decision, and that she died not more than six months after her father's death. It is important to notice the shortness of this period as it measures the duration of Ạli's alienation from Abu Bakr, for after the death of Faṭima, Ạli went at once to Abu Bakr and swore his allegiance. From that time on the " historic Ạli " accepted his status as one of the counsellors of the Caliph. The positions of primary leadership and responsibility, however,

[1] Ṭayalisi, *Musnad*, No. 61. Yaḳubi, *History*, ii, p. 141, says: " Faṭima, the daughter of the Apostle of God, came to Abu Bakr to ask for her inheritance from her father, but he said to her, ' The Apostle of God said, " I am of the company of the prophets, we will not have people inherit from us what we have left of money dedicated to pious purposes." ' Faṭima replied, ' Is it then that you will be heir to your father and that I will not be heir to my father, for surely the Apostle of God said, "A man will protect his child." ? ' " See also as-Suyuti, Tarikh-i-Khulafa, Trans. Jarret, p. 74.

[2] Bukhari, Ch. 64, No. 38, end; and Muslim, Ch. 32, No. 52. Cf. Muir, *Annals of Early Caliphate*, p. 65.

were given to others. Ụmar was made Chief Justice; Attab, the Governor of Mecca, was chosen to represent Abu Bakr at the annual pilgrimage; and Ụsamah and Khalid were the two outstanding generals. But we read that "the despatches were chiefly indited by Ạli."[1]

That Ạli had the personal respect of Abu Bakr and was able at times to influence him in his decisions is suggested by the fact that when Ụsamah returned from his successful expedition to Syria, and Abu Bakr was planning to lead the army against Tulaihah, a rebel who had set himself up as a prophet, Ạli held to the opinion, which he asserted strongly, that Abu Bakr should remain in Medina. To this the Caliph agreed, and sent Khalid in his place.

Ạli had his share also in the perquisites and privileges of the Caliph's courtiers. One of the captives brought back to Medina after the battle with the Beni Hanifa was a beautiful girl named Yamana. Mirkhond records a tradition,[2] that Muḥammad had said to Ạli, "a girl of the Beni Hanifa will fall into thy possession, and when she bears thee a son, call him by my name and give him also my surname." Accordingly, Abu Bakr gave this Hanifite girl to Ạli. Before the year ended, however, he purchased another girl, Sahba, the captive daughter of Bodeir, the chief of the Beni Taghlíb. He had already married, in this same year, Omamah, a girl from his own tribe. Omamah was Zeinab's daughter, a granddaughter of Muḥammad, and the deceased Faṭima's niece.

Such a year of matrimonial activity, the first year after Faṭima's death, will not impress some readers as exactly in accord with the picture of the simplicity of his life that is given by Ibn Athir[3]: "As an illustration of his plainness of living, it is recorded that when he married Faṭima, the Prophet's daughter, they had no bed save a ram skin to lie on at night, and to feed their camel from in the daytime. They had no servant. When he was Caliph

[1] Muir, *Annals of Early Caliphate*, p. 123.
[2] Mirkhond, *Rauzatu's-Safa*, ii, p. 199.
[3] Zaydan, *Islamic Civilization*, iv, Trans. Margoliouth, *Umayyads and Ạbassids*, p. 39, with reference to Ibn Athir, iii, 204.

some money came to him from Ispahan; this he divided into seven portions, and, as a loaf of bread remained over, he divided that also into seven portions. He wore a tunic too thin to protect him from the cold. Once when he was carrying a dirhem's worth of dates that he had bought, in a wrapper, some of his subjects offered to carry them for him; but he replied that this was the duty of the *pater-familias*. Once when asked to describe the proper condition of a Moslem, he replied, 'Pinched with famine, dry with thirst, blear-eyed with tears.'"

When Abu Bakr died he had designated Ụmar as his successor, and a tradition is related on the authority of A'isha that associates Ạli with Talha in raising objection to Ụmar's appointment. "When my father was very sick," she said, "two men entered and said to him, 'O Caliph of the Apostle of God, what will you say to your Lord when you approach him to-morrow, since you have appointed Ibn al-Khaṭṭab as Caliph over us?' Then my father said, 'Let me sit up.' Is it before God that you threaten me? Truly I shall declare before God that I have appointed over them the very best one of them.'"[1] If this tradition is true, then Ạli's prospects of enjoying high favour during Ụmar's Caliphate would not be the brightest. But Ụmar not only heard the criticisms that were made of himself, but he heeded them and showed a real desire that his faults should not stand in the way of the great service he considered that he had been called upon to render. After his inauguration as Caliph, when he mounted the pulpit, the very first words that he uttered were, "O God, I am violent, so do thou soften me; I am weak, so do thou strengthen me; and I am miserly, so do thou make me generous."[2] Such an attitude undoubtedly served to quiet the jealousies of the inner circle of the Companions.

Ạli continued to live in Medina, with much the same relations to Ụmar that he had enjoyed with Abu Bakr. We do not find that he took part, however, in any of Ụmar's great military campaigns. And on the literary side, while there is mention of

[1] Ibn Sa'd, *Tabaḳat*, III, i, p. 196, 1. 14.
[2] *Ibid*, III, i, p. 196, 1. 25.

his extraordinary knowledge of the Ḳoran,[1] yet the work of managing its official compilation and determining the authoritative text was not given to him, but to Zayd, who had been the amanuensis for the Prophet. He was highly esteemed for his knowledge of traditions, and it is said that Ạli had a scrupulous concern about relating only what he had actually heard the Apostle of God say. He called down a dire curse upon himself if he should do otherwise, and he said that he had heard the Prophet foretell that the time would come when there would be all kinds of traditions that would lead people from their faith and to believe even that it was not permissible to read the Ḳoran.[2] When questioned as to how he received this great knowledge of tradition, which was said to excel that of all the other Companions, Ạli replied, "For my part, whenever I asked the Prophet anything he revealed it to me, and when I kept silence he would begin telling me things."[3]

On various occasions, Ạli is said to have given advice to Ụmar that was readily accepted and thus to have maintained his position as unofficial counsellor at the Caliph's court. At the time the expedition was made against Jerusalem, Ạli advised Ụmar to go and he went; and when Ụmar hesitated as to whether he should personally lead the army to Madain, Ạli was one of those who dissuaded him from doing so; and before the battle of Nehawend, it was on Ạli's advice that Nu'mán ibn Muḳárin was placed in command.[4] In this year, A.H. 16, Ụmar is said to have first begun dating letters and papers as so many years "after the flight of the Prophet from Mecca to Medina," and some have also attributed this suggestion to Ạli.[5]

When Ụmar was assassinated and lay at the point of death, he appointed a commission of six members to meet and decide who should be his successor. Ạli was one of these six commissioners, which indicates that he had maintained his position as one of the

[1] *Ibid*, II, ii, p. 101; and Ṭayalisi, *Musnad*, No. 2096.
[2] Ṭayalisi, *Musnad*, No. 168 (edit. Haidarabad, 1321 A.H.).
[3] Ibn Sa'd, *Tabaḳat*, II, ii, p. 101.
[4] *Rauzatu's-Safa*, ii, pp. 209, 213, and 220.
[5] Ibn Sa'd, *Tabaḳat*, III, i, p. 102; and *Rauzatu's-Safa*, ii, p. 219.

counsellors of State. It would appear also that he had come to have high regard for Ụmar, as is shown by the tradition that when Ụmar's body was lying ready for burial, Ạli remarked, " There is no name on earth dearer to me than the one God has inscribed on his ledger for this man under the cover."[1]

Of the six commissioners who were to choose the new Caliph, Sa'd and Abdu'l-Rahman were brothers. At their first meeting, which was held in the public treasury, most of the six men were bent on nominating themselves. Finally Abdu'l-Rahmán said that he and his brother would withdraw their names, and as a consequence Abdu'l-Rahman was himself given the right to investigate the general feeling on the subject and to name the man who he felt would be most acceptable. When the meeting broke up they all agreed to abide by the final decision of Abdu'l-Rahman.

In the course of his investigation, Abdu'l-Rahman sent to the house of Ạli and asked him to answer this question, " If I should not name you, whom would you prefer ? " Ạli's answer was " Ụthman." Then the shrewd arbitrator sent a messenger with the same question to Ụthman, and his answer was " Ạli." He also summoned Talha and Zubair and asked them, " If you are not of sufficient calibre for the Caliphate yourselves, whom would you prefer ? " Zubair said, " Ạli," but Talha said, " Ụthman." Abdu'l-Rahman then asked his brother Sa'd whom he would prefer and he said, " Ụthman." In this way he had secured three votes for Ụthman and two for Ạli, and that very night he sent for them both to come and see him. He met them together and talked with them for a long time, and after his words of counsel he asked Ạli, " Do you agree that we should act according to the Book of God the Most High and according to the precedents established (Sunna) by His Apostle, and in agreement with what has been done by Abu Bakr and Ụmar ? " Ạli hesitated in his reply and said, " I will do so in so far as I can, according to my strength and ability." Some have said that he answered, " I hope I can do so, but I am not familiar with the administration of affairs." But when Abdu'l-Rahman asked Ụthman the same

[1] *Ibid*, III, i, p. 269.

question, his answer was, " I agree altogether with what you have said." In dismissing them at the close of their interview that night, Abdu'l-Rahman remarked, " If you have nothing more to tell me you may go home now and this matter will be decided to-morrow morning in the assembly."

The next morning, when the chief men of the Muhájirín and of the Ansár had gathered with others in the mosque, Abdu'l-Rahman led the prayer service and afterwards he addressed the assembly. First he spoke to the commissioners, " O commissioners, have you given me the right to appoint the Caliph ? " When they answered in the affirmative, he continued, " I have investigated this matter in so far as I could, so as not to feel a lingering preference for the one not chosen, no difference who may be chosen." He then asked Ạli to come forward, and taking him by the hand he repeated publicly the same question he had asked him the night before, and Ạli answered in the same way. After this, Ụthman was called forward and asked exactly the same question. But in answering, Ụthman accepted wholeheartedly, without any qualification as to his ability. Abdu'l-Rahman then looked upward and said, " O God, do thou witness, I have placed the burden of the Caliphate on the neck of Ụthman." He and the people proceeded immediately to give their allegiance to Ụthman. When, however, Ạli and Ạbbas hesitated about doing so, Abdu'l-Rahman reminded them of the words of the Ḳoran, " He who violates an oath violates it against himself." Accordingly, Ạli also came forward and gave his allegiance to Ụthman.[1]

As he began his administration, Ụthman had to face a new problem that had arisen from the effect of city life upon the Arabs. Ụmar's policy had been to unite the Arab tribes in Arabia, and he had forbidden them to till the soil, referring to the tradition, " Never has the ploughshare entered a house but humiliation has entered it also." But notwithstanding, many of the Arabs who had associated with him in the government had tasted the joys of city life and were fully ready to change their

[1] *Rauzatu's-Safa*, ii, p. 224.

desert dwellings for the more comfortable surroundings of the armed dictators in the newly conquered provinces. It has been estimated that there were about two hundred thousand of these Arabs whom Ụmar had looked upon as the nucleus of the empire. Consequently, Ụthman soon had to meet this problem of the urge of the Arabs to go and reside in the colonies. And he yielded to the pressure that was brought to bear upon him and allowed the Ḳuraish to leave Medina. They went to live in various cities in Egypt, Persia, Syria and Africa. They carried along with them an arrogant pride in their pure Arab blood. There were peoples dwelling in these other countries who had become Moslems but who were unwilling to be classified among the subject peoples. These communities soon resented the Arab assumptions of superiority and the systematic way in which Arabs were given offices that carried with them valuable perquisites. The result was that before long it was generally believed throughout the empire that Ụthman was definitely committed to the policy of allowing the native Arabs, particularly those of his own immediate family, to freely exploit the other people, and consequently there came to be a large element of malcontents.

Ạli had, in the meantime, remained in Medina and was still holding his *de facto* position as one of the counsellors to the Caliph. Those who were displeased with Ụthman's administration began to come to Ạli with their complaints. Ụthman's Prime Minister was his cousin Merwan, and the more rigorously he carried out the policy of undisguised favouritism for the Arabs, the more generally he was hated. First the people placed their hope on Ạli's mediation with the Caliph, but before long there was a strong desire for a change in administration.

This situation culminated in armed resistance in the twelfth year of Ụthman's Caliphate. It began with a concerted protest on the part of the troops that came from Egypt and Iraḳ. In so much as Ạli had received the complaints of these men and had presented their cause to Ụthman, in the light of later events, there were some who suspected that Ạli was himself involved in hostile plans against the Caliph. Mas'udi, however, does not consider that Ạli was in any way responsible for the murder of Ụthman. His detailed and unprejudiced story of the killing of Ụthman is as follows[1] :

" In the year 35 A.H., Malik ibn Harith al-Nakh'ai set out from Kufa with two hundred men, and Hakím ibn Jabala al-'Abdí set out with one hundred men of al-Basra, and six hundred Egyptian troops came that were under the command of Abdu'l-Rahmán ibn Ụdais al-Balawi. Al-Wáḳidi and other biographers relate that Abdu'l-Rahmán was among those who took part in the election under the tree, along with others in Egypt such as Ạmrú ibn al-Ḥamik al-Khuza'i,[2] and Sa'd ibn Ḥumrán at-Tujibi. Muḥammad, the son of Abu Bakr, was with them and had concerted with them in Egypt and had urged them to revolt against Ụthman, for reasons that would be too lengthy to explain. But the chief cause of discontent was on account of Merwan ibn al-Ḥakam.

" When they assembled at Medina they assembled at a place called Dhu'l-Khushub. Ụthman heard of their arrival and sent to Ạli ibn Abu Ṭalib and informed him. He asked Ạli to go to them himself and to give them his assurance that they would receive what they wanted in justice and good government. Ạli therefore went out to them and remained for a long parley. Finally they agreed to what he wanted and started to take their departure from Medina.

" But when the Egyptian troops came to a place called Ḥisma,[3] they saw a messenger coming toward them on a running camel. This man they recognised as Warash, who was one of the servants of the Caliph. They stopped him and compelled him to show them a letter that he was carrying. The letter was addressed to the son of Abu Sarh, the Governor of Egypt, and said to him : When the army returns to your province, cut off the hand of this one, kill the next one, and treat the third in such and such a way.'

[1] Mas'udi, *Muruju'l-Dhahab*, iv, p. 276 ff.
[2] Ibn Sa'd, *Tabaḳat*, VI, p. 15.
[3] *Ibid.*, I, i, pp. 17 and 28.

Thus the writer mentioned most of the soldiers and commanded such punishments as he wished.

"It was observed that the letter was in the handwriting of Merwán, and therefore they returned to Medina and got in touch with the discontented troops that had come from Iraḳ. They went also among the people in the mosque and told what had happened. They then set out against Ụthman and besieged him in his house. They shut off his water supply and after some time he came out on a high balcony and asked the people, 'Is there no one who will bring us water?' And he went on to say to them, 'Why do you seek to kill me? I have heard the Prophet say that it is not right to take the life of a Muslim, except for one of three crimes—apostasy, adultery after the marriage had been accomplished, or murder that is not in retaliation. Now I swear before God that I have not been guilty of any one of these crimes, neither in the time of ignorance nor in the years of Islam.'

"When Ạli knew that Ụthman was seeking water, he sent him three well-filled water skins, but the water had not reached him when a company of the freedmen of the Beni Hashim and of the Beni Umayyah clamorously surrounded the house, and with their swords in their hands they demanded the surrender of Merwan. But the Caliph refused to give up his favourite to them. Among the assailants were some of the Beni Zuhrah who had come to avenge Abdullah ibn Mas'ud, who was one of their confederates. There were others also of the Hudhail, who were of the tribe of Mas'ud, and there were a number of the Beni Makhzúm, with their clients, who had come on behalf of Ammár, and there were some of the Beni Ghaffár and their associates of the party of Abu Dharr. And finally there was Taim ibn Morrah and Muḥammad ibn Abu Bakr and still others whom it would be useless to mention.

"When Ạli saw that the Caliph's own life was in danger, he sent his two sons, Hasan and Husain, along with a good number of well-armed servants, with orders to defend the Caliph and to repulse the assailants. Zubair gave a similar order to his son

Abdullah, and Talha to his son Muḥammad. Other companions of the Prophet followed their example and sent their sons to the help of Ụthman. But some of those we have mentioned repulsed them from the house with a volley of arrows. The mass of people pressed forward so rapidly that Hasan was wounded. Those who were with them, fearing the excesses of the Beni Hashim and the Beni Umayyah, left them to get out of the way of those who were fighting in front of the house. Some of them took refuge in a (neighbouring) house that belonged to a family of Ansár.

"Among those who were able to reach Ụthman was Muḥammad ibn Abu Bakr, with two other men. Ụthman was in the same room with his wife and children, and along with his slaves, who continued fighting in his behalf. When Muḥammad ibn Abu Bakr seized Ụthman by the beard, the Caliph cried out, 'By God! Muḥammad, if your father could see you how it would grieve him!' At this Muḥammad let go and made his way to the door. But the two men who were with him entered the room and fell upon Ụthman and killed him. At the time (he was killed) the Caliph was holding a Ḳoran that he had been reading. His wife arose and cried out, 'The Commander of the Faithful is killed!' Then Hasan and Husain came in, with those who accompanied them of the Beni Ummayah, but they found the Caliph dead, and they wept when they saw what had happened. Ạli and Talhah and Zubair heard of this, as did also others of the Muhájirín and the Ansár. The mob withdrew and Ạli came into the house. He was evidently much grieved and said to his sons, 'How is it that the Commander of the Faithful was killed when you were at the door?' Then he slapped Hasan and struck Husain on the chest, and reviled Muḥammad ibn Talhah, and cursed Abdullah ibn Zubair. Talhah intervened and said to him, 'O Abu'l-Hasan, do not strike and revile and curse them. If the Caliph had surrendered Merwan to them he would not have been killed.' Merwan, however, had escaped with some of the Beni Umayyah. They made a diligent search for them, to kill them, but did not find them.

"Ali asked Uthman's wife, Na'ilah, the daughter of al-Ḳarafisa, 'As you were on the scene, you tell us who killed him?' She then explained how the two men had come upon him, and she told also about Muḥammad ibn Abu Bakr. And Muḥammad did not deny what she said, but declared, 'Before God, I did go in to him, and I intended to kill him, but when he spoke to me the way he did, well, I went out. I did not know that the two men remained behind him. Before God, I swear that I am not the cause of his murder. He has been killed, but I know nothing about the murder.'"

CHAPTER III

ALI THE FOURTH CALIPH

ALI, the cousin and son-in-law of Muḥammad, succeeded to the Caliphate in the month Dhu'l-Hijja, in the year 35 A.H.[1] Eleven of the outstanding chiefs, or knights, and "all the Companions of the Apostle of God who were in Medina" gave him their allegiance.[2] His acclamation as Caliph was in the Mosque of the Prophet in Medina, and he ascended the pulpit for the ceremony. Ashtar pledged the support of the people of Kufa, Talha and Zubair vouched for the Muhájirín, and Abu'l-Hit͟hám and Ukbah and Abu Ayyúb declared the loyalty of the Ansár.[3]

There were three influential men of the Ḳuraish, however, who held out against him. They were Marván ibn al-Hakam, Sá'íd ibn al-Aws, and Walíd ibn Ukbah. They protested to Ali that they were unwilling to recognize him as Caliph, because, at the Battle of Badr, he had killed the fathers of two of them, and in his criticism of the policy of Uthman, he had reviled the father of the other. They represented the Beni Manaf and in return for their allegiance they demanded that Uthman be revenged and that their own tribe be allowed to retain their holdings. This angered Ali and he told them that wherein he had injured them it was but right that he should do so, and as for avenging Uthman it would be impracticable, or indeed impossible, as it would mean a war with the tribes whose discontent had been the real cause of Uthman's death. In regard to their land rights, he said that they need expect no special consideration, but that he would deal

[1] Yaḳubi says Ali's inauguration was on "the seventh night" before the end of the month, i.e., about the 22nd (Tarikh, ii, p. 206). Mas'udi says it was the same day Uthman was killed (Tanbih, edit. de Goeje, p. 290). Ibn Sa'd says it was the day following the murder of Uthman, which he states was on Friday after eighteen nights had passed of the month Dhu'l-Hijja (Tabaḳat, III, i, p. 20).

[2] Ibn Sa'd, Tabaḳat, III, i, p. 20.

[3] Yaḳubi, Tarikh, ii, p. 206.

with them according to the Book of God and the *Sunna* of the Prophet.[1]

When this dissatisfaction was observed among the Ḳuraish, "Talhah and Zubair claimed that they had given Ạli their allegiance with aversion and not voluntarily. They set out for Mecca, and A'isha joined them. From Mecca they went to Basra, accompanied by A'isha, to seek vengeance for the blood of Ụthman. When Ạli learned of this he left Medina for Iraḳ. . . . He halted at Ḍhu Ḳár and sent Ạmmár ibn Yasír and Hasan ibn Ạli to the people of Kufa, to induce them to come with him. They joined him and he set out with them for Basra. There he met Talha and Zubair and A'isha, and those who were with them of the people of Basra, and some others, on the Ḍay of the Camel, in the month Jumadí II, 36 A.H. He defeated them and on that day Talhah and Zubair and others of their number were killed. The number of killed reached thirteen thousand.[2] Ạli remained at Basra for fifteen nights and then he returned to Kufa."[3]

In addition to this direct statement of the main facts of the conflict, as given by Ibn Sa'd, there are many points of human interest in the longer account of Yaḳubi.[4] Some of these will be more clearly appreciated if we recall that A'isha, the daughter of Abu Bakr and the favourite wife of Muḥammad, was perhaps the most popular and influential lady in Medina, but she had a long-standing dislike for Ạli. Thirty years had passed since the time when the Prophet went on his expedition against the Beni Muṣṭaliḳ. At that time he had decided which of his numerous wives should accompany him by casting lots, and the lot had fallen to her. She travelled in a litter that was carried by a camel, and on the return journey she had a grave misfortune. She was a little mite of a girl, scarcely sixteen years old, and had

[1] *Ibid.*, p. 207.

[2] Mas'udi's estimate of the number killed includes 13,000 among those who followed the Camel, and 9,000 from the followers of Ạli. He adds that the battle was fought on the 10th of Jumádi II, 35 A.H. (Tanbih, edit. de Goeje, p. 390), whereas Yaḳubi says that it occurred in Jumádi I (Tarikh, ii, p. 211).

[3] Ibn Sa'd, Tabaḳat, III, i, p. 20.

[4] Yaḳubi, Tarikh, p. 206 ff.

been married to the Prophet for more than five years. The litter in which she travelled was covered with curtains, and at one of the stopping-places near Medina she got left behind. Her camel had risen with the empty litter and had gone ahead with the caravan. According to her story, she sat down on the ground and waited until someone would come for her. A young man named Ṣafwán came along, riding a camel. He gallantly let A'isha ride the camel, and he himself walked ahead, leading it by the rein. But when the wife of the Prophet appeared in the camp, arriving in the company of this young man, there was much unfavourable comment. The chief accuser said, "Ṣafwán being handsome and young, it is no wonder that A'isha prefers him to Muḥammad." One woman who disliked her said she had often seen A'isha with Ṣafwán. The whole question was taken to the Prophet. And one of those whom the Prophet consulted as to what he ought to do was Ḁli. Ḁli advised him to put A'isha away, to repudiate her, but the well-known general, Usáma, maintained that she was innocent. To settle the matter the Prophet had a special revelation (Ḳoran xxiv, 11 ff.), in which he put the burden of proof rather heavily on her accusers, when he thus declared, as by divine inspiration, that no charge of adultery is valid unless it can be supported by four witnesses.[1]

But A'isha still remembered that Ḁli had advised the Prophet to put her away, and it was not to be expected that she would be one of those who would support him for the Caliphate. At the time when Ụthman was killed, she had gone on a pilgrimage to Mecca, and it was on her return journey that she received the news that Ḁli had been proclaimed the new Caliph. This turn of events she deeply resented, and entertained the idea at first that she should herself lead the opposition against him, but Umm Salmah, another of the Prophet's widows, to whom she ventured to make this suggestion, reminded her that "the virtues of women consist in hiding the eyes, in seclusion of themselves, and in the dragging of the skirts." But when she met Talhah and Zubair in Mecca she readily united with them in their plans against Ḁli,

[1] *Encyclopædia of Islam,* art. "A'isha."

and accompanied them to Basra. And on the way they met a certain Ya'la ibn Munyá, who was bringing 400,000 dinars from Yemen. This money they captured as a timely find which they were glad to use to gather further recruits.

When they arrived at Basra, Ụthman ibn Hanif, whom Ạli had sent there as governor, was at first unwilling to allow them to enter the city. Since, however, they solemnly declared that they came with no hostile intent and readily signed an agreement to this effect, he gave them permission to come into the city, and was apparently so well satisfied with their good will that he allowed his own men to lay aside their weapons of warfare. Then it was that Talhah and Zubair saw their opportunity, and treating their agreement as a scrap of paper, they seized the all too trustful governor and "cut his beard and moustache, and clipped his eyelashes and eyebrows, and proceeded to loot the treasury."

That evening, however, in Basra, when the time of prayer came, we read that Talhah and Zubair could not agree as to which one should take the lead, which was by no means an unimportant consideration, as it was a recognized prerogative of the Caliph. Each one of them seized and held back the other, while the people called to them, "Prayer! Prayer! O Companions of the Prophet!" But before either one could get ahead of the other, the appointed time of prayer had passed. It is further related that A'isha proposed that in the future they should take turn about and that her suggestion was accepted.

When Ạli started from Medina to Basra, he had four hundred horsemen, veteran troops of the Apostle, and before he reached Ḏhu Ḳár some six hundred men from Asad and Tai joined his force, and while he remained at this halting-place six thousand men from Kufa came as reinforcements. With this enlarged cavalcade he set out across the desert for Basra. Ạli himself could be easily distinguished by his high white Egyptian hat.[1] As to his personal appearance, Mas'udi says that "he was corpulent and partially bald, the hair of his head and beard was white, and he had large, dark eyes. His beard covered the upper

[1] Ibn Sa'd, III, i, p. 19.

part of his chest, and he did not dye his hair."[1] Almost all the writers mention that he had " a very large beard, white as cotton, which filled the space between his shoulders."[2] There was no doubt that he had reached the age that commanded deference and respect, and he was regarded as one of the four whom God himself had commanded Muḥammad to love.[3]

On the road he encountered the humiliated governor of Basra, who, after being despoiled of his whiskers and his treasury, had left the city in chagrin. When he met Ạli he remarked, " O Commander of the Faithful, you sent me here with a beard, and I have come to you now with the face of a boy."

They continued their journey until they came near Basra, when the army took their stand at a place called Khuráibah, and Talhah and Zubair came out with their followers from Basra and took position on the battlefield. Ạli first sent to them, saying, " What is it that you seek, and what do you want ? " They replied, " We seek compensation for the blood of Ụthman." Here Ạli was in a difficult situation, for the actual murderers of Ụthman had escaped, while those whose discontent and agitation had led to the tragedy were numerous and were among his most loyal supporters—in fact he may have been one of those himself. He answered with what was no more than a verbal acquiescence, " May God curse the murderers of Ụthman ! " This, however, was not deemed sufficient.

The followers of Ạli then drew up in ranks, and with the hope that the battle might even yet be avoided, Ạli commanded them : " Do not shoot the arrow, do not cast the lance, and do not strike with the sword." Thus they were to seek to avoid actual fighting. An arrow that was shot by the opposing side killed one of his followers, and when the man was brought to him, Ạli said, " Let God be witness ! " Another man was killed, and still he said, " Let God be witness.! " Abdullah ibn Budhail was then killed, and his brother carried him to Ạli, who again remarked, " Let

[1] Mas'udi, Tanbih, p. 297.
[2] As-Suyuti, History of the Caliphs, trans. Jarrett, p. 171 ; Ibn Sa'd, III, i, p. 16 ; and *Encyclopædia of Islam*, art. " Ạli."
[3] Tirmidhi, 46/20, and Wensinck, *H.E.M.T.*, p. 15.

God be witness!" But after this, fighting was judged to be unavoidable and the battle began in earnest.

The most desperate part of the conflict was where A'isha was mounted on a camel, a thoroughbred beast that had belonged to Ya'lá ibn Munyá. Of the Beni Ḍabba, who stood around her to protect her, there were about two thousand killed. And of the tribe of al-Azd, who rushed forward to take their places, there were two thousand seven hundred killed. No one was able, however, to seize the halter of A'isha's camel without forfeiting his life. The battle lasted until four hours after sunrise, and both Talhah and Zubair were put to death. When Ạli saw that his two chief opponents were killed and that their army was routed, his herald called out that permission was not given "to finish the wounded, or to pursue the retreating, or to defame those who turned back." Amnesty was proclaimed to all who would throw down their arms.

After the battle was over Ibn Ạbbas went to interview A'isha. In talking with him she was proud and haughty, and declared, "Twice, O Ibn Abbas, you have violated the Sunna, first, in that you entered my house without permission, and second, in that you seated yourself on my rug without my command." But when Ạli entered, he addressed her familiarly by a name the Prophet had sometimes called her, "Hello, red face (yá humaira'), are you not through with this journey?" She replied, "O Ibn Abu Ṭalib, you have gained the power, so grant me pardon." He then said to her, "Depart for Medina, and return to the house in which the Apostle of God told you to stay." She answered humbly, "I will do it."[1] Others have said that "seeing how much stronger Ạli's party was, A'isha suggested to him that she should stay with him and be his companion on subsequent expeditions against his enemies. But Ạli declined this offer and intimated that she had to depart."[2]

In the division of the spoils after the Battle of the Camel, Ạli is said to have made no distinction between the slaves and the free born. He is said to have buried the dead and to have waited

[1] Yaḳubi, *Tarikh*, ii, p. 213. [2] *Encyclopædia of Islam*, art. "A'isha."

three days before entering Basra, where he divided among the people the money he found remaining in the treasury. After spending a few days in Basra, he returned to Kufa, where he arrived in the month of Rajab, 36 A.H.

As we continue to follow the account given by Yaḳubi, we read of another Zubair whom Ạli had dismissed from his position as governor of Hamadán, who made representations to Ạli that he had much influence with one of the tribes that was following the leadership of Muáwiya. Against the advice of his friend and supporter, Ashtár, Ạli allowed this man Zubair to go to Muawiya and to carry to him a letter. When Zubair came to Muawiya, and was seated and the people were around him, he presented the letter from Ạli to Muawiya, who read it. Then Zubair arose and said, " O people of Syria, truly the one to whom a little does not bring advantage a great deal will not help. At Basra there was indeed such a battle that Islam could not suffer another like it and still continue. Therefore be earnest in serving God, O people of Syria, and consider what is best in regard to Ạli and Muawiya. Examine your own minds, for there is no one else to examine them except yourselves." He then ceased speaking, and Muawiya also said not a word. Then Muawiya did say, " You make me swallow with surprise, O Zubair."

But that same night Muawiya sent for Ạmr ibn Ạws. He wrote to him : " Since that which you have heard has happened in regard to Ạli and Talhah and Zubair and A'isha, and since Marwan, one of the fugitives from Basra, has taken refuge with us, and Zubair ibn Abdullah has come to me with a proposal in regard to the recognition of Ạli, I am most anxious that you should come to me. So come, by the blessing of the Most High God." When this letter reached Ạmr ibn Ạws, he called his two sons, Abdullah and Muhammad, and consulted with them. Abdullah said, " O Shaikh, the Apostle of God died, and he was pleased with you, and Abu Bakr and Ụmar died, and they were pleased with you, and now if you corrupt your faith for a minor material advantage, you will get that profit along with Muawiya, but to-morrow you will make your bed in Hell." Then Ạmr said to his son, Muḥammad, "What do you think?" He answered tersely, "Hasten to this affair, and be the head in it before you turn out to be the tail." And in the morning the father called his slave, Wardán, and said to him, "To horse! O Wardán," and then he said, "Dismount!" Thus Wardán mounted and dismounted three times, when he said to Ạmr, "You must be confused, O father of Abdullah, but if you will permit me I will tell you what is on your mind." He said, "Go ahead." And Wardán replied, "In your heart you are balancing the world and the hereafter. What I say is that your going with Ạli means the hereafter without the world, and your going with Muawiya means the world without the hereafter. . . . My opinion is that you should remain here in your house, and if the people of the faith are successful, then act in accord with their faith, but if the people of the world gain the advantage they will not be able to get along without you." Since, therefore, Muawiya had already sent for him, Ạmr felt that the world was calling for him, and he did not resist the appeal, but united with Muawiya in his plans.

When, in about three months, Muawiya had assembled his army, they numbered as many, perhaps, as a hundred and twenty thousand.[1] The fact that they were designated as "the people of Syria" does not mean that they were a non-Arab people, but rather the Arabs who had been carrying on the Muslim conquests in the West, and at the same time the Arabs who had gained most from the favouritism of Ụthman. As they marched down from the north, it was virtually to challenge Ạli's right to the Caliphate, but their battle cry or slogan was only "to avenge the murder of Ụthman." Ostensibly it was because Ạli was considered as having a share in the responsibility of Ụthman's death that this hostile force from the west did not consider him worthy of the Caliphate, and Muawiya carefully kept his own ambitions well in the background.

When they came into Mesopotamia, they established their camp near the Euphrates, in the valley of Siffín, not far from Raḳḳa.[2] Siffín was separated from the bank of the Euphrates

[1] Mas'udi, *Tanbih*, p. 290.

[2] *Encyclopædia of Islam*, art. "Ṣiffín."

by marsh land, overgrown with willows and full of water-holes. This marsh was seven or eight miles long and "an arrow shot broad," and there was only one paved road that led through it to the river. When Ali arrived with his army, by way of Ctesiphon and Raḳḳa, he found that Muawiya and the Syrians "were already encamped in the ruins of the city (of Siffín), which dated from the Roman period, and a detachment of troops from Abu'l-A'war held the road to the Euphrates. Ali attacked at a disadvantage but succeeded in gaining the approach to the river in the month Dhu'l-Hijja. But he generously allowed the Syrian water-carriers to come and draw water, which led to a period of fraternizing and negotiations for peace, with intermittent fighting, which was followed, however, by a truce during the sacred month of Muḥarram. It was after this, at the beginning of the month Ṣafar that the battle of Ṣiffín really began.

Mas'udi mentions that "they were at Ṣiffín 110 days, and there were ninety engagements."[1] This applies, of course, to the prolonged conflict in that vicinity and not to the duration of the battle itself, which continued about a fortnight. Mas'udi also asserts that of the ninety thousand troops that Ali had there were seventy thousand killed; and that of the one hundred and twenty thousand with Muawiya there were forty-five thousand killed. It this is true the last two weeks of the struggle must have been most sanguinary indeed, and it is not surprising that in the end "the people shrunk from the battle and called for peace."[2] At last, on the 13th of Ṣafar, or on the 17th,[3] the agreement was reached to abide by the decision of two arbitrators.

After the attempt to decide the issue by warfare, with so many engagements and for such a long period, most probably both armies were thoroughly exhausted, and in that case the so called agreement for arbitration ought not to be hard to explain. Nevertheless, volumes have been written about it. Some have said that Ali and his army had victory in sight and that they

[1] Mas'udi, *Tanbih*, p. 295.
[2] Ibn Sa'd, Tabaḳat, III, i, p. 21.
[3] Tabari (i, 3340) gives the 13th and Dinawari (p. 210, 1. 5) says the 17th.

made a mistake in agreeing to arbitrate. Certainly the man who was conspicuous as peace-maker, who is said to have suggested the idea of arbitrating the difficulty according to the Ḳoran, is most cordially hated by the friends of Ạli. He was Muawiya's esteemed counsellor, whom he had summoned before initiating his campiagn, Ạmr ibn Ạws, whom Yaḳubi represents as having sold his happiness in the hereafter by devotion to Ạli for advantages in this world by allegiance to Muawiya. He it was who suggested that some of Muawiya's men fasten manuscripts of portions of the Ḳoran to their lance heads and march forward, demanding a decision according to the book of God.

The story is told without elaboration by Ibn Sa'd,[1] "The people of Syria raised the Ḳorans to appeal to what was in them, a scheme which Ạmr ibn Ạws had suggested to Muawiya, who accepted it. The people shrunk from the battle and called for peace. They appointed two arbitrators. Ạli chose Abu Musa, al-Ashạrí and Muawiya chose Ạmr ibn Ạws. They wrote an agreement that they would meet at the beginning of the year at Adhruḥ and arrange for the government of the nation. Then the people dispersed. Muawiya relied on the friendship of the people of Syria and Ạli returned to Kufa, on account of difference of opinion and suspicion." Accordingly, "the people assembled at Adhruḥ in the month of Sha'bán, 38 A.H. Among those who were there was Sa'd ibn Abu Waḳḳás and Ibn Ạmr, and others of the companions of the Apostle of God. Ạmr insisted that Abu Musa take precedence over himself, so Abu Musa spoke first and deposed Ạli. After that Ạmr spoke and confirmed Muawiya (in Ạli's place) and expressed his allegiance to him. In view of this the people dispersed."

It has been suggested that an element of bias in favour of Ạli is shown in the story of the arbitration at Adhruḥ,[2] and that Ạli's admirers had added this story as an embellishment to explain the unsuccessful issue of the battle. Dinawari calls attention to the fact that there were readers of the Ḳoran (Ḳurrá') with

[1] Ibn Sa'd, Tabaḳat, III, i. p. 21.
[2] *Encyclopædia of Islam*, art. "Ṣiffín."

both armies and that they were eager advocates of peace,[1] and there is also a tradition recorded by Ibn Sa'd,[2] "in which we are told that the two armies were tired of war and reluctant to shed more blood, which induced Amr to propose to Muawiya to have the Korans displayed, and to summon the Irákís to the book of Allah, and thus effect a split among them."[3]

Among Ali's supporters against Muawiya were many Persians or non-Arabs who resided in the new cities in Mesopotamia, who had come to resent strongly the arrogance of the Arabs from Medina who had gone forth during Uthman's caliphate to rule the world.[4] There were also a number of the Kurrá', or readers of the Koran, who had been in open opposition to Uthman and some of his policies, and who now allied themselves to Ali. These bitter foes of Arab domination were ill disposed towards any compromise, and after the unfavourable arbitration, they decided that their purposes could no longer be served by loyalty to Ali. The summary statement of Ibn Sa'd is that this group of irreconcilables who "went out" from the army, the Khawárij,[5] "left Ali and his companions and those who were with him. They said, 'Judgment belongs to God alone,' and they set up their camp at Harura. This is why there are called the Haruríya. Ali sent to them Abdullah ibn Abbas, and others too, who disputed and contended with them. A large number did return, but a part of them stood firmly by their opinion and withdrew to Nahrawán, where they cut off the road. Besides that, they killed Abdullah ibn Khabbáb ibn al-Arith. Ali therefore set out against them and defeated them at Nahrawán. One of those killed was Dhu'l Thaddiyah. This was in the year 38 A.H. Ali then returned to Kufa. But the Khawárij did not cease to be on the alert for him from that day until he was killed."

Ali, who they had hoped would be their champion, had

[1] Goldziher, *Vorlesungen uber den Islam*, p. 189; and *Dinawari*, pp. 181, 204, and 205.

[2] Ibn Sa'd, Tabakat, IV, ii, p. 3.

[3] *Encyclopædia of Islam*, art. "Siffín."

[4] Zaydan, *History of Muhammadan Civilization*, Vol. IV, translated by Margoliouth, "Ummayads and Abbasids," p. 74.

[5] Ibn Sa'd, III, i, p. 21.

turned out to be their merciless foe. Resistance with an army was no longer practicable, for their defeat had been decisive. But they knew who was responsible for the killing of their fathers and brothers, and when they considered what had been the promise of the empire of Islam, now torn by civil strife, they came to look with particular hatred on the personal aspirations of the men whom they regarded as barriers to national unity The tradition which gives a detailed story of the plot which ended in Ạli's assassination,[1] though regarded by a recent writer as apocryphal,[2] is nevertheless accepted by al-Mubarrad, is repeated by Yaḳubi, is given also by Dinawarí, and is the obvious background of the account given by Mas'udi.[3]

"In the year 40 A.H. there was an assembly of the Khawarij at Mecca. They were conferring about the war and the rebellion. Three of them pledged themselves to kill Ạli and Muawiya and Ạmr ibn Ạws. They agreed that each was to pursue his man until he had killed him. The partners to the agreement were Abdu'r-Rahman ibn Muljam, of the family of Tujíb and the tribe of Murád; Hajjaj ibn Abdullah, Ṣarími, who was called al-Burak; and Zádawaih, a client of the Beni Ạnbar. Ibn Muljam declared, 'I will kill Ạli'; al-Burak declared, 'I will kill Muawiya; and Zádawaih declared, 'I will kill Ạmr ibn Ạws.' The seventeenth night of the month of Ramaḍan was the night arranged for the murders, though some say it was the twenty-first. Ibn Muljam went out against Ạli, and when he came to Kufa he went to Ḳuṭám, who was his cousin on his father's side. In the battle of Nahrawán, Ạli had killed her father and her brother also. She was one of the most beautiful women of her time, and Ibn Muljam asked for her in marriage. 'I will not marry you,' she said, 'unless you are generous with me.' 'You shall not ask anything,' he answered, 'that I will not give.' Her demand was for three thousand dirhems, a slave girl, a slave boy, and the death of Ạli. 'You shall have what you ask,' he said, 'except the

[1] *Ibid.*, p. 23-25.
[2] *Encyclopædia of Islam*, art. "Kharidjites."
[3] Al-Mubarrad, Wright's text, p. 548; Yaḳubi, *Tarikh*, ii, p. 251 ff.; Dinawari, pp. 227-229; and Mas'udi, *Muruju'l-Dhahab*, iv, p. 426 ff.

killing of Ạli, for I do not believe that you should plot against him.' 'His blood entreats me,' she replied, 'if you will pour it forth you shall gain my hand and person to your advantage. And even if you should be killed, your lot with God will be better than on earth.' He then exclaimed, 'I swear before God that this is indeed what brought me to this city, and I will leave here and I will not return until I have accomplished the deed. I will give you what you ask.' He left her presence, saying:

'Three thousand dirhems, a slave and a maid,
And killing Ạli with the poisoned sword;
No dowry more costly, but let it be paid,
For none will be braver than Ibn Muljam.'

"When he left, a man of the Ashja' met him, a man named Shabib ibn Najdah. He was also one of the Khawarij, and Ibn Muljam addressed him, 'Do you want to be distinguished in this world and the next?' 'Well, how so?' he asked. Ibn Muljam replied, 'Help me in the killing of Ạli.' 'May your mother grieve for you,' he answered, 'it is a shameful project. I have heard of the trouble he has suffered in Islam, and I know of his intimate association with the Prophet.' But Ibn Muljam reproached him, 'Woe to you, for God has cursed him. Understand that he condemned men who believed in the book of the Most High God, and that he put to death our brothers who were Muslims. It is on behalf of our brothers that we shall kill him.' They proceeded then together until they met Ḳuṭám herself at the Great Masjid (in Kufa), where she had pitched a tent for herself, in a place of religious retreat for Friday. It was the thirteenth night of mourning in the month of Ramaḍan. She told them that Mujáshí' ibn Wardán had been asked to help them kill Ạli, and thus she encouraged them and got them excited.

"Seizing their swords they went and sat in front of the gate of the vestibule through which Ạli would have to come on his way to the *masjid*, for he usually came every morning at the time for the call for prayer. Ibn Muljam, may God curse him, met al-Ashath in the masjid, and the latter said, 'May God expose you!'

Hajar ibn Ạdi heard this and added, ' You kill him, you one-eyed man, and God will be the one to kill you.' And at this juncture Ạli came and called, ' O people, come to prayers ! ' At once Ibn Muljam rushed upon him, aided by his companions, and together they cried out, ' Judgment is with God and not with you.' Ibn Muljam struck him a blow with his sword on the top of the head. Shabib's blow fell on one of the side posts of the door, and Mujashí' ibn Wardán ran away. Ạli shouted, ' Do not let the man escape ! ' and the people pressed hard upon Ibn Muljam, stoning him until they were able to seize him. . . . It is related that Ạli did not sleep that night, but continued walking back and forth from the gate of his house to his room, and that he kept saying, ' God be witness, I have not deceived nor been deceived ; truly it is the night appointed.' At one time when he went out several geese came upon some small boys, which frightened them so that they began to cry. The servants wanted to chase the geese away, but Ạli restrained them, saying, ' Let the boys cry, for they are weeping for my funeral.' "

He lived, however, through Friday and Saturday and did not die until Sunday night. Some say he was buried in the great cemetery beside the mosque at Kufa, but there is much difference of opinion as to the place of his burial and the modern Shi'ites generally consider that his body lies at Najaf, a few miles away from Kufa.

It is said that when Ạli died " they did not find more than six hundred dirhems, which was a sum that remained from his share of booty, and which had been designated to secure the services of a eunuch for the women's apartment. According to another account what remained amounted to only two hundred and forty dirhems, a Ḳoran and a sword."[1]

[1] Mas'udi, *Muruju'l-Dhahab*, iv, p. 434.

CHAPTER IV

ẠLI THE FIRST IMAM

A CAREFUL study of the Imams reveals the fact that very ordinary men have been made immortals. The best that we can do is to gather what we can from the earliest sources to enable us to determine what these men were in real life, in their unglorified and unsanctified existence. Yet at the same time it is necessary to endeavour to picture the halo that later legend has given them. Unless we go beyond what they were to what has been said about them, we will fail entirely to enter into the spirit of Shi'ite Islam and will not be able to explain the growth of the amazing and all-inclusive doctrines that are now considered fundamental to that faith.

The earliest traditions show that Ạli's claims to the caliphate were not regarded by his friends and supporters as merely political aspirations, but as his divine right. The teaching and agitation of a comparatively obscure figure in the history of Islam had much to do with the rise and spread of this point of view. As early as the caliphate of Ụthman, an itinerant preacher named Ạbd Allah ibn Saba' had travelled widely throughout the empire, as Tabari says, " seeking to lead the Moslems into error." According to Wellhausen he was said to have been a Jew before he became a Muḥammadan. Originally, he had come from Ṣana, in the Yemen, and he had worked in the Ḥijaz and in the new cities of al-Basra and Kufa, and had afterwards journeyed to Syria, and had ultimately settled in Egypt. In Egypt he had taken a leading part in the conspiracy in favour of Ạli, and had declared that Abu Bakr and Ụmar and Ụthman were usurpers. The malcontents during Ụthman's caliphate had been in secret correspondence with Ibn Ṣaba', and he had accompanied the troops that marched from Egypt to Medina immediately before the murder of Ụthman.[1] Ibn Sa'd makes only the remark that he was one of the readers of the Ḳoran who accompanied Ạli.[2] Mirkhond, in the Rauzatu's-Safá,[3] relates that this Jewish priest came to Medina and made a profession of the Muḥammadan faith with the hope that Ụthman would respect and honour him. He met, however, with disappointment, and soon began to associate with those who were dissatisfied, and he did not hesitate to openly censure Ụthman's administration. Finally, Ụthman asked, "Who is this Jew, after all, that I should bear all this from him ?" and gave orders that he should be compelled to leave Medina. Then it was that he went to Egypt where he was an active conspirator against Ụthman.

Part of the text of the protest of Ibn Saba' was that it is a saying of the Christians that Jesus will return, descending from heaven to earth. If, therefore, Muḥammad is to be considered superior to Jesus, he is more likely to return first, especially in the light of the verse in the Ḳoran (xxviii. 85), "Verily he who hath given thee the Ḳoran for a rule will certainly bring thee back home."

But another of his teachings that was more immediately influential was that every prophet has a *waṣi* (executor or plenipotentiary) and that Ạli was the waṣi of Muḥammad, and had indeed been so designated by him. When the people had disregarded the wish of Muḥammad, they had therefore committed a palpable injustice to Ạli. It became necessary, accordingly, for all the people to champion Ạli's divinely sanctioned rights and to obey him implicitly. In fact, the extreme or *ultra* Shi'ites (Ghul'at), who went so far as to claim that Ạli was himself divine, have been said to have derived this conception also from Ibn Saba',[4] who taught "that the Divine Spirit which dwells in every prophet, and passes successively from one to another, was

[1] Nicholson, *A Literary History of the Arabs*, p. 215, with reference to Tabari, i, 2,942, 2. Wellhausen, *Die Rel. Pol. Oppos. Partien*, p. 89 *seqq.* *Encyclopædia of Islam*, art. "Abd Allah b. Ṣaba'."

[2] Ibn Sa'd, *Tabaḳat*, vi, 163.

[3] Rauzatu's-Safá, trans. Rahatsek, II, iii, p. 160.

[4] Shahrastani, *Book of Religious and Philosophical Sects*, edit. Cureton, p. 132.

transferred at Muḥammad's death to Ạli, and from Ạli into his descendants who succeeded him in the Imamate."

Thus there was much discussion as to whether Ạli had actually received the designation (naṣṣ) of the Prophet at Ghadir Khum, and whether there were not other sayings of the Prophet also that should have been understood as expressing his intention that Ạli should have been his successor. Some of the oldest collections of traditions of orthodox Islam include sayings that appear to support this position of the Ạlids,[1] who were never able to accept the authority of the *ijmá'l-umma*, or agreement by the consent of the community. In subsequent periods they adapted themselves to the necessity of circumstances and recognized the ruling Caliphs and gave them their nominal allegiance, but they still maintained that one of the living descendants of Ạli was in point of fact the *rightful* Caliph (successor) or Imam (leader) of the people of Islam.

The most ordinary usage of the word *imam* was that of prayer leader, and this function was retained by the Caliph. The fact that the Prophet, in his last illness, had asked Abu Bakr to go and lead the prayers in his stead, was considered as contradicting the assertion that Ạli had been intended as his successor. By this act it was thought that any possible previous designation of Ạli had been abrogated. And Ạli was not given any special status as Imam during the caliphates of Abu Bakr or Ụmar or Ụthman. He was recognized and respected as an honoured counsellor and as one of the family of the Prophet, but he was not regarded as a spiritual pontiff. After he succeeded to the caliphate there is still no trustworthy evidence that he claimed to be more of a spiritual authority than other caliphs had been. In actual status, he was the one of the Companions of the Prophet who was chosen to succeed Ụthman, by the not unnatural consent of the community at the time, and who was murdered in the course of his efforts to overcome persistent and widespread rebellion against his authority.

[1] Tirmidhi, *Saḥih*, 46/31; as-Suyuti, *Táríkhu'l-Khulafa*, trans. Jarrett, p. 172 ff.; Guillaume, *The Traditions of Islam*, p. 61; and Wensinck, *Handbook of Early Muhammadan Traditions*, under "Ạli," "Ḥasan," "Ḥusain," etc.

But, unfortunately, by the time that even the earliest of either the *six* canonical or the *four* Shi'ite collections of traditions were compiled, Ạli had found his place in folklore and was celebrated by all kinds of legendary tales. For example, we may consider what the traditions relate about his valour in battle. At the Battle of Ṣiffín, he alone was said to have killed 523 men in one day.[1] When he accompanied the Prophet on his expeditions, "at Badr and at every *mashhad* (place of witnessing by martyrdom)," [2] he carried the standard. His honour as standard-bearer before Khaibar is also frequently mentioned,[3] which may well enough be true for there seems to have been no doubt of his loyalty and bravery. His great sword was called *Dhu'l-Faḳár*, the "owner of the vertebræ." It was a sword that had been captured at the battle of Badr from an unbeliever named Ạṣ ibn Munabbih, and it had been given to Ạli by Muḥammad.[4] With this sword Ạli could cut off heads with ease and he would sometimes dash at his opponents on horseback and hew their bodies in two, "the upper part rolling on the ground while the lower part remained on horseback"; or he would await the attack of the enemy, and by simply extending his arm he would knock down thirty-three assailants.[5] It is related that he seized a gate near the fort of Khaibar, "and used it as a buckler to guard himself, and it continued in his hand while he was fighting, until the Lord gave us the victory. Then he cast it from him, and verily I know that we eight men tried to turn over the same gate and we were not able to turn it over."[6]

We must be prepared to find exaggerated statements also in regard to Ạli's other personal virtues, for as Ahmad ibn Hanbal says, "there hath not come down to us regarding the merits of any one of the Companions of the Apostle of God what hath been transmitted concerning Ạli."[7] At times they are represented

[1] Mas'udi, *Murudju'l-Dhahab*, iv, p. 376.
[2] Ibn Sa'd, *Tabaḳat*, III, i, p. 4.
[3] Wensinck, *Handbook E.M.T.*, p. 16.
[4] Steingass, *Persian-English Dictionary*.
[5] *Encyclopædia of Islam*, art. "Ạli."
[6] As-Suyuti, *Tarikhu'l-Khulafa*, trans. Jarrett, p. 172.
[7] Ahmad ibn Hanbal, *Musnad*, i, p. 108, 114, and 118.

as so outstanding that it was for this reason that the Beni Umayyah were jealous of him and came to hate him. That he did have the special confidence of Muḥammad is acknowledged by all. His friends remembered that even his boyhood had been spent with the Prophet, whom he never deserted. He was one of the very first believers, perhaps the first after the Prophet's wife, Khadijah. They recalled that at the time of the expedition to Tabuk, when the Prophet had asked him to remain behind in Medina, he said to him, "Is it not fitting that you should be in the same relation to me that Aaron was to Moses?"[1]

However, like Aaron, on occasions when he was asked to undertake difficult administrative tasks, his answers sometimes betrayed a consciousness of his youth and a modest hesitancy. He is reported to have related, "When the Prophet sent me to Yemen as a judge, I said, 'O Apostle of God, do you send me to a people where there are old men of experience? I fear that I may not be scccessful.' But the Prophet answered, 'Surely God will establish your speech and guide your heart.'"[2] And Ụmar himself considered that Ạli was the best of all the judges of the people of Medina and the chief of the readers of the Ḳoran.[3]

Students of the Arabic language will observe with interest the assistance that Ạli is said to have given to Abu'l-Aswad ad-Duwali in the task of systematizing Arabic grammar. "Abu'l Aswad was one of the most eminent of the Tábís, an inhabitant of Basra, and a partisan of Ạli ibn Abu Talib, under whom he fought at the battle of Ṣiffín. In intelligence he was one of the most perfect of men, and in reason he was one of the most sagacious. He was the first who invented grammar. It is said that Ạli laid down for him this principle: the parts of speech are three, the Noun, the Verb, and the Particle, telling him to found a complete treatise upon it. . . . A scribe belonging to the tribe of Abdu'l-Ḳais was brought to him, but did not give him satisfaction; another then came and Abu'l-Aswad said to him, 'When

[1] Ibn Hajar, Vol. II, p. 1,208.
[2] Wensinck, *Handbook E.M.T.*, p. 15.
[3] Ibn Sa'd, *Tabaḳat*, II, ii, p. 101.

you see me open (fatah) my mouth in pronouncing a letter, place a point over it; when I close (damm) my mouth, place a point before (or upon) the letter; and when I pucker up (kasar) my mouth, place a point under the letter.' This the scribe did. The art of grammar was called *nahw* because Abu'l-Aswad had said, 'I asked permission of Ạli ibn Abu Ṭalib to compose in the same way (nahw) as he had done.' God knows best if this be true."[1]

Considerable pains have thus been taken to represent Ạli as no less mighty with the pen than with the sword. Hasan al-Basari called him "the scholar of God in this community.[2] "According to the historian, al-Wakidi, at the time of the appearance of Islam, among the tribe of the Ḳuraish, to which Muḥammad belonged, there were only six or seven men who could write. Among them were those who were afterwards the caliphs, Ụmar, Ụthman and Ạli. The Prophet is said to have been unable to write, but he had four secretaries who wrote the text of the Ḳoran as it was revealed on whatever came to hand—branches of palms, bits of leather, or dry bones. . . . There is a Muḥammadan tradition, also, which claims that Ạli, the last of the first four caliphs, had great skill in writing the Kufic characters. He was able to make the elongated *káf*, which is characteristic of that script, with such uniform exactness that it was scarcely possible, even with a compass, to distinguish any difference between the *káfs* that he had written."[3]

It is not unlikely, however, that Muḥammad could write, and at all events it would be misleading to over-emphasize the use of palm branches and bits of leather and dry bones by his secretaries. Probably no time was lost in transcribing what was so recorded, and we know that the number of copies of the Ḳoran was rapidly multiplied. Their newly acquired "book" was a source of Arab pride, and copies were produced in such a number and with such variation that the Caliph Ụthman felt the necessity of getting out an officially approved edition. And when a selected

[1] *Ibid.*, p. 102.
[2] Ibn Khallikan, *Biographical Dictionary*, trans. De Slane, Vol. I, p. 663.
[3] Goldziher, *Vorlesungen*, ch. v, sec. 3.

company from the army of Muawiya shrewdly advanced against the forces of Ali, with manuscripts of the Koran, or portions of it, attached to their lances, and demanded arbitration according to the "word of God," it would suggest that numerous copies were already extant.

There are traditions that affirm that Ali had a copy of the Koran of his own, a special copy which he had annotated according to conversations he had held with Muhammad. This additional writing on the margin of his own Koran is apparently all that Ali claimed to have, in the nature of revelation from the Prophet, that others did not have. As the question of the nature of this *Ṣaḥifa* that Ali referred to has a bearing on the later Shi'ite belief in the existence of a mysterious book that they called the *Djafr*[1], representative traditions on the subject are here recorded. First, it may be observed that the plural of the word *ṣaḥifa* is *ṣuḥuf*, and in the plural the term is used "for the one hundred portions of scripture said to have been given to Adam, Seth, Enoch, Abraham and Moses," which are referred to in the Koran (lxxxvii. 19), "this is truly written in *the books* of old, *the books* of Al raham and Moses."[2] In the singular the word *ṣaḥifa* means a written page, and in the following traditions it is used uniformly with the definite article or with the demonstrative pronoun, and should be translated *the writing* or *this writing*. In his chapter on *al-Ilm*, or Learning, al-Bukhari has cited a tradition that is referred originally to Abu Juhafa, who said, "I asked Ali, 'Is there any book with you?' He answered, 'No, none except the Book of God, or the understanding which is given a man who is a Muslim, or what is in *this writing*,' I said, 'What is in *this writing*?' He replied, 'Reason, and the separation of captives, and not killing the one who submits in unbelief.'"[3] A tradition attributed to at-Taymiya is mentioned twice by al-Bukhari,[4] in which the father of at-Taymiya reported that in a speech that Ali made he said, "There

[1] Huart, *Les Calligraphes et Les Miniaturiates de l'Orient Musulman*, 1908.
[2] *Encyclopædia of Islam*, art. "Djafr," by D. B. McDonald.
[3] Hughes, *Dictionary of Islam*.
[4] Bukhari, *Ṣaḥih*, text Leyden, III, 39. Tayalisi, *Musnad*, Haidarabad, 1321 A.H., No. 91.

is no book among us that we should read except the Book of God, the Most High, and what is in *the writing*." Then he said, "In it are instructions about the wounded, what to do with the older camels, and the extent of the sacred territory about Medina, that lies between Ạyr and Kadha." Ahmad ibn Hanbal, who has frequently given this tradition,[1] has mentioned the bounds of the sacred territory as lying between Ạyr and Thur. And he has attributed to Ạli the saying that whoever relates false traditions, or gives shelter to one doing so, upon him be the curse of God and of the angels and of all mankind ; God will not accept his offerings.

If Ạli was from ten to fifteen years of age at the time when he professed Islam, and if he was one of those who could write, with as much as we have of testimony from the traditions, it is not at all improbable that he did have a Ḳoran with marginal notes which he had made in his conversations with the Prophet. The purport of those notes is set forth in the traditions that have been cited. They are practical instructions and pronouncements, and have nothing mystical or peculiar about them, and they do not correspond at all with the elaborate claims made by the Shi'ites of later times for the secret book *Djafr*.

Typical of these later statements is the remark of al-Kulaini,[2] "that when the Apostle taught anything to Ạli, Ạli evolved from it a thousand other things."[3] He declares also that the *ṣaḥifa* in Ạli's handwriting was seventy cubits in length, as measured by the arm of the Apostle, and that it contained everything "permitted and forbidden," and everything necessary for mankind. And in the *Djafr*, or secret book, he assures us that there was to be found "the knowledge of the prophets, and of the representatives of the prophets, and of the scholars of the Beni Israel." Mas'udi shows how the later Imams were accustomed to refer at times to these secret books that Ạli was supposed to have left in their keeping.[4]

[1] Bukhari, *Ṣaḥih*, text Leyden, ch. 58, sec. 10 and 17.
[2] Ahmad ibn Hanbal, *Musnad*, Vol. I, pp. 81, 119, 122 and 126.
[3] Kulaini, *Usulu'l-Kâfi*, p. 85.
[4] Mas'udi, *Murudju'l-Dhahab*, Vol. VII, p. 382.

Belief in the existence of these sacred and secret books among the Imams was persistent, and later writers are more explicit in describing them. For example, in one of the popular books that Muḥammad Baḳir Majlisi wrote in the seventeenth century, the Hayatu'l-Ḳulub, or Life of Hearts,[1] it is related that at the time when Muḥammad appealed to the Nasárá (Christians) in Najrán in the Yemen to accept him as a prophet whose coming had been foretold by Jesus, a great book called the *Jáma'* was referred to in the course of the debate. It was supposed to be a collection of the writings of the 124,000 prophets. The first part was the book of Adam, " which related to the kingdom of the Most High, what he has created and what he has decreed in heaven and earth respecting things temporal and eternal. This book, which contained all sciences, was transmitted by the father of mankind to Shays." Shays added his contribution to the great work and handed it on to Idrís, and likewise there were the writings of Abraham, and Moses, and Jesus, until at last the time came for the great and final work of Ahmad (or Muḥammad).

A Persian manual on the lives of the Imams, which is a compilation from the voluminous works of Majlisi, was written in Persian and lithographed in Teheran in 1912. It is called the Tadhkiratu'l-A'imma, and here we find it stated that the Jafr-i-Jáma' is a book that the scholars agree that Ạli had in his possession, and that the part that now exists consists of twenty-eight portions, that each portion has twenty-eight pages, and each page twenty-eight divisions . . . " and no one beside God and the Imams knows the character in which it is written, unless the sinless Imams have taught it to him."

The same modern manual mentions also " the book of Ạli " (the ṣaḥifa), " which the Prophet dictated and Ạli wrote. It is seventy metres long and the width of a sheepskin. It is also called the Jáma', and it shows what things are permitted and what things are forbidden." Two other minor works of the same sort are the Jafr Abyaḍ (the white Jafr), which has fourteen

[1] Majlisi, *Hayatu'l-Ḳulub,* Vol. II, trans. Merrick, *Life and Religion of Muhammad,* p. 315.

portions, and each portion has fourteen divisions, etc., and the Writing of Fatima, with many traditions, to show that God taught Adam twenty-five of the divine names : Noah knew eight ; Abraham had six ; Moses had four ; Jesus had two ; and Ạaṣif ibn Barkhiá had one, whereas the Apostle of God knew seventy-two of these names, which he taught to Ạli.[1]

Collections have been made of maxims and aphorisms that are said to have originated with Ạli. A hundred of these were collected by the Persian poet Rashíd al-Dín and have been translated in German.[2] There are one hundred and sixty-nine of these moral sentences given in Ockley's *History of the Saracens*, (p. 339), and the following are a few of those that are quoted by as-Suyuti.[3]

In reply to one who persisted in asking him, " What is Fate ? " Ạli answered, "O questioner, hath the Lord created thee for what he hath willed, or what thou hath willed ? " He replied, " Indeed for what he hath willed." Ạli answered, " Then He will use thee as He thinketh fit."

It was said to Ạli, " What is generosity ? " He replied, " that from which the initiative proceedeth, for what cometh after a request is liberality and munificence."

A man went to Ạli and praised him and spoke extravagantly, and it happened that Ạli had heard somewhat of him before that, so he said to him, " Verily, I am not as thou sayest, yet I am above that which is in thy heart."

Once he said, " I make it incumbent upon myself when I am asked what I know not, to say God knoweth best."

On another occasion he remarked, " He who seeketh to do justice unto men, let him desire for them what he desireth for himself."

And seven things he said were of the Devil : excessive anger, excessive sneezing, excessive yawning, vomiting, bleeding at the nose, clandestine discourse, and sleeping during devotional exercise.

It is not, however, as a warrior, nor as a scholar, nor as a sage that the legendary Ạli has attained the greatest distinction.

[1] Tadhkiratu'l-A'imma, compiled from Majlisi, lithographed Teheran, 1912, p. 56 ff.
[2] *Ạli's hundert Spruche*, Fleischer, Leipsig, 1837.
[3] As-Suyuti, *Tarikhu'l-Khulafa*, trans. Jarrett, p. 185 ff.

"He is incomparable as a saint; he works miracles (karámát) which his adherents do not hesitate to compare to the miracles of the prophets (mu'djizát). . . . At Ṣahbá' God made the Sun to come back after it had set, to enable Ali to finish the *'asr* prayer; in the mosque of Kufa he restored the severed hand of a negro whom he had sentenced to the punishment which canonical law inflicts on thieves; the head of a Kharidjite who brought a charge before Ali against a woman, and, while doing so, indulged in crying, was changed by him into a dog's head; at his prayer, eighty camels which the Prophet had promised to a Bedouin rose out of the ground; when in the environs of Babylon a lion struck the inhabitants with terror, someone was charged by Ali to show his ring to the animal, and the lion disappeared; he raised somebody from the dead; and he reappeared, several centuries after his death, in a vision in order to blind his detractors."

But perhaps the most amazing instances of the exaltation of Ali are to be found in the descriptions of the *miráj* or ascension of the Prophet to heaven, in accord with the statement in the Koran (xvii. 1): "Glory to him who carried his servant by night from the sacred temple (of Mecca) to the temple that is more remote, whose precinct we have blessed, that we might show him of our signs." As Canon Sell has pointed out,[1] "this event has afforded to the imagination of the traditionists ample scope for the most vivid descriptions of what the prophet saw and heard. It is manifestly unfair to look upon these extravagant embellishments as matters of necessary belief. The most intelligent members of the modern school of Muslims look upon the *mi'ráj* as a vision, though the orthodox condemn such a view."

Certainly the orthodox Shi'ites most heartily condemn it. The second volume of Majlisi's *Hayatu'l-Kulub* has already been translated into English as the *Life and Religion of Muḥammad*, by Rev. James L. Merrick, and is characteristic and representative of the generally accepted Shi'ite beliefs. Majlisi says (p. 190) that "both Shi'ite and Sunnite traditions declare that the ascension was bodily, and not merely in the Spirit; in the state of wakeful-

[1] *Encyclopædia of Islam*, art. "Ali."

ness, not of sleep. On this head, among the ancient *ulamá* of the Shi'ites there was no disagreement. The doubts which some have entertained whether the ascension was bodily, or only in the spirit, have arisen from want of examining the subject, or from disbelief of its divine attestations, and listening to people who are without faith themselves." In his portrayal of all that Muḥammad heard and saw on his great night journey through the seven heavens, Majlisi mentions what was heard and seen of Ali[1]:

" It is related that Muḥammad declared that on the night of the ascension, the Most High commanded me to inquire of the past prophets for what reason they were exalted to that rank, and they all testified, We were raised up on account of your prophetical office, and the *imamate* of Ạli ibn Abu Ṭalib, and of the *imams* of your posterity. A divine voice then commanded, Look on the right side of the empyrean. I looked and saw the similitude of Ạli, and Hasan, and Husain, and Ạli ibn al-Husain (alias, Zainü'l-Abidín), and Muḥammad Baḳir, and Ja'far as-Sádiḳ, and Musa Kazim, and Ạli ibn Musa, ar-Riḍa, and Muḥammad Taḳi, and Ạli Naḳí, and Hasan Askarí, and Mahdí—all performing prayers in a sea of light. These, said the Most High, are my proofs, vicegerents, and friends, and the last of them will take vengeance on my enemies.

" The Prophet declared that when he performed the ascension, the angels inquired so particularly about Ạli that he began to conclude that Ạli was better known in heaven than himself. When I arrived, he continued, at the fourth heaven, I saw the angel of death, who said that it was his office to take the soul of every creature except mine and Ạli's ; your spirits, said he, the Most High will himself take away, by the hand of his power When I came under the empyrean, I saw Ạli ibn Abu Ṭalib standing there, and said to him, O Ạli, have you got here before me ? Whom are you addressing, said Jibraíl. My brother Ạli, I replied. This is not Ạli, said he, but an angel of the merciful God, whom he created in the likeness of Ạli ; and when those of us privileged to approach near the Deity wish to behold Ạli, we visit this angel.

And so Jesus and Moses and Abraham all inquired about Ạli and congratulated Muḥammad on having left so good a Caliph

[1] Sell, *Life of Muhammad,* C. L. S. for India, p. 72.

in his place.[1] And according to a book recently published,[2] the Apostle related, " On the night of the mi'ráj, on every one of the curtains of light and on every one of the pillars of the empyrean to which I came, I saw written, ' There is no God but God, Muḥammad is the Apostle of God, and Ạli ibn Abu Ṭalib is the Commander of the Faithful.' "

[1] Merrick, *Life and Religion of Muhammad*, p. 203.
[2] *Urjatu'l-Ahmadiyya*, by Shaikh Muhammad Ja'far, 1325 A.H., p. 193, Nos. 35 and 36.

CHAPTER V

THE SHRINE OF ALI AT NAJAF

IT is related on the authority of the Imam Ja'far Ṣadiḳ that Ạli had requested that he be buried secretly, because he feared that the Khawarij or others might desecrate his tomb.[1] But as there were few who knew the secret, some have thought that Ạli was buried in his own house in Medina. We find evidence of this idea in the travels of Thomas Forster in the sixteenth century,[2] for in his description of Medina he says that beyond the mosque of the Prophet "are two other sepulchres covered with green cloth, and in the one of them is buried Fatma, the daughter of Mahomet, and Ạli is buried in the other, who was the husband of the said Fatma." Others have said that Ạli was buried either in the courtyard of the mosque or in the public square at Kufa, while still others say that he was buried in Karkh, a quarter of the old city of Baghdad. But notwithstanding these various suggestions, the Shi'ite scholars are generally agreed, and it is the more popular belief, that Ạli ibn Abu Ṭalib, the fourth caliph and the first Imam, was buried in Najaf, which is a little more than four miles away from Kufa.

Ibn Jubayr tells us that "in the mosque at Kufa there is a pulpit which is surrounded by a circle of steps of sandal-wood. It is elevated above the court and is like a small mosque. This pulpit is a memorial to the Amiru'l-Muminín, Ạli ibn Abu Ṭalib, and it was at this place that the miserable and accursed Adbu'l-Rahman ibn Muljám struck him with a sword. People repeat a form of salutation here and pray and weep."[3]

But that the Shi'ite community as a whole have usually

[1] Majlisí, *Tofatu'z-Zá'irín*, lithographed in Persia, 1274 A.H., p. 53.
[2] Hakluyt, *The Principal Voyages of the English Nations*, edit. Everyman's Library, Vol. III, p. 195.
[3] *Travels of Ibn Jubayr*, Wright's Text, Gibb Memorial, Vol. V, p. 211.

regarded Najaf as the place where Ạli was buried is plainly indicated by the thousands of graves that are seen just outside the town. Any visitor will remember vividly that to the north and the east of the town there are "acres of graves and myriads of domes of various colours and in various stages of disrepair."[1] Whoever goes to Najaf will follow a road that approaches the town by a winding course through this vast cemetery, and if he has a well-informed Shi'ite guide he may be told that Abraham is supposed to have come to this village along with Isaac; that there had been many earthquakes in the vicinity, but that while Abraham remained there were no more tremors. On one night, however, Abraham and Isaac went to a different village, and sure enough Najaf was visited with another earthquake. When they returned the people were most eager for them to make Najaf their permanent dwelling-place, and Abraham agreed to do so on the condition that they would sell him the *wádí*, or valley, behind the village for cultivation. Isaac is said to have protested that this land was not fit for either farming or grazing, but Abraham insisted and assured him that the time would come when there would be a tomb there with a shrine, "at which seventy thousand people would gain absolutely undisputed entrance to Paradise, and be able also to intercede for many others."[2]

The valley that Abraham wanted to buy is called the Valley of Peace (Wadiu's-Salam), and it is related on the authority of the fourth imám that Ạli once said that this Valley of Peace is part of Heaven, and that there is not a single one of the believers in the world (i.e., the Shi'ites), whether he dies in the east or the west, but his soul will come to this Paradise. "As there is nothing hidden in this world from my eyes," Ạli went on to say, "I see all the believers seated here in groups and talking with one another."[3] And he mentioned also that there is a Wadíu'l-Barahut, "and whoever disbelieves in Muḥammad and his successors, of whatever nation he may be, will go there when he

[1] *Historical Mesopotamia*, a local guidebook that was issued by the "Times of Mesopotamia," 1912, p. 50.
[2] Majlisí, *op. cit.*, p. 108.
[3] Majlisí, *op. cit.*, p. 111.

dies." This declaration is with reference to the famous spring of Barahut in Ḥaramawt, which is said to be a fissure, 33 feet long and 25 feet broad, and that its entrance is filled with burning sulphur.[1]

The name of the town Najaf is explained in the traditions. At first there was a mountain there, and when one of the sons of Noah refused to enter the ark, he said that he would sit on this mountain until he would see where the water would come. A revelation came therefore to the mountain, "Do you undertake to protect this son of mine from punishment ? " and all at once the mountain fell to pieces and the son of Noah was drowned. In the place of the mountain a large river appeared, but after a few years the river dried up and the place was called Nay-Jaff, meaning "the dried river."[2]

Of the notices of Najaf in the works of the Arab geographers, the earliest is given by Ibn Ḥawḳal, who wrote in the tenth Christian century. Ibn Ḥawḳal states that the governor of Mosul, at some time from 292-317 A.H., "had built a dome on four columns over the tomb of Mashhad Ạli, which shrine he ornamented with rich carpets and hangings : also he surrounded the adjacent town with a wall."[3] The ordinary tradition about the founding of this shrine, however, is related by Mustawfi, who wrote in the fourteenth century[4] :

"Two leagues distant from Kufa towards the south-west lies Mashhad Ạli, the shrine of Ạli, the Commander of the Faithful, known as the Mashhad-i-Gharwá (the Wondrous Shrine). For when Ạli had received his death wound, in the mosque at Kufa, he gave it as his will that as soon as he was dead his body should be placed on a camel ; then the camel was to be given its head and set in motion, and wheresoever the beast knelt down, there they should bury his body. This being done, it came to pass that the camel knelt at the place where now is the Shrine, and here in

[1] *Encyclopædia of Islam*, Leyden, art. "Barahut."
[2] Majlisí, *op. cit.*, p. 111.
[3] Le Strange, *Lands of the Eastern Caliphate*, p. 76 *seqq.*
[4] Mustawfi, *Nuzhat al-Ẓulúb*, Gibb Memorial, Vol. XXIII, Text, p. 31 ; English trans. p. 38.

consequence was he buried. Now during the reigns of the Umayyad Caliphs his blessed resting-place could not be disclosed, and so it was also under the Abbasids until the reign of Harun-ar-Rashíd. But in the year 175 (791) Harun happened to go a-hunting in these parts, and his quarry fleeing from him took refuge in this very spot. And however much the Caliph urged his horse into the place, into it the horse would not go ; and on this awe took possession of the Caliph's heart. He made inquiries of the people of the neighbourhood, and they acquainted him with the fact that this was the grave of Ạli. Harun ordered the ground to be excavated, and the body of Ạli was discovered lying there wounded. A tomb was afterwards erected, and the people began to settle in its vicinity."

Perhaps the statement that Ạli's body was discovered lying there wounded, about 130 years after he had been killed, is one of the passages that may indicate that Mustawfi was himself a convinced Shi'ah. But he goes on to say that a hundred and ninety odd years later than this hunting experience of Harun ar-Rashíd's, " Ạdud-ad-Dawlah, the Buyid, in the year 366 (977), raised a mighty building over the grave, as it now exists, and the place has since become a little town, the circuit of which is 2,500 paces." We are informed by Ibn Athir that the great Buyid prince, the Ạdud-ad-Dawlah, and two of his sons were buried here. However, during a persecution of the Shi'ites in 443 (1051), this shrine, that had been built for only a little over seventy years, is said to have been burnt to the ground. But it appears to have been soon restored, at least before the time when the Wazir Nizam-al-Mulk accompanied Malik Shah on his visit in 479 (1086).[1] Mustawfi adds the observation that when Sultan Malik Shah, the Seljuk, visited Najaf, he noticed a minaret " which was all crooked, so that half rose straight from the ground and half was falling over. He enquired of the matter and was told that Ạli had once passed by here, when this minaret, to pay him respect, began to bend over : but the Caliph Ạli made a sign to it that it should remain thus."

[1] Le Strange, *op. cit.*, p. 77.

It is from the latter part of the twelfth century that we have a reference to Najaf in the account the famous traveller, Ibn Jubayr, has written of his visit to Kufa, for he mentions that he was told in Kufa that the Shrine of Ạli was at a point about a farsakh away, where the camel had stopped that carried Ạli's corpse, which was wrapped in a curtain.

In the thirteenth century Khulagu Khan captured Baghdad, and there was widespread destruction in the region round about. But apparently the Shi'ites themselves had invited and encouraged the coming of the Mongols, on account of various outrages that had been committed against their community. The Sunnite troops of Baghdad, under the command of the Caliph's son, had deliberately dishonoured the Shi'ites who lived in the village Karkh, by dragging their women out of their harems and carrying them on their horses' cruppers with their faces and feet bare in the public streets. "The Visier, who belonged to this sect, was outraged, and sent a letter to the Seyid Taj ud din Muḥammad, Ibn Nasir el Hoseini, the rais of Hillah, a famous seat of Shia influence, complaining, *inter alia*, that Karkh had been plundered, that the sons of the house of Ạli had been robbed, the people of the stock of Hashim made prisoners, and the dishonour which had formerly been put upon Hussain, the grandson of the prophet, in the plundering of his harem, and the accompanying bloodshedding, had been renewed. The Seyid replied in the names of all the relatives of the Prophet: 'The heretics must be put to death and destroyed, and their race be uprooted. If you will not side with us you will be lost. You will be despised in Baghdad, as henna, which delights women, is despised by rough men, and as a ring is despised by him who has had his hand cut off.' Khulagu at this time had captured the Ismaelite fortress at Alamut, and the Vizier wrote to him, pointing out the weakness of Baghdad, and inviting him to march thither."[1] Accordingly, when the Mongols came, we find that "during the siege of Baghdad some of the chief people of Hillah, where the Seyids or descendants of Ạli were influential, sent an embassy to

[1] Howarth, *History of the Mongols*, Vol. III, pp. 114-115.

Khulagu with their submission, and stating that it was a tradition among them, derived from their ancestors, Ạli and the twelve Imams, that he (Khulagu) would become the master of that district (i.e., of Irak Arab)." This explains why these Shi'ite communities in the vicinity of Baghdad were spared in the Mongol invasion, and this is the reason that, on Khulagu's command, one hundred Mongols were designated "to protect the tomb of Ạli at Najaf."[1]

When a little later the Mongol Il-Khans were doing everything possible to enhance the glory of their new city, Sultania, which was about one hundred miles from Kazvin, Uljaitu "entertained the project of transporting the bones of Ạli and Hussayn from Najaf and Kerbala respectively, and erected a superb building to receive the sacred remains." He did not live, however, to realize this scheme, and the building he had planned became his own mausoleum.[2]

As Mustawfi's fourteenth century description of Najaf had nothing to say about restorations, so also Ibn Baṭuṭa, who wrote about the same time, makes no mention of repairs to the Shrine after depredations by the Mongols.[3]

"We next proceeded to the city of Mashhad Ạli, where the grave of Ạli is thought to be. It is a handsome place and well peopled; all the inhabitants, however, are of the Ráfiza (or Shi'ah) sect. The inhabitants consist chiefly of rich and brave merchants. About the gardens are plastered walls adorned with paintings, and with them are carpets, couches, and lamps of gold and silver. Within the city is a large treasury kept by the tribune, which arises from the offerings brought from different parts: for when anyone happens to be ill, or to suffer under any infirmity, he will make a vow, and thence receive relief. The garden is also famous for its miracles; and hence it is believed that the grave of Ạli is there.

"Of these miracles the 'night of revival' is one: for, on the seventeenth day of the month Rajab, cripples come from the different parts of Fars, Rúm, Khorasan, Ịrak, and other places, and assemble in companies from twenty to thirty in number.

[1] Howarth, *op. cit.*, p. 132.
[2] Sykes, *History of Persia*, Vol. II, p. 235.
[3] Ibn Baṭuṭa, *The Travels of Ibn Baṭuṭa*, Trans. Lee, London, 1829, ch. iv, p. 32.

They are placed over the grave soon after sunset. People then, some praying, others reciting the Ḳoran, and others prostrating themselves, wait expecting their recovery and rising, when, about midnight, they all get up sound and well. This is a matter well known among them: I heard it from creditable persons, but I was not present at one of these nights. I saw, however, several such afflicted persons, who had not yet received, but were looking forwards for the advantages of this 'night of revival.'"

In so much as the Abbasid caliphate had been finally and completely overthrown by the Mongols, Baghdad itself very soon became a minor provincial town, and the elaborate system of irrigation that had sustained the surrounding region rapidly fell into disrepair. But for some fifty or sixty years, "while those survived whose education had been completed before Islam suffered this great disaster," there was a distinct survival of culture, so that during the period of the Jalá'ír or Il-Khaní dynasty there was unwonted literary activity.[1] Pilgrimages to the shrines of the Imams who were buried in the Baghdad vicinity were not prohibited, but in fact we observe that frequently these later Mongol princes bore the names Ḥasan and Ḥusain, which suggests their tolerant and sympathetic attitude toward the Shi'ite shrines.

Likewise the Shrine at Najaf does not appear to have suffered destruction during the raids of Timur. When in A.D. 1393 Timur definitely made up his mind to conquer Arab Ịraḳ, one of his stopping-places on the way to Baghdad was at the tomb of the saint at Ibrahim Lik, where he "paid his devotions and distributed alms." He arrived at Baghdad on the thirtieth of August and the people opened the gates of the town. The Jalá'ír sultan, Ahmad Khan, had fled towards Hillah. Timur's troops combed the surrounding country in search for the fugitive sultan, and finally they came up with him on the plain of Kerbala. It was a hot day and the fighting was indecisive, except that the sultan escaped. The Timurid chiefs, who were in pursuit, feared that they would perish with thirst, and retraced their steps until they reached the Euphrates, at a placed called "Makad" (perhaps mashhad), where Ḥusain, the son of Ạli, was killed.

[1] Browne, *Literary History of Persia*, iii, p. 172.

Here " each of them kissed the portal of the holy place and went through the ceremonies usual with pilgrims,"[1] which shows that the Timurid invaders also had no particular hostility toward the Shi'ites and were not disposed to dishonour their sacred places. Even eight years later, when the city of Baghdad was again taken and looted by the Timurids, and when there was a merciless massacre of the populace, we find that there is no mention of destruction to any of the outlying shrines.

After the death of Shah Rukh, Timur's third son, whose long reign continued from 1404-1447, the empire that had been extended with such widespread devastation began to disintegrate. Two dynasties of Turkomans, the Black Sheep and the White Sheep, came into supremacy, one after the other, and then finally the Uzbegs from Transoxiana gained the upper hand in this period of general warfare, pillage and anarchy. The theatre, however, of all these political movements was no longer at Baghdad, and consequently we find no references to damage done to shrines in that vicinity.

When the Safawid dynasty came into power, a dynasty with an aggressive Shi'ite propaganda, the vigorous Shah Ismaíl extended his authority through Khorasan as far as Herat, besides annexing the southern provinces, till in A.D. 1509 his dominions stretched from the Oxus to the Persian Gulf, from Afghanistan to the Euphrates. Then it was that there occurred a great revival of interest in the shrines near by Baghdad, and the ṣadruṣ'-ṣudúr, or chief of the Shi'ite clergy, who administered all pious foundations, was recognized as the highest judicial authority. It was only twenty-five years later, however, when this whole Mesopotamian region became a part of the Ottoman Empire, and a large share from the proceeds of the Shrine endowments went to Turkish rather than Persian authorities. Naturally, there was great rejoicing when Shah Abbas recovered the land of the sacred shrines in 1603, but it was lost again, this time to Murad IV, in 1638, and from that time for nearly three hundred years it continued under Turkish jurisdiction.

[1] Howarth, *History of the Mongols*, iii, pp. 662-665.

In the eighteenth century Nadir Shah undertook to weaken the influence of the Shi'ite hierarchy. It was with this end in view that he abolished the position of *ṣadru'ṣ-ṣudur*, but notwithstanding, the *imám-jum'a* of Isfahan was still generally regarded "as representative of the invisible imam of the house of Ạli, who is the true head of the Church."[1] The story was told me in Najaf that while Nadir Shah was not at first a true believer, and sought to do away with the Shi'ite schism and thus to reunite Islam, yet he was subsequently convinced as to the right of the claims of the imams by miracles that happened at the shrines.

For example, it had been commonly said that wine would turn to vinegar inside the walls of Najaf, and also that no dog would enter this city. Nadir Shah accordingly tried to take a bottle of wine along with him when he visited Najaf, and also undertook to make his own dog enter the city. But at the gates of Najaf, Nadir's dog made such violent resistance to their efforts to compel him to enter that they had to kill him, and sure enough the bottle of wine that was taken into the city did turn to vinegar. In consequence of these and other miracles, Nadir is said to have professed his belief in the Imams.

It is recorded that in 1794, Agha Muḥammad Khan, the founder of the Kajár dynasty, was so angry at the escape of his rival, Lutf Ạli Khan, that he cut off the hands and put out the eyes of the unfortunate and innocent secretary whom he had captured. "The next day, to atone for his cruelty, the Prophet having upbraided him in a dream, he gave the secretary mules, tents, and and equipment to go and spend the remainder of his days at the tomb of the holy Ạli," at Najaf.[2] This instance shows that although the Shrine was under Turkish jurisdiction, devotees and pilgrims were still accustomed to go there. Even after the great crusade of the Wahabites in 1843, when the Shrine at Najaf was looted and lost all its accumulated treasures, it still continued to be recognized as a place of pilgrimage, partly perhaps as an appreciated concession to the Shi'ites of Persia, and partly,

[1] *Encyclopædia Britannica*, 11th edit., art. "Shi'ites."
[2] Malcolm, *History of Persia*, Vol. II, p. 124, note.

doubtless, because its pilgrims were its chief source of income.

While during the Kajár dynasty the shrines of Mesopotamia were under the political authority of the Ottoman empire, the Shi'ite clergy who were resident in Najaf were less subject to interference from military or civil authorities than they would have been in Persia. They were not always content with the influence they exercised in Persia through their theological schools and their association with pilgrims. With Najaf as their centre, the old Shi'ite hierarchy, that had been suppressed by Nadir Shah, began again to reassert its authority, and on several important occasions they brought powerful pressure to bear that affected the decision of political questions in Persia. It was from Najaf that the command was issued in 1891 for *all believers* to cease using tobacco, in order to defeat a concession for a tobacco monopoly, and the consequence was that there was a serious riot in Teheran and the Persian government withdrew the concession. Also, at the time when the Persian constitution was adopted, there was a tacit recognition embodied in it that the hidden imam is the one in ultimate authority. As the Shi'ite clergy are his recognized representatives, this accounts for the number of the clergy who were members of the Parliament during the period of the Kajar dynasty.

At the time when the overthrow of the Kajar dynasty was being openly discussed, when the present ruler of Persia had achieved the virtual position of military dictator, he and his supporters seriously considered declaring Persia a republic. To this proposition the authorities at Najaf protested that a republican form of government would be contrary to Muḥammadan law and custom, but intimated that the law would allow a change of dynasty. Accordingly, after a few months of preparation, the Minister of War declared himself to be Shah of Persia, placed the crown on his own head, and founded the new Pahlevi dynasty.

As the Shrine at Najaf appears at the present time, lying beyond the acres of graves, there is a small town, of perhaps twenty-thousand inhabitants, that is enclosed within almost square walls. Above these walls one sees standing out conspicuously the gold-plated dome that rises above the tomb of Ạli. The interior is decorated with polished silver, with mirror work, and with ornamental tiles. Over the grave itself is a silver tomb, " with windows grated with silver bars and a door with a great silver lock," and in the courtyard there are two graceful minarets that are plated with finely beaten gold.[1]

The significance of the pilgrimage to the tomb of Ạli is based on traditions from the other Imams. Typical of these is the saying attributed to the Imam Ja'far Ṣadiḳ, " that whoever visits this tomb of his own free will and believing in the right of Ạli—that he was the Imam to whom obedience was required and the true Caliph—for such a pilgrim the Most High will register merit *equal to one hundred thousand martyrdoms*, and *his sins of the past and the present will be forgiven*." And when a visitor came in person to visit the Imam Ṣadiḳ, and remarked that he had neglected to go to the tomb of Ạli, the Imam rebuked him : " You have done badly, surely if it were not that you are one of our Shi'ite community, I would certainly not look towards you. Do you neglect to make the pilgrimage to the grave of one whom God and the angels visit, whom the prophets visit, and the believers visit ? " The pilgrim replied, " I did not know this." The Imam answered, " Understand that the Amiru'l-Muminín is in the sight of God better than all the Imams, and to him belongs the merit of the works of all the Imams, in addition to which he has the merit of his own works."[2]

Before making the visit to the Shrine, according to the Imam Ja'far Ṣadiḳ, the pilgrim should first bathe and put on clean clothing and afterwards anoint himself with perfume. The formal prayer of salutation that is given by al-Kulaini,[3] and which is very similar to that given by Ibn Babawaihi,[4] begins as follows :

Peace be unto thee, O Friend of God ;
Peace be unto thee, O Proof of God ;

[1] *Encyclopædia Britannica*, 11th edit., art. " Nejef."
[2] Majlisí, *Tofatu'z-Zá'irín*, p. 50.
[3] Kulaini, *Kafi*, Vol. II, p. 321.
[4] Ibn Babawaihi, *Man la yaḥḍuru hu'l-Faḳih*, p. 226.

Peace be unto thee, O Caliph of God;
Peace be unto thee, O Support of Religion;
Peace be unto thee, O Heir of the Prophets;
Peace be unto thee, O Guardian of the Fire and of Paradise;
Peace be unto thee, O Master of the Cudgel and the Brand-iron;
Peace be unto thee, O Prince of the Believers.

I TESTIFY that thou art the Word of Piety, the Door of Guidance, the Firm Root, the Solid Mountain, and the Right Road.

I TESTIFY that thou art the Proof of God to His Creation, His Witness to His Servants, His Trustee for His Knowledge, a Repository of His Secrets, the Place of His Wisdom, and a Brother of His Apostle.

I TESTIFY that thou art the First Oppressed and the First whose right was seized by force, so I will be patient and expectant. May God curse whoever oppressed thee and supplanted thee and resisted thee, with a great curse, with which every honoured king, every commissioned prophet, and every true worshipper may curse them. May the favour of God be upon thee, O Prince of the Believers—upon thy Spirit, and upon thy Body.

A complete translation of any one of these prayers of salutation would be tedious. In his *Manual for Pilgrims*, Majlisi gives eight long prayers that are appropriate at the time of the pilgrimage to Najaf,[1] and most of these prayers are attributed to different ones of the Imams and have been handed down for centuries, and have been used over and over again by hundreds of thousands of trustful pilgrims to the Shrine of Ạli at Najaf.

[1] Majlisí, *op. cit.*, pp. 58-92.

CHAPTER VI

HASAN, THE CALIPH WHO ABDICATED

ACCORDING to Masudi,[1] "Hasan ibn Ạli ibn Abu Ṭalib was proclaimed Caliph at Kufa two days after the death of Ạli, his father. It was in the month of Ramaḍan, 40 A.H. He sent his agents to al-Sawád and al-Jabal (Persian Iraḳ). Hasan killed Abdu'r-Rahmán ibn Muljám, as we have mentioned. Mu'áwiya entered Kufa after Hasan ibn Ạli had made peace, five days from the end of the month Rabí' I, 41 A.H. The death of Hasan when he was fifty-five years of age was caused by poison. He was buried in the Baḳi'a cemetery beside his mother, Faṭima, the daughter of the Apostle of God."

After the murder of Ạli it is related by Ahmad ibn Hanbal[2] that it was Hasan who addressed the people, declaring: "A man, indeed, left you yesterday, whom those who preceded him did not excel, and whom those coming after will not equal, for the Apostle of God had surely *designated* him." Whether this was true in the case of Ạli has already been discussed,[3] and we wish now to consider whether there is evidence that Hasan was thus formally designated to succeed Ạli.

It is very probable that the idea of divine right, expressed by each Imam designating his successor, was not clearly discriminated at first from other ideas of succession. The custom of the tribes of Arabia was to choose the next man in importance in their community, with an eye to his actual authority and capacity for leadership. This was undoubtedly the principle that had determined the appointment or election of the successive caliphs, Abu Bakr, Ụmar, and Ụthman. It may well be considered, also, that Ạli came into the Caliphate at a time when circumstances

[1] Mas'udi, *Muruj al-Dhahab*, Vol. V, p. 1.
[2] Ahmad ibn Hanbal, I, 199.
[3] See Chapter I and the Ghadir Khum tradition.

had brought him to the front, independent of any question of heredity or of special designation. It could have been naturally anticipated, therefore, that after the death of Ạli, Mu'áwiya would succeed to the Caliphate, for as governor of the province of Syria under Ụthman, he had proved himself to be an exceedingly capable administrator.

But Islam was no longer a united Arabian community, to be governed solely by the ancient customs of the tribes. Ideas of succession by heredity had come to be familiar to those who had shared in expeditions of conquest against the Byzantine Empire in the west, and also to those who had made up armies of occupation in the vanquished empire of the Persians. And there was the teaching of Ibn Saba', that Ạli, as Muḥammad's *wasí* (or executor), had received from the Prophet a certain divine light or spirit that he could transmit to whom he chose. And during the four years of Ạli's caliphate the Moslem empire had been divided. They had been years of civil strife which had drawn sharp lines between the East and the West. The arbitration plan that was provided for in the armistice after the battle of Ṣiffín had failed to effect any united sentiment. For a time the two rival caliphs, Ạli and Mu'áwiya, had publicly cursed one another in their prayers. The whole community was exhausted by the years of warfare, and while both sides were recuperating, there was continued tension and uncertainty, such as to make stability of government impossible.

It was in this time of general confusion that Ạli was assassinated, and we know that Hasan was acknowledged almost immediately in Kufa as Ạli's successor. According to the accepted Shi'ite tradition,[1] before Ạli died, in the presence of his family, the "people of the Household," and the leaders of the Shi'ites, he gave to Hasan the (secret) books and his personal armour. He then addressed him: "O my son, the Apostle has commanded me to give you the designation, and to bequeath to you the secret books and the armour, in the same way that he gave them to me. And when you die you are to give them to your brother Husain."

[1] Kulaini, *Usul al-Káfi*, p. 110.

At this point Ạli turned to Husain, and said to him: "The Apostle has commanded you to give these (secret) books and the armour to this son of yours" (i.e., Ạli ibn Husain), and at the time Ạli took the little boy's hand in his own. Then he said also to the boy, "The Apostle of God commanded me to tell you to give these (secret) books and this armour to your son, and to convey unto him, from me, the salutation of the Apostle."

That Ạli actually accomplished any such comprehensive designation of the four succeeding Imams is scarcely probable. Other traditions that are given in the same connection are less ambitious. One narrator says that Ạli said to Hasan, "Come near to me so that I may whisper to you what the Apostle of God whispered to me, and confirm to you what he confirmed to me," and so it was done. Again it is related that Ạli called Hasan the *waliu'l-amr*, in the sense that he gave him his authority to command; and that he called him also the *waliu'l-dam*, in so far as he left it to his judgment as to whether he should avenge his blood. In this connection he is said to have remarked, "If you forgive my murder, then it is forgiven, and if you kill my murderer, let him be killed with only one stroke."

Perhaps the most reliable Shi'ite account of what occurred after the death of Ạli is that which is given by Abu Hanifa ad-Dinawari (A.D. 895), who wrote the *Kitabu'l-Akhbár al-Tiwál*, or Book of Long Histories. This book is most important, as it is written from the Shi'ite point of view, earlier than any of the canonical traditionists, a full hundred years before the Moslem invasion of India, and as a matter of fact Dinawari died only twenty-two years after the last Imam is supposed to have disappeared. According to the account of Dinawari,[1]

"Ạli was buried at night. Hasan offered the prayer, and repeated the *takbír* five times. No one knows where he was buried. They have related—And when Ạli died, Hasan went to the largest *masjid* and the people gathered about him and gave him their allegiance. Then he spoke to the people as follows:

'See what you have done, you have killed the Amiru'l-

[1] Dinawari, Abu Hanifa, *Kitab al-Akhbar al-Ṭiwal*, edit. Guirgass, p. 230.

Muminín, but before God, observe that he was killed on the same night that the Ḳoran descended, and on the night the book (al-kitáb) was taken up and the pen became dry, the same night in which Moses ibn Imrán died, and the night in which Jesus was taken up.'

They have related—And when Mu'áwiya heard of the killing of Ạli, he began to get ready and sent on in advance (an army under) Ụbaidullah ibn Ạmr ibn Kuraiz. Then he seized Ạyn al-Tamar, and came down to Anbár, with Ctesiphon as his objective. This news reached Hasan ibn Ạli when he was at Kufa, and he therefore set out for Ctesiphon, intending to meet Ụbaidullah ibn Ạmr ibn Kuraiz. When he arrived at Sábát, however, he saw that some of his companions were faint-hearted and he withdrew from the battle and camped at Sábát. There he arose and said to the people :

'O people, truly I awoke this morning without malice toward any Muslim, and I perceive that you share this feeling with me. I believe, indeed, and you will not oppose me in the opinion, that the one you dislike from those who have united together (al-jamá'a) is more worthy than what you love from the separate group (al-farḳa) ; and also I perceive that most of you have given up the fight and have grown fearful of the battle. It is certainly not my desire to lead you to what you dislike.'

When his companions heard this, some of them looked significantly at others. Then some of those who had sympathized with the Khawárij declared, 'Hasan has spoken blasphemy, as his father blasphemed before him.' Then one of their number rushed towards him, and they jerked his prayer rug from under him, and seized his clothing, and pulled off the cape from his shoulder. He called, therefore, for his horse and mounted and cried out, 'Where are Rabai'a and Hamdán ?' They then hastened to him and drove away the people from him. He started to flee towards Ctesiphon, but a man was waiting for him, one of the Khawárij sympathisers, a man called Jarráḥ ibn Ḳabaiṣ, from the Beni Asad. (This man was hidden) in the darkness of a covered passage, and when Hasan came upon him, he stood up before him with an iron-pointed stick, with which he pierced him in the thigh. But Abdullah ibn Khaṭal and Abdullah ibn Zabyán fell upon the Asadí and killed him.

Hasan, severely wounded, proceeded until he came to Ctesiphon. There he took up his abode in the White Palace, where he was cared for until he recovered. He then prepared for a meeting with Ibn Ạmr.

Mu'áwiya had approached as far as Anbar, where Ḳais ibn S'ad ibn Ụbáda had camped with his troops on the side of Hasan. Mu'áwiya, therefore, surrounded him.

Hasan had departed (from his army at Sábát), and when Abdullah ibn Ạmr arrived, he took his stand and called out (to Hasan's army): 'O people of Ịráḳ, truly I also am not anxious for battle, but I am in command of the advance guard of the army of Mu'áwiya, who has halted at Anbár with the troops of Syria. Therefore, convey to Abu Muḥammad, i.e., to al-Hasan, my desire for peace, and say to him on my behalf, "Before God, I swear to protect your life and to value highly the company that is with you."' When the people heard this they ceased fighting and abhorred the idea of battle.

Hasan had given up the war and returned to Ctesiphon, where Abdullah ibn Ạmr besieged him. And when Hasan saw that some of his companions were fearful, he sent Abdullah ibn Ạmr a statement of the conditions on which he would surrender his claim to the caliphate to Mu'áwiya. The conditions were: (1) that Mu'áwiya should not seize any of the people of Ịraḳ in retaliation, (2) that the Arab and the non-Arab should be protected, (3) that Mu'awiya should overlook whatever their offences had been, (4) that he should give to him (Hasan) the tribute of Ahwaz as an annual grant, (5) that he should give to his brother Husain ibn Ạli an annual grant of a thousand thousand dirhems, and (6) that he should honour the Beni Hashim in his favours and gifts in the same way that he would honour the Beni Abdu'l-Shems.

Abdullah ibn Ạmr wrote these conditions to Mu'áwiya, and Mu'áwiya wrote them all out with his own hand and sealed them with his seal. He then gave Abdullah, to give to Hasan, a formally written statement of these conditions and deceptive promises. And he had all the leaders of the people of Syria witness to them. Abdullah brought the agreement to Hasan and Hasan assented to it.

In accordance with the agreement, Hasan wrote to Ḳais ibn S'ad concerning the peace and to order him to give up the authority to Mu'áwiya and to return to Ctesiphon. When the letter containing this command reached Ḳais ibn S'ad, he stood up before the army and said, 'O people, you can choose one of two possible courses of action, either to fight the battle without the Imam, or submission to the authority of Mu'áwiya.' The army chose to submit to Mu'áwiya. They marched on, therefore, to Ctesiphon, and Hasan accompanied the army from Ctesiphon to Ḳufa, where Mu'áwiya came and the two met. Hasan confirmed to him personally the conditions and stipulations, and then he departed with the 'people of the Household' for the city of the Apostle (al-Medina).

Mu'áwiya required the people of Ḳufa to recognize him as Caliph, and accordingly they gave him their allegiance. He then appointed Mughairah ibn Shu'bah as their governor, and set out with his army on his return to Syria."

A similar account of Hasan's brief caliphate is given by Yaḳubi,[1] who was contemporary with Dinawari, and who also wrote from the Shi'ite point of view. He has added, however, a few interesting details. For example, when Jarrah, the Asadí, wounded Hasan with the iron-pointed stick, "he seized him by the beard and twisted it, and pounded his throat till he almost strangled him." And he tells us that Hasan was terribly exhausted, that sickness oppressed him, and that he was wholly discouraged, for the people had deserted him and Mu'áwiya had captured Ịraḳ and had thus succeeded in establishing his authority. It was therefore when he was very ill and when he saw that he had no more power that he made peace with Mu'áwiya. When he did so, he entered the pulpit (probably at the time when he returned to Kufa), and after praising God, he said:

"O people, surely it was God who led you by the first of us, and who has spared you bloodshed by the last of us. I have made peace with Mu'áwiya, and 'I know not whether haply this be not for your trial, and that ye may enjoy yourselves for a time' (Ḳoran, xxi. 111)."

As-Suyuti says that Hasan sent to Mu'áwiya, "offering to resign the government to him on the condition that the caliphate should revert to himself after him," but the translator of as-Suyuti observes that he has not been able to find this stipulation mentioned elsewhere.[2] Perhaps the two books that are most referred to in Persia at the present day for details about the lives of the Imams are the *Jannatu'l-Khulud*, "Perpetual Gardens," which gives the biographical data for each Imam in tabular form, and the Rauḍatu'sh-Shuhadá, "Garden of the Martyrs," which is frequently read at the services for weeping in memory of the

[1] Yaḳubi, *History*, edit. Houtsma, Vol. II, p. 254.
[2] As-Suyuti, *Tarikh al-Khulifa*, trans. Jarrett, p. 194.

Imams.[1] These books give little additional information about Hasan's abdication. They mention that he had forty thousand troops at first, as against Mu'áwiya's sixty thousand, but that Mu'áwiya was successful in bribing Hasan's commanding officers. They both show a conscious effort to justify the Imam, and to throw the blame on the cupidity of particular commanders and on the repeated disloyalty of the people of Kufa.

There is uncertainty as to the exact length of the short period that Hasan served as Ạli's successor. Masudi says that it was six months and three days,[2] and describes him as "the first caliph to depose himself and surrender his authority to another." The accepted Shi'ite statement is that "his caliphate lasted for ten years and six months, that for fourteen months he himself exercised the caliphate, and for nine years and four months he resigned it to Mu'áwiya out of policy (taḳiya), and in order to preserve the lives, property, and families of his followers from the aggressions of Mu'áwiya and his companions." The fourteen months that he is said to have exercised the caliphate, when compared with Masudi's statement, leaves a discrepancy of almost eight months. This is explained by the fact that during the time when Mu'áwiya and Ạli were each claiming the caliphate, when Mu'áiwya had sent Busr with three thousand men to secure for him the allegiance of Mecca and Medina, and Ạli had afterwards sent an army of four thousand to relieve the two sacred cities and to reverse their allegiance, Mecca had sworn fealty to Ạli, and Medina, strange to say, had declared allegiance to Hasan, while Ạli was still living.[3] If the later Shi'ites dated the beginning of Hasan's caliphate from this first acknowledgment in Medina it would account for the difference of seven or eight months.

There are few apologetic explanations of untoward events in the early history of Islam that have not been incorporated in the traditions. One of the most striking examples of this tendency

[1] *Jannát al-Khulúd*, table number nine; *Rauḍat al-Shuhadá*, by Hasan Wa'iz-i-Kashifi (910 A.H.), ch. vi, pp. 107-117; and Browne, *Persian Literature under Tartar Dominion*, pp. 441 and 503-4.

[2] Mas'udi, *Tanbih wa'l-Ishraf*, Bibliotheca Geo. Arab., Vol. VIII, p. 300.

[3] Muir, Sir William, *Annals of the Early Caliphate*, p. 409; and Mas'udi, *Muruj al-Dhabab*, Vol. V, p. 57.

to explain why things turned out adversely for the "people of the Household," by citing sayings of Muḥammad as predictions that such things would happen, is the tradition that Masudi says he found in several books of history, namely, that the Apostle had said, "The Caliphate after me will be for thirty years."[1] As-Sayuti mentions this supposed prediction, and his translator observes that Muḥammad died in the year 11 A.H. and that Hasan's abdication occurred in the year 40 A.H., "Whence it is plain," says al-Bukhari, that not only was Muḥammad a prophet but Hasan was his rightful successor."[2]

Another interesting characteristic of the traditions about the Imams is that there is almost invariably some unique circumstance connected with each Imam's birth. Ạli is said to have been born in the Kaaba itself, and while this was not said of Hasan, yet we read that he was born in the house of Ạli and Faṭima in Medina, which was the only house that was allowed, by the angel Gabriel, to have a door opening into the courtyard of the mosque of the Prophet.[3]

Among the traditions that describe Muḥammad's fondness for his two grandchildren, Hasan and Husain, is one that ascribes remarkable foresight to the Prophet, when he had taken little Hasan with him into the pulpit and declared to the people, "Verily this son of mine is a prince, and perchance the Lord will unite through his means the two contending parties of the Muslims."[4] The two grandchildren are said to have resembled both their father and their grandfather, but in different ways. Hasan resembled Muḥammad from his belt upwards, and was like Ạli from below the belt; whereas Husain resembled Ạli in his upper half and Muḥammad in the lower.[5]

But whatever his superficial likeness to the Prophet may have been, the records show clearly that Hasan lacked the moral force,

[1] Mas'udi, *op. cit.*, p. 7.
[2] As-Suyuti, *Tarikh al-Khulifa*, trans. Jarrett, p. 191.
[3] *Jannát al-Khulúd*, table number nine.
[4] As-Suyuti, *op. cit.*, p. 191; al-Bukhari, 53/9; Tirmidhi, 46/30; Ṭaylisi, No. 874; and Wensinck, *H.E.M.T.*, under heading "Hasan."
[5] *Jannát al-Khulúd*, table number nine; al-Bukhari, 61/23; Tirmidhi, 41/60 and Ṭayalisi, No. 130.

the courage, the self-discipline, and the intellectual capacity to be a successful leader of his people. As he has been summarily estimated in the Encyclopædia of Islam,[1] " sensuality and a lack of energy and intelligence seem to have been the fundamental features of his character. After the premature death of Faṭima, he was not on particularly good terms with his father and brothers. He spent the best part of his youth in making and unmaking marriages ; about a hundred are enumerated. These easy morals earned him the title *miṭlāḳ*, 'the divorcer,' and involved Ạli in serious enmities. Ḥasan, moreover, proved a thorough spendthrift ; he allotted to each of his wives a considerable establishment. We thus see how the money was scattered during the caliphate of Ạli, already much impoverished."

The Shi'ites themselves acknowledge that Hasan had sixty wives and numerous concubines, for we read that " the wives to whom he was legally married numbered sixty, besides concubines and temporary wives. The numbers three hundred and nine hundred have also been given. But he divorced many of them. On this account his Excellency was called *al-miṭlāḳ* (or the man who divorces many wives)."[2] Complaint had been made to Ạli by prominent men that Hasan " was continually marrying their daughters and continually divorcing them," and Ạli's only answer had been that " they should refuse to give him their daughters to wife."[3]

During his period of retirement in Medina, there is little of actual achievement to relate. Mu'áwiya paid his expenses and he continued his dissipation, in consequence of which he is said to have died of tuberculosis when he was about forty-five years of age.[4]

But aside from matters of actual history, whether it be on account of his recognized inferiority or for other reasons, there are a smaller number of miracles attributed to Hasan than to most of the other Imams. There are only sixteen mentioned,[5] of which the following are representative.

[1] *Encyclopædia of Islam,* art. by H. Lammens on " Hasan."
[2] *Aḳa'id ush-Shi'ah,* Bk. IV, ch. ii.
[3] Muir, *op. cit.*, p. 418, note.
[4] *Encyclopædia of Islam,* art. " Hasan."
[5] Khulasat al-Akhbar, chap. xxx, " Imám Hasan."

1. One day Hasan was out in a date grove with one of the children of Zubair. The child wished for dates. There were none on the tree, but Hasan prayed, and the tree produced ripe dates at once.
2. When challenged to do something unusual, he once raised the dead. On another occasion he let his challenger see a vision of three men, chained to a rock, from the crevices of which fire gushed forth. The three (i.e., Abu Bakr, Ụmar and Ụthman) were thus suffering punishment for not having recognized the right of Ạli.
3. In Medina, one time he let his whip fall, and a negro brought it to him. In return for this kindness he prayed for the negro, whose skin was immediately made white.
4. A certain Zabir of Ju'fa had been opposed to Hasan's making peace with Mu'áwiya. In reply to his protest, Hasan told him of the tradition that the Prophet had said, "My son is a prince, through whom the Lord will unite two contending parties of the Muslims." But the man appeared not to be convinced, so Hasan made a motion and uttered a sound, and behold the Prophet himself came before them. Hasan therefore appealed to him, and the Prophet told Jabir to believe that the Imam was right in what he did. Ạli and Hamza and Ja'far appeared along with the Prophet, and as Jabir stood amazed, he saw them all ascend up into the sky.
5. The confusion of another doubter was miraculously brought about, when the man in question said, in ridicule of Hasan, "Pray that I may be changed into a woman and my wife into a man." Hasan was angered and took him at his word. He prayed for just that and so it happened. After a time, however, the two came and humbly repented, and they were restored to their former state.
6. A man came from Mu'áwiya to ply Hasan with difficult questions. He asked him first, "What is the difference between truth and folly?" Hasan answered, "The difference between truth and folly is the breadth of four fingers" (i.e., the distance measured by the fingers between the eye and the ear).

The account that is ordinarily given of Hasan's death, and the account that the Shi'ites accept is that after several unsuccessful attempts, he was finally poisoned.[1]

[1] Yaḳubi, *History*, Vol. II, p. 266; Mas'udi, *Muruj al-Dhahab*, Vol. V, p. 2 ff.; *Jannát al-Khulúd*, table number nine; and the *Rauḍat al-Shuhadá*, ch. vi, pp. 107-117.

As the story goes, arrangements had first been made with Hasan's table servant to poison his food. The servant wrote that he had tried three times and that nothing had happened. A messenger was sent with a letter to the servant and with a vial of such deadly poison that it was said a drop of it in the sea would kill the fish. This particular poison, *zar-i-haláhil*, was described by a Persian shaikh as a liquid that a peculiar animal (perhaps a skunk) emits sometimes on a hillside, and it is of such virulence that it will kill any other animal it strikes, and if it falls on the ground, it makes crevices in the surface of the earth. But the messenger was hungry and got down from his camel to eat, and when he had eaten he was seized with a violent stomach-ache. As he lay there in misery a black wolf came and devoured him. His camel, however, went on in safety, and the letter and the vial of poison for Hasan's servant were given to Hasan himself, at a time when he was entertaining some of his friends. When he read the letter he placed it under the rug on which he was sitting, and would not say anything about it, though his friends urged him to do so. He had turned pale, however, and one of his more intimate companions managed to get the letter, and when he and some of the others had read it, in the indignation of the moment, they immediately killed the table servant, whose fell purpose had been thus disclosed.

At another time, in Medina, one of Hasan's wives had been induced to try and poison him. She had been deceived by Marwan, as the Shi'ites relate, into thinking that Yezid, the Caliph's son, was eager to marry her. But of course he could not do so while Hasan was still living. In this way they got her consent to undertake to give Hasan poison.

On her first attempt she put the poison into honey and it made him violently sick. He surmised what had happened and went to the near-by tomb of Muḥammad, where he prayed, and rubbed himself on the tombstone. By and by he felt easier and considered that he had been miraculously healed. But from that time on he was gravely suspicious of this particular wife, Ja'dah, the daughter of al-Ashath ibn Ḳais. She was sometimes called Asama.

She tried again to poison him, but this time she put the poison in ripe dates, which she brought to him in a basket. As a matter of precaution Hasan insisted that she partake of the dates first. As she was aware which dates were poisoned, she took a handful of those she knew were safe. Hasan, on the contrary, got about seven of the dates that were poisoned, and it was only a short time until he was suffering the severest agony. He was able to wend his way again, however, to the Prophet's tomb, where he was once more miraculously restored to health.

After this experience his nerves were shaken and he told his companions that for several years he had not enjoyed good health in Medina and that he had decided to go to Mosul. One reason for the decision was his desire to get away from the wife whom he feared. But in Mosul there was a blind man who was at enmity with him, who took occasion to poison the metal tip of his staff, and one day as he came before the grandees for alms, as Hasan was sitting with his legs crossed, having but one foot on the ground, the blind man managed to bring the point of his staff on top of Hasan's foot, and to press it in with all the weight of his body. The surgeons declared that the blind man's staff had been poisoned, but they gave him immediate attention and the wound was not fatal.

But Hasan had not found the peace of mind he wanted in Mosul and returned to Medina, where he arranged to live without having anything to do with the wife whom he suspected, and to observe the greatest precautions about his eating and drinking. Notwithstanding, Asama came at night, with a poison that had been made with powdered diamonds. She found that Hasan and his family were all asleep. Beside Hasan was the vessel that contained his drinking water, and her thought was to put the poison in that water. This vessel was corked with a cloth that was tied tight and sealed. But the cloth was moist and she rubbed the poison well into it. Apparently it seeped down into the water all right, for when Hasan had his daughter break the seal to give him a drink, very soon afterwards he became so desperately ill that he was almost literally turned inside out. At all events, the graphic descriptions say that he cast off his liver in little bits, in as many as a hundred and seventy pieces. A Persian shaikh remarked that modern doctors say that this would be impossible, and that thus some doubt has been thrown on the details of the story of Hasan's martyrdom.

The traditions tell us that when Hasan was dying, he predicted that the one who had given him the poison would not attain her object, and accordingly we find it related that after the deed had been done, Mu'áwiya sent her this message, "I value the life of Yezid, otherwise we would surely arrange with you to marry him."[1]

The story is told that in compliance with Hasan's request,[2] they took his body to the place where the Prophet had been buried. He had forewarned his friends that probably A'isha would protest and not allow him to be buried there, in which case they were to take him to the Baḳi'a cemetery, and bury him beside his mother. When, therefore, they took Hasan's body to the Prophet's tomb, Marwan carried the information to A'isha, and she came out to protest. She was mounted astride on a mule. She declared that it would be a dishonour to the Prophet to bury Hasan there. This so angered Hasan's half-brother, Ạli's third son, Muḥammad, the son of the Hanifite woman, that he answered her, "When you came out against my father, you were mounted on a camel; now that you come to insult us, you are mounted on a mule; and the next time you come out to disgrace Islam, you will be mounted on an elephant." Provoked by this abuse, A'isha turned to the Beni Umaiyya and asked if they would stand by and hear her so disrespectfully addressed. They asked what they should do, and she replied, "Shoot your arrows into the corpse!" This they did, seventy arrows in all, and after that the Ạlids buried Hasan in the Baḳi'a cemetery, as he had requested, beside his mother, Faṭima.

[1] Mas'udi, *op. cit.*, p. 3. [2] Dinawari, *op. cit.*, p. 235.

CHAPTER VII

HUSAIN, THE IMAM WHO WAS KILLED IN BATTLE

ALI is said to have preferred Husain to Hasan, saying, "Hasan is a spendthrift, thinking of nothing but the pleasures of the table and of entertaining, but as for Husain, *he is mine and I am his.*"[1] They were both along with Ạli at the time of the uprising in Medina against Ụthman, and when Ụthman was killed, Ạli was either actually displeased with them both, or else he feigned displeasure, because they had been so near at hand and yet had not prevented Ụthman's murder. During the lifetime of Hasan we do not find that the people expressed any preference for Husain, and there is no mention of any sect that believed that the Imamate should have passed directly from Ạli to Husain because of outstanding personal qualifications. When Hasan abdicated, Husain also retired with him to Medina, and for the remaining years of Mu'áwiya's reign he refused to allow himself to be induced to lead in any active opposition.[2]

The suggestion to constitute the Caliphate an hereditary office was made to Mu'áwiya by his able assistant, al-Mughairah ibn Shu'bah, who is said to have been the earliest Muḥammadan forger of false coins. It was on his advice that homage was obtained for Yezíd while Mu'áwiya still lived.[3] This aroused considerable indignation among the Ạlid party in Kufa, who were waiting only for the death of that dominant and efficient leader in Damascus, Mu'áwiya, until they would reassert the claims of the Prophet's household.

Following the account given by Mas'udi for the straightforward story of the martyrdom of Husain,[4] and omitting for the

[1] *Encyclopædia of Islam*, art. "Ḥusain."
[2] Dinawari, Abu Hanifa, *Kitab al-Akhbar al-Ṭiwal*, edit. Guirgass, pp. 234, 235, 238.
[3] Zaydan, *Umayyads and Abbasids*, trans. Margoliouth, p. 61.
[4] Mas'udi, *Muruju'l-Dhahab*, Vol. V, p. 127 ff.

moment the mass of legendary material the Shi'ites have added, we read that when Mu'áwiya died, the people of Kufa sent to Husain and professed their desire to pay homage to him and declared that they would be loyal. He would have not a mere party in his favour, so they said, but they would restore the whole union of the tribes. Husain himself had not as yet paid homage to Yezíd, and had managed to go from Medina to Mecca.

Mu'áwiya is said to have foreseen some such development, for on his deathbed he cautioned Yezíd, "As for al-Husain, the restless men of Ịraḳ will give him no peace till he attempt the empire; but when thou hast gotten the victory, deal gently with him, for truly the blood of the Prophet runneth in his veins."[1]

From Mecca Husain sent his cousin Muslim to Kufa, saying, "You go on ahead to the people of Kufa, and if what they have written to me is the truth, let me know and I will overtake you." In agreement with this commission, Muslim started out from Mecca about the middle of the month of Ramaḍan, and he entered Kufa on the fifth of Shawwal. The deputy governor of Kufa at the time was Nu'man ibn Bashir, al-Ansarí.

Muslim entered the city secretly and put up in the house of a man called Ạwsaja. News of his arrival soon got abroad, however, and twelve thousand men, some say eighteen thousand, declared to him their readiness to swear allegiance to Husain. Muslim therefore sent word of this to Husain and urged him to come.

But when Husain was ready to comply with Muslim's request, Ibn Ạbbas came to him and protested, "Cousin, I understand that you are planning to go to Ịraḳ, but let me assure you that the people there are faithless and will not support you in battle. Pray do not act thus hastily, and in case you are determined to fight this tyrant, and if you do not like the idea of remaining in Mecca, then set out for Yemen. There you would be in retirement and there are your brothers and your true helpers. That is the place for you to stay, and from there you could publish your proclamation, and from there also you could write to the people of Kufa and to those in sympathy with you in Ịraḳ. They could then

[1] Muir, *Annals of the Early Caliphate*, p. 304.

dismiss their governor. If they should persevere in this and drive him out from them, there would then be no one to oppose your coming to them. But if they should fail to do this, you could still remain in your place until God would make the way clear. And you would be where there are strongholds and mountain passes."

"Cousin," Husain replied, "I recognize the truth and friendliness of your advice, but on the other hand, Muslim has written me that the people of the great city had pledged themselves to acknowledge my right and to defend me. I must therefore consent to go among them." "But they are a people," Ibn Ạbbas interrupted, "with whom I have had experience. They were companions of your father and of your brother. If you start fighting to-morrow with their governor, as soon as you begin your undertaking, Ibn Ziyád will hear of your expedition, and will succeed in frightening them so that they will be afraid to support you. Before God, I bear you witness that the very ones who wrote you are your enemies. At any rate, if you refuse my warning and are determined to go, I pray you not to take the women and the children, for I solemnly declare that I am afraid that you will be killed as Ụthman was killed, and his women and children saw it happen." "If indeed I die on the battlefield," said Husain, "I witness before God that that will be better than to live in dishonour in Mecca."

When Ibn Ạbbas got this final answer, he left his presence, distressed and disheartened.

Ibn Zubair had also heard that Husain was planning to go to Kufa, and he likewise came to see him. But he was personally jealous of Husain and nothing would please him more than the departure of his rival. When therefore he came into his presence he said, "O father of Abdullah, what are your plans? I have been afraid at times that you were giving up the holy war of this people against those who oppress them, and who treat with contempt the honest servants of God." Husain informed him, "I am planning to go to Kufa." He replied, "May God prosper you! Truly, if I had as many supporters as you have in that place

I would prefer Kufa to any other city." Then he feared that perhaps he had been too insistent, and he added, "On the other hand, if you remain in your camp, and if you ask us and the people of the Hedjaz to recognize you as Caliph, we will gladly do so and will obey you, for you are more worthy of that office than Yezíd or the father of Yezíd."

When Yezíd heard what was under way he made Ụbaidullah ibn Ziyád the military governor of Kufa. Accordingly, Ụbaidullah left Basra in great haste and arrived at Kufa the following day at noon. As he entered the city, he mingled with his officers and his family, and he wore a black turban that covered his face, and he rode on a mule. The people were expecting the arrival of Husain, and in response to the salutes of Ibn Ziyád they called out, "Peace to the son of the Prophet, may his way be prospered!" And as the company advanced, Nu'man ibn Bashir, who was the deputy governor of the city, and who had taken refuge in the fortress, shouted to him, "O son of the Prophet of God, what difficulty has arisen between thee and me, that you should come to my city before all others?" To this Ibn Ziyád replied, as he raised the covering from his face, "My dear Numan!" And Numan knew him and opened the door to him.

When Muslim heard of the arrival of Ibn Ziyád, he changed his residence and went to stay with Hani ibn Ụrwa, al-Muradí. But Ibn Ziyád found out where he was and sent Muḥammad ibn al-Ashath to ask Hani about him. Here the accounts differ. Mas'udi says that Hani sent Ibn Ziyád a disrespectful reply, in answer to which the latter had Hani brought before him, and he struck him in the face with a rod, struck him a blow that broke his nose and split open his eyebrow and tore his flesh. He then broke the rod over his head. But the companions of Hani heard the commotion and started the cry, "Our master is killed!" Ibn Ziyád did not kill him, therefore, but had him imprisoned near by, and his companions dispersed. But Yaḳubi explains the matter differently.[1] He said that when Ibn Ziyád came to

[1] Yaḳubi, *History*, edit. Houtsma, Vol. II, p. 228.

Kufa, he heard that Hani was seriously ill, and as he was one of his particular friends, he went at once to inquire for him. But Hani had conspired with Muslim, that he and his company should hide within the house, and when Ibn Ziyád came, he would receive him himself in the courtyard, "and when Ibn Ziyád comes and is seated, I will call, 'Bring me some water!' and on this signal you will come out and kill him." But although Hani gave the signal three times, Muslim and his men failed to act. Ibn Ziyád's suspicions were aroused and he arose and left abruptly. It was after this, according to Yaḳubi, that he sent and demanded Muslim, specifying certain conditions on which he would be safe.

However this may be, fighting ensued near the house of Hani, and Muslim gave the rallying signal for the friends of Husain to assemble, shouting "O Mansur!" Immediately eighteen thousand men gathered together, and Muslim led them against Ibn Ziyád, who had taken refuge in the fortress. But these men were no sooner assembled than they began to disperse, and Muslim found that he had scarcely one hundred men, and hence he withdrew to a quarter of the city called Kanda. When he arrived there he had only three men who still followed him, and then he passed in through a door, and behold there was not a man left.

Perhaps this statement that Mas'udi has recorded is an exaggerated representation of the perfidy of the people of Kufa. At least we know that Yaḳubi says simply that in the fighting that ensued at the house of Hani, Ibn Ziyád captured Muslim, killed him, and dragged him by the feet in the bazaar, and that he also killed Hani for having rendered assistance to Muslim.[1]

But Mas'udi goes on to say that when Muslim found himself utterly deserted by his followers, he got down from his horse and walked confusedly through the streets, not knowing where to turn, when he came to the house of a slave woman, who belonged to al-Ashath ibn Ḳais. He asked this woman for a drink of water, which she brought for him, and as she gave it to him, she asked him who he was. When he told her she waited on him and gave him shelter. But her son came home and

[1] Yaḳubi, *op. cit.*, p. 229.

learned about the refugee and his hiding-place, and early in the morning this son went and told Ibn al-Ashath, who immediately informed Ibn Ziyád. "Seize him and bring him to me," was the reply, and to accomplish this Ibn Ziyád sent Abdullah al-Sulami, with a force of seventy men. These men rushed heedlessly upon Muslim at the door of the house, but Muslim resisted them so effectively with his sword that he succeeded in driving them out. They came upon him a second time, but again he put them out. When they saw the difficulty they were having, they climbed up the outside walls of the house and threw stones down upon him, also baskets of reeds that they had set on fire. When he perceived what they were doing, he cried out, "What a multitude has gathered to kill Muslim ibn Ạḳil!" With sword in hand, therefore, he dashed out on to the road and fought desperately. First he exchanged blows with Bukair ibn Ḥumran al-Amarí. Bukair's blow hit Muslim on the mouth and lashed both his lips. But in return, Muslim struck him one blow on the head and another on the shoulder, and the latter blow cut close to the heart. And as he struck these mighty blows, he kept reciting a verse of poetry, which was to the effect that he did not fear death, but only lest he should be the victim of falsehood or wrong desire.

Muḥammad ibn Ashath approached him and assured him of protection, and he trusted his life to him. They mounted him on a mule and brought him to Ibn Ziyád.

At the gate of the palace, he saw a vessel of fresh water and asked for a drink. When they gave it to him, he put it to his lips, but the blood from his mouth filled the cup, so he poured it out and asked for another. He put this second cup to his lips, but his teeth fell into it and it was again filled with blood. "Praise be to God!" he exclaimed, "if he has not destined me this means of living, I will not drink." They took him, therefore, before Ibn Ziyád, who had him beheaded, and his body was hung up in Kufa on the same day that Husain was to start out from Mecca, the eighth of Dhu'l-Ḥijjah, 60 A.H., and his head was sent to Damascus. He was the first of the Beni Hashim, as Mas'udi says, whose body was suspended to the public gaze and whose head was sent to Damascus.

When Husain reached Kádisíya he was met by al-Hurr ibn Yezíd al-Tamímí, who asked him, "Where are you going, O son of the Apostle of God?" Husain replied, "I wish to go to this great city." He informed him then of the killing of Muslim, with all its gory details, and said, "You had better return, for there is no hope of your success." When they started to return, however, the brothers of Muslim said to him, "Before God we swear that we will not return until we have taken vengeance, or until we perish in the attempt." But Husain answered, "Life without you would mean no more to me," and he continued on the march.

Yaḳubi says that this Hurr ibn Yezíd had been sent by Ibn Ziyád, and that he forbade him to return to Medina.

At this juncture they saw a troop of cavalry approaching, troops of Ibn Ziyád, under the command of Ụmar ibn S'ad ibn Abu Wakkas. They turned, therefore, towards Kerbala, with their small body of five hundred horsemen, which consisted of members of Husain's family, and followers, and about one hundred other men. And when he saw the number of their enemies and that there would be no escape, Husain cried out, "O God, judge between us and this people, who indeed summoned us and promised to defend us, but who are now fighting against us."

To complete Mas'udi's graphic story, Husain "did not cease fighting until he died, may God be pleased with him. And the man who gave him the fatal blow was an Arab of the Beni Madhhij, and it was this man who cut off his head and who took it to Ibn Ziyád. Ibn Ziyád ordered him to take the head to Yezíd ibn Mu'áwiya, and when he came into the presence of Yezíd, who was sitting with the Abu Barza al-Aslamí, and the head was placed before Yezíd, he struck it on the mouth and said, 'We have taken the lives of those who were dear to us, but who became rebellious and unjust.' And Abu Barza protested, 'Withdraw your staff, for have I not seen the mouth of the Prophet on this mouth in a kiss?'

"All the troops that took part in the battle that brought

about the death of Husain were from Kufa. There was not a single Syrian among them. And those who died with Husain, on the tenth day of Muharram, were eighty-seven people. Among them was his oldest son, Ạli ibn al-Husain. Hasan's sons, Abdulla and Ḳasim and Abu Bakr, were also killed. And the brothers of Husain that were killed, all of them sons of Ạli (but not of Faṭima), were Abbas, Abdulla, Ja'far, Ụthman, and Muḥammad the Younger.

" Husain had reached the age of fifty-five (some say fifty-nine). On his body they counted thirty-three strokes of the lance and thirty-four blows of the sword. Zoráh ibn Sharík gave him the severest blow with the sword. There were four Ansarí who perished with him, but all the rest were from various Arab tribes. Ụmar ibn S'ad ordered his horsemen to trample the body of Husain underneath their horses' feet, for he had lost eighty-eight men in the conflict."

While Mas'udi, who has been called the Heroditus of Islam, was not disposed to sacrifice a good story in order to adhere too scrupulously to the bare facts of history, nevertheless, this description of the death of Husain, which has been translated with some condensation, and with a few sidelights from Yaḳubi, is distinctly different from the more legendary accounts of later Shi'ite writers.[1]

In the earlier traditions there is not much recorded about Hasan or Husain, except as it had to do with Muḥammad's affection for them as his grandsons.[2] On one occasion when he was speaking, the little boys stumbled and fell, and the Prophet is said to have stopped to lift them up. It is considered that they both resembled Muḥammad in their personal appearance. And Tirmidhi and Ibn Madja and al-Dárimi all mention a time when the Prophet took them with him on his riding mule. And Muslim has recorded that Muḥammad once said that Allah intends to purify Ạli, Faṭima, Hasan and Husain. There is also the tradition related

[1] *Ḳanun-i-Islam*, by Ja'far Sharíf, trans. Herklots, 1832; *The Miracle Play of Hasan and Husain*, by Sir Lewis Pelly; and the *Rauḍat-al-Shuhadá*, ch. vii, p. 117-130.

[2] Wensinck, *H.E.M.T.*, p. 94.

by Ahmad ibn Hanbal,[1] that Muḥammad had told Ạli with distress that Gabriel had just appeared to inform him that Husain would be killed on the banks of the Euphrates, which will be recognized as typical of many of the traditions that appear in the works of later Shi'ite theologians.

There has been much discussion as to what was done with the head of Husain. Ibn Khallikan[2] points out that it was in Ascalon that the head of Husain, the grandson of Muḥammad, was interred before its removal to Egypt ; and that al-Afdal Shahanshah built the " Chapel of the Head " at Ascalon. Ibn Baṭuṭa[3] remarks that " from Jerusalem I paid a visit to Ascalon, which was in ruins. In this place was the *mashhad* (place of martyrdom), famous for the head of Husain, before it was removed to Egypt." In Cairo there is a mosque of the Ḥasaneyn,[4] where, during the month of Muharram, there are particular days when dervishes go solemnly around a sacred tomb that is said to contain the head of the martyred Husain.

But the Shi'ites of Persia look with the greatest reverence upon the plain of Kerbala, where Husain's body was trampled under foot. They recall that one of his wives was the daughter of Yezdegird, the last Sassanian king, and look upon his death at Kerbala as a great national calamity, which they have kept fresh in their memories by frequent services of weeping, and by the widespread Persian Miracle Play in the month of Muharram. The shedding of the blood of Husain, the grandson of the Prophet, on the plain of Kerbala, has also come to be regarded as having a sacrificial value. This is evidenced in the development of doctrine and in the growth of pilgrimage customs that are distinctive of the Shrine of Husain.

1 Ahmad ibn Hanbal, *Sunan*, I, p. 85.
2 Ibn Khallikan, trans. de Slane, i, p. 615, note.
3 Ibn Baṭuṭa, *Travels*, trans. Lee, ch. v, p. 20.
4 Lane, *Manners and Customs of the Modern Egyptians*, edit. Everyman's Library, p. 219.

CHAPTER VIII

KERBALA, THE MOST SIGNIFICANT SHI'ITE SHRINE

WHEN we visited Kerbala, I remember leaving the hotel in Baghdad at four o'clock in the morning, and how we dashed across the desert at top speed in an old-fashioned "Model T" Ford car. Shortly before six o'clock we went more slowly in heavy sand, as we wound our way through groves of date palms that surround the sacred city. It was summer time, and here and there we saw folks who had spent the night under the trees. They were lighting their samovars to make ready the early morning tea, or were leaning over a little stream of water in an irrigating ditch, vigorously washing their teeth with sticks that they had softened on one end.

The city lay three or four miles further on, within the gardens, and without any protecting wall. Accordingly, a few minutes later we were seated at a coffee-house, almost opposite the Shrine of Husain, and were making a hearty breakfast of hot Persian bread, tea and ripe dates. Strange to say, in the Persian *coffee-house* one always drinks tea, for there is rarely anything else available. I had gotten out of the car to take a photograph on the main street, which approaches the Shrine, but from this angle the view of the golden dome was spoiled by the conspicuous clock-tower.

From where I sat in the coffee-house I could see the delicate and intricate designs of the tile work on the Shrine entrance and on the minarets. Across this entrance was the iron chain which marked the barrier beyond which the "unclean unbeliever" must not pass. A visit to this Shrine with faith in Muḥammad as a prophet, and in Husain as the God-appointed Imam, is a momentous and significant undertaking, for it entitles the pilgrim to such privileges as that the roof of his house will never fall on his head, and that he will never be drowned or burned or injured by wild beasts. But for one who was not a believer to go beyond those forbidding chains was an offence that might very likely be punished by death, as the result of mob violence, for such an act would be regarded as a desecration of the sacred area around the tomb.

As I thought how easy and incidental my coming to Kerbala had been, I realized that a mere traveller belongs in an entirely different category from the pilgrims. There were some of these pilgrims in the coffee-house, who had just come out of the bath. They sat there, with their bright red towels wrapped about their naked bodies, and busied themselves sipping tea. In a few moments they would don clean clothes and make the *ziarat*, or formal visitation, with scrupulous regard to all the ceremonial regulations.

One old man, with a kindly, trustful face, was letting his tea get cold, for he went on saying his prayers. And every time he prostrated his head to the ground, his forehead touched a little clay tablet. Several shops in the main street had hundreds of these tablets, presumably for sale, but I was told that one of the Imams had said that to sell the clay that had been taken from the area made sacred by the blood of Husain would be like selling his very flesh. But when we left Kerbala, the chauffeur gave twenty cents for a box of matches, and he took several of these little clay tablets as the change. Pedlars of these tablets would bring a hundred or so of them on a tray, as a nominal present to a likely looking pilgrim, saying that he would not name a price, but that he would collect the price from him on the Judgment Day. It is because they usually get their reward in this life, however, that the custom has come to be such a nuisance to the wealthier pilgrims. Indian merchants arrange to buy these tablets at about Rs. 3 per hundred, and in many places in Kerbala there are cellars that are literally full of them.

The clay for these tablets is supposed to be taken from the spot where Husain was killed. A rosary of this clay is the one most commonly used. It consists of thirty-four beads, and with this rosary the devout believer utilizes his spare moments in saying " God is great " thirty-four times, and " Thanks to God " and " Praise to God," each thirty-three times. When a Shi'ah dies, he is most fortunate if he can have a necklace of clay beads around his neck, a clay ring on the forefinger of his right hand, an armlet of clay on each of his arms, and a little of the dust that is swept from the tomb should be bound in a cloth and gripped in his right hand, and it is well if the sheet, in which the body is wrapped for burial, should have words of the Ḳoran written upon it with this clay.

The most authoritative guide-book for Shi'ite pilgrims is the *Tofatu'z-Za'irín*, or " A Present for Pilgrims," which was written by that voluminous and popular writer, Muḥammad Baḳir al-Majlisí, in the sixteenth century. This book specifies very particularly that it is only the clay from the sacred area around the tomb of the Imam Husain that has healing properties. The seventh Imam, Musa ibn Ja'far, is said to have declared that people should not take the clay from his grave, or from the graves of any of the other Imams, except only the grave of the Imam Husain, for he maintained that God had given that particular clay healing value for the Shi'ites and their friends.[1] It is believed, and the accepted traditions from the Imams confirm the belief, that if a man is ill and about to die, and if with unfeigned faith in the Imam Husain, he eats a small pinch of this clay, he will live. But the eighth Imam, Ạli Riḍa, said, " To eat the clay from a tomb is generally forbidden, for it is like eating the blood of a corpse, except in the case of the Imam Husain, when it is a remedy for every disease. And for one square mile from the tomb the clay is efficacious." This promise of the Imam Riḍa is declared to be true, with the provision, however, that if it is God's will that a man should die, then even eating this clay will do no good. Any one who keeps a tablet of this magic clay on his person is said to be protected from disease and misfortune. If a man eats the forbidden flesh of the pig, and dies, the Imam Riḍa gave it as his opinion that he would refuse to conduct his

[1] Majlisí, *Tofatu'z-Za'irin*, p. 146.

funeral service unless the offender had on his person the clay from the tomb of the Imam Husain. And if evil spirits or unbelievers of *jinns* should pass a man who has this clay with him, it is believed that they would perceive a sweet fragrance, though the man himself might not be conscious of it.

The clock in the tower said it was three o'clock (i.e., three hours after sunrise), and sure enough, as I looked at this tower, I saw the makeshift repair work that had been done with petrol tins that Kermit Roosevelt had noticed.[1] I then walked over to the forbidding chains and looked eagerly into the courtyard. How I wished I could go inside and spend the whole day studying the tile work and reading the inscriptions. I had what had been gleaned from the Arab geographers in Le Strange's indispensable book, *The Lands of the Eastern Caliphate,* where the author pointed out that there must have been some sort of a shrine here even previous to A.D. 850, for it was then that the Caliph Mutawakkil had earned the lasting hatred of all the Shi'ites by ordering the Shrine of Husain to be destroyed by flooding the place with water. Afterwards we read that the site was ploughed and sown, and that the pilgrimage was forbidden under heavy penalties.[2] That some sort of a building was again erected, early in the tenth century, probably, is indicated by the references of Istakhri and Ibn Hawḳal,[3] but a few years later, when the Buyid dynasty came into power, not assuming to displace the Abbasid caliphs, but at the same time effectively relieving them of their secular authority, the Aḍud ad-Dawlah, the same prince who built the Shrine of Ạli at Najaf, put up a magnificent memorial to Husain, here at Kerbala in A.D.979. But as the power of the Buyids was of short duration, we read that in the year 1016 the dome of this splendid shrine was burned down. The next traveller to visit Kerbala, apparently after the dome had been restored, was Malik Shah, in 1086.

There is no description of Kerbala and the Shrine of Husain, however, that is earlier than that of Mustawfi, in the fourteenth

[1] Roosevelt, Kermit, *War in the Garden of Eden,* p. 76.
[2] Browne, *Literary History of Persia,* i, p. 290.
[3] Le Strange, *Lands of the Eastern Caliphate,* p. 78.

century.[1] This also is far from satisfactory, for in addition to ascribing the original building to the Aḍud ad-Dawlah, the author remarks merely that in his own time a small town had grown up around the shrine, 2,400 paces in circuit. But Ibn Baṭuṭa, who wrote at about the same time, mentions an influential theological school, and gives some particulars about the shrine. "The holy threshold of the actual tomb," he says, "which the pilgrims kissed on entry, was of solid silver; the shrine was lighted by numerous gold and silver lamps, and the doorways were closed by silken curtains." As to the little town, he adds that "it was then mostly a ruin, from the ceaseless fighting of rival factions among its inhabitants, but it stood among many groves of date palms, well watered by canals from the Euphrates."

I was standing there at the entrance, wondering how best to get at the historic points of interest, when I heard what sounded like antiphonal singing. A caravan of pilgrims was arriving, under the escort of a professional guide. As they approached, they were chanting after their leader a special pilgrimage psalm of salutation, the same, I thought, that has been translated as follows by Garcin de Tassy[2]:

"Que l'Éternel daigne accepter les vœux que je forme pour le repos de l'àme glorieuse des deux braves imams, des deux martyrs bien-aimés de Dieu, les innocentes victimes de la méchanceté, les bien heureux Abou Mohammad el-Haçan et Abou Abd-Allah el-Hoçain; et pour tous les douze imams, les quatorze purs et les soixante-douze martyrs de le plaine de Kerbela."

There they were, the weary pilgrims, arriving from distant places. They had not come in cars, but had been from four to eight weeks on the road, rising every day at sunrise and spending eight to twelve hours riding their mules. There were men and women, most of whom looked as though they were villagers, or perhaps artisans or shopkeepers. Interestingly conspicuous among them were several old women, grandmothers whose life ambitions were now being realized. I studied their faces as they

[1] Mustawfi, *Nuzhat al-Qulub*, trans. Le Strange, Gibb Memorial, XXIII, ii, p. 39.
[2] Garcin de Tassy, *L'Islamisme*, p. 266.

passed by, wending their way to a near-by caravanserai. There was something sternly serious about it all.

Could we realize what this pilgrimage meant to them? All their lives, whenever a child was circumcised, whenever a couple was married, whenever anyone died, a priest had been called in and some part of the tragic story of what happened at Kerbala had been recited, while everybody wept. They knew the marvellous blessings the Imams had solemnly promised to all who would make this pilgrimage. And were not these promises written in books and had they not heard them read every night or so on the journey? From childhood they had heard that there are 4,000 angels surrounding Husain's grave, angels that are weeping day and night, and whatever pilgrim comes from any place, even from the frontiers, these angels go to meet him. If he falls ill, they go to his assistance, and if he dies, they go to his grave and pray for his forgiveness. They had been told that God himself is responsible for all the material needs of the pilgrims, and that he will pardon his sins for fifty years. Most of them had come with little money, and they knew just how many days they could afford to buy bread in Kerbala and still have enough money left for the return journey. There were gratuities also that must be sparingly given, for their money had come from family savings that had been accumulated slowly, the kind of money that goes into insurance policies in countries where religious pilgrimages are no longer in vogue.

The analogy suggested by the insurance policy is useful, for the pilgrimage manual promises not only additional years of life to those who pray with faith in this shrine, but stipulates what one might call insurance benefits, that anyone who makes this pilgrimage with great eagerness will have the merit of 1,000 pilgrimages to Mecca, and of 1,000 martyrdoms, and of 1,000 days of fasting, and for freeing 1,000 slaves. The following year, also, the devils and evil spirits will in no way harm the pilgrim, but God himself will be responsible for him. And if he should die, the angels will see to burying him, and on the Resurrection Day, he will rise with the followers of the Imam Husain, whom he will recognize by the flag that he will carry in his hand, and the Imam will triumphantly escort his pilgrims directly to Paradise. Or, according to another statement, if the pilgrim dies in Kerbala, we learn that the angels will wash his body and take him to Paradise, where there are ten thousand dirhems awaiting him in compensation for what he spent on the pilgrimage. On the day of resurrection, also, all those who are buried in any one of the shrines of the Imams, no difference what sins they may have committed, will be subject to no examination, but will be tossed, as it were from a sheet, directly into Paradise, and the angels will shake their hands in congratulation.

For here on the plain of Kerbala, according to the best authorities, the body of Husain was trampled under foot by the four thousand mounted troops of Ụmar ibn S'ad. Here, with sixty-two, or seventy-two, of his companions of the "people of the Household" (of the Prophet), he gave his blood to mingle with the soil. It is thus that Kerbala has become sacred to that great group of Muḥammadans whose first loyalty was always to the family of the Prophet. They commemorate the death of Husain in their Muḥarram procession, which is the climax of a sort of passion play in which they act out all the tragic events that occurred at Kerbala.

It is not strange that the traditions relate remarkable things about so sacred a place. On the authority of the sixth Imam, the Prophet Muḥammad is said to have remarked that the angels brought the sacred dust of Jerusalem to Kerbala, knowing that Husain was to be buried there, and that it was a full thousand years beforehand that they began to prepare the place for his burial. The fourth Imam, who was Husain's own son, is said to have given out the information that the virgin Mary came miraculously from Damascus to Kerbala, and that Jesus was born at the very place where Husain is buried, and that the same night she returned with the child to Damascus. We read also that Ạli passed across the plain of Kerbala with some companions, and when he arrived at the place where Husain was to be killed, he said, "Truly two hundred prophets, and two hundred repre-

AIR VIEW OF THE SHRINE OF HUSAIN IN KERBALA, WITH THE TOMB OF ABBAS IN THE BACKGROUND

Facing p. 95] *[Royal Air Force Official—Crown Copyright Reserved*

sentatives of prophets, and two hundred sons of prophets have longed to be buried here.[1]

We know that the *há'ir* or "enclosed area" that is sacred to Husain in Kerbala was mentioned by Tabari as early as A.D. 915, and that there was at that time a cult of official priests of Kerbala, "who were supported by endowments founded by Umm Músá, mother of the Caliph al-Mahdi."[2] It was when Tabari was only twelve years old that the Caliph Mutawakkil had attempted to do away with the graves of Husain and his companions by flooding them with water. But according to Shi'ite tradition, the immediate area containing the graves was miraculously kept dry, and it is this area that is designated in their guide-books as the *há'ir*.[3]

The photograph taken from the air shows that there are two shrines in Kerbala, both of which are considered as lying within this sacred area. They are very similar, for each has minarets, a clock tower, and a large covered pavilion; each has a surrounding *sahn*, or courtyard, with groups of rooms like those in a caravanserai; and the two central buildings are of nearly the same shape and size, with space to allow the pilgrim who enters to make the *tawáf*, or circumambulation of the tomb. But there are also distinguishing features between the two shrines that are immediately observed. The one in the foreground has three minarets instead of two. This is the Shrine of Husain, the dome of which gleams forth in the sunlight, resplendent with its gold plate. The shrine in the background of the picture was built in honour of Ạbbas, the half-brother of Husain, and its dome is of that lustrous blue tile that is so pleasing against the clear Persian sky, and that appears like a massive turquoise when you see it under a cloud. This Ạbbas is said to have been most courageous in battle, and the tradition has grown up that the most dangerous place to take a false oath is at his shrine, for as a Shi'ite friend explained, "he was not an Imam, who would be expected to have mercy, but a most exacting man of valour."

[1] Majlisi, *op. cit.*, p. 164.

[2] *Encyclopædia of Islam*, art. "Há'ir," by Herzfeld; also art. "Meshhed Ḥusain."

[3] Majlisi, *op. cit.*, p. 162; and *Miftah al-Janan*, p. 366.

The best way to appreciate the significance of both of these shrines is to read an account of the final suffering of Husain and his immediate followers. If we follow the direct narrative of al-Dinawari (A.D. 895),[1] who was one of the earliest and best of the historians with Shi'ite sympathies, we read that the companions of Husain did not cease killing and being killed until there remained only the people of his immediate household. Of these, the first one to advance and fight was Husain's son, Ạli Akbar, who did not cease fighting until he was killed. He was struck by a lance and knocked to the ground, and afterwards killed by the sword. One after another, six more of them were killed in individual combats, and among them were Abdulla, the son of Muslim, and Ḳasim and Abu Bakr, two sons of Hasan.

They say that when Ạbbas ibn Ạli saw this, he said to his brothers, Abdulla and Ja'far and Ụthman, "Charge with me, and defend your master until you die fighting before him!" They charged, therefore, all together, and threw themselves between the Imam Husain and the enemy, to protect him with their persons. But one after another, Abdulla, Ja'far and Ụthman were killed. Ạbbas, however, still stood by the Imam Husain, to fight in front of him and to move with him wherever he went, until he also was killed. The Imam Husain was then alone, and Malik ibn Bishar al-Kindí came forth against him and struck him with a sword on his head. He was wearing a *burnus*, a cloak of silk and wool, apparently over his head, and the sword cut this garment and wounded him on the head. He then put aside the cloak, and called for a cap and put it on with a turban and sat down. He called a small boy, perhaps the one who brought the cap, and had him sit with him on a rock. But while this boy sat on the rock with the Imam Husain, he was shot by a man of the Beni Asad, with a broad-headed arrow that killed him. Husain remained a long while, sitting there, for every tribe relied on the other and hated to advance to kill him. He was thirsty, however, and called for a vessel of water, but when he was ready

[1] Dinawari, *Kitabu'l-Akhbár al-Ṭiwál*, p. 268; and Yaḳubi, *History*, edit. Houtsma, ii, p. 253 and p. 289; and A. Nöldeke, *Das Heiligtum al-Husains zu Kerbala*, Berlin, 1909.

to drink, a man called Huṣain ibn Numair shot him with an arrow that entered his mouth and prevented him from drinking. He set the vessel down. When the people saw this they withdrew, but when he stood up to walk to the river, they took a position between him and the water, and he returned to his former place. A man from the people shot an arrow that stuck in his back. He removed the arrow, but Zur'ah ibn Sharík struck him with a sword. Husain tried to ward off the blow with his hand, but the sword made quick work with his hand. At last, Sinán ibn Aws al-Nakha'í came forth against him and thrust him with a lance, and he fell. Ḥawlí ibn Yazid al-Aṣbaḥi then fell upon him to cut off his head, but his hands trembled, so his brother, Shibal, cut off the head and handed it over to Ḥawlí.

It is more than a thousand years since this tragedy occurred at Kerbala, and tens of thousands of pilgrims are still coming every year. Chiefly from Persia, but to some extent from almost all parts of the Muḥammadan world, they come to visit these sacred tombs. They often carry with them the remains of particular ones of their relatives, who stipulated in their wills that they were to be buried in Kerbala. To the right of the entrance to the Shrine of Husain there is a stairway that leads to a huge underground vault that is perhaps two hundred yards long. The bodies of foreign pilgrims are brought in boxes, and those that are accepted for burial here are kept in stacks in this vast sepulchre. There is a similar arrangement for burial in connection with the Shrine of Ạbbas, and I was told that bodies were not placed in either of these great underground caverns for less than a fee of five hundred rupees. Inside the Shrine of Ạbbas, and next to his grave, the guide points out the Treasure Chamber of the Martyrs, where the sons of Husain and others of his household are buried.

At the entrance to the Shrine of Ạbbas, the visitor is warned by a verse in large characters, "Do not put your feet on this threshold irreverently, for this is the place for the prostration of angels and emperors." The dome here is not of gold, for they say that Nadir Shah, who built it, was admonished in a dream, in which he thought that he saw Ạbbas, who is usually called Abu Fazl, and that he heard him say, "As I am younger than Husain, and am the dust of my master's feet, so in your construction you should consider the difference between the master and the slave." Inside the shrine, however, are many fine Persian rugs, which have been given by merchants, whose names are woven in the corners. There are silver and gold chandeliers hanging inside the dome, and the grave itself is surrounded by a simple silver grating. Within the grating, on the tomb itself, lies a turban and a sword, which tradition affirms were used by Ạbbas in his last heroic struggle. But perhaps the most significant thing to be seen here is a black, round patch on the ceiling of the dome, for the story is related that this is the head of a man who took a false oath in this shrine, and at once his head left his body and went smash up against the ceiling. At least, the story emphasizes the fact that the great majority of the Shi'ites will hesitate to swear falsely in the name of Abu Fazl. Pilgrims to his tomb go around the grave three times, and when they come under the black spot on the ceiling they confess their sins and pray for God's mercy.

But surrounding the grave of the Imam Husain, in the shrine with the gold dome, there are two gratings. The inner one is of gold and the outer one of elaborately carved silver. This silver grating was given by Nasir-i-din Shah, and bears his name. The pilgrims bring offerings of money and of jewellery, which they place inside these gratings. Particularly at times when they make sacred vows, which are made conditional on the Imam's assisting them in their desires, they have their presents deposited within the golden grating. At intervals the gratings are opened and the treasures are removed and officially appraised before they are sold as part of the revenue of the shrine. This opening of the tomb chamber is something of a ceremony, and representatives of the civil government take pains to attend.

A fortunate eye-witness of this official collecting of the treasures and sweeping of the tomb told me what he saw. He said that first two priests were chosen by lot. First they bathed themselves, for their ceremonial purification, in a tank of cold water in the courtyard. Then their bodies were wrapped in white sheets, like grave clothes, which each man had fastened with strings at his neck, wrists and ankles. This was not only in order that their clothing should be ceremonially clean, but that they might not even be suspected of carrying away in their clothing any of the treasures they would collect. Thus arrayed, they prostrated themselves before the tomb and made their way on all fours inside the grating. First they brushed the dust from the various treasures they found, taking care not to scatter it, for the dust itself is valuable. After a few minutes white mice were seen scurrying about the tomb. They had been attracted there by a special bread that is put inside the grating sometimes by men who have lost their positions, and who want the Imam to intercede for them. When the priests who were sweeping noticed these white mice, they called out in a loud voice, "Behold the angels are working with us!" and the people broke forth in a prayer of salutation to the Imam, for according to tradition the angels can transform themselves into any form they choose. After about three hours of this careful dusting and sweeping, along with the collecting and sorting of the treasures, the jewellery was brought out and with it a quantity of the sacred dust, which they had carefully gathered. The precious ornaments, necklaces, earrings, etc., were turned over to the Shrine treasury, as part of the regular income, and the priests took the sacred dust to wrap up in little bits of cloth. A small amount of it, wrapped in a cloth, is called a *surreh*, and is readily sold to pilgrims, for it is considered that if a little of this dust is buried with a man, the forgiveness of his sins is assured.

At the conclusion of the ceremony there was what is called a *rauda khwání*, or memorial service, in thanksgiving. There was no word or spirit of rejoicing, however, but simply a rehearsal of the tragic happenings at Kerbala so long ago. Devoted shrine attendants marched around the tomb and beat their bare shoulders with iron chains, to which nails and small knives were fastened.

Naked to their waists, and glistening with perspiration, they passed round and round, shouting "Husain! Husain!" in honour of their martyr of martyrs, and their trusted mediator or intercessor on the Day of Judgment.

CHAPTER IX

THE IMAM ẠLI ASGHAR, ZAIN AL-ẠBIDIN

AFTER the death of Husain the Ạlid party was divided on the question of succession. Should the next Imam be the surviving son of Ạli, Muḥammad, who was not a son of Faṭima but of the Hanafite girl? History represents this Muḥammad as a man of more force of character than either Hasan or Husain, and there was a large party who supported him for the Imamate. They were known as the Kaisánís, and they have been fully described by both Sunnite and Shi'ite authorities.[1] They accepted the doctrine that had been formulated by the Saba'ites, that there is a divine spirit that dwells in all prophets, and that passes from one to another.[2] This spirit was transferred as they said, at Muḥammad's death to Ạli, and from Ạli it went to his descendants who succeeded him in the Imamate. They believed that the millennium was at hand and that the number of Imams was limited to four, i.e., Ạli and his three sons, Hasan, Husain and Muḥammad. Professor Nicholson has given a translation of some verses from al-Kuthayyir that are quoted by Shahrastáni in his description of the Kaisánís[3]:

Four complete are the Imams,
  of Kuraish, the lords of Right:
Ạli and his three good sons,
  each of them a shining light.
One was faithful and devout;
  Kerbala hid one from sight;
One, until with waving flags,
  his horsemen he shall lead to fight,
Dwells on Mt. Radwa, concealed;
  honey he drinks and water bright.

[1] Ibn Khaldun, *Mukaddama*, Arabic text, Quatremète, Part I, p. 357 Ạlamu'l-Huda (Sayyid Murtaḍa), *Tabsiratu'l-Awwam*, ch. xix.

[2] Shahrastání, *Religious and Philosophical Sects*, edit. Cureton, p. 132.

[3] Nicholson, *A Literary History of the Arabs*, p. 216.

But the other faction of the Ạlids recognized that Muḥammad ibn Hanifiyya was in no sense a descendant of the Prophet, and they asserted that Husain had actually designated his son Ạli to be his successor in the Imamate.[1] While the theory of the Imamate involves the necessity of each Imam designating his successor, it will be observed that wherever possible this designation follows the recognized order of heredity. As Husain's oldest son, Ạli Akbar, had been killed at Kerbala, the succession fell to another son, Ạli Asghar, or "Ạli the Younger," who was afterwards called Zain al-Ạbidín, the "Ornament of the Pious." He was one of the five survivors of Husain's family after the slaughter at Kerbala, the others being his aunt, his brother Ụmar, and his two sisters.

According to Ibn Sa'd,[2] Ạli Asghar was not less than twenty-three years of age at the time when his father was killed, and it was because he was ill and had not taken part in the fighting that Ụmar ibn Sa'd had spared his life. Ḍinawari describes him as "a boy,"[3] but it is probably misleading to associate him with his brother Ụmar, who was just four years old, as one of Husain's "two little sons."[4] The five survivors of the Family of the Tent were taken to Ubaidulla ibn Ziyád, the governor of Kufa, and he sent them on their journey to Yezíd at Damascus. They travelled across the desert in the same caravan with the man who carried the head of their father. And when they arrived, we read that it was at the very time they entered the presence of Yezíd, that the head of Husain was brought in and cast before the Caliph. With this spectacular introduction, Shimr ibn Dhu'l-Jushan addressed the Caliph as follows:

"O Amiru'l-Muminín, it has fallen to our lot to bring the heads of the men of the people of the Household, and sixty men from his *shi'at*, or party. We went out to them and demanded of them that they should either halt, according to the order of our commander, Ubaidulla ibn Ziyad, or else fight. We went to them in the morning at sunrise and we surrounded them on all

[1] Kulaini, *Usul al-Kafi*, pp. 110 ff. and 220 ff.
[2] Ibn Sa'd, *Tabaḳat*, V., p. 156, l. 25.
[3] Dinawari, *Kitab al-Akhbar al-Ṭiwal*, p. 270.
[4] Muir, *Annals of the Early Caliphate*, p. 441.

sides, but when the sword overpowered them, they began to take refuge in the plea that they were without fault, like pigeons taking refuge from the falcons. It all took a very short time, like the sewing of a seam or the period of a nap, and we got the last of them. Their bodies were dishonoured and naked, their clothes mixed with sand, their faces stained with the earth, the winds blew upon them, their pilgrims were the eagles, and their visitors the buzzards."[1]

After some delay in Damascus, the five survivors were permitted to return to their home in Medina, and when they arrived they told all the gruesome details of what had happened at Kerbala. Thus a splendid opportunity was afforded for someone to arouse the indignant people against the Umayyad oppressors, who had unnecessarily shed the blood of the direct descendants of the Prophet.

It was Abdulla ibn Zubair who took advantage of this opportunity. He was a man in his early sixties, an opportunist perhaps, and ambitious in a selfish way, but nevertheless a man with real capacity for leadership. He had been associated with Husain and Abdu'l-Rahman in their refusal to comply with Mu'áwiya's request that they approve his appointment of Yezíd as his successor. The fact that he encouraged Husain to go to Kufa has been attributed to insincerity of friendship, on the belief that he foresaw what would happen and realized that when Husain was well out of the way, he would then have his great opportunity. However this may be, when the people of Medina were furiously excited by the atrocities the survivors had been relating, Abdulla, who was, on his mother's side, a grandson of Abu Bakr, spoke to the inhabitants of Medina who assembled in the mosque, and emphasized especially the treachery of the Kufans. The result was that the people of Medina, and later the inhabitants of Mecca also, acclaimed Abdullah ibn Zubair as their Caliph. He was himself, however, content with the title, the "Protector of the Holy House."

The two cities therefore united in revolt against Yezíd, each appointing a separate commander. Abdulla established his

[1] Dinawari, *op. cit.*, p. 271.

headquarters in Mecca, and devoted his energy to arousing all Arabia against the Umayyads. But very promptly, in the year 63 A.H., according to Yaḳubi, Muslim ibn Ụḳba was sent from Damascus on a punitive expedition against Mecca and Medina. This expedition appears to have been more in the nature of a raid, for while we do not hear that the army of Ibn Zubair was defeated, we know that several of the leaders in the rebellion were killed and that the inhabitants of Medina were subjected to violence and rapine, and also that the mosque of the Prophet was desecrated.[1]

After three days of destruction and bloodshed in Medina, Muslim sat in state and gave opportunity for those whose lives had been spared to come before him and declare that they were ready to be the slaves of Yezíd. And among those who came was Ạli ibn Husain, and Muslim gave him a seat with him on his own carpet, and said, "The Caliph gave me special instructions concerning you." Then Ạli answered, "Truly I disapproved entirely of what the people of Medina did." Muslim therefore took him to his house in honour.[2]

Afterwards, part of Muslim's army, now under the command of Husain ibn Numair, marched on to attack Mecca. In the course of the siege they resorted to shooting firebrands and the sacred Kaaba was set on fire, and much destruction was wrought in the city.[3] This siege of Mecca is said to have lasted sixty-four days,[4] when suddenly word came of the death of the Caliph Yezíd, which meant that the attacking army returned to Damascus and Abdulla ibn Zubair had opportunity to reorganize his forces. He kept his army busy with numerous expeditions against the Kharijites, rebuilt the Kaaba, and as he had been acknowledged as Caliph in the Hedjaz, in Ịraḳ, and in southern Arabia, he was able to maintain a rival court in Mecca for as long a period as nine years.

But the people in Kufa were not satisfied either with Marwan,

[1] Ya'ḳubi, *History*, edit. Houtsma, Vol. II, p. 298 ff.
[2] Dinawari, *op. cit.*, p. 276 ; Cf. Mas'udi, *Muruj al-Dhahab*, Vol. V, pp. 162-164.
[3] Ya'ḳubi, *op. cit.*, p. 300.
[4] *Encyclopædia of Islam*, art. "Abd Allah ibn Zubair."

who had succeeded Yezíd in Damascus, or with Ibn Zubair, who had established his authority in Mecca. The Kufans had come to believe that they had made a fatal mistake. " 'What excuses,' they were asked, 'would they have when they would come before God, and how would they be able to look the Prophet in the face, when they had slain his grandson?' There was no way of atonement but by avenging Husain's death. The appeal was successful, but as they were few in number, a letter from Sulaiman ibn Surad, now chosen with a few others as their leaders, was sent out far and wide to all the members of the Shi'ah sect, and many heartily responded and promised aid. They appointed five men, who had been companions of the Prophet, to consult as to what should be done. They met in Sulaiman's house and agreed that the trouble suffered in Kufa was on account of their action towards Husain, and that they must therefore repent and seek for pardon. Sulaiman told the people that their first duty was to repent and then act. They bowed their heads and sought pardon, and stood up and drew their swords and upheld their lances, and unanimously agreed to clear the earth of the murderers of the family of their Prophet, and to make an end of them and their frivolous rulers, and to appoint Zain al-Abidín as Caliph.[1]"

These "Penitents," led by Sulaiman, went first to a place called al-Warada in Ịraḳ, "to avenge the blood of Husain," and to carry out what God commanded the Beni Israel, when he said "Be turned then to your Creator, and slay the guilty among you; this will be best for you with your Creator" (Ḳoran, ii. 51). It was their intention to depose the two rivals, Marwan and Abdulla ibn Zubair, and to make Ạli ibn Husain the Caliph. A multitude of the people had followed Sulaiman, and Marwan sent Ubaidulla ibn Ziyad against them, with the promise that if he would subdue Ịraḳ, he would be made governor of that province. He soon encountered Sulaiman, therefore, and did not cease waging war against him until he killed him.[2]

As soon as Sulaiman had been killed, the uprising in Kufa

[1] Canon Sell, *Ithna Ạshariyya*, p. 6, quoting *Sahifatu'l-Abidín*, p. 85.
[2] Ya'ḳubi, *op. cit.*, Vol. II, p. 306.

subsided, but nevertheless, the cry for vengeance for the blood of Husain would not be suppressed. A man who had been associated with the Kharijites, al-Mukhtár ibn Abu Ubaid, came to Kufa and professed to represent Zain al-Abidín, who was still in Medina. He soon gained the authority of a popular leader in Kufa and took sudden vengeance on the men who had been responsible for the killing of Husain and his followers at Kerbala. Shamir and Ụmar ibn Sa'd were both executed, and he sent their heads to Zain al-Abidín. And after gaining the victory over Ubaidulla ibn Ziyad in the battle on the Zab, in which Ubaidulla was killed, Mukhtar had his head taken to the very place in the palace in Kufa where Ubaidulla had received the head of Husain.

Ibn Zubair, however, did not consider that Zain al-Abidín was in any way responsible for these actions of Mukhtar, for while he steadily pursued the latter, until he defeated him and killed him in battle, he left Zain al-Abidín unmolested in Medina. The Imam had received overtures from Mukhtar, but he had disdained to answer the letter, and had publicly denounced Mukhtar in the Mosque of the Prophet at Medina.[1]

For two or three years longer Ibn Zubair was able to retain his authority at Mecca, but because of his wars with the various Shi'ite factions, his strength was waning, and the cause of the Umayyads was correspondingly strengthened, so that in 73 A.H., when the famous Hajjáj besieged Mecca, Ibn Zubair was defeated and slain.

It was during this period of disturbed political conditions that the divergent theories of the Caliphate received the most attention. One of the mooted questions was the attitude to be taken towards the "two Shaikhs," Abu Bakr and Ụmar. All aspirants for leadership among the Shi'ites were required to express themselves as to whether they regarded these first two Caliphs as usurpers. Also the question of the right of succession, as between Muḥammad ibn Hanifiyya, the half-brother of Husain, and Zain al-Abidín, the son of Husain, was a living issue and created factions, some of which came to be regarded as separate sects. The efforts of

[1] Mas'udi, *Muruj al-Dhahab*, Vol. V, p. 172.

the Shi'ite party to gain the temporal power in the Muḥammadan empire had been repeatedly disappointed, and the final result was that they modified their theory of the Imamate and came to regard the Imams as primarily spiritual guides and intercessors.

It was shortly after the death of Ibn Zubair that Muḥammad ibn Hanifiyya went along with Zain al-Abidín to Mecca to see if they could not determine which of the two really had the right of succession. "Muḥammad said that he was the most worthy, as he was the son of Ạli ibn Abu Ṭalib. But Zain al-Abidín replied to his uncle, 'Fear God and make no such claim,' and accordingly they agreed to appeal to the Black Stone (hajaru'l-aswad). Muḥammad prayed for a sign, but no answer came; then Zain al-Abidín prayed, and the stone was so agitated that it nearly fell out of the wall of the Kaaba. Then came, in eloquent Arabic, the answer that he was the true Imam after Husain, to which decision Muḥammad consented."[1] After this settlement at the Kaaba, Zain al-Abidín returned to Medina, where he led a quiet and retired life, with only a few intimate friends who visited him for religious purposes.

Most of the biographers who have mentioned anything about the private life of Zain al-Abidín, have called special attention to the fact that his mother was a Persian princess.[2] Ibn Khallikan has related the story that when the Moslem army came to Medina

[1] Canon Sell, *op. cit.*, p. 11, quoting *Sahifat'l-Abidín*, p. 184.

[2] Ibn Khallikan, Arabic text, *Bulak*, Vol. I, p. 347. To this statement concerning Zain al-Abidín's mother and her sisters, Ibn Khallikan adds the interesting story from the Kamil of al-Mubarrad, that shows the unfortunate status of the sons of slave mothers, on the one hand, and the recognition of the value of the Persian royal blood on the other. An unnamed man of the Kuraish related: "I was associated with Sa'id ibn Musayib, and one day he asked me, 'Who are your uncles on your mother's side?' I answered, 'My mother was a slave,' and I saw that when I said this he despised me. I was silent, however, and one day Salím the son of Abdulla ibn Ụmar al-Khattab came to see him. When he went away I asked, 'And who is his mother?' He said, 'A slave.' On another day Ghasim came and sat with him, and when he went away, I asked, 'O uncle, who is this man?' He said, 'Do you not know your own people; that is strange, for this is Ghasim the son of Muhammad ibn Abu Bakr.' I said, 'And who was his mother?' He said, 'A slave.' Some time afterwards Ạli ibn Husain came and greeted him and soon went away. I said, 'O uncle, who is this?' He replied, 'He is the man whom all Muslims must recognize, Ạli ibn Husain ibn Ạli ibn Abu Ṭalib.' I asked, 'Who was his mother?' He replied, 'A slave.' Then I said, 'O uncle, you looked with contempt on me when I told you that my mother was a slave, so what do you have to say about these men?' After that he always respected me very highly."

with the women and children they had captured from Persia, during the Caliphate of Ụmar ibn al-Khattab, there were among the captives three daughters of the Persian king, Yezdigird. The other captives had for the most part been sold as slaves, and Ụmar commanded that these three young women should also be sold. Ạli ibn Abu Ṭalib was present, however, and objected, "The daughters of kings should not be treated like the daughters of common men." In reply, Ụmar inquired, "In that case, what is best to do with them?" Ạli answered, "Their value should be determined by consultation, and then, whoever is willing to pay that price should take them." When accordingly their value had been determined, Ạli took them himself, and gave one of them to Abdulla, the son of Umar, one to his own son, Husain, and one to Muḥammad, the son of Abu Bakr. And all of these Persian women gave birth to sons for their Moslem husbands. Abdulla's son was named Salím, Husain's son was called Ạli, Zain al-Abidín, and Muḥammad ibn Abu Bakr's son was known as Ghasim. It was for this reason that Zain al-Abidín was sometimes spoken of as "the son of worthy parents," and it was pointed out that the Prophet had said that God had chosen the Kuraish as the best of the Arabs and the Persians as the best of the non-Arab peoples. There is a tradition, also, that one time someone said to Zain al-Abidín, "You are the kindest of men to your mother, but we do not see you eating with her out of the same dish." To this he answered, "I fear that I should put my hand upon something she had set her eyes upon, and thus I might displease her."[1]

After the death of Ibn Zubair, Zain al-Abidín lived on quietly in Medina for approximately twenty years longer.[2] During the

[1] Ibn Khallikan, *op. cit.*, p. 347. The author remarks that Zain al-Abidín's thoughtfulness was decidedly different from the experience of Abu'l-Musin with his grandson, who says: "I had a daughter who was sitting with me at the table. When she drew her hand out from her sleeve it was like the blossom of the date tree, and whenever her eyes fell upon a choice morsel, she asked me to take it or presented it to me. Then I gave her in marriage, and in due time a small son of hers was sitting with me at the table. When he drew his hand from his sleeve, I saw it was like the black stub of the date branch, and, may God be my witness, whenever I wanted a particularly good bite of food he took it before me."

[2] Mas'udi, *Muruj al-Dhahab*, Vol. V, p. 368.

time when others had been continuing the struggle for political supremacy, he had become widely known for his extreme sorrow, after the killing of his father, and for his remarkable devotion in prayer. It was this latter characteristic that earned for him the name Zain al-Abidín, " the Ornament of the Pious," which is the name that is said to be recorded for him in Paradise. And he is represented as one of the five or six most copious weepers in the world's history. Adam wept in repentance for three hundred years, Noah wept for the iniquity of the peoples, Jacob and Joseph wept for forty years on account of their separation, John the Baptist wept in fear of Hell, Faṭima wept excessively for her father, and so it was that Zain al-Abidín had wept for Husain and those who perished with him at Kerbala. The story is told that at times his grief was so excessive that one day when he was praying on the roof, a stranger passed and water struck him in the face. It had shot out from a drain pipe when it was not raining, and he learned on inquiry that at times the Imam wept so copiously that his tears would run off from the roof in the drain pipes.

Every night he was said to repeat seventy *takbir* in prayer, and to read the entire Ḳoran through once. And so pleasing was his voice that the men who carried heavy skins of water along the street below would stand entranced and listening. Owing to his repeated prostrations, calloused places had formed on his knees and on his forehead that were said to be like the foot of a camel. One of his most remarkable experiences was the time when the Devil assumed the form of a dragon and tried to distract him in his prayer by biting his foot. The Imam felt great pain but he did not look up until he had finished praying, when he perceived that it was the Devil annoying him and ordered him away.

His self-control must indeed have been remarkable, for once when a slave spilled a dish of thick soup all over the Imam's head and neck, he refrained from reprimanding him, but on the contrary, he graciously gave him his freedom.

In praise of his generosity, it is said that he would himself go out at night and carry bags of wheat, or flour, to houses where he knew the people were hungry, that he fed from one to three hundred families this way every night, and that they would not know who brought the food. And in the daytime he would have a hundred sheep a day killed for meat, which would be distributed to the people. But much of his time he spent sitting on an old piece of matting, fasting all day, or eating a little barley bread. One writer mentions that he claimed to get nourishment from merely the smell of food.

A man who was poor and in debt came to him and asked for something to eat, and he gave him what he had at hand, a loaf of very hard bread. The man found it hard to bite and traded it at a fisherman's shop for a most unpromising looking fish. But when he opened the fish he found an exquisite and exceedingly valuable pearl, the sale of which enabled him to settle his accounts and to live in comfort.

In his personal appearance the Imam Zain al-Abidín is described as much like Ạli. He was about the same height, had reddish hair, a white face and neck, and a large chest and stomach—the latter being explained as a sign of valour. He was the first one of the Imams to have only one wife, by whom he had one son, Muḥammad Baḳir, who succeeded him in the Imamate. But he had fourteen other children by his numerous and unenumerated concubines.

An incident that is said to have provoked the jealousy of Hishám ibn Ạbd al-Malik occurred when both he and the Imam had gone on pilgrimage to Mecca. They were making the circumambulation of the Kaaba, and had come to the place where the pilgrims press forward to kiss the black stone. Hishám found that in his pilgrim's garb he was not distinguished from the rest of the crowd, whereas he was the son of the Caliph. He was amazed and chagrined also to see the crowd voluntarily make way for another, the Imam Zain al-Abidín. To make matters worse, the poet, Farazdaḳ, was present and celebrated the incident in verse, which aggravated Hishám exceedingly. The Shi'ite traditionists declare that Hishám then arranged that he should be poisoned.[1]

He died in 94 or 95 A.H., during the caliphate of Walíd, while Hishám was still a young man. Zain al-Abidín, however, was fifty-seven years of age, and it is well within the range of probability that he died a natural death. He was buried next to his uncle Hasan in the Baki' cemetery in Medina. The years of his life are enumerated as follows: two years with Ạli, ten years with Hasan, ten years with Husain, and thirty-five years as the Imam.

[1] These details may be found in the *Tadhkiratu'l-A'imma,* ch. vi, p. 130 ff., and in the *Jannatu'l-Khulud,* table No. 9. The stories of the miracles are given more at length in the *Khulasatu'l-Akhbar,* ch. 32. These books represent what is actually taught and believed rather than what can be historically determined.

CHAPTER X

THE IMAM MUḤAMMAD AL-BAḲIR, "THE AMPLE"

MUḤAMMAD AL-BAḲIR succeeded to the Imamate as a spiritual function during the last year or so of the caliphate of Walíd. This was the culminating period of the glory of the Umayyads at Damascus. "The arts of peace prevailed; schools were founded, learning cultivated, and poets royally rewarded; public works of every useful kind were promoted, and even hospitals established for the aged, lame and blind."[1] The new Imam, who lived quietly in Medina, as his father had done, was recognized as the leading interpreter of the Shi'ite faith for about nineteen years. The time of his death, however, is difficult to determine with certainty, for Yaḳubi places it as early as 117 A.H., while Mas'udi says that he lived as late as 125-126 A.H.[2] The date 113 A.H., the one preferred by Stanley Lane-Poole in his *Muḥammadan Dynasties*,[3] is probably at least ten years too early.

Muḥammad al-Baḳir is said to have been highly esteemed for his learning as well as on account of his noble birth. According to Ibn Khallikan, he received the appellation *al-Baḳir* (the Ample) because he collected an ample fund (tabaḳḳar) of knowledge,[4] but Yaḳubi says that he was called al-Baḳir because he split open (baḳara) knowledge, that is, he scrutinized it, and examined into the depths of it.[5]

[1] Muir, *Annals of the Early Caliphate*, p. 447.

[2] Ibn Sa'd (*Tabaḳat*, v, p. 238) gives traditions that he died in 114, 117 or 118 A.H. Yaḳubi (*History*, ii, p. 284), says that he died in 117 A.H. Mas'udi (*Muruj al-Dhahab*, vi, p. 17) gives it as his opinion that Muhammad Baḳir died in the reign of Walid II (125-126 A.H.), though he mentions that others say that he died in the previous reign of Hisham (105-125 A.H.), and that still others assert that it was not until the following reign of Yazid III, or as late as 126 A.H.

[3] S. Lane-Poole, *Muḥammadan Dynasties*, p. 72.

[4] Ibn Khallikan, trans. de Slane, Vol. II, p. 579.

[5] Yaḳubi, *History*, Vol. II, p. 384.

He was born at Medina on Tuesday, the third of the month of Safar, 57 A.H., and is said to have been three or four years old on the day his grandfather, Husain, was killed. His mother was known as Umm Abdulla, and was a daughter of Hasan, the son of Ạli ibn Abu Ṭalib.

In his life of respectable and scholarly retirement at Medina, the Imam al-Baḳir was frequently called upon to explain particular teachings in regard to the Imamate. A synopsis of his teaching in the *Ma'athiru'l-Báḳir* is given in Canon Sell's *Ithna 'Ashariyya*, an interesting part of which may well be quoted, as it shows the emphasis at this early period on the intellectual and spiritual character of the Imamate.[1]

" A man one day said to him, ' Was the Prophet heir to all the knowledge of the prophets ? ' He replied, ' Yes ' ; then he was asked whether he had inherited it. He said he had. He was then asked if he could raise the dead to life, restore sight to the blind, and cleanse the leper. He said, ' Yes, by the valour of God Most High.' He therefore put his hand on the eyes of a man and blinded him completely, and then restored his sight. Many more such stories are told.

" He discoursed fully on many topics, such as the nature of the soul of man, the qualities of the *ulama* (the learned) and the nature and attributes of God. He discouraged arguments about the divine nature, saying that it was not possible for men to understand it. One day a Mu'tazilí leader asked what the anger of God meant. He said it was simply punishment, but that this anger was not to be compared to the anger of men. God's nature did not change. He defined a *Rasul* as a prophet who hears the voice of the angel (of revelation) and sees the angel in a bodily form or in a dream ; a *Nabi*, he said, is a prophet who also hears the voice of the angel under the same conditions, but does not see him ; and the *Imam's* condition is like that of the Nabi and not like that of the Rasul. He said that the Imams were pure and that the ' men of the House ' were free from sin ; that all the world was under their rule, that through them the eye of God's mercy

[1] Canon Sell, *Ithna Ạshariyya*, pp. 18-19.

falls on men ; and that, if they did not exist, men would perish, and that they should not fear though worthless fellows might deny all this.

"The Imam Baḳir, in defending his claims to the Imamate before the Caliph Hishám, quoted this verse: 'This day have I perfected your religion unto you and fulfilled my mercy upon you and appointed Islam to be your religion' (Koran, v. 5). He went on to say that the open revelation being thus perfect, the Prophet had made known other secret matters to Ạli. From amongst the men of 'the House,' Ạli had appointed one special person as his confidant, to whom this heritage of the knowledge of secret things came down. Hishám replied that as God allowed no partner in the matter of knowing the secret things, how could Ạli make such a claim? In reply Baḳir repeated many sayings of the Prophet, showing the mutual relationship between himself and the high position accorded to Ạli. On hearing all this Hishám was silent for a while, and then permitted Baḳir and his companions to return home. Neither the pomp nor the power of the Caliph influenced the Imam, who boldly and without fear answered all the questions put to him."

In 122 A.H., we are told by Ibn Khallikan,[1] Zaid, the brother of Muḥammad Baḳir came forward in his own behalf and summoned the people to espouse his cause. This occurred in the reign of Caliph Hishám. Yusuf ibn Ụmar al-Thakafi, the governor of the two Ịraḳs, dispatched al-Ạbbas al-Murri with an army against the insurgent chief. Zaid was struck by an arrow that was shot by one of al-Murri's soldiers, and he died of his wound. His body, however, was fastened to a cross and set up in the Kunasa of Kufa, and his head was carried to the different cities of the empire and there exposed.

When speaking of this uprising of Zaid,[2] Mas'udi says that in the year 121 or 122 A.H., Zaid consulted with his brother, Muḥammad ibn Ạli ibn Husain, who warned him not to put any

[1] Mas'udi, *Muruj al-Dhahab*, Vol. V, p. 467 ff.; and *Tanbih*, edit. de Goeje, p. 323.
[2] Ibn Khallikan, trans. de Slane, Vol. III, p. 274.

reliance on the people of Kufa, with details of how they had treated the people of the Household formerly. Zaid, however, did not heed his brother's warning but led the people of Kufa in another vain rebellion, with the results that have been mentioned. This warning that was given by Muḥammad Baḳir is treasured by the Shi'ites as an illustration of his supernatural knowledge. But it should be observed that if this warning was given at about the time when Zaid rebelled, then any earlier dates assigned for the death of Muḥammad Baḳir are obviously incorrect.

Shahrastani mentions[1] that a disagreement had arisen between Zaid and his brother Muḥammad Baḳir because Zaid had been following the teaching of the Mu'tazilite, Wasil ibn Ạṭá. Zaid had quoted something from those who attributed error to Ạli in killing the deserters, and who had said that Ạli had motives that were different from those the people of the Household assigned to him. He had also asserted that the status of an Imam was conditional upon his appearing publicly to claim his rights. And in answer, Muḥammad Baḳir said to Zaid, "Your faith then is merely in your father, as such, for according to your theory he was not an Imam, for he certainly never came forth to assert his claims."

There is uncertainty about the cause as well as the time of the death of Muḥammad Baḳir. Some say that he was poisoned by Ibrahim ibn Walíd, but according to the ordinary account,[2] another Zaid, his cousin, the son of al-Hasan, quarrelled with the Imam over the question of his inheritance. He seized him by his clothing and was about to stab him, but agreed however that they should go to the *ḳazi*, or judge. When the judge gave his decision in favour of the Imam, Zaid carried the case to the Caliph Hisham. Influenced by Zaid's false accusations, Hisham sent a present of gold to the Governor of Medina, with instructions that he should secure the Imam's inheritance, or the documents involved, and send the same to him. Apparently the Imam was

[1] Shahrastani, *Kitab al-Milal wa'l-Nihal*, edit. Cureton, p. 116 ff.
[2] Majlisi, *Tadhkiratu'l-A'imma*, p. 136.

ready for such an emergency, however, for he gave the Governor a box that contained spurious documents. These were sent to the Caliph, but when they were shown to Zaid he recognized that they were not genuine. According to the Shi'ite story, the Caliph gave Zaid a saddle that had been treated with poison, and Zaid managed matters so that this saddle was given to the Imam, who used it and died from the effects of the poison. But to show how the divine judgment intervened to thwart Zaid's plans, it is further related that Zaid immediately fell ill, and that he lost his mind " so that he did not say his prayers until he went directly to the punishment of God."

Stories of the miracles wrought by the Imams are accepted as authentic by the great majority of the Shi'ites and are recorded at length in their most popular books as convincing proofs of the authority the Imams exercised. To Muḥammad Baḳir they have attributed thirty-one of these miracles.[1] After having predicted the death of a man two days before the event, the Imam asked one of the friends who was much impressed, " Do you not know that we see from near at hand and from afar, both what is hidden and what is evident ? None of your works are concealed from us, and it is thus therefore that you must look upon us as your protectors." On another occasion the Imam accurately predicted the dismissal of the Governor of Medina two or three days beforehand.

It is related that the Prophet had said to his companion, Jabir ibn Abdulla al-Ansári,[2] " When you run across my descendant, Muḥammad Baḳir, give him my salaams," and they say that when Muḥammad Baḳir first met Jabir he immediately told him of the Prophet's behest.

One of the best stories is that of a son who was sorely distressed because his wealthy father had hidden his money and had died without leaving anyone information as to where it could be found. The Imam gave the disappointed son a letter, which he was to take to the Baki' cemetery, where he was instructed to stand and

[1] Sayyid Muhammad Mahdi, *Khulasatu'l-Akhbar*, Kerbala, 1297 A.H., ch. 33.
[2] Jabir ibn Abdulla al-Ansari was one of the well-known "companions" of the Prophet. Cf. Ibn Sa'd, *Tabaḳat*, III, ii, p. 114.

shout, " O Darján ! " (the name of a jinn) and a person would appear whom he was to inform as to his wishes. He was to tell this person that Muḥammad Baḳir had sent him, and he would then tell him whatever he desired. What he asked was that he might speak with his dead father, and almost at once the father appeared, and he recognized him, although his complexion had been affected by the smoke and fire of Hell. In the interview, however, the father confessed his sin, told him where his treasures were buried, and ordered him to give fifty thousand dinár to the Imam Muḥammad Baḳir.

The Imam Ja'far Sadiḳ was a son of Muḥammad Baḳir, and he is said to have related, " My honoured father came to the valley of Feruz and commanded that they put up the tent. Then he walked forth until he came to a dry date palm. He began praising God, and he uttered something I have never heard. Then he commanded, ' O palm, give me what God has put upon thee ! ' At once the palm brought forth fruit and the ripe dates fell, some red and some yellow. He ate of them and we also ate. Abu Umayya al-Ansari was with us, and my father said, ' O Abu Umayya, this is the miracle of Maryam, for she shook a dry palm and ripe dates fell.' " This reference is to the Ḳoran (xix. 25), where Mary, in travail with Jesus, heard a voice saying, " Grieve not thou, thy Lord hath provided a streamlet at thy feet, and shake the trunk of the palm-tree toward thee : it will drop fresh ripe dates upon thee."

One of Muḥammad Baḳir's rival claimants to the Imamate was Abdulla ibn Ạli ibn Abdulla ibn al-Husain, and the story is told that a delegation of seventy-two visitors came to Medina from distant Khorasan. They were men of wealth and had many jewels with them. They said it was their desire to determine who the Imam was. First they went to see Abdulla, who undertook to prove to them that he was the rightful Imam by showing them the armour, the ring, the cane and the turban of the Prophet. As they took their departure they said they would return the next day, but as they were leaving Abdulla's house, a man who was in the service of Muḥammad Baḳir addressed them by their proper names and invited them to the house of his master. Later, as the seventy-two visitors sat in his presence, the Imam Baḳir requested his son Ja'far to bring him his ring. This he took in his hand and waved it slightly as he muttered certain words, and to the amazement of all, apparently from the ring itself, fell the armour and the turban and the staff of the Prophet. He put on the armour, placed the turban on his head, and took the staff in his hand. After thus exhibiting them, he removed the turban from his head and took off the armour, and, as he moved his blessed lips again, they all returned to the ring. He proceeded, therefore, to assure his visitors "that there has never been a true Imam who did not possess the treasure of Ḳárún."[1] Thus convinced, they acknowledged his right to the Imamate and gave him many valuable presents.

Sayings attributed to the Imam Muḥammad Baḳir by Ibn Sa'd[2] would indicate that he was of a peace-loving disposition. "Do not quarrel with one another," he said, "for quarrelling discredits the Ḳoran." And that he had the knack of answering questions in such a way as to please his Umayyad protectors is shown by a conversation he is reported to have had with Jabir. The latter asked him, "Is there any one of you people of the Household who has been guilty of the sin of Polytheism?" He answered, "No." Jabir then asked, "Is there any one of you people of the Household who returned to life?" He said, "No." Again Jabir asked, "Is there any one of you people of the Household who defames Abu Bakr and Ụmar?" He replied, "No, but rather each one has loved and trusted and prayed for them."

While it is of course possible that the Imam, Muḥammad Baḳir, may have been poisoned at the age of fifty-seven, as the Shi'ite authorities say, and that he may thus have attained the distinction of a martyr (shahíd), it must still be observed that he had reached an age when his death from some other cause would not have been improbable. The very uncertainty as to when and how he died

[1] Ḳárún (Ḳoran xxviii and Numbers xvi) is the biblical Korah, who treated the Israelites contemptuously because of his pride in his immense wealth. Cf. *Encyclopædia of Islam*, art. "Ḳárún."

[2] Ibn Sa'd, *Tabaḳat*, II, p. 236.

goes to show that very little is known of the closing years of his life. It is related that he requested that he be buried in the tunic in which he prayed, and his son said that like the Prophet he was buried in three garments. From the point of view of history, both his life and death were inconspicuous. Other matters were attracting public attention. The active uprising against the Umayyads was getting under way, so that the exact time of the cessation of the nominal authority of the peaceful Imam, Muḥammad al-Baḳir, and of the succession of his equally peaceful son, appears to have been overlooked or ignored.

CHAPTER XI

THE RISE OF THE 'ABBASIDS

THE Umayyad persecution was getting unbearable and discontent had become so widespread that there were few indeed who were satisfied with the idea of the Imam being merely a spiritual guide. The sanctimonious aloofness of the Imam, Zain al-Abidín, and likewise of the Imam, Muḥammad al-Baḳir, was looked upon by other factions of the Hashimids as evidence of the futility of expecting guidance or help from the division of the family known as the Imámís. The Kaisánís especially, who were the descendants of those who had supported Ạli's son by the Hanifite woman, were eager for an aggressive movement against their oppressors. And it was because both he and they wanted action that Zaid, the brother of the Imam Muḥammad Baḳir, had listened to the invitation of the people of Kufa to lead them in rebellion.

The last of the Umayyad caliphs was Marwan II, who ruled from 127-132 A.H. As governor of Armenia and Adhherbaijan for twelve years, he had frequently been involved in fighting with warlike tribes in the Caucasus, and in acquiring this military experience he had worked out a plan for the reorganisation of the Moslem troops. "In place of divisions consisting of the different tribes he created regular, paid troops under professional commanders; and the men levied for military service were divided into smaller divisions which possessed much greater mobility and strength than the long Arab battle lines."[1] When he was thus equipped with his reorganized army, Marwan observed that Ibrahim ibn Walid, the new Caliph, could not be regarded as secure in his office, as he had gained support only in southern Syria. Quick to

[1] *Encyclopædia of Islam*, art. "Marwan ibn Muhammad."

see his opportunity, Marwan decided to come forth himself, not to claim the caliphate, but to champion the rights of the sons of the murdered Walid II. In the campaign that followed he defeated his military rival, Sulaiman ibn Hisham, who commanded the Caliph's troops, but when Sulaiman retreated to Damascus he there put to death the two sons of Walid II, and then managed to withdraw with his troops to Palmyra. Marwan had declared that he was fighting in the interest of these boys, but now that the boys were dead, as he was supported by the powerful tribe of the Ḳaisís, without delay or hesitation, he entered Damascus and received for himself the homage of the people as Caliph.

Once the die was cast, Marwan encountered serious opposition, first in Syria and later in Iraḳ, and his military skill and the loyalty of his supporters were taxed to the extreme. And it was while he was still occupied in these conflicts that he heard of a precarious situation in the distant province of Khorasan. The Umayyad governor at Marw is said to have written the following verses to Marwan to inform him of the dangerous state of affairs :

" I see the coal's red glow beneath the embers,
  And 'tis about to blaze !
The rubbing of two sticks enkindles fire,
  And out of words come frays.
' Oh ! is Umayya's House awake or sleeping ? '
  I cry in sore amaze."[1]

The reasons for the trouble in Khorasan were, first the growing distrust of the Umayyads that prevailed throughout the empire, and also the fact that the discontented non-Arab Muslims had hit upon a new basis for the establishment of a new dynasty. A persistent effort had been made in Khorasan to arouse sympathy for the people of the household of the Prophet, not so much for the Imams, who had in recent years chosen to follow the policy of non-resistance, but for other branches of the Hashimids that were more aggressive and influential.

[1] Translation by Nicholson, *L.H.A.*, p. 251. The original may be found in Mas'udi, *Muruju'l-Dhahab*, vi, p. 62 ; in Yaḳubi, *Tarikh*, edit. Houtsma, ii, p. 408 ; and in Dinawari, *al-Akhbar aṭ-Ṭiwál*, edit. Guirgass, p. 356.

The Abbasids did not trace their descent from Muḥammad, but from his uncle, al-Abbas, who had supported Ạli after the death of Muḥammad in preference to himself. And when Ạli was finally made Caliph after the death of Ụthman, he appointed Abbas's son, Abdulla, as governor of Basra. But the family could not look back with pride to Abdulla, for when Ạli wanted him to render an account of the money he had received, he took offence and left Basra, and at the same time carried away a sum of money that has been estimated at six million dirhem. He fled to Mu'áwiya, who was shrewd enough to include him among the young nobles to whom he gave large annual stipends, and thus under the protection of the Umayyads he devoted the remainder of his life to literary work. He is mentioned as "the real founder of Ḳoranic Exegesis," though it sometimes appears that he had little more integrity as an historian or traditionist than he had had fidelity as an administrator.[1]

This renegade's son, however, Ạli ibn Abdulla ibn Ạbbas,[2] was the pride of the Abbasids. Born the same night that Ạli was assassinated, A.H. 40 (661), he was later esteemed as "the handsomest and most pious Ḳuraishite of his time." But he could ill abide the way the Umayyad rulers and their agents were vigorously persecuting the entire Hashim clan. Plotting secretly against the Umayyads, in the caliphate of Walid I, he was apprehended and consequently banished to a village called Ḥumaima, in the province of Sharát, on the border between Arabia and Palestine. He lived in this village until his death in A.H. 117, and it was here that his son, Muḥammad, organized and maintained the headquarters of the Abbasid faction.

At their headquarters in Ḥumaima they were close enough to Damascus to realize fully that the Umayyads had lost their fighting strength by allowing the Arab tribes to settle in the cities, where they had wasted their native vigour in dissipation, and where their arrogance had made the Arab name despised.

[1] See art. "Abd Allah b. Ạbbas," in the *Ency. of Islam*; also Nicholson, *L.H.A.*, p. 145.
[2] See art. "Ạli b. Abd Allah b. Ạbbas" in the *Ency. of Islam*.

As has been pointed out, " it was the lust of conquest more than missionary zeal that caused the Arabs to invade Syria and Persia, and to settle on foreign soil, where they lived as soldiers at the expense of the native population whom they inevitably regarded as an inferior race. If the latter thought to win respect by embracing the religion of their conquerors, they found themselves sadly mistaken. The new converts were attached as clients (Mawáli, sing. Mawlá) to an Arab tribe: they could not become Moslems on any other footing. Far from obtaining the equal rights which they coveted, and which, according to the principles of Islam, they should have enjoyed, the Mawáli were treated by their aristocratic patrons with contempt, and had to submit to every kind of social degradation, while instead of being exempted from the capitation tax paid by non-Moslems, they still remained liable to ever increasing exactions of Government officials. And these 'clients,' be it remembered, were not ignorant serfs, but men whose culture was acknowledged by the Arabs themselves—men who formed the backbone of the influential learned class and ardently prosecuted those studies, Divinity and Jurisprudence, which were then held in highest esteem. Here was a situation full of danger."[1]

At this point, when the discontent with the Umayyad military oppression was at its height, a strange coincidence brought about a union between the two most powerful branches of the Hashimids. The Imam, or leader, of the Kaisánís at the time was Abu Hashim, the son of Muḥammad ibn al-Hanafiyya. He had been called to Syria to visit the Caliph Hishám. The Caliph was aware of the agitation the Kaisánís had been carrying on in distant Khorasan, and he feared Abu Hashim as a capable leader of rebellion. Accordingly he arranged that poisoned milk should be given to him. Zaydan relates that " Abu Hashim felt the poison in him as he journeyed, and turned aside to Ḥumaima, the headquarters of the Ạbbasid faction, and was entertained in the house of their leader, Muḥammad ibn Ạli ibn Abdulla ibn Abbas. And when Abu Hashim saw that he was about to die, it is said that he

[1] Nicholson, *L.H.A.*, p. 247-248.

bequeathed his right to the Caliphate to Muḥammad,[1] in the presence of witnesses from the Kaisánís. When Abu Hashim died, with this assurance of the support of the Kaisání faction, Muḥammad carried on his propaganda with greater zeal and confidence. But he also died before attaining his objective and handed on his claims to the Caliphate to his son, Ibrahim.

"Ibrahim now began to dispatch emissaries, beginning with Khorasan, in whose inhabitants he placed greater reliance than in those of any other province, because the bulk of the Kaisání faction were to be found in Khorasan and Iraḳ, and the inhabitants of both provinces had repeatedly assisted the Ạlids. Sending out the same emissaries as had been employed by Abu Hashim, he told them to obtain oaths of allegiance *to the family of the Prophet,* without specifying whether Ạlids or the Ạbbasids were meant. The people of Khorasan, wearied with the Umayyad despotism, were quite ready to promise allegiance to the family of the Prophet, supposing that the sovereignty would be shared by the two branches."[2]

The first of the emissaries sent by Ibrahim to Khorasan was Bukair ibn Mahán, who went to Marw and announced that after the death of Muḥammad, Ibrahim had been proclaimed as his successor. This mission was in A.H. 126, and was successful in that Bukair returned with large gifts of money to advance the Abbasid cause. This occurred just a few months before Marwan was proclaimed the Umayyad Caliph in Ḍamascus. But Bukair died the following year and Abu Salama was sent to Khorasan in his stead. There he carried on the agitation so successfully that the next year, when Ibrahim sent the nineteen-year-old soldier, Abu Muslim, to organize his supporters into an army in Khorasan, in one day he was joined by the inhabitants of sixty

[1] "This statement, though found in the oldest Arabian historians, is strongly doubted by more recent investigators, and is to be ascribed to the invention of the followers of the Ạbbasids, who desired to prove in this way the claim of the Ạbbasids to the Caliphate" (K. V. Zettersteen, *Ency. of Islam,* art. "Abu Hashim"). The force of this doubt would seem to be broken, however, by the admitted fact that Abu Hashim did die at Ḥumaima, and it is not improbable that this coincidence did have something to do with the subsequent united effort of the Kaisánís and the Ạbbasids against the Umayyads.

[2] Zaydan, *Umayyads and Ạbbasids,* trans. Margoliouth, p. 146-147.

villages near Marw. And it was but a short time after this that the Umayyad Governor, Naṣr ibn Sayyár, wrote frantically to the Caliph Marwan that the rebel leader, Abu Muslim, was in command of an army of two hundred thousand men. It was a long way from Marw to Damascus, but the spirits of the non-Arab Moslems, particularly the warlike tribes of Persia, were intensely gratified when they heard that this new army of people of the country, led by Abu Muslim, had driven the Umayyad governors and the Caliph's regular troops from Marw and Nishapur. Almost at once the movement took on the character of a widespread appeal for the union of the house of Hashim against the Umayyads, which proved a popular slogan. Even some of the Imámís were led to hope that perhaps the house of Ạli would come back to their rightful authority.

In the meantime, the newly acclaimed Umayyad Caliph Marwan was putting forth every effort to quell the uprisings in the Yemen and in Iraḳ. Word came that Abu Muslim was remaining in control of everything in Khorasan, but that his armies, under other commanders, were steadily advancing towards the West. Marwan sought to strike at the centre of the whole movement by arresting Ibrahim, the recognized leader of the Ạbbasids at Ḥumaima. He is said to have strangled him, as some say, by having his head put into a bag of lime until he died.[1] But Ibrahim had two brothers, Abu'l-Abbas and Abu Ja'far, both of whom escaped to Khorasan. And very soon these two brothers returned, supported by Abu Muslim's victorious troops, to lead the insurgents in their final struggle in the West, and to themselves become the first two of the Ạbbasid Caliphs.

Their way had been prepared for them in Kufa by propaganda that had been carried on for more than twelve years, and when the army arrived from Khorasan they found the city was decorated in black, the accepted colour of the Ạbbasids, and the people who crowded to the mosque wore black clothes and black turbans and carried black banners. One of the most zealous of the leaders in Khorasan, Abu Salama, led the prayers, after which he

[1] Yaḳubi, *Tarikh*, edit., Houtsma, ii, p. 409.

announced that Abu Muslim had now made it possible for the world of Islam to shake itself free from the Umayyads, and declared that it was to this end that he called upon them to recognize Abu'l-Ạbbas, the brother of the murdered Ibrahim, as their rightful Imam and Caliph. The excited crowd expressed their approval with enthusiasm, and as they gave their allegiance to Abu'l-Ạbbas, they took up his battle cry, " O men of Khorasan, revenge the death of Ibrahim ! "

Marwan was at the time advancing towards Kufa with an army of 120,000 men, and he encountered the army from Khorasan at a point on the Greater Zab river, and the Battle of the Zab lasted for two days. It was a closely contested struggle, and tradition says that the day was turned when Marwan's horse ran away without its rider, which gave rise to the rumour that Marwan had been killed, and that consequently his army fell back and gave way and fled. The rumour was not true, however, for Marwan managed to escape, though he was eagerly pursued from place to place, until he was eventually discovered and killed at an isolated Christian chapel on the Nile. So fell the last of the Umayyads, except Abdu'l-Rahman, who continued to maintain the family authority in Spain.

Abu'l-Ạbbas came back in triumph and made a speech in the mosque of Kufa, where he established his capital. In this speech he called himself *al-ṣaffah*, " the pitiless bloodshedder," thus expressing his intention to kill all the Umayyads. The massacre of the inhabitants of Mosul was typical of his thoroughness in this undertaking, for it was on his command that his brother, at the head of four thousand Khorasan troops, fell upon the people of Mosul on Friday and killed " eighteen thousand men of Arab extraction, and after that he killed all their slaves and their freedmen, until he had completely annihilated them."[1] But during his short rule of less than four years, he was kept fully occupied in meeting numerous insurrections and in ruthlessly killing those who were suspected of disloyalty.

The famous Mansur (Abu'l-Ja'far) was his successor as Caliph.

[1] *Ibid.*, p. 429.

He it was who built the new capital, the round city of Baghdad, with its four great gates that faced the roads that led respectively to Kufa, to Basra, to Syria, and to Khorasan. The latter was called the Gate of Good Fortune, because the dynasty of the Abbasids owed its origin to the armies of Khorasan.[1]

But Mansur was dominated by a jealous fear that led him to put to death many of his most capable leaders. Among these was Abu Muslim, whom he had always distrusted. For we read that early in his brother's reign he had gone to Khorasan and Abu Muslim "had not exerted himself to show him courtesy or respect, and had not shown pleasure at his arrival." And on returning from Khorasan he had warned his brother, "While Abu Muslim is alive, you are not established in the Caliphate."[2]

Accordingly, Mansur was eager to get Abu Muslim within his power, and finally succeeded in luring him to come with his army to Iraḳ. Mansur had established himself at a place that Chosroe Anoshirwan had built near Persepolis, and he sent word to Abu Muslim, who was camping near by, that he wanted to see him personally about several matters concerning which it would be difficult to write. The appointment was made, and in the meantime Mansur instructed his doorkeeper that Abu Muslim was coming and to remove his sword when he entered the inner room. At this discourtesy Abu Muslim was offended, but notwithstanding he gave the attendant his sword and went and sat down in the room where he thought he would be alone with Mansur. But Mansur had arranged that three trusted men should remain in hiding near by, and he had instructed them, "When I clap my hands three times, come out upon Abu Muslim and cut him to pieces." Accordingly few words were exchanged until Mansur clapped his hands and the deed was done.[3]

It should be said in justice, however, that Abu Muslim was accustomed to rule in Khorasan in much the same way that Mansur did in Iraḳ. It is said that he "shrank from employing no means, either against the adversaries of the Ạbbasids or

[1] Mas'udi, *Muruju'l-Dhahab*, vi, p. 171.
[2] Dinawari, edit. Guirgass, p. 373.
[3] *Ibid.*, p. 377.

against his personal enemies or rivals, and removed all that was in his way either by force or artifice."[1] The art of the ruler appeared to be to strike and strike first, and it may well be that when Abu Muslim saw the trap he had stepped into he thought less about the ingratitude of Mansur for his services in Khorasan than he did of his own regret that he had been outwitted.

But in these troublous times that gave rise to the new dynasty of the Ạbbasid Caliphs, and with the many instances that occurred of assassination on suspicion during the reign of Mansur, what was the life of the Imam Ja'far Sadiḳ? What was his status as "*Imam*," and how did it happen that he was allowed to live on in Medina?

[1] And in his religious beliefs, yielding possibly to his personal ambitions, he seems to have united Islam with the ancient belief in metempsychosis. He pretended that he was himself an incarnation of the divinity, and the Veiled Prophet of Khorasan, Háshim al-Muḳanna' was one of his pupils. He had come to have more sympathy with the 'Ạlids, and several of the later Shi'ite sects trace their origin back to Abu Muslim. See the *Encyclopædia of Islam*, art. "Abu Muslim."

CHAPTER XII

THE IMAM JA'FAR AṢ-ṢADIḲ, "THE TRUTHFUL"

THE Imam most frequently cited as an authority on points of law or tradition is the Imam Ja'far aṣ-Ṣadiḳ. Kulaini says that he lived sixty-five years (83-148 A.H.), which was a longer life than that of any of the other Imams.[1] All the biographers mention that his mother was Umm Farwa, the daughter of Kázim, who was the grandson of Abu Bakr aṣ-Ṣadiḳ, "the Truthful."[2] For it was Abu Bakr who had said, "Let there be truth among you, it leads to freedom."[3] The Imam Ja'far was likewise called aṣ-Ṣadiḳ for his veracity.

For his mother he had a high regard, and on her authority he related that his father had said, "O Umm Farwa, I pray to God for the sinners among the Shi'ites day and night, a thousand times, for we Imams endure the misfortunes that happen in the light of what we know of the coming reward, whereas they suffer without such knowledge."[4]

Little is recorded of the personal appearance of Ja'far, except that "his face and his body were white, his nose was somewhat bent, and his hair was black."[5] Of his domestic life also little is said, but we know that he had ten children, seven of whom were by his two legal wives, Faṭima and Umm Walad, and the three others were "from various mothers," or as we read elsewhere, from women whom he held as concubine slaves.[6]

Whether as a matter of principle or of discretion, in the exciting and distressing times in which he lived, the Imam Ja'far managed

[1] Kulaini, *Usul al-Kafi*, p. 193. Cf. also Majlisi, *Tadhkiratu'l-A'imma*, pp. 139-148, and *Anvaru'l-Bahár*, Vol. II, p. 79; and Ya'ḳubi, *Tarikh*, ii, p. 458.

[2] Mas'udi, *Muruju'l-Dhahab*, Vol. IV, p. 182.

[3] Tayalisi, *Musnad*, edit. Haidarabad, 1321 A.H., p. 3, tradition No. 5.

[4] Kulaini, *Usul al-Kafi*, p. 193.

[5] Majlisi, *Tadhkiratu'l-A'imma*, p. 139.

[6] *Aḳa'id ush-Shi'a*, Bk. IV, ch. iii; *Jannatu'l-Khulud*, table xiii; and Majlisi, *Anvaru'l-Bahár*, Vol. XI, p. 134.

to keep entirely out of politics. Mas'udi mentions that when the Ạbbasid leader, Ibrahim, was killed by Marwan II, Abu Salama, the chief agitator, feared that this would mean the failure of their undertaking, and he attempted therefore to induce Ja'far aṣ-Ṣadiḳ to come to him in person, and to openly declare his claim to the Imamate, and to accept the allegiance of the people of Khorasan. The Imam Ja'far, however, called for a lamp and burned Abu Salama's letter, and said to the messenger who brought it, "Tell your master what you have seen." At the same time he repeated this verse[1]:

> When one lights a fire, are its flames for another?
> Or does one gather wood in the rope of another?

Shahrastani has paid Ja'far aṣ-Ṣadiḳ a high tribute. "His knowledge was great in religion and culture, he was fully informed in philosophy, he attained great piety in the world, and he abstained entirely from lusts. He lived in Medina long enough to greatly profit the sect that followed him, and to give his friends the advantage of the hidden sciences. He then visited Iraḳ, but he never came out publicly to claim the Imamate and never discussed the Caliphate with anyone. For he who is drowned in the sea of knowledge does not covet anything, and whoever rises to the summit of truth has no fear of degradation. Another saying is, Whoever is devoted to God withdraws from mankind, but whoever seeks attachment to other than God, truly desires will ravish him. On his father's side the Imam Ja'far was connected with the 'tree of prophecy,' and on his mother's side with Abu Bakr."[2]

Perhaps there may be something in the tradition that as-Sayuti records, that the Imam Ja'far once exclaimed, "I am quit of anyone who mentions Abu Bakr or Ụmar otherwise than favourably."[3] Some such attitude towards his mother's people, or the ability to appreciate the true merits of the first two Caliphs may have helped him avoid the suspicions of the various Caliphs of his

[1] Mas'udi, *Muruju'l-Dhahab*, Vol. VI, pp. 93-96.
[2] Shahrastani, *Book of Religious and Philosophical Sects*, ed. Cureton, p. 124.
[3] As-Suyuti, *History of the Caliphs*, p. 125.

time—the Umayyads, Hisham, Walíd, Ibrahim and Marwán; and the Ạbbasids, as-Saffah and al-Mansur.

A story that is told by Kulaini,[1] however, would suggest that he was not always left in peace. For it is said that the Caliph al-Mansur instructed the governor of Medina to burn down the Imam's house. The fire reached the hallway, when the Imam came out and drew a line before it, and boldly stamped on the flames, exclaiming, "I am of the sons of Isma'il, I am a son of Ibrahim, the Friend of God," whom the Ḳoran represents as having escaped the fire in safety (Surah lxv. 69). The orthodox Shi'ites look upon this as a miraculous escape for the Imam, but other readers consider that the element of truth in the story may simply be that at one time the Imam's house took fire and he easily stamped out the flames before they did any damage.

On the question of the Caliph al-Mansur's attitude toward the Imam Ja'far, Ibn Khallikan relates that "al-Mansur wanted his principal men in Iraḳ. But for Ja'far this would have meant leaving him home in Medina, and he therefore asked Mansur to excuse him. This Mansur refused to do. He asked then for permission to remain in Medina a little longer to settle the affairs of his property, but this also Mansur refused. The Imam then said to the Caliph, "I have heard my father relate from his father, from his grandfather, the Apostle of God—may God bless him and his household and give them peace—that 'the man who goes away to make a living will achieve his purpose, but he who sticks to his family will prolong his life.' Mansur asked, 'Truly, did you hear this from your father, and from your grandfather, the Apostle of God?' The Imam said, 'Before God, I declare that I did.' Therefore Mansur excused him from the number of persons whom he required to go and live in Iraḳ, and appointed his place of residence in Medina, and gave him permission to remain there with his family."[2]

Nevertheless, the Imam was apprehensive when Mansur sent for him at the time Muḥammad ibn Abdulla was killed. He

[1] Kulaini, *Usul al-Kafi*, p. 194.
[2] Ibn Khallikan, edit. Buluk, 1284 A.H., Vol. II, p. 112.

prayed, " O God, make level for me the rough ground, and soften his disposition toward me; give me the good I hope for and turn me from the evil that I dread." It appears also that this prayer was answered, for when he entered his presence, the Caliph rose to meet him and showed him honour and favour, " and rubbed his beard with perfume and sent him to his own house." When he was questioned later as to his sympathy for Muḥammad ibn Abdulla, he repeated a verse from the Ḳoran (Surah lix. 12), " If they were driven forth they would not share their banishment; if they were attacked they would not help them, or if they help them they will surely turn their backs: then would they remain unhelped." Mansur was satisfied and replied, " Even without this promise from you, it is sufficient."[1]

From the descriptions we read of the way the Imam Ja'far aṣ-Ṣadiḳ entertained generously there in his beautiful garden in Medina, receiving visitors of all persuasions, it appears that he conducted a kind of forum or Socratic school. Several of his pupils had important contributions to make in the future development of jurisprudence and theology. In later years two of these pupils, Abu Ḥanifa and Malik ibn Anas, the founders of two of the recognized schools of law, gave their judgment to the people of Medina that the oath they had taken to Mansur could not be considered binding since it was given under compulsion. It is related that another of his pupils, Waṣil ibn Ạta, the founder of the Mu'tazilite sect, brought up theories for discussion which led to his being dismissed from the Imam Ja'far's classes. And Jabir ibn Hayyan, who became famous as an alchemist, was also his pupil.[2]

Perhaps the most interesting of all his pupils was Abu Ḥanifa, who gave public lectures at Kufa that attracted much attention. In giving decisions, he claimed the right to exercise the privilege of deduction (ḳiyas), and of using his own judgment (ra'y) to supplement the traditions, and for this departure he was severely criticised by rival scholars in Mecca and Medina. His decisions

[1] *Ibid.*, p. 112.
[2] Zaedán, *Umayyads and Ạbbasids*, p. 152; and Huart, *Arabic Literature*, p. 313.

were on points of the law of Islam, however, rather than in any official capacity, for he steadfastly refused to enter the service of the government as a judge. Thus it was that as a literary or academic jurist he was able to carry on his work in Kufa under both the Umayyads and the Ạbbasids. It is probable, moreover, that he strongly sympathized with the Ạlids and resented the way in which they had been set aside.[1]

One is surprised to observe that these two contemporary scholars were able to carry on their teaching in their respective cities, Abu-Ḥanifa in Kufa and Ja'far aṣ-Ṣadiḳ in Medina, for so long a period in such troublous times. The two men were on friendly terms, and it appears that each of them endeavoured to sustain a reputation for knowing almost everything.

Ibn Khallikan tells of a joke that the Imam Ja'far got on his rival savant. The Imam asked, "What would you say is the proper fine for one who breaks the front molars (rubá'iyát) of a deer?" Abu Ḥanifa answered, "O son of the Apostle of God, I do not know about that." To this the Imam replied, "Can you then pretend to learning when you do not know that a deer has no front molars, but only the incisors (thanáyá)?"[2]

On another occasion, Abu Ḥanifa remarked that if the Imam did not teach three things he would be able to accept him. The first was that good is from God and evil is from the deeds of the slaves of God, "whereas I say that the slave has no choice, but both good and evil are from God." The second was that in the final judgment the Devil suffers in the fire, "whereas I say that the fire will not burn him, in so much as the same material will not injure itself."[3] The third was that it is impossible to see God in this world or the next, "whereas I say that anyone who has existence may be seen, if not in this world, then in the next." But at this point Shaikh Buhlúl, who was one of the Imam's companions, picked up a clod of earth and smote Abu Hanifa

[1] *Encyclopædia of Islam,* art. "Abu Ḥanifa."
[2] Ibn Khallikan, edit. Buluk, 1284 A.H., Vol. II, p. 113.
[3] Iblis and the djinn are said in the Ḳoran to have been created from fire (nár), in surahs xviii, 48; vii, 11; and xxxviii, 77, whereas man was created of clay (tín). Cf. MacDonald in the *Encyclopædia of Islam,* art. "Malá'ika."

on the head, declaring, as he made a hasty departure, "All three points are refuted." Abu Ḥanifa made a complaint against him to the Caliph, who called Buhlúl before him and asked, "Why did you throw the clod of earth at Abu Ḥanifa?" He answered, "I did not throw it." Abu Ḥanifa protested, "You did throw it." But Buhlúl replied, "You yourself have maintained that evil is from God and that his slave has no choice, so why do you upbraid me? And you have said also that the same material will not injure itself. Accordingly, therefore, as you are from the dust of the earth and also the clod that struck you was from the dust of the earth, tell me how it could injure you? You have claimed also that you can see God, affirming that anything that has existence may be seen. Show me, I pray thee, this pain that has existence in your head?"[1]

Nevertheless, Abu Ḥanifa was highly esteemed by those who sympathized with the cause of the Imam Ja'far aṣ-Ṣadiḳ, for they heartily endorsed a remark that he made concerning the Caliph Mansur and all such oppressors, whether of the Beni Umayya or of the Beni Ạbbas. For Abu Ḥanifa had eloquently declared that if such men would build a *masjid* (Moslem house of prayer) and command him to the simple task of counting the bricks he would not do it, "for they are dissolute (fásiḳ), and the dissolute are not worthy of the authority of leadership." Ultimately, Mansur heard of this remark and cast Abu Ḥanifa into prison, where he remained until his death. It was his suffering on account of this statement that gained for him the friendship of the Shi'ites.[2] The statement was based, they say, on the verse in the Ḳoran (Surah ii. 118), where God said to Abraham, "I am about to make thee an Imam to mankind," and Abraham asked, "Of my offpsring also?" but God answered, "My covenant embraceth not the evildoers." Later Shi'ite theologians, such as Majlisi, insist that this verse shows clearly that the dissolute or evildoer (fásiḳ) is not qualified to be an Imam, and it is their delight to point out that Baidawi and Zamakhshari and Abu

[1] Majlisi, *Tadhkiratu'l-A'imma*, p. 130.
[2] *Ibid.*, p. 130.

Ḥanifa so nearly agree with them in their interpretation of this verse in the Ḳoran.[1]

On the question of the freedom of the will (iráda), which was much under discussion at the time, the Imam Ja'far aṣ-Ṣadiḳ taught " that God the Most High has decreed some things for us and he has likewise decreed some things through our agency: what he has decreed for us or on our behalf he has concealed from us, but what he has decreed through our agency he has revealed to us. We are not concerned, therefore, so much with what he has decreed for us as we are with what he has decreed through our agency."

As to the question of the power (ḳadr) of directing one's own actions, the Imam took a middle position, which is neither compulsion (jabr) nor committing (tafvíz) the choice to ourselves. He was accustomed to say in prayer, " O God, thine is the praise that I give thee, and to thee is the excuse if I sin against thee. There is no work of merit on my own behalf or on behalf of another, and in evil there is no excuse for me or for another."[2]

Ya'ḳubi remarks in regard to the Imam Ja'far aṣ-Ṣadiḳ, that " it was customary for scholars who related anything from him to say ' the Learned One informed us.' " When we recall that Malik ibn Anás (94-179 A.H.), the author of the *Muwatta'*, was contemporary with the Imam Ja'far, at least a century before the time of al-Bukhari and Muslim, it is significant to find that it is the Imam Ja'far who is credited with stating what came to be regarded as the most important principle to observe in judging traditions: " What is in agreement with the Book of God, accept it, and whatever is contrary, reject it."

In making further reference to the Imam Ja'far in his " History,"[3] Ya'ḳubi has recorded a number of pithy sayings or proverbs that have been ascribed to him. A few examples of these, though they lose by translation, are the following:

" There are three classes towards whom mercy is required,

[1] *Ibid.*, p. 118.
[2] Shahrastani, *op. cit.*, p. 124.
[3] Ya'ḳubi, *Tarikh*, edit. Houtsma, Vol. II, p. 458 ff.

the rich who have become poor, the noble who have been abased, and the scholar who is the butt of the ignorant."

"Whomsoever God removes from the degradation of sin to the exaltation of piety, he it is whom God makes rich without property and noble without the help of family."

"Whoever fears God, God makes all things fear him; and whoever does not fear God, God makes him fear all things."

"Whoever is content towards God with little in the way of bounty, God will be content towards him with little in the way of works required."

It is related also by the same author that the Imam Ja'far said, "There are two friends, and whoever follows them will enter Paradise." Someone asked, "Who are they?" He said, "The acceptance of that which you dislike when God likes it, and the rejection of that which you like when God dislikes it." The questioner asked, "Who is able to do this?" He replied "Whoever flees from the fire to Paradise."

Once the Imam Ja'far remarked that God had revealed to Moses, "If you put your arm in the mouth of a serpent up to your elbow, it will be better than asking something for someone to whom it could not be given." On another occasion he said, "Beware of association with five sorts of people, first, the fool, for he wants to help you but he will really injure you; second, the liar, for he is like a mirage, making the distant appear near and near to be distant; third, the dissolute or evildoer, for he will sell you for his own food or drink; fourth, the miser, for he will leave you more in need than you were; and fifth, the coward, for he will give you up and save himself by paying the ransom."

On caravan journeys it is customary to cover the sordid pack-saddle of the load animal with a rug and bright coloured bedding. From this custom the Imam derived an illustration, saying: "Believers will show love and love will be shown to them, so as to conceal their pack-saddles."

And at times the Imam gave such sage advice as this, "Whoever is angry with you three times but does not speak evil of you, count him as your friend; but whoever seeks that you should show him the friendship of a brother, while he himself does not befriend his brother, or associate with him or invite him to his home, know that he will surely injure you."

It has been pointed out that as the Imam Ja'far lived at the close of the Umayyad dynasty and at the beginning of the rule of the Ạbbasids, while both these parties were fully occupied with the problems of resisting one another, he had opportunity to give his attention to interpretations of the divine commands. It is to his declarations on such matters that later theologians most frequently refer. But it is difficult to determine whether he actually committed these statements to writing. At the present day it is generally considered that the works which bear his name are later forgeries,[1] though Ibn Khallikan says that "he composed a treatise on alchemy, augury and omens; and the Sufi, Abu Musa Jabir ibn Haiyan of Tarsus, compiled a work of two thousand pages, in which he inserted the problems of his master, Ja'far aṣ-Ṣadiḳ, which formed five hundred treatises."[2]

While many traditions used by later Shi'ite theologians to establish the doctrine of the Imamate are traced to the Imam Ja'far aṣ-Ṣadik, one of the most interesting and far-reaching is that mentioned by Mas'udi. It was ascribed by the Imam to Ạli ibn Abu Ṭalib, who is said to have related "that when God wished to establish Creation, the atoms of creatures and the beginning of all created things, he first made what he created in the form of small particles. This was before he stretched out the earth or raised the heavens. God existed alone in his authority and power. So he cast forth a ray of light, a flame from his splendour, and it was radiant. He scattered this light in the midst of invisible atoms, which he then united in the form of our Prophet. God the Most High then declared unto him, "You are the first of those who shall speak, the one with the power of choice and the one chosen. To you I have trusted my light and the treasure of my guidance. For your sake I will form

[1] *Encyclopædia of Islam,* art. "Dja'far ibn Muhammad aṣ-Ṣadiḳ."

[2] Ibn Khallikan, *op. cit.*, p. 113. Cf. D. B. MacDonald, *Encyclopædia of Islam,* art. "Djafr"; also Ibn Khaldun, Quatremere's text, ii, p. 191; and De Slans' translation, p. 224.

spacious channels, give free course to the waters, and raise the heavens. For your sake I will give rewards and punishments, and assign men to Paradise or to the Fire. *I will appoint the people of your household for guidance.* I will bestow upon them the secrets of my knowledge: no truth will be hidden from them and no mystery concealed. I will designate them as my *proof* to mankind, as those who shall admonish men of my Power and remind them of my Unity." Then God took the testimony of the creatures to the fact that he was the Preserver of all and the one who is perfect in his Unity. When this testimony had been secured, God added to the sagacity of mankind the power to recognize that he had chosen Muḥammad and his family, and had made them understand that guidance is through him, and that the *light* is with him. The Imamate also is with Muḥammad and his family. It is given as a rule of righteousness, and the Imams are the *intercessors* provided.

"Thus God concealed creation in his mystery and hid it in the secrets of his knowledge. But the time came, however, when he arranged the universes and stretched out time. He stirred up the waters and obtained the foam, and caused the vapour to move. His throne floated on the water. He stretched out the land on the back of the water: he drew forth the vapour and with it he made the sky. He summoned the earth and the heavens to obey him and they accepted his dominion. He formed the angels from lights he had created and spirits he had originated.

"He established the prophecy of Muḥammad upon the foundation of his Unity, and announced it in heaven before he was commissioned as a prophet on earth.

"God then created Adam, declaring his nobility to the angels, and showing them how God had given him priority of knowledge from the time he first knew them, in that God had given him the names of things. God indicated that they were to bow down to Adam as to the *Mahráb* (prayer niche), or to the Kaaba, or to the sacred door (of a shrine) or to the Ḳiblah (the direction of prayer). The good spirits and the angels of light were to bow down before him. God then informed Adam of his responsibility and showed him the rare treasure he had committed to him, when he designated him as the Imam among the angels. Now Adam was so highly favoured in the praise of God because he had been endowed with our light. But God kept this light concealed under the veil of time until he exalted Muḥammad in holiness.

"It was Muḥammad who declared his message both privately and publicly, and preached to mankind openly and in secret. He proclaimed the *warning*, according to the agreement which God had made with him at the time of Creation, and before his human birth. By what had fallen upon him of the flame from the atoms of the original light, he was guided to what was secret with God and comprehended it clearly. But those who remained in the bondage of ignorance or indifference would be the objects of God's displeasure.

"The light descended," the Imam Ja'far went on to say, "upon our most noble men, and shone through our Imams, so that we are in fact the lights of Heaven and of Earth. To us is salvation committed, and from us are the secrets of science derived, for we are the destination that all must strive to reach. Our *mahdi* will be the final Proof, the Seal of the Imams, the Deliverer of the Imamate, the Apex of the Light, and the Source of all good works. We are the most noble of all mankind, the most exalted of all creatures, the Proofs of the Lord of the Worlds, and those who cling to our friendship will be favoured in this life and in death they will have our support."[1]

Much freedom has been taken in relating traditions from the Imam Ja'far concerning the light of Muḥammad, as is illustrated by the following version from Mulla Muḥammad Taḳi, Khawnsárí.[2] "It is related that the Imam Ja'far aṣ-Ṣadiḳ handed down a tradition from his father, that Ạli ibn Abu Ṭalib had said that God had created the *Light of Muḥammad* before he created Adam or Noah or Abraham or Isma'il or any others. Along with this Light of Muḥammad God created twelve curtains. The names of these were Power, Greatness, Generosity, Prosperity, Mercy,

[1] Mas'udi, *Muruju'l-Dhahab*, Vol. I, p. 55.
[2] *Khulasat al-Akhbar*, ch. xxviii.

Benevolence, Dignity, Guidance, Exaltation, Prophecy, Purity and Intercession. The Light of Muḥammad was concealed for seven thousand years in the curtain of Power, and Muḥammad said, Praise be to him who is self-sufficient and never in need! It was within the curtain of Dignity for six thousand years, and Muḥammad said, Praise be to the High and the Great! It was within the curtain of Guidance for five thousand years, and Muḥammad said, Praise be to the God of the Great Throne! It was within the curtain of Exaltation for four thousand years, and Muḥammad said, Praise be to the Lord of all that changes! It was within the curtain of Prophecy three thousand years, and Muḥammad said, Praise be to the Master of ancient kingdoms! It was within the curtain of Purity for two thousand years, and Muḥammad said, Praise be to the Lord who is exalted and praised!

"Then God revealed the name of Muhammad on a tablet, and the Light was on the Tablet for four thousand years. Then it was in the *Ạrsh* (the ninth heaven) and remained on the leg of the Throne for seven thousand years, until God placed it in the loins of Adam. Thence it passed to Noah, and thus it came on down to Abdu'l-Muṭṭalib and from him to Abdulla (Muḥammad's father). When God sent the Light to Muḥammad he gave him six miraculous garments—the Shirt of Acceptance, the Cloak of Congratulation, the Trousers of Kindness, the Belt of Love, the Shoes of Fear, and the Staff of Dignity. And God said to him, Go near unto mankind, and declare among them, *there is no God but God*.

"Now this Shirt of Acceptance was made of six things. The body of it was of precious stones, both sleeves were of pearls, the girdle was of yellow crystal, the two gussets were of coral, the lap was of green emerald, and the collar was of light. It was out of regard for this shirt of Muḥammad's that God had accepted the repentance of Adam. It was because of it also that Solomon's seal had power at a distance, and that God saved Jonah from the stomach of the huge fish, and rescued the prophets from various physical plagues. Such was the shirt of the Prophet!"

Fantastic as these conceptions may seem to those who have not been familiar with them from their childhood, it is nevertheless important to observe that this comprehensive claim that the celestial light substance had been received into the souls of the Imams was most probably first enunciated during the period of the Imamate of Ja'far aṣ-Ṣadiḳ, for there is much in the subsequent development of Shi'ite theology that is dependent upon this belief.

The Imam Ja'far died in the tenth year of the reign of the Caliph Mansur, 148 A.H. (765 A.D.). On this date of his death the authorities are agreed. He had worn a signet ring with the inscription, "God is my Master and my Defence from his Creation." He had lived to be sixty-four or sixty-five years old. Nevertheless, the story is told that on the Caliph's order he had been given poisoned grapes and died. Thus he became a martyr, dying the appropriate death for an Imam, for with the exception of Ạli and Husain and the Mahdi, all the rest of the twelve Imams are said to have been put to death by poison, which is consistent, not with any law of probability, but with the accepted traditions that none of the Imams should die a natural death.

The Imam Ja'far was buried in the Baki' cemetery at Medina, in the same place with his father and his grandfather. For centuries there has been a marble slab over their grave and on this is written:

> "In the name of God the Merciful and Compassionate,
> Praise be to God who sustains the nations, and who gives life to dead bones!
> Here is the tomb of Faṭima, daughter of the Apostle of God, and Queen of the women of the world;
> Here also is the tomb of Hasan ibn Ạli ibn Abu Ṭalib;
> Here also is the tomb of Ạli ibn al-Husain;
> Here also is the tomb of Muḥammad ibn Ạli;
> Here also is the tomb of Ja'far ibn Muḥammad;
> May God favour them all!"

CHAPTER XIII

MEDINA, THE CITY OF THE PROPHET AND HIS FAMILY

"MEDINA is but a small town, being less than half the size of Mecca, its lands, however, are more fruitful, and the climate is very warm. There are running streams here, and it possesses cultivated fields and gardens and date groves, also the dates of the kind called *Bardí* and *Ajwah* are better here than in any other country. The inhabitants are for the most part dark-skinned, and the men have their occupation in commerce.

" In honour of Medina many traditions have been recorded. Among the rest in the *Maṣábiḥ* it is reported that the Prophet said, *Verily Abraham sanctified Mecca and made it a sanctuary but I have sanctified Medina, making a sanctuary all that lies between (the limits of) its calcined rocks. It is incumbent that no blood shall be shed there, and none shall wear weapons of war, and no place shall be enclosed there, except indeed for forage.* Further, the Prophet said, *At the gates of Medina are angels, so that the plague cannot enter the city, nor Ad-Dajjál (Antichrist)* : and again he said, *He who can compass to die in Medina, let him die there, for verily I will intercede for any who shall die there.* And again he said, *The last place of the places of Islam to come to ruin will be Medina.*"[1]

This fourteenth-century description, written by Mustawfi, a convinced Shi'ite, makes no mention of the sorry state of the Tomb of Muḥammad at the time of his visit, and for the preceding one hundred years. For from the time of the fire in A.D. 1256, when the Mosque of the Prophet was almost completely destroyed, " the rubble was not even cleared away from the tombs, but

[1] Mustawfi, *Nuzhatu'l-Qulub*, English trans. by G. le Strange, Gibb Memorial, Vol. XXIII, 2, p. 12. Cf. Goldsack, *Selections from Muhammadan Traditions*, Madras, 1923, p. 144.

remained there for over two centuries." Eventually, in A.D. 1279, the Maluk Sultan, al-Mansur Kalá'ún, "marked the site of the Prophet's tomb with a dome that was covered with plates of lead," but it was not until after this modest structure had been struck by lightning, in the year A.D. 1481, when the library and many manuscripts of the Ḳoran perished, that anything like a restoration was undertaken. This restoration was in A.D. 1484, and at that time the dome over the tomb was enlarged and a brass railing was provided to surround its immediate area. In A.D. 1492 however, this new mosque, with its beautifully reconstructed minaret, al-ra'isíya, was also struck by lightning and destroyed.[1]

During the rule of the Saffawid dynasty in Persia (A.D. 1502-1736), with long periods of war between Persia and Turkey, Shi'ite pilgrimages to either Mecca or Medina became extremely difficult. In fact they were discouraged and prohibited by Shah Ạbbas and others of the Saffawid rulers in the interest of the development of the shrines within the Persian borders, in order thus to retain within the country the large sums of money the pilgrims were accustomed to spend. We find also traditional sayings, attributed to the Imams, that minimize the importance of actually going to Medina and emphasize "the sufficiency of the prayer of visitation at a distance." One tradition says that God has a number of angels who go about in the earth, "so that if any one of my people sends me a greeting, I will receive it." The Imam Muḥammad Baḳir recommended that anyone who was unable to visit Medina should fast three days, and then, on his own roof, or out in the open desert, he should repeat the prayer of visitation to the Prophet. And Majlisi says, on good authority, that this special prayer is acceptable at the tomb of any of the Imams; or at the tomb of one who is regarded as a saint, or out in the open desert.[2]

By the close of the eighteenth century the Turks had taken Persian Iraḳ and were in control in the Hedjaz. Except in Shi'ite countries the Turkish Sultan became the recognized Caliph.

[1] *Encyclopædia of Islam*, art. "Madina."
[2] Majlisi, *Tafatu'z-Zá'irín*, p. 36.

The pilgrimage cities were administered on a revenue basis. The pilgrimages regained their popularity and many thousands went from Persia also to the shrines at Najaf, Baghdad, Kerbala and Samarra, to seek the intercession of the Imams who are buried in these several places. And those who went on the great pilgrimage to Mecca were scrupulously careful to also visit Medina, to pray at the tomb of the Prophet, and at the tomb of his daughter, Faṭima, and at the one tomb that served for the four Imams—Hasan, Zayn al-Abidín, Muḥammad Baḳir and Ja'far aṣ-Ṣadiḳ.

These pilgrimages were profitable to the Turkish government and to the local inhabitants of the sacred cities, but the idea of thousands of Moslems coming from all parts of the world to invoke the intercession of their dead Prophet and of the Imams stirred up the ire of powerful tribes of Wahhábís in the Hedjaz, who assumed the role of reformers, and declared that such worship even at the tomb of the Prophet was forbidden. They attacked Medina, therefore, in the year A.D. 1804, and "took the town, plundered its treasures, and prevented pilgrimages to the tomb of Muḥammad. An attempt to destroy the dome over the tomb failed, but the great treasures in pearls, jewels, etc., presented by pious visitors to the mosque, were carried off."[1]

It was some years after the restoration of the Turkish authority in A.D. 1818 that the Sultan Abdul Majid made elaborate provision for the rebuilding of the Mosque of the Prophet at Medina. It was under construction from A.D. 1848-1860, and was built at an estimated cost of "seven hundred thousand pounds," but it has been suggested that this sum probably included the value of the jewels deposited by the Sultan in the Shrine and also the amount of "the embezzlements of the officers in charge of the work."[2] This is the mosque that is still standing and that has been described by the modern travellers, Burton (1853), Wavell (1908), Batanuni (1910), and Rutter (1928).

Up until 1918 Mecca and Medina were under Turkish adminis-

[1] *Encyclopædia of Islam*, art. "Madina."
[2] Rutter, *The Holy Cities of Arabia*, Vol. II, p. 237.

tration, but by the terms of the peace at the conclusion of the World War, Turkey relinquished her suzerainty in favour of Husain, the new King of the Hedjaz. But Husain was unable to maintain his authority, for again the Wahhábís became masters of the situation and took control of Mecca and Medina. When this news became known to the Shi'ites in Persia, all their shrines were draped in black, a gesture of horror that meant " Dust on our heads ! " for they feared the worst, i.e., that the tombs of the Prophet and his family in Medina would all be destroyed. And they had reason to fear, for the main point that distinguished the Wahhábís from other Muslim communities is their consistent opposition to the practice of invoking the intercession of saints. " This matter involves one Islamic ideal—the recognition of the unity of the Deity. The Wahhábís regard the employment of such intercession as polytheistic, and since the devout visit the graves of deceased saints in order to secure their intercession, the Wahhábís go to the length of desecrating or destroying the tombs."[1]

As far as the tomb of the Prophet was concerned, the Wahhábí occupation of Medina has not been so disastrous as was anticipated. The Wahhábí religious leaders were anxious enough to throw down the dome and rebuild the *Haram* so as not to include the Prophet's tomb. But their leader, Ibn Sa'ud, exercised the statesman's restraint, for fear of arousing the hostility of the entire Islamic world. Thus the tomb of the Prophet has so far been spared, but the religious zeal of the Wahhábís was allowed full scope in the destruction of the shrines and tombs in the Baki' cemetery. The appearance of the cemetery, after this work of destruction was completed, has been described by Mr. Rutter: " When I entered the Bakia the sight which I saw was as it were a town which had been razed to the ground. All over the cemetery nothing was to be seen but little indefinite mounds of earth and stones, pieces of timber, iron bars, blocks of stone, and a broken rubble of cement and bricks, strewn about. It was like

[1] Margoliouth, art. " Ideas of Modern Islam," *Moslem World*, July, 1930, p. 239.

the broken remains of a town which had been demolished by an earthquake. Against the western wall lay great stacks of old wooden planks, and others of stone blocks, and of iron bars and railings. This was some of the scattered material, which had been collected and stacked in order. A few narrow paths had been cleared in the rubble, so that visitors might make their way to the further parts of the cemetery ; but other signs of order there were none. All was a wilderness of ruined building material and tombstones—not ruined by a casual hand, but raked away from their places and ground small."[1]

An Egyptian has also described what he saw : " And they destroyed in Medina all the graves to be found in al-Baki' (the cemetery where many of the Prophet's Companions lay), likewise the Mosque of Hamsah, the Prophet's uncle, with his tomb at Uhud."[2]

What this desecration signifies to an orthodox Shi'ite can be imagined from the descriptions of the Baki' cemetery that were written before the time of the Wahhábís. Mustawfi writes, " The cemetery of Medina, called Baki', lies to the westward of the town, and here is seen the grave of Ibrahim, the Prophet's (only) son, also the graves of his daughters. The Caliph Ụthman also was buried here ; and the Commander of the Faithful, Hasan ; and Ạbbas, the uncle of the Prophet ; also the Imams Zayn-al-Abidín and Muḥammad Baḳir, and Ja'far Ṣadiḳ—the blessing of God be upon them one and all."[3] And Ibn Jubayr mentions that " there is a lot that contains the graves of the wives of the Prophet, and adjoining this is a small lot in which are the graves of three of his children. Close by are the graves of Ạbbas ibn Abdu'l-Muṭṭalib and of Hasan ibn Ạli. The latter has a dome which stands high in the air. It is near the Baḳi' Gate, which we have mentioned, on the right, as one would go out. The head of al-Hasan lies towards the feet of al-Ạbbas. Their two graves are broad and elevated from the ground, are faced with slabs of beautiful stone, are ornamented with plates of nickel, and are

[1] Rutter, *op. cit.*, p. 256.
[2] Margoliouth, *op. cit.*, p. 240.
[3] Mustawfi, *Nuzhatu'l-Qulub*, p. 15.

bound with star-headed nails, all of which give a most pleasing effect. The grave of Ibrahim, the son of the Prophet, is of the same kind."[1]

The Significance of the Pilgrimage to Medina

Many years before guide books were published for travellers in Europe or America, there were books written to direct Muḥammadan pilgrims as to the proper procedure when visiting these various sacred cities. One of the most esteemed of these books for the Shi'ites is the *Tofat az-Záirín*, "A Present for Pilgrims." This book of over four hundred pages was written in the seventeenth century by the most influential of Shi'ite theologians, Mulla Muḥammad Baḳir Majlisi (d. 1111/1699). It is not like modern guide books, however, in giving interesting bits of history and geography, and indicating what is sufficiently extraordinary to deserve the traveller's attention. For the Shi'ite pilgrim's objective in making long treks across the desert lands of the east is not the satisfaction of travel or sightseeing, primarily, but to attain merit in the sight of God and to have his sins forgiven. Accordingly, Majlisi's book is an authoritative manual for attaining merit through pilgrimages. Much attention is given to appraising the relative value of visits to the different shrines, to the ceremonial observances that are required, and to the efficacy of special prayers at specified times and places.

For example, this is the manner in which the significance and importance of the pilgrimage to Medina is established. According to several of the Imams, Muḥammad himself said, "Whoever visits me while I am alive or after my death, on the Day of Judgment I will be his intercessor." At another time he is reported to have said, "Whoever goes on the pilgrimage to Mecca and does not visit my tomb in Medina, I will punish him on the Day of Judgment; but I will be under obligation to intercede for the believer who visits my tomb, and my intercession

[1] *Travels of Ibn Jubayr,* Wright's text, revised by M. J. de Goeje, Gibb Memorial, Vol. V, p. 196. For translation see art. "Ibn Jubayr's Visit to al-Medina," by Dwight M. Donaldson, *J.A.O.S.*, Vol. 50, p. 39.

will assure him of Paradise." Again it is related that Muḥammad said, "Whoever dies in the sanctuary in Mecca, or in Medina, will not be judged on the Day of Judgment, for he dies as one making a pilgrimage to God, and on the Day of Judgment he will be raised up along with those who were martyrs in the battle of Badr." And they say the Prophet declared still more positively, "Whoever visits my tomb, his sins will be forgiven and he will not be poverty stricken."

A frequent expedient to establish the importance of visiting a particular shrine is a reference to some conversation that one of the Imams is said to have had. We are told that the eighth Imam, Ạli ibn Musa ar-Riḍa, was asked, "Which is the better, that we should make the pilgrimage to Mecca and not visit the tomb of the Apostle, or that we should visit the tomb of the Apostle and not make the pilgrimage to Mecca?" To this question the Imam replied, "What would you say in this case? We Shi'ites recognize the visitation of the tomb of the Imam Husain as better than the pilgrimage to Mecca, then why should we not recognize the pilgrimage to the tomb of the Apostle as better also?"[1]

Regulations for Visiting the Mosque of the Prophet

On entering the city of Medina the pilgrim is expected to take a bath, and ordinarily he should do so again before entering the mosque. When he crosses the threshold of the Door of Gabriel, he must stand in the open court and offer a prescribed prayer for entrance (*Tofatu'z-Za'irín*, p. 27), after which he repeats the *takbir* ("God is great!") one hundred times. He may then go inside the covered part of the mosque, into what is called the *rauzat*, or garden, between the pulpit and the mausoleum, and stand at a point "above (to the west of) the head of the Prophet, and before the second pillar, which faces the head of the Blessed One." He must then face the *ḳiblah*, or direction of prayer, which in Medina is to the south, and offer the Prayer of

[1] Majlisi, *Tofatu'z-Zá'irín*, pp. 24-26.

Visitation. This is the approved Shi'ite procedure, for it is said that the sixth Imam, Ja'far aṣ-Ṣadiḳ, said, " Go near the pillar which is to the right of the tomb and face towards the *ḳiblah*, in which case your left cheek will be towards the tomb and your right cheek towards the *mambar* (or pulpit)."

The appropriate Prayer of Visitation to be offered at this place by Shi'ite pilgrims is said to have been given by the eighth Imam, Ạli ar-Riḍa, and it is distinguished from the prayer employed by the Sunnites in that it emphasizes the purity or sinlessness of the Apostle[1] and his Household.

> " Peace be upon thee, O Prophet, and the mercy and blessing of God be upon thee !
> Peace be upon thee, O Abu'l-Ḳasim !
> Peace be upon thee, O Leader of the first and the last !
> Peace be upon thee, O Ornament of the Day of Judgment !
> Peace be upon thee, O Intercessor on the Day of Judgment !
> I testify that there is no God but the one God and he has no partner ;
> I testify that thou art his Servant and his Apostle ;
> Thou did'st bring his message and did'st fulfil what he entrusted.
> Thou did'st warn thy people and did'st put forth great effort until thou did'st fully accomplish thy purpose.
> Peace be upon thee and upon thy Household, *pure as they were in life and pure also in death.*
> Peace be upon thee and upon thy brother
> (Ạli was so called), thy *wasi*, thy cousin, the Commander of the Faithful ;
> and upon thy daughter, the Leader of the women of the two worlds ;
> and upon thy sons, Hasan and Husain, the greatest mercy and blessing be upon them.
> Let the most perfect benediction be upon them, the most pure salutation, and to thee be our greeting and the mercy and blessing of God."

But if for some reason the Shi'ite pilgrims are not allowed to stand and offer their prayer in the place recommended by the Imams, or as Majlisi remarks significantly, " if *taḳiyah* (dissimula-

[1] It is interesting to compare this prayer, as given by Majlisi (*op. cit.*, p. 31), with the prayer used by the Sunnites, as translated by Garcin de Tassy in *L'Islamisme*, p. 282, and by Burton, *Pilgrimage to Mecca and Medina*, Vol. I, p. 317.

tion) is necessary, the pilgrim is to go in front of the face of the Prophet, and offer the Prayer of Visitation there, after the manner of the Sunnites." At this place there is a small window, through which it was possible for Burton to look in and see "a curtain, or rather hangings, with three inscriptions in gold letters, informing readers that behind them lie Allah's Apostle and the first two Caliphs." The same writer mentions that "the Persians have sometimes managed to pollute the part near Abu Bakr's and Ụmar's graves by tossing through the aperture what is externally a shawl intended as a present for the tomb." At least, Persian Shi'ites have been accused of attempting such desecration, provoked perhaps at the necessity for dissimulation, when they were not permitted to pray at the point they considered most appropriate. The Sunnite Arabs have thus found excuse from time to time for a general slaughter of the Persian pilgrims.

The tradition is related, however, that the Imam Zayn-al-Abidín stood at this point by the grave of the Apostle, where he offered his Prayer of Visitation and repeated his testimony, or confession of faith. After this he stood with his back to the grave, by the thin green marble slab that is near by. He then leaned on the wall of the mausoleum and faced the *ḳiblah* and prayed:

"O God, I trust my affairs to thee and at the tomb of Muḥammad, God be gracious unto him and his Household. I support my back upon him, and I face the *ḳiblah* which thou did'st favour for Muḥammad.

"O God, since I have lived until morning, I am not sufficient in myself to accomplish the good I wish, and I am not able to put away from myself the evil that I would refrain from, but I have lived until morning, and all things are in thy hand. There is no one more in need than I am. Behold me in need of that good which thou dost send down to me (Ḳoran xxviii. 24).

"O God, give me good from thee, and no one can prevent thy gift.

"O God, I take refuge in thee, for thou mayest change my lot, and thou mayest change my body, or lessen thy bounty towards me.

"O God, honour me with virtue, and exalt me with thy favour, and build me up with assurance. And for this give me gratitude."

There is a pillar included within the mosque which is said to contain a portion of the date palm against which the Prophet leaned when he preached there, before there was any mosque. At this pillar the Shi'ite pilgrim is advised to repeat the Surah al-Ḳadar eleven times and to make six prostrations in prayer. On the authority of the Imam Ja'far aṣ-Ṣadiḳ he is to go also to the pulpit Muḥammad used, the *mambar*, and to rub his face and eyes on the sides of the pulpit, for they are said to cause the healing of eyes. "Stand by the pulpit and offer prayers of thanksgiving and petition, for the Apostle said, Between the pulpit and my house is a garden (rauzat), which is one of the gardens of Heaven, and my pulpit is the Door of Paradise."

There are further instructions for the visit to the Baḳi' cemetery, and prayers appointed to be read at the tombs of Faṭima, Hasan, Zayn al-Abidín, Muḥammad Baḳir, and Ja'far aṣ-Ṣadiḳ, for they are all counted among the "fourteen" intercessors for the Shi'ite world. But the pilgrim to the Baḳi' cemetery to-day sees no golden domes and no richly ornamented tombs. The whole area, the resting place of so many of the Household of the Prophet, is but a desolate waste. It remains as a place of weeping, but the formal prayers invoking their intercession are no longer said at the tombs of the Imams in Medina.

CHAPTER XIV

MUSA KAẒIM, "THE FORBEARING"

MUSA KAZIM was born during the struggle between the Umayyads and the Ạbbasids. He was only four years old when Abu'l-Ạbbas aṣ-Saffah, "the shedder of blood," came to the throne as the first Ạbbasid caliph. For twenty years he was under the authority of his father, who died, or perhaps was poisoned, ten years before the end of the long reign of Mansur. The Imamate of Musa extended through the ten remaining years of the caliphate of Mansur, and included the ten years of the rule of Mahdi, the year and some months of the reign of Hádi, and about twelve years of the reign of Harún ar-Rashid. Thus for thirty-three years he was Imam, which was eight years longer than his father, Ja'far aṣ-Ṣadiḳ, had held this coveted but precarious distinction.

His mother, Hamidah, like Khaizarán, the influential wife of the Caliph Mahdi, was originally a Berbery slave,[1] though some writers say she was from Andalusia,[2] whose women were said to have been the most beautiful in Spain. Ya'ḳubi does not attempt to decide this question,[3] but speaks of her as Umm Walad, "the mother of sons," which entitled her, of course, to special dignity and favour among the other wives and concubines who made up the household of the Imam Ja'far.[4]

With six brothers and nine sisters, Musa grew up in a large

[1] Majlisi, *Bahāru'l-Anvār*, Vol. XI, p. 172, quoting Kulaini, *Usulu'l-Kāfi*, p. 182.

[2] *Tadhkiratu'l-A'imma*, pp. 144, 148.

[3] Ya'ḳubi, *Tarikh*, edit. Houtsma, ii. p. 499.

[4] The distinction between the legal wives and the "personal female slaves" has been hard for the chroniclers to maintain. The *Aḳa'idu'sh-Shi'a* says the Imam Ja'far had twenty-eight legal wives in addition to concubines (Bk. IV, ch. iii), but the *Jannātu'l-Khulud* (table xiii), mentions only two as wives, but says there were many concubines.

family. Isma'íl, his oldest brother, was designated to succeed his father as the Imam, but he greatly disturbed the whole Shi'ite community by dying before his father. This was a coincidence that had not been provided for and it gave rise to much startling speculation as to the nature of the "Imamate."

The most damaging suggestion was that Isma'il was the last of the Imams, the seventh, and those who chose this explanation denied that he died before his father's death. They admitted that he had disappeared, but insisted that he would return, as he was not really dead but God had concealed him until the time when he should be manifested. Others accepted the fact of his death and continued the imamate down to Isma'íl's son. This whole group who conceived the idea of the visible imamate ceasing with the death of Isma'íl or his son were known as the Seveners, *Sab'íya*, and they may be identified with the Isma'ilís. "Karmatians, Faṭimids, Assassins, and the Isma'ílís of India, Persia and Central Asia are groups through which the Sevener movement finds its place in secular history, but the Druses also and in a way the Mutáwila and Nusairís may also be traced back to the old Sab'íya."[1]

The orthodox Shi'ites, the "Twelvers," assert that while the Imam Ja'far aṣ-Ṣadiḳ had appointed his eldest son Isma'il to succeed him, in so much as Isma'il was found to be addicted to drunkenness, Musa, who was the fourth of the seven sons, had been designated as the next Imam. The dispute that resulted brought about a radical division in Shi'ite Islam, as has been pointed out by Ibn Khaldun.[2] Various sects and sub-sects arose from the continued discussion of the vexed question of the right of succession. These are described in detail by Shahrastani,[3] and an early statement of the various divisions of the Isma'ílís, written from the orthodox Shi'ite point of view,

[1] *Encyclopædia of Islam*, art. "Sab'íya."

[2] Ibn Khaldun, "Prolegomena," in *Notices et Extraits des Manuscrits de la Bibliotheque Imperiale*, Arabic text, Vol. XVI, Part II, p. 355; trans., "The Shi'ah Imamate," in *The Moslem World*, Jan., 1931.

[3] Shahrastani, *Book of Religious and Philosophical Sects*, edit. Cureton, p. 145 ff. Cf. German translation, Haarbrucher, Halle, 1850, and English translation of pertinent sections in the *J.A.O.S.*, Vol. II, pp. 263-272.

may be found in chapter xix of the *Tabsiratu'l-Ąwwám*, by Sayyid Murtaḍa, the Alamu'l-Huda, who died in 436/1044.

The first of the twenty-three miracles that are attributed to the Imam Musa relates that another of his older brothers, Abdulla, immediately made his claim to the Imamate. But Musa directed that a large pile of firewood should be collected in the courtyard of a *serai*, where his friends, including his brother Abdulla, were invited to assemble. As they sat repeating traditions turn about, the Imam Musa ordered the wood to be set on fire, and before them all he went and stood in the flames, but without injury to himself or his clothing. He then challenged his brother Abdulla, if he really felt his claim to the Imamate to be genuine and approved of God, to submit it to the same test. But the traditionist relates that Abdulla changed colour and left the assembly.[1]

What Musa's life was in Medina, as he shared in his father's scholarly retirement, in tremendously exciting times, can be imagined more easily than ascertained. Not much of historical value can be gained from the miracles attributed to him in his young manhood, as for example, on the occasion when a certain Ya'ḳub ibn Saraj was told by Ja'far aṣ-Ṣadiḳ to salute his master, as he pointed to Musa al-Kaẓim. Ya'ḳub did so, and the boy Musa commanded him to change the name he had given yesterday to his daughter, as it was displeasing to God. And Ya'ḳub relates that it was true that he had given a name to a daughter the day before, and that the Imam Ja'far told him to do as Musa said, as it would be to his advantage.

Perhaps the chief characteristic of the time in which Musa lived was that the learning and culture of the Greeks and the Persians had brought out in unfavourable contrast the simplicity and comparative ignorance of the Arabian tribal life. The Arabs, as such, had suffered in their prestige by the despiteful treatment of the Umayyads. National or tribal superiority was no longer accorded to them. On the contrary, indeed, a movement that got its name (al Shu'úbiyya) from a verse in the

[1] *Khulasatu'l-Akhbár*, ch. xxxv.

Ḳoran (xlix, 13), asserted the superiority of the tribes or peoples (shu'úban) on the basis that "the noblest of you in the sight of God are they that do most fear him." They claimed "that the Persians, it might be, or Greeks, were in every way superior to the Arabs, both in arts and sciences, and even in what these claimed as especially their own, the study of genealogies and the practice of the virtues of the desert."[1]

This increased influence of Persians and Greeks, with its bolder disdain for the Arabs, gave rise also to teachings that were regarded as heretical or atheistic, *zandaḳa*, by individuals "who managed more or less adroitly to conceal under the veil of Islam old Persian religious ideas. Sometimes indeed they did not consider any disguise to be necessary, but openly set up dualism and other Persian or Manichaean doctrines, and the practices associated therewith, against the dogma and usage of Islam. Such persons were called Zindíqs."[2] The Caliph Mahdi and Hádi and Harun ar-Rashíd were thorough and persistent in their efforts to stamp out these forms of heresy. Moreover, at the same time, along with the increased Persian influence, the Ạlids, who felt generally that they had been ill treated and deceived by the Ạbbasid branch of the house of Hashim, were ever ready to create disturbances in different parts of the empire.

The Imam Musa knew that each of the Caliphs was on the alert to discover in him any signs of disloyalty, and he may frequently have been apprehensive as to what his fate might be, especially if he believed the report that Mansur had brought about the death of his father. Habitual anxiety, however, does not appear to have seriously interrupted his domestic life, for we know that he had a large family of eighteen sons and twenty-three daughters. "He had no legal wife," according to the Jannatu'l-Khulud (table xiv), which makes the blunt statement that "all his children were from slaves, whose names are not known, but this does not affect their nobility, for the essential consideration is their father." Without giving any

[1] Muir, *The Caliphate, Rise, Decline and Fall,* 1915, p. 475.
[2] Nicholson, *Literary History of the Arabs,* p. 372.

reason for it, Ya'ḳubi records that Musa ibn Ja'far decreed that his daughters should not marry, and that none of them did marry except Umm Salma, who was married in Egypt.[1]

He was mild and patient in his temperament, however, and was called *al-Kazim,* "the forbearing," and *Abdu'l-Salih,* "the Holy Servant." In illustration of his religious rather than political interest, which was characteristic of all the Imams since Husain, we read "that he entered one evening into the mosque of God's Apostle (at Medina) and, just as the night was setting in, he made a prostration which lasted until morning, and during that time he was heard to request without intermission, 'O thou who art the object of our fear! O thou whom it becometh to show mercy! Let thy kindly pardon be granted to me whose sin is so grievous!'"

We read also in the notice given him by Ibn Khallikan of his generosity and benevolence, "that when a man had spoken ill of him he sent him a purse containing one thousand dinars," and "that he used to tie up in packets sums of three hundred, or four hundred, or two hundred dinars and distribute them in the city of Medina." It may have been this generosity which brought him under suspicion when the Caliph Mahdi had him arrested and brought to Baghdad. But as Ibn Khallikan further relates, "this Caliph had a dream in which Ạli ibn Abu Ṭalib appeared to him and said, 'O Muḥammad, were ye ready therefore, if ye had been put in authority, to commit evil in the earth, and to violate the ties of blood?' Ar-Rabi (Ibn Yunus, the gifted favourite of al-Mansur) relates in these terms what followed: 'He sent for me at night and that put me in great dread. I went to him and found him chanting the above verse and no man had a finer voice than he. He said to me, "Bring me Musa ibn Ja'far." I did so and he embraced him, seated him by his side and said to him, "Abu'l-Hasan, I have just seen in a dream the Commander of the Faithful, Ạli ibn Abu Ṭalib, and he has recited to me such and such a verse; give me the assurance that you will not revolt against me or against any of my children."

[1] Ibn Khallikan, trans. de Slane, iii. p. 463.

He answered, "By Allah, I am incapable of revolting." "You say the truth," replied the Caliph, "give him three thousand pieces of gold and restore him to his family in Medina." I arranged the affair of his departure that very night, lest some obstacle might turn up, and before morning the man was on his journey.'"[1]

If this story is true the Imam was back in his home in Medina at the time of the Ạlid uprising during the reign of al-Hádi, which had resulted from the uncivil treatment of some of the family of the Prophet who were accused of drinking wine. For this offence "they were paraded with halters about their necks in the streets of the Holy Cities. The family thereupon broke out into rebellion, and some hard fighting was needed before peace could be restored."[2] This trouble, however, appears to have been primarily among the Khariji faction of the Ạlids, and as far as we know the Imam Musa was not molested. Persistent in his devotions, he declared in his pious discourses[3]:

"How base is the world for a people, unless God give them joy; and how great is that people always, if God is not angry with them."

And he was regarded as having divinely given powers of healing. Once he saw a woman who was surrounded by a group of children. They were all crying. The Imam asked, "Why do you weep?" The woman answered that the cow on which they depended had fallen and died. The Imam made two prostrations in prayer, and then he went and put his blessed finger on the cow, and she arose and stood up. The woman exclaimed, "Behold it is Jesus the son of Mary!"[4]

In the caliphate of Harun ar-Rashíd the Imam Musa was repeatedly subject to suspicion and disfavour. It is said that on one occasion ar-Rashíd took umbrage at an apt retort from the Imam when they were together before the tomb of the Prophet in Medina. With the desire to show his own family

[1] Ibn Khallikan, *op. cit.*
[2] Muir, *op. cit.*, p. 473.
[3] Ya'ḳubi, *op. cit.*, p. 499.
[4] *Khulasatu'l-Akhbar*, ch. xxxv.

relationship to the Prophet, Harun had said, "Salutation unto thee, O Prophet of God, unto thee who art my cousin!" But as he faced the tomb, the Imam said, "Salutation unto thee, O my dear father!" At this Harun was disconcerted and remarked, "Abu'l-Hasan, such glory as thine is truly to be vaunted of."[1]

This occurrence would be sufficient to explain his first summons from Harun ar-Rashíd to come to Baghdad. There he was kept in prison, and al-Khuzai, the chief of the palace guards, has related a vision the Caliph had which led him to release the Imam. "A messenger came to me from ar-Rashíd," he said, "at an hour in which I never before received his visits; he pulled me from the place where I was and would not even allow me to change my clothes. This put me in great fear. When I arrived at the palace a servant went before me and informed ar-Rashíd of my presence. The Caliph ordered me to come in and I found him sitting up in his bed. I saluted him, but he kept silent for some time; so my mind was much troubled and my fears greatly augmented. At length he said, 'Do you know why I sent for you at such an hour?' I answered, 'By Allah, I do not, Commander of the Faithful.' 'Know,' said he, 'that I just had a dream in which it seemed to me as if an Abyssinian came to me with a javelin in his hand and said to me: "Let Musa ibn Ja'far be set at liberty this very hour, otherwise I shall slay thee with this javelin." Do you, therefore go and get him set free.' I replied, 'Commander of the Faithful, shall I then liberate Musa the son of Ja'far for the third time?' 'Yes,' said he, 'go and set Musa ibn Ja'far at liberty. Give him thirty thousand dirhems and say to him in my name, If you would like to remain with us you will obtain from me whatever you desire, but if you prefer going to Medina you have permission to do so.' I went to the prison in order to take him out, and when he saw me he sprang up on his feet, thinking I had received orders to treat him in a manner he should not like, but I said to him, 'Fear not, the Caliph has ordered me to set

[1] Ibn Khallikan, *op. cit.* Cf. E. H. Palmer, *Haroun ar-Rashíd*, p. 129.

you at liberty, and told me to give you thirty thousand dirhems and to deliver to you this message, If you would like remaining with us, you will obtain whatever you desire, but if you prefer going to Medina you have free permission to do so.' I then gave him money, set him free, and said to him, 'I see something in you extraordinary, what is it?' He replied, 'I shall tell you. Whilst I was alseep, behold the Apostle of God came to me and said, "O Musa, thou hast been imprisoned unjustly, so recite the words I am going to repeat to thee, for assuredly thou shalt not pass all this night in prison."' I replied, "For thee I should give up father and mother, what must I say?" "Repeat these words," said he:

> "O thou who hearest every voice!
> O thou who lettest no opportunity escape!
> O thou who clothest the bones with flesh
> and who wilt raise them up after death!
> I invoke thee by thy holy name, and by that
> great and awful name which is treasured up
> and closely hidden, by that name which no
> created thing shall ever know!
> O thou who art so mild and whose patience
> is never equalled!
> O thou whose favours never cease and can
> not be numbered, set me free!"

'So you see what happened.'"[1]

As to what may have led to his final imprisonment, we find that it is stated by al-Fakhri that "there were some of the relatives of Musa ibn Ja'far who were envious of him and carried false reports about him to ar-Rashíd, saying, 'The people are paying him the *khums*, or one-fifth of their property, are accepting the Imamate, and he is about to come forth against you.' They brought this report to ar-Rashíd so frequently that it made him anxious and agitated. And he gave the accuser money to the amount of the income to be derived from the district. But he did not enjoy the fruits of it, for the money was not collected, when he took seriously ill and died. And in that year ar-Rashíd

[1] Mas'udi, *Muruju'l-Dhahab*, vi, p. 308; and Ibn Khallikan, *op. cit.*

went on the pilgrimage, and when he arrived in Medina, he arrested Musa ibn Ja'far, and brought him to Baghdad in a litter, and imprisoned him under the care of al-Sindi ibn Sháhik."[1] This agrees with Majlisi's statement, on the basis of the most reliable Shi'ite traditions, that "Harun took him from Medina ten days before the end of the month Shawwal, 177 A.H. Then Harun set out for Mecca and took him with him, and returned by Basra, where he imprisoned him with Isa ibn Ja'far. Afterwards he took him to Baghdad and imprisoned him with al-Sindi ibn Sháhik." Majlisi goes on to say that "the Imam died in his prison and was buried in the cemetery of the Ḳuraish."[2] And al-Fakhri adds, "Ar-Rashíd was at Raḳḳa and sent orders that he should be put to death. They then brought a number of reputable men to Karkh to act as coroners and to testify publicly that he had died a natural death."[3]

Ya'ḳubi also mentions this coroners' inquest,[4] "He (Musa) was in prison at the order of ar-Rashíd, in the custody of Sindi ibn Sháhik, who sent for the servant Masrur, and he assembled the leaders and the writers, the members of the house of Hashim, and the judges, and whoever was in Baghdad from the descendants of Ạli ibn Abu Ṭalib. Then he showed the face of the Imam and said to them, 'Do you know this man?' They said, 'We know him well, he is Musa ibn Ja'far.' Again he asked, 'Do you see any wound upon him, or anything that looks like he was killed?' They answered, 'No.' Then the body of the Imam was washed and wrapped and taken out and buried in the cemetery of the Ḳuraish on the western side of the city."

[1] Al-Fakhri (Ibnu'l-Ṭiḳṭiḳá), in the *Adab al-Sultaniyya, Chrestomathie Arabe*, Silvestre de Sacy, i, text, p. 7, and translation, p. 6.
[2] Majlisi, *Baharu'l-Anvar*, Vol. XI, p. 214.
[3] Al-Fakhri, *op. cit.*
[4] Ya'ḳubi, *Tarikh, op. cit.*

CHAPTER XV

ẠLI AR-RIDA, THE IMAM INVOLVED IN POLITICS

AFTER Harun ar-Rashíd had ruthlessly destroyed the influence of the Barmakids, the Arab loving and Persian hating al-Faḍl ibn al-Rábí again became the vizier. And of the Caliph's two sons, Amín and Ma'mun, the Arab party were exceedingly eager for the former to succeed to the throne, because he was of purely Arab origin, whereas his brother Ma'mun had a Persian mother, a slave named Marádjil. But Harun ar-Rashíd recognized in Ma'mun the more capable ruler. In his quandary as to how he might avoid division in the empire, he sent his executioner, al-Mesrur, to fetch from prison the aged Yahya, whose counsel he felt he needed. To the noble old Barmakid, bereaved by the killing of Ja'far, the impetuous and violent Caliph explained his position: "The Prophet of God, on whom be peace, died without a testament, when Islam was yet in the vigour of youth, and the faith was fresh. The Arabs were united, and God had granted security and honour after peril and abasement. Then were the quarrels for succession, with the melancholy results you wot of. For me, I intend to regulate my succession, and to let it pass into the hands of one whose character and conduct I approve, and of whose political capacity I am assured. Such an one is Abdullah (Ma'mun); but the Beni Hashim incline to Muḥammad (Amín) to further their own desires, capricious, extravagant, and sensual though they know him to be, and ever subject to the influence of women. Now, if I show my preference for Abdullah, I let loose against me the hatred of the house of Hashim; but if I make Muhammad my only heir, I fear it will bring trouble on the State."[1] Accordingly, in 183 A.H., the year in which this same executioner, al-Mesrur,

[1] E. H. Palmer, *Haroun Alraschid*, p. 119.

was thought to have brought about the death of the Imam Musa Kaẓim in the prison of al-Sindi, Harun-ar-Rashíd arranged to publicly proclaim Amín as his successor in Baghdad, "with the guardianship of the holy cities and the spiritual headship of Islam," but Ma'mun was to rule the eastern provinces, "where the Persian element prevailed," and with his capital at Merv. And in case of the death of either Amín or Ma'mun, the survivor was to govern the entire empire.[1]

Nine years later, 192 A.H., Harun set out for Khorasan, accompanied by his son Ma'mun. There had been repeated rebellion and widespread discontent in Khorasan, and the objects of the journey were to quell this rebellion and to establish Ma'mun in his new authority. Amín remained in Iraḳ, but his watchful friend, the vizier Fadl ibn Rábí, went along with Harun ar-Rashíd. Ma'mun had with him his chief adviser, Faḍl ibn Sahl.

When they had made the long and tedious journey along the course of the Elburz mountains, and had passed over the pass at the modern Sharífabád, they arrived at Naugawn, the largest town in the district of Tus. Here the Caliph Harun ar-Rashíd was suddenly taken seriously ill, and the same night he died. Perhaps his death was due to the exertion of the journey, at a time when he was trying to conceal a physical disability from which he had been suffering. Or, as others explain, he had an attack of nervous heart failure, when he realized that he had arrived unwell at Tus, the place where it had been foretold that he was to die. He was buried in a garden, at a place called Sanabad, about one mile from Naugawn. Immediately afterwards his vizier, al-Faḍl ibn Rábí, left hastily to return to Baghdad and ordered back the army that was coming with reinforcements.

"Mamun was furious at this defection of Faḍl ibn ar-Rábi', and he had at his side Faḍl ibn Sahl, whose devotion to the Persian cause was only equalled by his hatred to his namesake Amín's vizier. This man pointed out to his master that he must prepare for a decisive struggle, and that his brother had, by his

[1] *Aṣru'l-Ma'mun*, by Ahmad Firíd Rifá'í, Vol. II, p. 244. Cf. *Encyclopædia of Islam*, art. "Harun al-Rashíd"; also E. H. Palmer, *op. cit.*, pp. 115-116.

minister's act in depriving him of his troops, really aimed a blow at his succession to that part of the inheritance which his father had left him. He also reminded him of the powerful influence which Persia had exercised in the elevation of the Ạbbasids to power in Abu Muslim's days, and, in fine, urged him to strengthen his position by conciliating the Persian people, and then to aim at grasping the whole and undivided sovereignty for himself."[1]

Accordingly, Ma'mun made peace in Khorasan, and gave diligent attention to ingratiating himself with his subjects in that province. At the same time he adhered scrupulously to the sworn compact he had made with his father at Mecca, and recognized his brother Amín as Caliph. But when al-Faḍl ibn al-Rubá'í returned to Baghdad he soon persuaded Amín to ignore his part of the agreement, and to appoint his son Musa to succeed him in place of Ma'mun. This was done in 194 A.H. It was on this provocation, therefore, that Ma'mun prepared to send his armies from Khorasan to maintain his own right to the Caliphate. These armies, strengthened by thousands of Persian supporters who preferred Ma'mun to Amín, were under the able command of the generals Harthama and Ṭahír. The crisis of the fighting came in the siege of Baghdad, which was long and difficult (196-198 A.H.), and ended only when Ṭahir sent the head of Amín to Ma'mun in Khorasan, as " a proof that the war was now really at an end."[2]

While Ma'mun was declared Caliph at this time, according to the agreement, which was strengthened by the victory of his troops, yet it was nearly six years before he ventured to return personally to Baghdad. During this period he continued to be influenced strongly by his vizier, Faḍl ibn Sahl, whose Persian and Shi'ite sympathies were well known. Finally, as a master stroke of diplomacy, in his opinion, he arrived at the decision to attempt to conciliate the Shi'ites by designating their Imam as his successor to the Caliphate.

[1] E. H. Palmer, *op. cit.*, p. 126.
[2] Le Strange, *Baghdad during the Ạbbasid Caliphate*, p. 310.

The Shi'ite Imam at the time was Ạli ar-Riḍa, the son of Musa al-Kaẓim. He also had a Persian mother, a slave girl named Tukhtam, whom Hamida had herself chosen for her son Musa Kaẓim.[1] We learn from the same source that the boy Riḍa required a very great deal of milk. When the mother was asked if her milk was sufficient, she answered, "Truly it is not because my milk is not sufficient, but he wants it all the time, and consequently I am falling short in my prayers." His father, with his numerous concubines and no legal wife, his eighteen sons and his nineteen daughters, was apparently somewhat negligent about keeping the family records, for the birth of Ạli ar-Riḍa is placed by several writers as late as 153 A.H.,[2] but the date usually accepted by Shi'ite authorities is the eleventh of Dhu'l-Ḳa'dah in the year 148 A.H.[3] He was thus twenty or twenty-five years old when he succeeded his father as Imam in Medina, and it was about eighteen years later, when the Caliph Ma'mun was not entirely sure of his personal following in Iraḳ, that he undertook to ingratiate himself with the numerous Shi'ite parties by designating Ạli ar-Riḍa as his successor to the Caliphate.

The Caliph Ma'mun was far away in Merv and he sent to Medina for Ạli ar-Riḍa to come to him at his distant army headquarters. The Imam answered Ma'mun's summons, and set out from Medina in the year 200 A.H., making a beginning on the long journey to Merv, which lay in what was at that time the extreme north-eastern corner of Persia. In so doing he was abandoning the policy of his three immediate predecessors, for the Imam could not be the heir apparent to the Caliphate without becoming inextricably involved in politics. He took pains, however, to indicate that it was not at his desire, but that he was acting only in accord with the summons he had received.

In the long list of miracles attributed to him,[4] he is represented as a thoughtful and likeable man, in spite of the showy piety

[1] Majlisi, Muhammad Baḳir, *Anvaru'l-Bahār*, Vol. XII, p. 3; Cf. also Ibn Babawaihi (d. 431 A.H.), *Uyunu'l-Akhbari'l-Riḍa*, p. 11.
[2] Ibn Khallikan, Arabic text, Bulaḳ, Vol. I, p. 348; and Mas'udi, *Muruju'l-Dhahad*, vii, p. 61.
[3] Kulaini, *Usulu'l-Kafi*, p. 200; and Majlisi, *op. cit.*, p. 1.
[4] Majlisi, *op. cit.*, p. 6, ff.

that his position naturally fostered. Reyyan ibn Salt relates: "Before setting out on a journey to Iraḳ, I went to say farewell to Riḍa. I wanted to ask him to give me one of his shirts to use as my shroud, and some pieces of money coined in his name to make rings for my daughters. But I was so overwhelmed with grief at the time of saying farewell, that I forgot my request and left him without asking anything. However, as I left he called to me and said, 'Do you not want one of my shirts to keep as your shroud? And would you not like some pieces of money for rings for your daughters?' I said that I had intended to ask him for these things, but that my sorrow had prevented me. He then went to his place of prayer and got a number of dirhems which he handed me, and when I counted them I found there were thirty." Byzanti relates: "Once Riḍa sent a donkey for me and I went to see him. I stayed until it was late at night, and after a while he rose and said, 'I do not think that you will be able to go back to-night.' I said, 'Yes, I think I can.' But he said, 'No, you had better spend the night with me, and in the morning, by the blessing of God, you may go.' He called a maid servant to spread his own bed for me—with his mattress, his pillow, and his blanket. And as I thought about this I was feeling rather vain, when suddenly he said to me, 'O Ahmad, when Zaid ibn Sahwan was ill and Ạli visited him he felt puffed up and boasted to others. You must not feel proud and boastful, but humble yourself before God and depend on him.'" Muhammad ibn Ghaffar relates: "I had a debt that was so large that I thought there was no one who could pay it except ar-Riḍa. In the morning I went to his house, and when I had gotten permission I went in. As soon as I was seated he said, 'O Abu Muhammad, we know your need, and we will have to satisfy it and pay your debt.' When night came food was brought and he asked whether I could spend the night with him. I told him that if he would satisfy my want it would be better for me to go. He then took a handful of money from beneath the carpet on which he was seated and gave it to me. I went near the lamp and saw that the coins were gold, and on the one

I examined was written: 'O Abu Muhammad, here are fifty dinars, twenty-six of which are for paying your debt, and the remaining twenty-four are for the expenses of your wife.' But in the morning, however much I searched for this coin, I could not find it, though the total number was fifty dinar."

When he set out on his long and arduous journey from Medina to Merv, the Imam first made a farewell pilgrimage to Mecca, then he went to Basra so as to reach Baghdad without going to Kufa.[1] From Baghdad he went north, up over high mountain passes to Kermanshah and Hamadan. He travelled by short stages to ar-Rayy, the Greek Rhages, which was near the site of the present Teheran. From there the patient caravan, bearing the incarnate Light of Muḥammad, continued due east for about a month until it reached the city of Tus. From Tus they travelled on to the city of Merv, in what is modern Turkestan. It is possible, and in fact almost certain, that the Imam travelled much more slowly than the time required for successive daily stages from Baghdad to Merv, a period of from two to three months, for he was lavishly entertained and consequently much delayed along the way.

On his arrival in Merv he found the Caliph Ma'mun had not changed his mind, but treated him with the highest honour and put elegant lodgings at his disposal. Shi'ite writers maintain that he was forced to accept Ma'mun's proposal, but that he had expressed his strong preference to be free from all secular administrative duties.[2] According to Ya'ḳubi it was on the 27th day of Ramaḍan, in the year 201 A.H., that he was officially designated as Ma'mun's "heir apparent," *walí'ạhd,*[3] and the Caliph had the Imam's name included with his own on gold and silver coins. The inscription on these coins is well worthy of notice: "The King of God and the Faith, al-Ma'mun, Amir and Khalifa of the Faithful, and ar-Riḍa, Imam of the Muslims."[4] This meant

[1] Kulaini, *op. cit.*, p. 201.
[2] Sell, *Ithna Ạshariyya,* Madras, p. 32.
[3] Ya'ḳubi, *Tarikh,* edit. Houtsma, Vol. II, p. 545; also Mas'udi, *Tanbih wa'l-Ishraf*, edit. de Goege, pp. 249, 250.
[4] Sell, *op. cit.*, p. 32.

more than that the Imam was to be official chaplain to him, for Ma'mun summoned the descendants of Ạbbas, men and women, to come to him at Merv. It was an assembly of thirty-three thousand, including both adults and children, and when they were all gathered together, the Caliph called for Ạli ar-Riḍa and gave him the place of honour among the greatest of the nobles. He then announced to those whom he had summoned, that he had carefully considered all the descendants of Ạbbas and also the descendants of Ạli, and that he had not found in his time anyone more worthy or more fit to be his successor than Ạli ar-Riḍa. He therefore took him by the hand and publicly acknowledged him as his successor.[1] He then gave him his daughter Habíb in marriage. He also sent abroad the command that the wearing of black and the use of black flags should be discontinued, and that hereafter the use of green should be substituted, green being the colour of the house of Ạli, whereas black had been the insignia of the Ạbbasids.

This momentous action was of course reported to the Arab party in Baghdad, who had long been ill-disposed towards Ma'mun. The scions of the family in Iraḳ perceived that by this appointment the principal authority in the empire would very likely be taken from them. They got together, therefore, and proclaimed that for thus bequeathing the Caliphate after his death to the Imam Riḍa, who was not of their immediate family, Ma'mun himself was declared deposed, and they swore allegiance to Ibrahim ibn Mahdi, who was the uncle of Ma'mun, as their new Caliph. This proclamation took place on the fifth of Muharram, in the year 202 A.H.

While the Imam Riḍa was with Ma'mun in Merv, al-Faḍl ibn Sahl arranged for a conference on religions, to which he invited the leaders of different sects, including Zoroastrians and Christians and Jews, that they might hear what the Imam had to say and that he also might hear what they said. The first conference,[2] when the Imam was seated beside Ma'mun, led to other meetings.

[1] Kulaini, *op. cit.*, p. 201.
[2] Ibn Babawaihi, *Uyunu'l-Akhbári'l-Riḍa*, ch. xii, pp. 87-100.

One of these was devoted to the discussion of the Divine Unity, when a scholar from Khorasan, Sulaiman al-Merví, took a leading part in the deliberations (ch. xiii); another conference took up the question of the sinlessness of the Prophets, and the answer to the Imam's statement was made by Ạli ibn Muhammad ibn al-Jahm (ch. xiv); and this led to another conference on the same subject (ch. xv), when the Caliph Ma'mun took considerable part in the discussion himself. Unfortunately the reports we have of these conferences from Shi'ite sources were not written until nearly two hundred years after the event, and it was apparently easier for the writer, Ibn Babawaihi (d. 431 A.H.), to supply appropriate sayings for the Imam than to invent intelligent replies for his opponents, whether Jewish, Christian, or Zoroastrian. It is possible that Theodore Abú Qurra, the Bishop of Harran,[1] may have been the unidentified "Catholicos" in one or more of these conferences and that his report of a "mujádala," or debate, before the Caliph Ma'mun may be genuine. His report, however, like that of Ibn Babawaihi, is notably weak in stating his opponents' positions, and whereas the one report refers only vaguely and inaccurately to the Taurát and the Injíl, the other is perhaps equally unscholarly in its references to the Ḳoran.

At the most, the Imam Riḍa could not have remained in Merv more than about a year, for when Ma'mun heard that his uncle Ibrahim had been proclaimed Caliph in Baghdad, he decided that it was time for him to return from Khorasan and assert his rights in person. He set out, therefore, in the same year, on his return journey to Iraḳ (202 A.H.). He was accompanied, as Ya'ḳubi mentions definitely,[2] "by ar-Riḍa, who was his heir-apparent, and by al-Faḍl ibn Sahl, who was known as Lord of the Two Highest Offices," i.e., vizier and commander-in-chief. But when they reached the town of Sarakhs, the vizier, who was in the same hostel with Ma'mun, was assassinated in his bath by Ghalib ar-Rúmí and Sarráj al-Khádim, who had a number of people

[1] Guillaume, "A Debate between Christian and Moslem Doctors," *J.R.A.S.*, Centenary Supplement, 1924, p. 233.

[2] Ya'ḳubi, *Tarikh*, ii, p. 548.

as their supporters. All of those in any way connected with the murder were immediately put to death by Ma'mun, which lends weight to the suggestion that the cause was the jealousy of members of the Arab party,[1] rather than that Ma'mun had himself arranged it because of his suspicion that Faḍl had been withholding information in regard to the unfavourable military situation in Iraḳ.[2] And in one or two days, when the army reached the district of Tus, Ạli ar-Riḍa died in the village called Naugawn, in the beginning of the year 203 A.H. Ya'ḳubi, who gives the Shi'ite point of view, says that "his sickness was no more than three days, and it was reported that Ạli ibn Hisham had given him a pomegranate that was poisoned. Al-Ma'mun, however, showed great grief at the time of ar-Riḍa's funeral."[3] Mas'udi says that Riḍa's death was "on account of grapes which he had eaten, as he had eaten too many. Some say, though, that he was poisoned."[4] He is commonly pictured as eating poisoned grapes.

Ibn Babawaihi relates various reasons that have been assigned to Ma'mun for poisoning the Imam ar-Riḍa, and shows also the circumstances in which ar-Riḍa is said to have designated his son Muhammad as his successor in the Imamate.[5]

Thus Ạli ar-Riḍa died and was buried far off from Medina, the home of his forefathers of the household of the Prophet. In Sanabad, about a mile from the village where he died, they placed him in a grave inside the tomb of the most celebrated of the Ạbbasid caliphs; for it was in this same garden spot that Ma'mun had buried his father Harun ar-Rashíd ten years before. At this time, on his long delayed return to Baghdad, he stood in the same place and offered the funeral prayer for the Imam whom he had hoped to make a Caliph.

[1] *Encyclopædia of Islam,* art. "Ma'mun."
[2] *Encyclopædia of Islam,* art. "Ạli al-Riḍa."
[3] Ya'ḳubi, *Tarikh,* ii, p. 550.
[4] Mas'udi, *Muruju'l-Dhahab,* vii, p. 61.
[5] Ibn Babawaihi, *Uyunu'l-Akhbari'l-Riḍa,* chaps. lix-lxi.

CHAPTER XVI

THE DISTANT SHRINE AT MASHHAD

Significance of the Pilgrimage

THE fact that the Imam Ạli ar-Riḍa was buried in such a distant place as Ṭus has received its full share of attention in the Shi'ite traditions. Even the Prophet Muhammad is said to have remarked, "A part of my body is to be buried in Khorasan, and whoever goes there on pilgrimage God will surely destine to Paradise, and his body will be *harám*, forbidden, to the flames of Hell; and whoever goes there with sorrow, God will take his sorrow away."

Ạli, the Amiru'l-Mu'minín, is represented as having a clear prophetic vision, when he said, "One of my children will be cruelly poisoned in the land of Khorasan. His name will be the same as mine, and his father's name will be Musa." But to compensate for the suffering that was to come to this particular one of his offspring, Ạli went on to give the assurance that "whoever goes to visit his tomb, God will forgive all his past and future sins. Though his sins be as many as the stars, as the drops of rain, or as the leaves of the trees, they will all be forgiven."

And Musa, the father of Ạli ar-Riḍa, is said to have declared very definitely, "My son Ạli will be killed by poisoning, with cruelty and deceit, and he will be buried beside the tomb of Harun ar-Rashíd." As he continued to show that whosoever should make the pilgrimage to the tomb of his son Ạli should have the merit of seventy thousand pilgrimages to Mecca, Musa ibn Ja'far made the statement, "Whoever sits at his shrine for one night is as though he had gone to the seventh heaven to meet God." This statement was challenged with the surprised inquiry, "As though he had gone to meet God"? "Yes," the

Imam went on to explain, for in the four corners of the seventh heaven are Noah, Abraham, Moses and Jesus; and on the right side of God himself are Muhammad and Ạli, and on the left are Hasan and Husain. These are the four who, on the Day of Judgment, will cast the rope that is fastened to the foot of the throne of God to all pilgrims to any of the shrines of the Imams, and will draw them up to sit with them in the seventh heaven."[1] Many such traditions are inscribed in the shrine at the present time. This last one may be seen on a cornice opposite the Golden Porch of Nadir.

Historical Sketch of Mashhad

It was in the beginning of the ninth century of the Christian era that the Imam Ạli ar-Riḍa died at Ṭus. To Ya'ḳubi, who wrote during the latter part of the same century, we owe the knowledge of the fact that Ṭus was at that time the name of a district rather than of a particular city. Its two principal towns were Naugawn and Tabarán, and of the two Naugawn was the larger and the one most frequently called Ṭus. The Arab inhabitants of the district were of the tribe of Tay, but the majority of the people were Persians.[2] It was in Naugawn, therefore, that both Harun ar-Rashíd and the Imam Riḍa died, although it was Tabarán which became the celebrated city of Ṭus in later years. This opinion, based on the statements of Ya'ḳubi, is confirmed also by the stages given by Ibn Rustah from Nishapur to Ṭus, which indicate that the destination was at that time Naugawn rather than Tabarán.[3]

When Harun ar-Rashíd came to Ṭus, he stopped for the night in the house of Hamíd ibn Ghutbah at-Tay'í, who was the governor of the district, and who had a house and garden at Sanabad, a mile from Naugawn. As he had requested, he was buried in a room of this house, and his son, Ma'mun, ordered a tomb to be built above his grave. Thus when the Imam Riḍa died in the

[1] Majlisi, *Tafatu'z-Záirín*, p. 314 ff.

[2] Ya'ḳubi, *Kitabu'l-Buldán*, edit. de Goeje, p. 277; and Le Strange, *Lands of the Eastern Caliphate*, p. 389.

[3] Ibn Rustah, *Kitab al-A'lák an-Nafisa*. edit. de Goeje, p. 172.

same town of Naugawn, and was buried in the same tomb, it was said of him[1]:

> "He entered the house of Hamid ibn Ghutbah at-Tay'í
> And he entered the tomb of Harun ar-Rashíd."

In the tenth century we observe that the adjacent quarter of Tabarán had a fortress "which was a huge building, 'visible afar off,' as Muḳaddasi writes, and the markets of this half of the town were well supplied." Also we note that at this time "the neighbouring tombs of Sanábádh were already in the fourth (tenth) century surrounded by a strongly fortified wall, and the shrine, as Ibn Hawḳal reports, was constantly thronged by devotees. A mosque had been built near the tomb of the Imam Riḍa by the Amír Fáiḳ Ạmid-ad-Dawlah, than which, says Muḳaddasi, 'there is none finer in all Khorasan.' The grave of Harun ar-Rashíd had been made by the side of that of the Imam, and many houses and a market had been built in the vicinity of the great garden."[2] But this first building, however magnificent it may have been when Ibn Hawḳal and Muḳaddasi saw it in the tenth century, was destroyed shortly after its completion by the Amir Sabuktagin because of his determined opposition to the Shi'ites. For several years after this the tomb was left in neglect and ruin, for there was such general fear of religious persecution that no one undertook to rebuild it.

But early in the eleventh century, it is said that Sultan Mahmud, the son of Sabuktagin, saw Ạli, the Amiru'l-Mu'minín, in a vision and that Ạli said to him, "How long shall this remain as it is?" He understood that Ạli referred to the *mashhad*, or place of martyrdom, of the Imam Riḍa, and he erected a creditable building with a high dome. The work was done under the direction of the governor of Nishapur in A.D.1009, but this second building also was soon destroyed by the ravages of Turkish tribes and robbers.[3] That the destruction was thorough-

[1] Ibn Babawaihi, *Uyunu'l-Akhbari'r-Riḍa*, ch. 59.
[2] Le Strange, *Lands of the Eastern Caliphate*, p. 389.
[3] *Maṭla'u'sh-Shams*, by Mirza Muhammad Hasan Khan (I'timadu'd-Dawla), Vol. II, p. 49.

going would be indicated by the fact that no inscriptions are to be found in the present shrine that date back that early.

In the twelfth century, in the reign of Sultan Sanjar, Seljuki, a man named Abu Ṭahír, Ḳumi, restored the building, either with his personal funds or at the expense of the Sultan. But before this new structure had stood for a hundred years, it was damaged seriously, though not destroyed, at the time of the invasion of the Mongols. For in A.D. 1220, after Telegu Khan had slaughtered the inhabitants of Nishapur, he came with hordes of his followers upon Tus, and did the same thing again. He destroyed the city of Tus (old Tabarán), and sacked the shrine at Mashhad, where were the tombs of Ạli ibn Musa ar-Riḍa and of Harun ar-Rashíd. They did not completely destroy the shrine, however, for several inscriptions in the tomb room of the present mausoleum are dated 612 A.H. (A.D. 1215), or five years before this Mongul invasion.[1]

There was, however, a restoration and rebuilding of the shrine early in the fourteenth century, in the government of Sultan Muḥammad Uljaitu, who was the first of the Shi'ah party of the Moguls. We read in Howarth's *History of the Mongols* that Uljaitu's mother had taught him the Christian faith, and that he had been baptized with the name Nicholas, but that after his mother's death his wife had persuaded him to become a Mussulman. During his reign he " enjoined observance of the commandments of religion and the precepts of Muḥammadanism, while an adherence to the *yassa* of Ghazan was also required." And the funds that accrued from the shrine endowments were spent according to the will of the founders, and it was at this time when the shrine revenues were available, that the tomb of the Imam Riḍa at Mashhad was restored. While the faith of Uljaitu fluctuated many times, especially when he was sorely displeased with the discussions between the Hanifites and the Shafi'ites on marriage regulations, yet on his later coins the blessing of

[1] Sykes, Sir Percy, *History of Persia*, Vol II, p. 935 ff. ; *Maṭla'u'sh-Shams*, Vol. II, p. 50 ; and Le Strange, *op. cit.*, p.; 90.

God is invoked, not only upon Ạli, but upon all the twelve Imams.[1]

The traveller Ibn Batutah visited the reconstructed shrine a few years later on in the fourteenth century (A.D. 1333), and relates that he found Mashhad "a large and well-peopled city, abounding with fruits." Over the tomb, he wrote, "is a large dome, adorned with a covering of silk, and golden candlesticks. Under the dome, and opposite to the tomb of ar-Riḍa, is the grave of the Caliph Harun ar-Rashíd. Over this they constantly place candlesticks with lights, but when the followers of Ạli enter, as pilgrims, they kick the grave of ar-Rashíd, but pour out their benedictions over that of ar-Riḍa."[2] Mustawfi also, who was contemporary with Ibn Batutah, refers to Sanabadh by the name Mashhad, and says "the shrine has become a little town," and speaks appreciatively of the friendliness of the people to strangers, and of the abundance of the fruits."[3]

After these accounts had been written, however, only a few years elapsed until, in the devastating raids of Timur Lang (Timur the Lame), which began in Khorasan in A.D. 1380, both Ṭus and Meshed again suffered severely. Fortunately Timur's son, Shah Rukh, was made governor of Khorasan and busied himself at once with the task of rehabilitation. And after the death of Timur, particularly at the time of the rebellion in Samarkand, in so much as he anticipated an extensive advance in that direction, he thought it only prudent to organize and reduce to order such places as had already been conquered. In the year A.D. 1405, he at first contemplated rebuilding Ṭus, but found that those whom the sword had spared had settled round about Sanábád, where they had already built for themselves mud houses. He made an effort, through his officials, to persuade them to return to Ṭus, but they were unwilling to do so. For they looked upon the place where they had settled as a place of refuge, and accordingly, after securing the permission of Shah Rukh, they built walls and fortifications about their

[1] Howarth, *History of the Mongols,* Vol. III, pp. 535-536, 557-559, and 580.
[2] Ibn Batutah, Lee's trans., ch. xiii, p. 95.
[3] Mustawfi, *Nuzhatu'l-Qulub,* trans. Le Strange, p. 149.

houses, and this is the place that has become the famous city of Mashhad, whereas Ṭus (on the site of old Tabarán) has been completely abandoned.[1]

It was the wife of Shah Rukh who provided the money for building adjacent to the shrine a magnificent mosque, which is known by her name still, the Masjid-i-Gauhar Shád, and has been called " the noblest mosque in Central Asia."[2] Inscriptions may yet be seen in this mosque that mention her as the original donor, but there are other inscriptions that attribute the completion and further ornamentation of it to Shah Sultan Husain, Safavi. On one of the earliest inscriptions, dated 821 A.H., which was in the time of Gauhar Shád, there is a tradition that the Prophet Muhammad had declared, " In a mosque a believer is like a fish in water, but an unbeliever is like a cooped-up chicken."

We have no record of any further destruction that occurred to the shrine of the Imam Riḍa until the time of the severe earthquake that cracked the main building during the reign of Shah Sulaiman I of the Safavi dynasty. Sir John Chardin was in Isfahan when the reports of the earthquake came and he made the following entry in his traveller's diary for the eleventh of August, A.D. 1673 : " On the 11th, there arriv'd two Expresses, one upon the Heels of the other, with bad news, to-wit, That two thirds of Metched, the Capital of Corasson, which is the Choromithrene ; one half of *Nichapour*, anoth great Town of the same Province, and a little town near *Nichapour*, had been overthrown by an earthquake. That which most sensibly touched the *Persians*, and particularly the Devout Part of them, was the Damage that had happened to the Mosque of *Metched*, in which is the tomb of *Imam Reza*, and is a *Magnificent* Mosque, and Famous through all the East. The Dome thereof was quite broke down, but the rest of the Edifice remain'd as was said, pretty entire. The King immediately sent Post, a Person of Quality, to take a more particular Account of the Damage ;

[1] *Maṭla'u'sh-Shams*, Vol. II, p. 54.
[2] Sykes, Sir Percy, *History of Persia*, Vol. II, p. 235.

and soon after, he despatch'd two other Lords, with his Orders to the Officers of the Province, in so great a Calamity."[1]

Two months later, Chardin observes : " On the 9th (of October), I went to the House of the King's Goldsmiths, which is in the Royal Palace, to see them make some Gilt Plates in the Form of Tiles, which were to cover the Dome of the Mosque of *Imam Reza* at *Metched*, which an Earthquake had flung down as I before related. A thousand men, as was said, were employed in repairing this Mosque ; and they worked at it with so much Diligence and Application, that it was to be finished by the latter end of December. These Plates were of Brass, and square, Ten Inches in Breadth, and Sixteen in Length, and of the Thickness of two Crown-Pieces. Underneath were two Barrs three Inches broad, solder'd on Cross-wise, to sink into the Parget, and so serve as Cramp-Irons to fasten the Tiles. The upper part was gilt so thick, that one would have taken the Tile to have been of Massif-Gold ; Each Tile took up the weight of three Ducates and a quarter of Gilding, and came to about ten Crowns Value. They were ordered to make Three thousand at first, as I was told by the Chief Goldsmith who was Overseer of the Work."[2]

This repair of the golden dome by the order and in the time of Shah Sulaiman is mentioned by an inscription on the dome itself, and the concluding statement of this inscription is : " Shah Sulaiman Husaini was enabled to cover with gold this heavenly dome, to ornament it and to put it in thorough repair, when it had received injury by a severe earthquake in this sacred place in the year 1084/1673, but the date of this repair, when complete, was in 1086/1675."[3] An inscription on the door leading into the mosque from the golden porch indicates that Shah Sulaiman repaired the Masjid-i-Gauhar Shád at the same time.[4]

On a panel of the frieze of the interior of the golden dome there is an inscription that commemorates the fact that Shah

[1] *Sir John Chardin's Travels in Persia*, Argonaut Press, 1927, . 62.
[2] *Sir John Chardin's Travels in Persia*, p. 112.
[3] *Maṭla'u'sh-Shams*, Vol. II, p. 127.
[4] *Maṭla'u'sh-Shams*, Vol. II, p. 139.

Ạbbas the Great " was privileged to come on foot from Isfahan, the capital, on a pilgrimage to the shrine, and was fortunate in having the opportunity to contribute to the adornment of this dome from his well gotten wealth in the year 1010/1601, and the work was finished in 1016/1607." In the eighteenth century Nadir Shah also repaired the Golden dome, and made other substantial gifts to the Shrine.

The principal gifts made by Shahs of the Ḳajár dynasty were the Reception Room and the Golden Porch, which were donated by Fath Ạli Shah, and later improved and ornamented by Nasirú'd-Din Shah, in the year 1250/1848.

The last serious injury to the Shrine was the Russian bombardment in 1911. The city was being looted by robbers who had taken up their headquarters in the sacred area, and declared themselves in rebellion against the constitutional form of government. As the Persian authorities did not have sufficient soldiers in the city, it is said that they authorized the Russians, who had a large number of troops in Khorasan, to undertake to restore order. From a convenient point outside the city they bombarded the shrine area, where the rebels had made their headquarters, and in a few minutes there was a considerable damage done to the domes and higher buildings, and it is estimated that about one hundred people were killed, mostly non-combatants, and the majority of the robbers made good their escape. Devotees of the Shrine throughout Persia have bitterly resented this desecration, and they observe the annual anniversary of its occurrence with a spirit of deprecation, in which they are not slow to point out that the grave afflictions that have come upon Russia since 1911 must be a Divine punishment for their having violated the sanctity of the tomb of the Imam Riḍa. Not only had they fired upon it, but they had occupied it for several days, walking about with their boots on, and had let their dogs in too.

Affection of the People for the Imam Riḍa

The very vicissitudes through which Mashhad has passed have contributed to the affection with which the people in general regard the Imam Riḍa. In the sacred city farthest away from Sunnite interference, after a period of many years in which traditions have grown more wonderful it is not surprising that many amazing deeds have been attributed to him. "Rain fell in answer to his prayers, and he indicated for which province every rain cloud was destined; he caused a gold coin to come from a rock by rubbing it with a piece of wood; he informed Abd Allah ibn Mughíra of a prayer which the latter had made at Mecca; he knew what passed in the hearts of men and gave many examples thereof; he knew beforehand the hour of men's deaths. In mid-winter he made the grass grow in a garden and the grapes ripen. The third hour of the day is sacred to him; his intercession is invoked for a favourable journey by land or sea, and in order to be delivered from the sufferings of exile."[1] And besides all this, the pilgrimage city that was farthest away from the centre of Islamic culture could not be reached except by a long and fatiguing journey of eight or nine hundred miles, so that it was a means of rare merit and a sign of extreme devotion to visit the shrine of the Imam Riḍa in distant Mashhad.

A Description of the Sacred Shrine

A central avenue (Khiabán),[1] running approximately from the north-east to the south-west, extends through the entire length of the city. The visitor may enter the Shrine area from either the Upper or the Lower gate on this avenue, or by way of the covered Bazaar.[2] There is a water channel[3] in the middle of the broad avenue, but the plane trees which were planted here many years ago and which were spoken of as "some straggling trees remaining" when Fraser saw them in 1825,[2] have now grown to such huge proportions that many of them have fallen. Round about the entire Shrine district a boulevard is being built to afford a convenient and necessary detour for traffic. The making of the southern half of this boulevard has served also

[1] *Encyclopædia of Islam*, art. "Ạli ar-Riḍa," quoting a summary of miracles given in the Jannatu'l-Khulud, table xv; and art. "Meshhed," by M. Streck, with valuable references.

[2] Fraser, James B., *Journey into Khorasan*, 1825, p. 444.

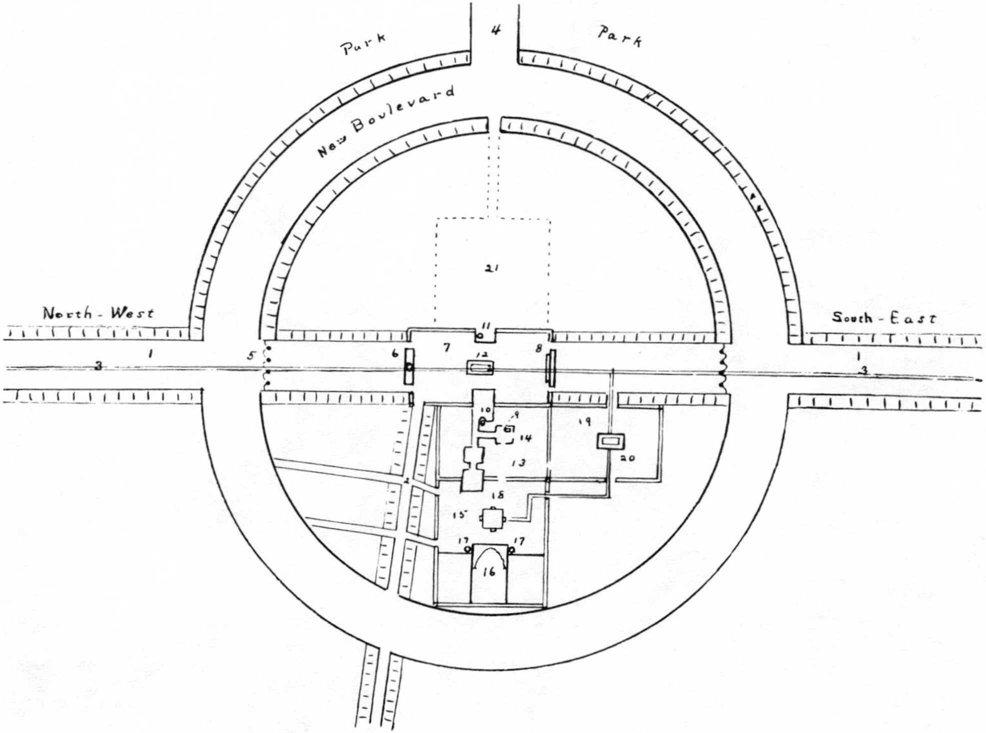

PLAN OF THE SHRINE IN MASHHAD

Facing p. 178]

to open up a section that was badly congested with inferior buildings, such as old hostels and bath-houses, that have been a real menace to the health of the city. And marvellous to relate, the northern half of the new boulevard has been cut directly through the extensive cemetery, where for many generations devout Shi'ites have buried their dead, with implicit faith that on the Judgment Day they would rise with the Imam and be saved from eternal punishment by his intercession. The ditches that were made on each side of the broad new street, so that trees could be planted and irrigated, were dug through six or eight layers of graves, the stones of which have been removed and utilized for curbing or paving purposes. The remainder of the old cemetery, covering about ten acres to the north, is being cleared off and made into a park, which is bisected by the new Tabbasi Avenue,[4] which goes directly from the Shrine into the heart of the quarter of the city which was old Naugawn.

On arriving at the barrier[5] on the Upper Avenue, beyond which wheeled traffic and all unbelievers may not pass, one can see the delicate tile work on the arched gateway[6] that leads into the Old Court,[7] which measures 277 by 105 feet. Beyond this gateway is a comparatively crude-looking tower for the clock, which counts the hours and half-hours from sunrise to sunrise. Across the old court and leading to the Lower Avenue is a similar gateway,[8] surmounted by another tower which is not for a clock but for those who beat the kettle-drums and blow trumpets at sunrise and sunset. This is called the *niḳárah khánah*, or kettle-drum house. Beating the kettle-drums to celebrate the advent of the day and the setting of the sun, and as a royal salute, has been customary in Persia from ancient times.[1] Inside the

[1] The use of the kettle-drum by the Parthians to frighten their enemies is mentioned by Plutarch (Crassus, xxiii, 10), and the custom of employing the kettle-drums in a royal salute was prevalent in Europe in the Middle Ages. They were used also at the time of the triumphal entry of Edward III into Calais, 1347, and the "nakares" are mentioned by Chaucer in the Knight's Tale (line 2514) among the musical instruments employed in the tournament. (*Encyclopædia of Islam*, art. "Kettledrum.") The beating of the kettle-drums in the Shrine at Mashhad, however, to greet the rising of the setting sun, suggests that it is a custom that has survived from practices connected with the special veneration of the sun in Persia in pre-Islamic times.

Old Court the visitor is struck with the gleaming gold on the lofty dome above the tomb.[9] This effect is intensified as he looks upon the glistening minaret that rises above the Golden Porch,[10] and as he glances across to the opposite minaret above the Porch of Ạbbas.[11] Slightly to the west of the centre of the court is a water tank,[12] which in recent years has been supplied, not from the channel running on the avenue, but from pipes that come from a clean reservoir on the western side of the city.

The large area behind the Old Court is taken up by the main building of the Shrine,[13] which has about fifteen rooms and various alcoves and passages. The tomb room[14] is about 34 feet square, and the Golden Dome above it rises to a height of 82 feet. At the present time there is nothing to indicate the tomb of Harun ar-Rashíd except an unmarked pillar in the corner of the room that is closest to the tomb of the Imam. The custom of cursing the deceased Caliph is not so uniformly observed as formerly. At the command of Nasiru'd-Din Shah the interior of this dome was decorated with excellent mirror-work, and the walls are ornamented with broad panels of valuable tiles, on which are inscribed verses from the Ḳoran and favourite traditions.

The customary entrance to the tomb is from the East, but in each of the four directions there is a niche or hallway where the pilgrims may stand and offer the prescribed prayers, and on the walls of these hallways are many inscriptions that celebrate the magnificence of the Shrine. An interesting and highly imaginative one of these is at the place of prayer "below the foot of the Blessed One," where one may read:

Gabriel came from Heaven, and likewise a hauri,
To go round about the sacred Shrine of the Imam;
And they deliberately gave their wings to the edge of the shears
In the hope that they might thus be able to tarry.

Another verse in praise of the Shrine declares that "in order to appreciate its full height and glory the Heavens use the Sun and the Moon as binoculars."

The tomb is protected by three steel gratings, one within the other. There is a sarcophagus of wood, plated with gold, that bears the name of Shah Ạbbas. Surrounding this is the first grating of plain steel, which is protected by a screen of copper wire to receive the gifts that are there deposited by devoted pilgrims, gifts that it is customary for the Shrine authorities to remove a few days before *Nő Ruz* (New Year's day) and to sell at auction. The second steel grating is ornamented with gold and jewels and has an inscription that marks it as the gift of Shah Husain, Safaví; and the third or outer grating, also of steel, is decorated with a delicate inscription of the whole of the Surah *Insan* (Ḳoran lxxvi). The second and third gratings each have gold balls at the corners, and above the tomb there is a wooden roof, which is covered with gold leaf, and from beneath there are golden hanging ornaments that are also set with jewels.

Pilgrims make their way around the tomb, starting at the point to the south which is described as "before the Face of the Blessed One,"[1] where they pray for peace upon the Imam, whom they call the Stranger, the Martyr, the Oppressed, the Sinless, the Poisoned, the Bereaved, the Grieved, and the Guide and Protector of the followers of the right way. They pass then to the East, " at the foot of the Blessed One," where they pray for peace upon the Imam again, but they include in their prayer the curse, " God kill him who killed thee! And God curse those who oppressed thee by their hands and their tongues." They then go " behind the Head of the Blessed One," and again ask for peace upon the Imam, this time as the heir of Adam, Noah, Abraham, Moses, Jesus, and Muhammad. Finally they pray " above the Head of the Blessed One," at the West, " *Be thou for me a mediator before God on High*, a Saviour from Hell fire, on Earth a Support, and on the Road of Life an Assurance, and in the Grave a most intimate Friend and Companion, and the mercy of God and His blessing be upon thee."

[1] It is the Muhammadan custom, at the time of burial, to lay the corpse on its right side, facing the Ḳiblah.

Behind the Shrine building is the *Masjid* of Gohar Shad,[15] the entire area of which, including its courtyard, measures 181 by 164 feet. It has a magnificent blue dome,[16] flanked by two minarets,[17] all of blue tile and all rising to a height of 140 feet. The interior of the mosque is 116 feet long, 41 feet wide, and 87 feet high, and to each side of this great corridor there are enclosed rooms that are called "places for the night." Thus the shape is not unlike a cathedral, except for the great open front, with its arch and minarets, which are decorated with tile work in such intricate designs that they make an altogether delightful harmony of colours. And on the massive dome of blue tiles, that seems to change its tint with the varying light of the sky, appears the Moslem creed, declaring the Unity of God and proclaiming Muḥammad as the Apostle of God. And at the base of the great dome are inscribed the first 39 verses of the Surah *Ya Sín* (Ḳoran xxxvi), to which the Shi'ites ascribe such importance.

In the middle of the courtyard of the mosque is a raised stone platform,[18] about 37 feet square, and with fountains on each side. It is called the *Masjid* of the Old Woman, in memory of a supposed old lady who long refused to sell this particular piece of land.

To the east of the main Shrine building is the New Court,[19] which was built in the time of Fath Ạli Shah. It also has a water tank in the centre,[20] for a bountiful supply of water is greatly appreciated by the crowds of pilgrims, not only for their convenience and comfort, but to enable them to perform their ceremonial ablutions in any one of the three great courts. Throughout the month of Ramaḍan and on nights preceding holidays all the courts of the Shrine are brilliantly illuminated. There are now electric lights on the domes and the minarets so that their graceful outlines and lustre and colour may be seen any night, not alone from almost all parts of the city, but by pilgrims and travellers who may be coming over the mountains some fifteen miles away.

The boulevard that is being made around the Shrine district

has given new importance to the area north of the central avenue. The large old building behind the Porch of Ạbbas has been occupied by the oldest of the many theological schools, that of Mirza Ja'far. This building is being remodelled to serve as a library and museum, which travellers who are not Moslems will be free to visit, for it is to have an entrance from the boulevard. When this building is completed, the famous old carpets, the wealth of jewels, and the many handwritten copies of the Ḳoran, and numerous manuscripts of rare books, that have been kept for years in the vaults of the Shrine, will be systematically arranged and displayed. The new building will accommodate the library that is kept at present in three rooms of the main Shrine building, and the rumour is that the number of books on general subjects is to be largely increased so as to give it more of the character of a public library.[1]

The Income from Shrine Properties

In the year 1900 a catalogue of the various properties belonging to the Shrine of the Imam Riḍa was published by the Azamu'd-Daulah. A very small edition of this book was issued, however, and it is only intelligible to those who take great pains to unravel what is evidently its intentional obscurity. Large grants of property were made to the Shrine by successive rulers of Persia and official registers have been kept which are called " tomárs," or rent rolls. These give the annual income in cash, or in produce, for the many fields, gardens, shops, bath houses, mills, etc., that are included in confusing detail. There is no summary given anywhere in the book to show the total value of the income from these properties, and consequently it has been necessary to classify, condense, and summarize these records, with the result that the total annual income at that time appeared to be approximately $235,000. But after this estimate was made, one of the

[1] This new catalogue (1930) is arranged by subjects and can be much more readily consulted than the list of the books that appears at the end of Vol. II of the *Matla'u'sh-Shams*.

Persian newspapers in Meshed[1] published a statement of the account of the Shrine income and expenditures for the year 1878, which gave the total as $250,000. The present Shah of Persia, Shah Riḍa, the founder of the new Pahlevi dynasty, has succeeded in virtually taking over the administration of all the ecclesiastical lands and endowments throughout the country, with the result that the National Bank of Persia now handles the money for the Shrine in Meshed, and it is said that the annual income has already increased considerably.

Officials and Servants of the Shrine

When the first good snow falls there is general rejoicing in Mashhad, for it is the failure of winter rains and snow that causes hard times and famine. Accordingly, when the first snow falls, it is customary for the chief officials of the Shrine to go themselves and shovel it off the flat roof at the base of the Golden Dome. This is a public expression of their gratitude to the Imam when the people joyfully see the prospect for another year of plenty. The highest of the officials in rank is the *Mutawali Bashí*, the Superintendent in Chief, who is appointed by the Shah to administer the Shrine business, and who has usually been expected to pay the central government ten per cent. of the Shrine's total receipts. Next comes the Assistant Superintendent, *Naib at-Tauliya*, who is the high priest of the sons of Aaron, so to speak, for he must be a lineal descendant of the Imam. His office is therefore hereditary, like that of the *Ka'im Maḳám*, who serves as the President of the Board of Trustees. In addition to these three there are six or eight officers with executive or clerical duties who receive stipulated salaries and perquisites. Several of these men have grown rich from the continued privilege of administering the income from the Shrine properties.

As great a drain, however, on the Shrine's income has come from

[1] The *Chaman* published this account in a "special issue" in 1923, in an article protesting against the misuse of Shrine money.

the very large number of servants and attendants. Until recently there were seven hundred doorkeepers registered on the pay roll, each to draw $25.00 annually and 1,000 lbs. of grain. These doorkeepers were divided into courses or watches, each watch to be on duty for twenty-four hours every fifth day. Their duties were those of ushers and guards. Besides these there were one thousand attendants at double the pay of the doorkeepers, who were divided similarly into five watches. The night when each watch was on duty they received also a dinner of *pilau*, the delicious dish of boiled rice and mutton that is so popular in the near East, which was ordinarily served to them on the Golden Porch. The attendants' usual duties were to see that the sufficient quantity of water[1] was thrown at once on any spot in the courtyard or in the corridors that might perchance have been polluted, also to light candles, help in the sweeping, etc. And whether a doorkeeper (darbán) or an attendant (khádim), each of these seventeen hundred servants had the right also to bury as many as five of his relatives in the Shrine cemetery. At the present time, however, these regular employees have been reduced in number, by the order of the ruling Shah of Persia, so that there are now scarcely one-third as many as there were five years ago.

But in addition to the regular employees there is a considerable number of those who use the Shrine area as their place of business. There is a regular class of preachers (wu'áẓu) who go and sit at the numerous pulpits that are scattered about in the courtyards and corridors. Then there are the readers who have committed the Ḳoran to memory (ḥufáẓ), dividing it into thirty portions and reciting one part a day, sometimes on their own account but more frequently by contract on behalf of several others. Also there are some forty or fifty readers of prescribed prayers for the pilgrimage (ziyárat khánán), who accompany the groups of unlettered pilgrims as they "ask permission to enter" the Shrine, and as they make their salutations to the Imam at the appointed

[1] The amount of water that is necessary to pour on a spot that has been polluted, in order that it may be cleansed, is the contents of a vessel measuring three cubits each way.

places when they go around his tomb. These men who read the prayer-book receive gratuities.

Until recently there have also been prayer writers, who sat in the old Court and wrote special prayers, which the ignorant purchasers bound on their arms, or on the arms of their children, in the hope that they would ward off disease or bring good fortune. Sometimes "solicitors," whose real business was to arrange temporary marriages for the male pilgrims, would be engaged in the ostensible occupation of writing prayers. But ordinarily when a man wishes to procure a temporary wife, he goes to the little room adjacent to the north-east corner of the Tomb Room, to the room called the *Masjid* of Women, where he tells a woman agent that he wishes to take a temporary wife (*zan-i-mut'ah* or *zan-i-síghah*), and an arrangement is concluded with the agent to have a girl meet him there the next day, when the two go out to find a theological student to give them a paper certifying that they are married for a day, or a week, or a month or so if they desire. These temporary marriages are not looked upon as immoral, as they are fully provided for by the *shariat*, or religious Law, in accordance with the teaching of the Ḳoran and the example of the Prophet and the Imams.

Pedlars of talismans of all sorts also frequent the courts of the Shrine, imposing on the credulity of the hundred odd thousand of pilgrims who visit the city every year. It should be mentioned to the credit of the present administration of the Shrine, however, that in response to a growing public sentiment, these less reputable parasites—the prayer writers, solicitors, and pedlars of talismans—are no longer free to carry on their work openly within the immediate area of the Shrine.

Mashhad, a City independent of the Shrine

With the rapid advance in education throughout Persia, the Shrine at Mashhad is steadily waning in influence. The increase in its annual income, mentioned above, does not mean that it is more popular, but indicates rather that the Government has been ferreting out its assets and scrupulously administering its resources as a public foundation for more useful purposes. A large new hospital, modern school buildings for boys and for girls, substantial contributions towards new streets, the plan for the museum and an enlarged library—all these activities go to show a different point of view on the part of the government towards the Shrine endowments. It is not confiscation, but it is a virtual appropriation of these properties and their incomes for more useful and more practical purposes. That families of descendants from the Prophet, through the Imams, should be maintained in comparative luxury at public expense is no longer generally accepted. The expedient of requiring almost all Persians to wear the adopted national hat has been most effective as a direct blow at these privileged classes who were distinguished by their turbans.

There is perhaps a majority of the people in Mashhad who sympathise heartily with this new point of view, and those who object are finding it increasingly difficult to resist the radical change of sentiment that is clearly evident among all classes. The divine right to nobility, independent of intellectual or moral attainments, meets with ridicule. Several European travellers who visited Mashhad in the last century observed that it was the Shrine that made the city, but Mashhad's significance as the capital of Khorasan and as a city well located for commerce should not be overlooked, and in recent years it has certainly been growing more and more independent of the Shrine. With its splendid cantonments to the south, its aviation field to the east, its newly developed residence district near the Government House, its hundreds of improved buildings along the broad new avenues, its regular motor transport service to all the principal cities of the province, and to Russia and Afghanistan and India, its hospitals, schools, cinemas, public parks, libraries, restaurants, water works, motor buses, and the big new theatre, the modern Mashhad may be truly said to have become a city in its own right, and, according to the new census, a city of 130,000 population, which makes it the largest of the sacred cities of Islam, and the fourth largest city in Persia.

CHAPTER XVII

IMAM MUḤAMMAD TAḲI, THE PROTÉGÉ OF THE CALIPH MA'MUN

THE Muhammadan Empire was by no means at peace when Ma'mun returned to Baghdad. Nasr ibn Shabath held out in Syria, Egypt also was in rebellion, and the notorious Babak, leader of the Khuramiyya, was terrorizing Adherbaiján. Likewise, in the regions of the Persian Gulf, there were depredations by the az-Zuṭṭ, the Ját tribes from India who are said to have been the original Gipsies.[1] Moreover the Caliph had not gotten well on his way to Baghdad when the Harurís broke out in rebellion in Khorasan.

When he arrived, however, he came as a conqueror who was in no sense a suppliant. Nevertheless he showed a disposition to be merciful to those who had opposed him or who had been disloyal, and to conciliate in so far as he could the various factions in the empire. His deceased brother Amín's former vizier, Faḍl ibn Rabí, who had always worked against him, was pardoned and allowed to retire in peace. Those who sympathized with the Caliph's tendency to side with the Ạlids saw him clothed in green as he entered the city. Not only was Ma'mun himself so arrayed but likewise " his officers and his troops and all the people."[2] However, before a month had passed, in public assembly he changed his green apparel for the Ạbbasid black, and bestowed black garments upon his commanders, and the leaders of the principal families, and all his government employees. In so doing he acknowledged that while he was out in Khorasan he had bet on the wrong colour. Whether this conviction had come to him shortly after leaving Merv and led to his having a hand in bringing about the death of the Imam

[1] Rifá'í, *Asru'l-Ma'mun*, Vol. I, p. 270; and Le Strange, *Lands of the Eastern Caliphate*, pp. 245, 331.

[2] Yaḳubi, *Tarikh*, edit. Houtsma, Vol. II, p. 551.

Riḍa, as later Shi'ites have maintained, or whether in the sudden death of the Imam and in the extreme unpopularity of the Shi'ite parties in Baghdad he but read the signs of the times and found that they pointed to black as the colour with the better omen, is a question that may never be conclusively determined.

On the journey from Merv, his own vizier, Faḍl ibn Sahl, had been killed in his bath. He was a Zoroastrian who had become a Moslem and who had a strong Persian loyalty and Shi'ite sympathy. It was largely due to his influence that Ma'mun had appointed the Imam Riḍa to be his heir apparent and had given him his daughter Umm Habíb in marriage. A similar question arises in connection with the death of Faḍl ibn Sahl, was Ma'mun himself the instigator of this murder, or did the Arab party take this means to get rid of the vizier they hated? It would be of interest if we could know how Hasan ibn Sahl, who was governor of Arabia and Iraḳ, would have answered this question when he heard of his brother Faḍl's death and received the heads of the supposed murderers. The Caliph had sent him a letter of condolence on the death of his brother and had promised to appoint him as the next vizier. But all we know is that Hasan ibn Sahl went temporarily insane, or was so regarded for a time, and next we hear that he had recovered and had promised his daughter in marriage to the Caliph.

As part of Ma'mun's policy to conciliate and retain all the strong men he could, he reappointed Hasan ibn Sahl as governor of Iraḳ, and in this capacity the latter co-operated handsomely in the literary and cultural interests of the Court. For in spite of the fact that there was warfare and political turmoil in all directions during the reign of Ma'mun, the period marks perhaps the apex of the Oriental renaissance. There was freedom for speculation and discussion, eagerness in translating the Greek classics, and official encouragement of poetry, art, and science.

Most significant for the life of the Imam Muhammad Taḳi was the fact that Ma'mun's favour towards the Shi'ites persisted even after he had replaced the green colour with the black.

Indeed he took that action as a political necessity and against his personal preference. For not only were prominent Shi'ite Persians appointed to responsible positions, but particular public favour was shown to the family of the deceased Imam Riḍa. One of his brothers was chosen to preside at the annual pilgrimage, and it was but a short time until the Caliph married his own daughter Umm Faḍl to Muhammad Taḳi, the son of Ạli Riḍa. According to Yaḳubi he bestowed upon the bridegroom one hundred thousand dirhems, and said, "Surely I would like to be a grandfather in the line of the Apostle of God and of Ạli ibn Abu Ṭalib."

Muhammad Taḳi (the Pious), who was sometimes also called Jawád (the Generous), was nine years of age (some say seven) at the time of his father's death. He was living in Medina at the time and there were many Shi'ites who took account of his youth and were in doubt as to whether he was really the Imam. However, a number of the learned and prominent men from all quarters came to the annual pilgrimage, and they were so impressed with him that their doubts were dispelled. Kulaini relates that the *mutawali* (superintendent of the Shrine) gave him an examination that lasted for several days, in which he answered thirty thousand questions to their great amazement.[1] He was not the son of his father's legal wife, Umm Habíb, the daughter of Ma'mun, but his mother was a concubine whose name and origin is uncertain. According to Kulaini her name was Habíbí, and she was a Nubian, but the same authority mentions that it was the opinion of others that she was Khaizarán, a girl from Rum (or the Byzantine empire). The statement is also recorded that she was of the household of Mary the Copt, who was the slave mother of the Prophet's little son Ibrahím.[2]

The Shi'ite account of the Caliph's first meeting with this boy Muhammad Taḳi is an unusually pretty story.[3] He had come apparently to Baghdad shortly after the death of his father, and

[1] *Khulasatu'l-Akhbár*, ch. 37, miracle No. 15.
[2] Kulaini, *Usulu'l-Káfí*, p. 203.
[3] Majlisi, *Baharu'l-Anvár*, Vol. XII, p. 95; and the *Khulasatu'l-Akhbár*, ch. 37, miracle No. 16.

one day when Ma'mun was out hunting with his falcons he passed through a village where a group of boys were playing. Among them was Muhammad Taḳi, who was then nearly eleven years old. When the Caliph's cavalcade approached the boys ran away hurriedly, but the young man stood his ground. Ma'mun looked upon him and stopped and asked him, "Boy, what kept you from running away with the others?" Muhammad replied quickly, "O Amiru'l-Muminín, the road was not so narrow that I should fear there would not be room for you to pass, and I have not been guilty of any offence that I should be afraid, and I considered that you were the sort of man who would not injure one who had done no wrong." The Caliph was much pleased, and after he had gone on a short distance one of his falcons brought him a tiny fish, which Ma'mun concealed in his hand and returned and asked the boy, who was still standing where he had met him, "What have I in my hand?" The young Imam answered that the Creator of living things had made fish to live in the sea, but that sometimes the little fish came up into the clouds, and that his falcon had brought him one of these little fish.

It was soon after this that the Caliph called together a great assembly that met for several days, when all sorts of questions were put to the precocious young Imam, who astonished them all with his judgment and learning. Then it was that Ma'mun announced that he thereby formally gave him his daughter in marriage with a large dowry. At this, we are told, the Imam lowered his head, and the Abbasids, who were jealous of him, "died" in chagrin.[1]

Thus the Caliph Ma'mun showed his continued interest and regard for the Shi'ites and made the son of the deceased Imam Riḍa his special charge or protégé, and the boy would come from time to time to the royal palace for study and conversation with the learned men he would meet there. Unfortunately the traditionists have emphasized the miraculous in his attainments

[1] Majlisi, *Baharu'l-Anvár*, Vol. XII, p. 92; and the *Tadhkiratu'l-A'imma*, p. 155.

to the exclusion of incidents that might have shown his scholarship. It is disappointing, for example, to read the testimony of Yahya ibn Akihám, who was one of the men who quizzed him closely before accepting him as the Imám, and to discover that all he has to relate is that when he asked him, with apology for his directness, "Who is the Imám?" the reply was, "I am." He then asked, "By what proof?" and Muhammad Taḳi's cane spoke, "My master is this man, the Imam of the Age and the Proof of my Lord."[1]

A year or so after the wedding the Caliph permitted him and his young wife to go and live in Medina. To this the Abbasid leaders were altogether agreeable for they hated to see the preference that was shown to him in Baghdad. In Medina he lived simply, after the manner of previous Imams, for about three years, meeting those who came to pay him their respects, generously giving to the poor, and avoiding participation in public affairs. He performed miracles also, many of them of the same nature as those ascribed to other Imams, such as predicting that a particular slave girl would bear a man a son, or causing a tree to bear fruit in the time it took him to say his several prayers at the tomb of the Prophet, or rejoicing the heart of an old woman by bringing her dead cow to life again.

His married life with the Caliph's daughter Zainab, who was later known as Umm Faḍl, is reported to have been unhappy, for the conduct of this his legal wife "was not conducive to the friendship and the mutual love which should exist between husband and wife. In order to create enmity against him she used to write to her father disparaging letters about her husband, saying that he associated with slave girls. He rebuked her for making such charges and for *making unlawful what God had made lawful.*"[2]

From Medina he and his wife returned to Baghdad in time to be present at the Caliph's magnificently celebrated wedding, when seven years after his betrothal, Ma'mun married Burán,

[1] *Khulasatu'l-Akhbár*, ch. 37, miracle No. 10.
[2] Sell, *Ithna Ashariyya*, Madras, 1925, from *Tufatu'l-Mutaḳin*, p. 66.

the eighteen-year-old daughter of the Governor, Hasan ibn Sahl. It was a gay occasion for the holy Imám to witness, for, instead of rice, seed pearls were thrown upon the bridegroom, and these were picked up and given to the bride, who had already been arrayed in a robe of lustrous pearls by no less a personage than Zubaida, the widow of Harun ar-Rashíd. " The bridal chamber was lighted with candles of costly ambergris," and the bride's father, the most wealthy and influential Persian of the age, " to mark his gratitude for the royal favour, spent fabulous sums in presents to all around. Balls of musk were cast amongst the crowd who rushed about to catch them. In each was the name of an estate, slave-girl, steed, or other prize, which fell to the lot of him who caught it. Dresses of honour were conferred on all, and so this festival, unparalleled in its magnificence, came to an end."[1]

One difficulty that occurred later in Baghdad between the Imám Taḳi and Umm Faḍl involved the royal family in considerable embarrassment. According to a tradition that is attributed to Hakimah, the sister of the Imám Riḍa, Umm Faḍl told her that once a strikingly beautiful woman had come to see her and had informed her that she also was the wife of the Imam Taḳi. And Umm Faḍl said that in her distress, as she wept on her pillow that night, her jealousy changed to sheer anger, and she arose and went to her father and complained that her husband had not only contemptuously dishonoured her, but that his conduct was an insult also to her father and to the Abbasid dynasty. " It happened," she explained to Hakimah, " that my father was under the influence of liquor, and he seized his sword and called for his horse and his retainers, and went at once to the Imám's house. There he found the offender asleep, and he slashed him with his sword repeatedly, so that the bystanders thought that he had cut him to pieces. But the next morning, when sober, the Caliph deeply regretted what he had done and sent to inquire for the Imám's health, and the messenger returned to say that he had seen him engaged in his morning prayers as

[1] Muir, *The Caliphate, Rise, Decline and Fall*, p. 503.

usual. The Caliph, however, sent again to make more particular inquiry, and learned that the Imám said that a special shirt he wore must have protected him. Nevertheless, to express his shame and sorrow, the Caliph sent the Imám as presents the horse he had ridden and the sword he had wielded the night before. And in addition," Umm Faḍl continued, " he severely rebuked me, and declared that if I ever came to see him again with complaints against my husband, he would refuse to see me as long as I lived."[1]

During the eight years the Imám lived in Baghdad he was principally engaged in teaching. Some of his sayings that are remembered are mentioned by Ibn Khallikan.[2] One of these was in favour of early rising, namely, " that Ạli ibn Abu Ṭalib had said that once when Muḥammad sent him to Yemen, he said to him, ' O Ạli, he is never disappointed who asks for good (from God) ; and he never has a motive for repenting who asks (His) advice.' " Again he related that the Prophet had said, " Make it a point to travel by night, for more ground can be got over by night than by day." And on another occasion he reported that Muḥammad had said to Ạli, " Rise betimes in the name of God, for God hath bestowed a blessing on my people in their early rising." And it is said that Muḥammad Taḳi himself used to declare, " Whosoever gaineth for himself a brother in God, hath gained for himself a mansion in Paradise."

It was during this time that the Imám Taḳi was teaching in Baghdad that the Caliph Ma'mun fell more and more under the influence of the Mu'tazalites, and especially of their leader, Ḳádí Aḥmad ibn Abu Du'ád. He was finally urged in 212/827 to proclaim publicly the dogma of the creation of the Ḳoran. " Persians now ruled the provinces, and worse, the memory of Muawia was formally cursed in public (826) ; the following year the pre-eminence of Ạli was proclaimed with equal official solemnity ; and to the horror of all true believers in the mission of the Prophet, it was also declared that the Ḳoran was no longer

[1] *Khulasatu'l-Akhbár*, ch. 37, miracle No. 17.
[2] Ibn Khallikan, trans. de Slane, Vol. II, p. 580.

to be deemed *an eternal and uncreated book.* This last was a stroke at the foundation of Islam, and was destined to exert a long and important influence.

" It is related that Ma'mun had received from Kabul a volume entitled *The Eternal Reason,* which attempted to undermine Islam by teaching that reason is the only source of religion, and that revelation cannot be the sure ground upon which to base a universal cult. To seek and develop this religion of reason and conscience became thereafter his persistent effort. He insinuated doubts at first by means of discussion, at which no one was permitted to appeal to revelation, but only to reason. Thus, unconsciously, Ma'mun began a process by which that implicit faith which had been at once the foundation and the inspiration of Islam, which had nerved its warriors in their terrible warfare, and had brought the nation out of its former obscurity to the foremost position among the peoples of the world, was to be taken from them."[1]

But as has been pointed out, the liberal Mu'tazalites were exceedingly intolerant in their treatment of the orthodox,[2] and were bent on forcing them to accept the syllogism, God created all things, the Ḳoran is a thing, so therefore the Ḳoran is created. To gain this admission from them the chief judges and lawyers were severely catechised, scourged and imprisoned. But the Ạlids, however, were treated with the greatest consideration,[3] and it is especially noteworthy that the Imam Taḳi was not arrested or annoyed in any way during the reign of Ma'mun. The position he held makes it difficult to suppose that he was able to avoid discussing these theological questions, so the more probable explanation is that he made the desired concessions to the opinions of the party in power, which was a procedure that his Shi'ite followers would have no difficulty in explaining by their doctrine of legitimate dissimulation (taḳíya) for prudential purposes.[4]

[1] Gilman, *The Saracens,* Story of the Nations series, pp. 384, 385.
[2] Moore, *History of Religions,* Vol. II, p. 438.
[3] *Encyclopædia of Islam,* art. " al-Ma'mun."
[4] Kulaini, *Usulu'l-Káfi,* p. 316.

But Ma'mun was forced to leave Baghdad in 215/830 on his great campaign against Theophilus. The immediate cause of this war is obscure. It has been suggested that the Byzantine Emperor had been supporting the rebel Bábak and that he had encouraged the emigration of thousands of Persian Christians from the Caliph's dominions.[1] Others have said that it was because the Emperor had refused to allow the philosopher, Leo of Thessalonica, to accept the Caliph Ma'mun's invitation to go to Baghdad.[2] In any event the war was carried on for two full years, and Ma'mun died suddenly in a town near Tarsus, the Apostle Paul's birthplace, in Cilicia. There in Tarsus, in accordance with his own request, the free-thinking Caliph had the *salát* said over his body with the burning of incense and candles, a custom that was in imitation of the practice of the Christians of the time.[3]

After the death of Ma'mun, the Imám Muḥammad Taḳi went with his family back to Medina, where they remained only a little more than a year, however, when the new Caliph, Ma'mun's brother, Mu'tasim, sent for them to come to Baghdad. This was in the beginning of the year in which the Imam died, 220/835, and while there is no evidence to show that his relations with the new Caliph were lacking in cordiality, yet statements are to be found in the books most commonly read by present day Shi'ites[4] that say he was poisoned by his wife, Umm Faḍl, on the instigation of Mu'tasim. But there is no agreement in the details of these charges, some saying that his wife gave him a poisoned handkerchief when he was in bed, while others say she gave him poisoned grapes. Still others say that Mu'tasim himself sent the Imám poisoned sherbet to be given by the hands of a servant, while others say that the Caliph invited him to his house, where poison was mixed with the food. In the comprehensive account of his life in the *Baharu'l-Anvár*,[5] is found the testimony of the older

[1] Finlay, George, *History of the Byzantine Empire*, Everyman's Library, pp. 141, 142.
[2] Dilman, *The Saracens*, Story of the Nations Series, p. 386.
[3] *Encyclopædia of Islam*, art. "Masjid," Vol. III, p. 344.
[4] *Aḳayidu'sh-Shi'sh*, Mishkát, iv; and *Tofatu'l-Mutaḳin*, p. 63 ff.
[5] Majlisi, *Baharu'l-Anvár*, Vol. XII, p. 78 ff.

and more authoritative books, such as the *Irshádu'l-Mufíd* and the *Kashfu'l-Ḳamah,* that " although some say he was poisoned we have found no tradition to confirm it."

" He was buried," as Kulaini observes,[1] " in Baghdad, in the cemetery of the Ḳuraish, beside the grave of his grandfather, Musa al-Kaẓim." The funeral service for him was repeated by al-Wathik, the son of the Caliph Mu'tasim.

[1] Kulaini, *Usulu'l-Káfí,* p. 203.

CHAPTER XVIII

THE SHRINE OF KAZIMAIN, "THE TWO KAZIMS," AT BAGHDAD

ANYONE approaching Baghdad from the north or the west will be impressed by the sight of the four golden minarets at Kazimain, the Shrine of the Two Kazims, Musa ibn Ja'far and Muḥammad Taḳí. These two saints were respectively the Seventh and the Ninth of the Twelve Imams, at whose tombs the Shi'ite Muhammadans are accustomed to seek healing and to invoke intercession for the forgiveness of their sins. Across the arched gateway, in the wall that surrounds the Shrine, are suspended huge chains, which indicate that the area within is sacred and that unbelievers are not to enter. The visitor who is forbidden entrance, however, may look through the gate and see the minute patterns in the tile work on the front of the building, or may climb up to a neighbouring roof, as did the writer and his wife, to get a better view. Moreover, recent years have afforded a new avenue of approach from the air, which is free to all faiths, and the photograph from above discloses the whole plan of the Shrine.

The present building dates back only to the beginning of the sixteenth century, and has been kept in excellent repair. This building represents the restoration of Shah Ismaíl I (1502-1524), though when the Turkish Sultan, Sulaiman the Great, captured Baghdad and remained there for four months in 1534, he visited the sacred places of the Shi'ites, and is said to have contributed to the further ornamentation of the Shrine at Kazimain. The tiles for the double cupula, however, were provided in 1796 by Shah Agha Muḥammad Khan, who was the first of the Persian Kadjár dynasty. In 1870, Naṣr al-Din Shah had these golden tiles repaired on one of the domes and on the minarets. It is

THE SHRINE OF KAZIMAIN AS SEEN FROM THE AIR

Facing p. 198]

interesting that the dates of all these alterations are clearly indicated by inscriptions.[1]

If we bear in mind that the two Imams who are buried here died in the beginning of the eighth century, it will be evident that there are seven hundred years of the history of their tomb to account for previous to the comparatively modern restoration of Shah Ismaíl I. The Imams lived in the early days of Baghdad, while the walls of Mansur's Round City on the western side of the Tigris were still standing. There were cemeteries to the north and north-west that went by various names—that of the Syrian Gate, that of the Abbasids, and that of the Straw Gate.[2] The two Imams were buried immediately to the west of this later cemetery, but by the time Yaḳubi wrote the whole northern district was designated in a general way as the cemetery of the Ḳuraish.[3] The Shi'ites assert that both of these Imams were poisoned, or put to death in some other way, at the instigation of the reigning caliphs, but it is significant that in the case of Muḥammad Taḳí, the funeral service was read by a representative of the royal family,[4] which undoubtedly distinguished the Imam as an important person, at whose grave some sort of a mausoleum would be built.

But as to the importance attached in the early times to the visitation of this tomb, the only information available is on the questionable authority of traditions that have been attributed to the Eighth and Tenth Imams. These traditions are answers they are said to have given when they were asked by their followers concerning the merit of pilgrimages to Kazimain. It is related that the Imam Riḍa, whose life in Baghdad was during the caliphate of Harun ar-Rashíd, told his Shi'ite followers to say their prayers of salutation to his father, the Imam Musa Kazim, "outside the walls of the Shrine, or in the near-by mosques," if the Sunnite authority and prejudice in Baghdad was too great for them to do so at the tomb itself. He said the merit of so doing

[1] *Encyclopædia of Islam,* art. "Kazimain."
[2] Ibn Sa'd, *Tabaḳat,* VII, ii, pp. 68, l. 18; 99, l. 13; 90, l. 21; and 80, l. 11.
[3] Yaḳubi, *Tarikh,* edit. Houtsma, Vol. II, p. 499.
[4] Kulaini, *Usulu'l-Kafi,* p. 203.

was the same as the pilgrimage to the tomb of the Imam Husain at Kerbala, or to the tomb of the Prophet Muḥammad at Medina, or to the tomb of Ạli at Najaf. From this we infer that a building of some sort was recognized at that early date as marking the tomb of the Imam Musa and that it was surrounded by a wall. Further statements are said to have been made a few years later by the Imam Ạli Naḳi, whose period in the imamate began during the later part of the caliphate of Mu'tasim, and who enjoyed the greater indulgence that was shown the Shi'ites until the period of reaction against them and the Mu'tazalites under the Caliph Mutawakkil. He is said to have given the following particular instructions for visiting this Shrine:

"When you wish to visit the tomb of Musa ibn Ja'far and the tomb of Muḥammad ibn Ạli ibn Musa, first you must bathe and make yourself clean, then anoint yourself with perfume and put on two clean garments, after which you are to say at the tomb of the Imam Musa:

Peace be upon thee, O Friend of God!
Peace be upon thee, O Proof of God!
Peace be upon thee, O Light of God!
O Light in the dark places of the Earth!
Peace be upon him whom God advances in thy regard!
Behold I come as a pilgrim, who acknowledges your right,
Who hates your enemies and befriends your friends,
So intercede for me therefore with your Lord.

"You are then free," said the Imam Ạli Naḳi, "to ask for your personal needs, after which you should offer a prayer in salutation to the Imam Muḥammad Taḳi, using these same words."

Majlisi, who has included these traditions in his instructions for modern pilgrims to this Shrine, makes the observation in explanation of the unusual brevity of the prescribed prayer, "that it was necessary in those times to take great care in dissimulation (taḳiyah) that the Shi'ites should not suffer injury."[1]

Another tradition that dates from the same century in which these two Imams died is attributed to a certain Hasan ibn Jamhúr, who said:

[1] Majlisi, *Tofatu'z-Zá'irín*, pp. 308 ff.

"In the year 296 A.H., when Ạli ibn Ahmad ibn al-Frát was vizier, I saw Ahmad ibn Rabí', who was one of the Caliph's writers, when his hand had gotten infected so that it had a bad odour and turned black. Everyone who saw him had no doubt but what he would die. In a dream, however, he saw Ạli, and said to him: 'O Amiru'l-Muminín, will you not ask God to give me my hand?' Ạli answered, 'I have many things to do, but you go to Musa ibn Ja'far and he will ask this for you from God.' In the morning they got a litter and carpeted it, gave him a bath and anointed him with perfume. They had him lie down in the litter and covered him with a robe. Then they carried him to the tomb of the Imam Musa, whose assistance he sought in prayer. The afflicted man took some of the earth from the tomb and rubbed it on his arm up to the shoulder and then bound the arm up again. The next day, when he opened the bandage, he saw that all the skin and the flesh of the arm had fallen off, and that only the bones and veins and ligaments remained. The bad odour, also, had ceased. When the vizier heard of this they took the man to him to testify to what had happened. In a short time the flesh and skin grew back again, and he was able to resume his work of writing."

Majlisi adds the comment that "in every period there are so many miracles (mu'jizát) and demonstrations of power (karámát) at the tomb of these two saints (or sinless ones) that there is no need of describing cases in times past, for in our own time there are so many of these instances occurring and recurring that to recount them would be a lengthy process."[1]

After the Abbasid caliphs had fallen more and more under the authority of the commanders of their armies of Turkish mercenaries, there was a rising of the Buyids (or Buwaihids) in Persia; and in A.D. 946 the Caliph Mustakfi was blinded by the Buyid Prince, Mu'izzu'd Ḍawla, who set up the blinded Caliph's son, al-Muḳtaddír, as a nominal ruler while he exercised the actual authority himself. Ibn Athir has related that "the Buyids were fanatical adherents of Ạli and were firmly convinced that the Ạbbasids were usurpers of a throne that rightfully belonged to others."[2] They did not take over the caliphate, but in addition to retaining for themselves the authority and perquisites of the government of the provinces, they proclaimed the first ten days

[1] Majlisi, *op. cit.*, p. 309.

[2] Ibn al-Athir, *Kamil*, viii, p. 177.

of the month of Muharram as a period of public mourning for the Imam Husain,[1] and they frequently enriched the sanctuary at Kazimain with their gifts. The Caliph Ṭái' is reported to have led the Friday prayers in the Kazimain mosque,[2] so that in the period of the revival of the Shi'ite influence under the protection of the Buyids, we are certain that the Kazimain Shrine was regularly visited by pilgrims and served as "the rallying place of the heterodox party."

It was during this period that the four great works of the Shi'ite traditionists were compiled. Kulaini died in Baghdad in A.D. 939, after completing his monumental work, *The Compendium of the Science of Religion* (*al-Káfí fí Ịlm ad-Dín*), which is perhaps the most highly esteemed of all the Shi'ite source books. Ibn Babuwaihi had come to Baghdad from Khorasan in 966, where he devoted himself to teaching and writing. His *Every Man His Own Lawyer* (*Kitáb man lá yadhuruhu'l-Faḳíh*), is also one of the four most authoritative books on Shi'ite law and tradition. And sixteen years after the death of Ibn Babuwaihi, aṭ-Ṭusi also came from Khorasan to teach in Baghdad, where he wrote the remaining two of the four great books of traditions that lie at the basis of Shi'ite theology and jurisprudence, *The Correcting of Judgments* (*Tahdhíb al-Aḥkám*) and the *Examination of Differences in Traditions* (*al-Istibsár*).

At this time of greater boldness on the part of the Shi'ites, riots with the Sunnís were not infrequent in Baghdad. In one of these disturbances in 1051, the Sunní leader was killed in a fight that had ensued when the Shi'ites ventured to put an inscription laudatory of Ạli above one of the city gates. The indignation of the Sunnis was so great that in the tension of the situation after their leader's funeral, they rushed as a mob into the Shrine of Kazimain and plundered the tombs of the two Imams. "After carrying off the gold and silver lamps and the curtains which adorned these sanctuaries, the rioters on the following day completed their work by setting fire to the buildings. The great

[1] Browne, *Persian Literature in Modern Times*, p. 31.
[2] Le Strange, *Baghdad during the Abbasid Caliphate*, p. 162.

teak-wood domes above the shrines of the Imams Musa and Muḥammad were entirely burnt.[1] This fact that the domes were at first of teak-wood has something to do doubtless with the number of times they were burned.

It was shortly after the burning of the Shrine in 1051 that the Seljuk Sultans displaced the Buwaihids as military dictators in Persia and " protectors " of the Caliphs in Baghdad. They had learned what they knew of Islam in the distinctively Sunni atmosphere of Bukhara. Nevertheless, when they came to Baghdad, no injury was done to the Shrine at Kazimain. And when Sultan Malik Shah visited it in 1086, it had apparently been repaired from the damages of the fire of thirty-five years before.[2]

Ibn Jubayr, who gives a detailed description of Baghdad in 1184, in his *Travels*,[3] mentions the tomb of Musa ibn Ja'far, but he does not speak of it as Kazimain, and he makes no reference to the tomb of the Imam Muḥammad Taḳi, which would suggest that Shi'ite influence was at that time at such a low ebb that this shrine, so close to the city of Baghdad, had been abandoned as a place of regular pilgrimage.

Notwithstanding, before another hundred years had passed, when the domes of the Shrine had again been destroyed by fire, we find that its repair was regarded as of sufficient importance to be the one and only enterprise that the short-lived Caliph Záhir had been able to undertake. And Ibn Tiḳtaḳa, who mentions thiṣ repair of the domes in his *Kitab al-Fakhri*,[4] is known to have succeeded his father as supervisor of the sacred towns of the Shi'ites in the Baghdad vicinity, so that it is possible that the minority community, while by no means free, may have enjoyed certain prescribed and restricted rights. Their headquarters, however, were no longer in Baghdad but in Hilla, and greater importance was given to Najaf and Kerbala as places of pilgrimage.

[1] Le Strange, *op. cit.*, p. 164.
[2] Le Strange, *op. cit.*, p. 163.
[3] Ibn Jubayr, *Travels*, Wright's text revised by de Goeje, p. 226.
[4] Ibn Tiḳtaḳa, *Kitab al-Fakhri*, p. 163.

When the Mongols came with their overwhelming force in 1258, they wrought almost complete devastation in and around Baghdad. There is said to have been an understanding, however, that the holy cities of the Shi'ites should be spared, and in fact Kazimain was the only one of these shrines that suffered. This was due perhaps to the destruction of the western part of the city first. It may have been during the subsequent siege of the fortress on the eastern side of the Tigris that the deputation of Shi'ites from Hilla arrived and arranged with Khulagu Khan for the special protection of Najaf and Kerbala. However that may be, we know that the city of Baghdad was utterly ruined by the Mongols, and that the tombs of Kazimain were burned. "Nearly all the inhabitants, to the number, according to Rashid ad-Din, of 800,000 (Makrizi says 2,000,000) perished, and thus passed away one of the noblest cities that had ever graced the East—the cynosure of the Muḥammadan world, where the luxury, wealth and culture of five centuries had been concentrated. . . . The booty captured, we are told, was so great that Georgians and Tartars succumbed under the load of gold and silver, precious stones and pearls, rich stuffs, gold and silver vessels, etc., while as to the vases from China and Rashan (i.e., porcelain), and those made in the country of iron and copper, they were deemed scarcely of any value, and were broken and thrown away. The soldiers were so rich that the saddles of their horses and mules and their most ordinary utensils were inlaid with stones, pearls and gold. Some of them broke off their swords at the hilt and filled up the scabbards with gold, while others emptied the body of a Baghdadian, refilled it with gold, precious stones and pearls, and carried it off from the city."[1]

The death of the last of the Abbasid Caliphs, Mustasim, has been so celebrated in literature that what actually happened is obscure.

There are numerous accounts of how Khulagu Khan was disgusted when he saw that in his avarice the Caliph had gathered

[1] Howarth, *History of the Mongols*, iii, pp. 126, 127.

gold which he had been unwilling to spend either in defence of the city or to effect favourable terms of capitulation. Marco Polo relates the story that when Khulagu Khan entered Baghdad he found to his astonishment a town that was filled with gold, and in his indignation he gave orders that the avaricious Caliph should be " shut up in this same town, without sustenance ; and there, in the midst of his wealth, he soon finished a miserable existence."[1] This story is based on the narrative of Mirkhond, of Joinville, and of Makakia, the Armenian historian, and as Howarth remarks, it has provided " one of those grim episodes which Longfellow delighted to put into verse " :

I said to the Caliph, " Thou art old,
Thou hast no need of so much gold ;
Thou should'st not have heaped and hidden it here,
Till the breath of battle was hot and near,
But have sown through the land these useless hoards,
To spring into shining blades of swords,
And keep thine honour sweet and clear."

* * * * * *

Then into his dungeon I locked the drone,
And left him there to feed all alone,
In the honey cells of his golden hive ;
Never a prayer, nor a cry, nor a groan,
Was heard from those massive walls of stone,
Nor again was the Khalif seen alive.

But other records suggest that there were discussions about the propriety of killing the holy Khalif. An astrologer, Husam ad-din, pointed out dire portents that would happen if the Caliph's blood was shed. But we are told that another astrologer, a Shi'ah, Naṣr ud-din, from Tus, remarked that no such things had happened when John the Baptist, the Prophet Muḥammad and the Imam Husain were killed. We are told in fact that " it is probable that Khulagu would have spared the Caliph's life, impressed by the lugubrious prognostications of the faithful Mussulmans about him, if he had not been dissuaded from this course by the Shi'ahs who were with him, and who had a bitter resentment against the Ạbbasid dynasty." One notable fact in

[1] *Travels of Marco Polo the Venitian*, ch. viii.

this connection is that the life of the Caliph's vizier in Baghdad was spared. He was Muayid ud-din Alkamiya, who was known to have been favourable to the Shi'ites, and who was also reported to have sent his submission to Khulagu, and to have invited him to invade the country. However this may be, the Caliph was put to death on the 21st of February, 1258. "Wassaf and Novairi say he was rolled up in carpets and then trodden under by horses so that his blood should not be spilt. This was in accordance with the *yasa* of Jingis Khan, which forbade the shedding of the blood of royal persons."

But the Caliph's vizier, whose life was spared, "retained his post as vizier, the reward doubtless of his dubious loyalty." Various prominent Persians, as distinguished from Arabs or Turks, were appointed to important positions in the new administration of affairs, and among the first buildings to be rebuilt was the Shrine of the two Imams, at Kazimain.[1]

After the fall of the last of the Ạbbasid Caliphs, Baghdad was never rebuilt on its former scale of grandeur. The Il-Khans, who were the descendants of Khulagu, held the city for 82 years—not as a capital, however, but merely as the chief town of the province of Iraḳ. It was near the close of their period of authority that the traveller Mustawfi visited Baghdad (1339), and at that time he mentioned seeing the shrines of Kazim and of his grandson, Taḳi, the Seventh and Ninth Imams. He observed that Kazimain was a suburb by itself, about six thousand paces in circumference.[2]

About that time the Mongol tribe of Julayr wrested the power from the Il-Khans, and their chief, Shaikh Hasan Buzurg, made his residence in Baghdad in 1340, as the town best suited for his tribal headquarters.

Fifty odd years later, in A.D. 1393, in connection with his widespread conquests, Timur spent three months in Baghdad. It happened to be in the summer that he besieged and captured the city, and the Persian chronicler in the *Zafar Nameh* remarks

[1] Howarth, *op. cit.*, pp. 127-131.

[2] Mustawfi, *Nuzhatu'l-Qulub*, Eng. trans. Gibb Mem. series, Vol. XXIII, ii, p. 42.

that "the heat was so intense, that as for the fish in the water, the saliva boiled in their mouths; and as for the birds in the air, from the fever heat their livers were cooked and they fell senseless."

The horrors of the taking of the city are described in graphic detail. So thoroughly had all avenues of escape been closed that when the wind accelerated the flames that filled the air, there were many people who threw themselves into the water, to escape the fire or the sword. It was a time when the slave market was such that an old man of eighty and a child of twelve sold for the same price, and the fire of hate waxed to such a heat that the garment of the wealthy merchant and the rags of the sick beggar burned the same way. Individual soldiers in bands of the troops had been commissioned to each get a head, but some who were not content with one head got all they could tie to their belts. It is mentioned, however, that such of the men of learning and rank as were able to appeal to Timur himself were granted his protection and shared his bounty, but the general carnage was hideous. When the inhabitants had been thus almost annihilated, their habitations were dealt with. Only the mosques, the schools, and the dormitories were spared. Accordingly, we read that Timur left Baghdad on account of "the vile odour of the carcases of the dead."[1]

Nevertheless, when Timur took his departure, we are told that he ordered that the city should be rebuilt. The Shrine at Kazimain, however, was not restored. After the death of Timur, there was a brief reoccupation of Baghdad by the Julayrs, who were displaced by the "Black Sheep" Turkomans, who held the city from 1411-1469. They in turn were driven out by their rivals, the "White Sheep" Turkomans. It was therefore after a long period of neglect, when the city had been held by successive generations of half-savage tribes, that Shah Ismaíl I, of the Safawi dynasty captured Baghdad in 1508, and it was in 1519 that he completed the rebuilding of the Shrine at Kazimain much

[1] *Zafar Nameh*, by Sharifu'd-Din Ạli Yezdí, edit. Calcutta, 1887-8, Vol. II, pp. 363-369.

as it stands to-day. With the rise of Shah Ismaíl there is an interesting and significant story of the revival of Persian Shi'ite power, which belongs in the history of Ardebil in Adherbaijan rather than in a description of the Shrine of the "Two Kazims" at Baghdad.

The population of the present town of Kazimain is estimated at from six to eight thousand, and we are told that frequently from twenty-five to thirty thousand pilgrims visit the Shrine in one day. If viewed from a point of advantage, this Shrine with its twin domes of gleaming gold is one of the prettiest sights in Baghdad; and if studied in its historical associations throughout the last eleven hundred years, it affords a thrilling resumé of the changing fortunes of the far-famed city of the Arabian Nights.

CHAPTER XIX

THE IMAM ẠLI NAḲI, WHO WAS TWENTY YEARS A PRISONER

IN the first half of the ninth century of the Christian era, Rome, Constantinople and Baghdad yielded to the rising power of foreign peoples. On Christmas Day, A.D. 800, Pope Leo III placed the imperial crown on Charlemagne, the great King of the Franks. In 843, by the Treaty of Verdun, "the territorial Empire was divided into three separate kingdoms. The Western Franks, speaking a Romance tongue, were, in the still distant future, to form the nation-state which we call France; the Eastern Franks, Teutonic in speech, were to become the historical Germany; and a middle kingdom was to include for a brief period, Burgundy, Lorraine and Italy."[1]

In the Byzantine Empire Theophilus (829-842) was forced to maintain his authority at great hazard by employing armies of Persians and Armenians. Likewise in Baghdad during this period, fearful of the plots and counterplots of the conflicting national elements in Islam, the Caliphs, Ma'mun and Mu'tasim, and their immediate successors put their chief dependence on hired Turkish troops. For greater personal security they founded a new military city at Samarra, some sixty miles north of Baghdad, where they made their headquarters. But before long their Turkish generals, whose armies suppressed the repeated Moslem insurrections, began to dictate and became the true rulers, while the Caliphs were guarded as little more than useful puppets in the prison city of their own making. It was at this time, when the imperial authority in Islam was rapidly passing into the hands of the Turks that the tenth Imam, Ạli Naḳi, lived.

There is uncertainty as to whether he was born in 827 or 829,

[1] *Christianity in the Light of Modern Knowledge*, a Collective Work, publ. Harcourt, Brace and Company, 1929, p. 532.

and equally good authorities differ.[1] If we prefer the earlier date, he was little more than seven years old when his father died. According to the authorities cited, his mother was a concubine, who was called Samanah, the Maghribiyya, or Westerner, but in the more popular manual in Persian, the *Akayidu'sh-Shi'a* (Mishkat iv), her name was Susan (Lily), and she was called Durrah-i-Maghribiyya, the Pearl of the West, which would indicate that she was a captive from one of the Christian nations.

As the boy grew into manhood he lived in Medina and occupied himself in teaching. Gradually, he attracted pupils in large numbers from the provinces where the adherents of the house of the Prophet were strongest—Iraḳ, Persia and Egypt. During the seven or eight years that remained of the Caliphate of Mu'tasim after the death of the Imam Muḥammad Taḳi, and throughout the five years of the next Caliph, Wathik, we do not hear that the young Imam was molested. One of the traditions he is said to have related, that had been written in the Saḥifa by the hand of Ạli ibn Abu Ṭalib at the dictation of the Apostle of God, and inherited by the Imams from generation to generation, was that the Prophet had defined *faith* (ímán) as contained in the hearts of men, and that their *works* (a'mál) confirm it, whereas *surrender* (islám) is what the tongue expresses which validates the union.[2]

During the Caliphate of Mutawakkil, however, a reaction set in against all freethinking, with systematic persecution of both the Mu'tazalites and the Shi'ites. Only the strictly orthodox were exempt. In the year 851, when the Imam was nearly twenty-five years old, the Caliph Mutawakkil ordered the pilgrimages to the shrines of Ạli and Husain to be stopped. Then it was that he had the mausoleum of Husain totally destroyed.

At this period the Caliph came to be suspicious also of the young Imam Ạli Naḳi. But on one occasion at least, according to Mas'udi, the Imam is said to have saved himself by a shrewd answer to an artful question that the Caliph put to him. Mutawakkil asked, " What does a descendant of your father have to

[1] Kulaini, *Usulu'l-Káfí*, p. 206; and Majlisi, *Baharu'l-Anvár*, Vol. XII, p. 100.
[2] Mas'udi, *Muruju'l-Dhahab*, vii, p. 382.

say in regard to al-Abbas ibn Abdu'l-Muttalib ? " He answered, " What would a descendant of my father say, O Governor of the Faithful, in regard to a man whose sons God has required his people to obey, and who expected his sons to obey God ? " The Caliph was so pleased with this reply that he commanded that he be given one hundred thousand dirhems.[1]

And in the same connection Mas'udi quotes another incident, one which is derived originally from al-Mubarrad, and which Ibn Khallikan has incorporated in his description of the Imam Ạli Naḳi (*Abu'l-Hasan al-Askari*).[2] " Secret information having been given to al-Mutawakkil that the Imam had a quantity of arms, books, and other objects for the use of his followers concealed in his house, and being induced by malicious reports to believe that he aspired to the empire, one night he sent some soldiers of the Turkish guard to break in on him when he least expected such a visit. They found him quite alone and locked up in his room, clothed in a hair shirt, his head covered with a woollen cloak, and turned with his face in the direction of Mecca ; chanting, in this attitude, some verses of the Ḳoran expressive of God's promises and threats, and having no other carpet between him and the earth than sand and gravel. He was carried off in that attire, and brought, in the depth of night, before al-Mutawakkil, who was then engaged in drinking wine. On seeing him the Caliph received him with respect, and being informed that nothing had been found in his house to justify the suspicions cast upon him, he seated him by his side and offered him the goblet which he held in his hand. ' Commander of the Faithful,' said Abu'l-Hasan, ' a liquor such as that was never yet combined with my flesh and blood ; dispense me therefore from taking it.' The Caliph acceded to his request and asked him to repeat some verses which might amuse him. Abu'l-Hasan replied that he knew by heart very little poetry, but al-Mutawakkil having insisted, he recited these lines :

They passed the night on the summits of the mountains,

[1] Mas'udi, *op. cit.*, pp. 206 ff.
[2] Ibn Khallikan, trans. de Slane, Vol. II, p. 214.

protected by valiant warriors, but their place of refuge availed them not.

After all their pomp and power they had to descend from their lofty fortresses to the custody of the tomb.

O what a dreadful change! Their graves had already received them when a voice was heard exclaiming:

Where are the thrones and the crowns and the robes of state?

Where are now the faces of the delicate, which were shaded by veils and protected by the curtains of the audience hall?

To this demand the tomb gave answer sufficient. The worms, it said, are now revelling upon these faces.

Long had these men been eating and drinking, but now they are eaten in their turn.

"Every person present was filled with apprehension for Abu'l-Hasan's safety; they feared that al-Mutawakkil, in the first burst of indignation, would have vented his wrath upon him. But they perceived the Caliph weeping bitterly, the tears trickling down his beard, and all the assembly wept with him. Al-Mutawakkil then ordered the wine to be removed, after which he said: 'Tell me, Abu'l-Hasan, are you in debt?' 'Yes,' replied the other, 'I owe four thousand *dinars*.' The Caliph ordered the sum to be given him, and sent him home with marks of the highest respect."

Yahya ibn Harthama, the captain of the guard, is reported to have related his experience as follows: "The Caliph Mutawakkil sent me to Medina with orders to bring Ạli ibn Muḥammad to answer certain accusations that had been made against him. When I arrived, his household made such wailing and lamentation as I had never heard. I tried to quiet them and assured them that I had received no orders to do him any harm. And when I searched the house where he lived, I found only a Ḳoran, books of prayer and such things. So while I took him away, I offered him my services and showed him very high respect.

"But one day on the journey, when the sky was clear and the Sun just rising, Ạli put on a cloak when he mounted his horse and knotted the animal's tail. I was surprised at this, but it was only a little while afterwards that a cloud came up and there was a regular torrent of rain. Then Ạli turned to me and said, ' I know that you did not understand what you saw me do, and that you imagine that I have had some unusual knowledge of this affair. It is not, however, as you supposed, but as I was brought up in a desert, I know the winds that come before rain. This morning the wind blew which does not deceive, and I noticed the odour of rain and so prepared for it.'

" On our arrival in Baghdad, our first visit was to Ishaḳ ibn Ibrahim, of the family of Tahir, who was the governor of the city. He said to me, ' O Abu Yahya, this man (Ạli) is a descendant of the Apostle of God. You know Mutawakkil and have influence with him, but if you urge him to kill this man, the Prophet himself will be your enemy.' I replied that I saw nothing in the conduct of Ạli except what was altogether praiseworthy. I went on to Samarra, where I saw Waṣif, the Turk, for I was one of his intimate friends. ' I swear before God,' he said to me, ' if a single hair of the head of this man falls, I will myself demand satisfaction.' I was somewhat surprised at the attitude taken by these men, and when I informed Mutawakkil of what I had heard in praise of the Imam, he gave him a handsome present and treated him with all sorts of honour."[1]

Mas'udi also remarks, " In the Akhbaru'l-Zamán (his great work that is no longer extant) we have already described the occasion when Ạli ibn Muhammad refuted the false prophetess Zainab in the presence of al-Mutawakkil by descending into the den of the lions, and how they crouched at his feet, and how Zainab then gave up the claim that she was a daughter of Ḥusain ibn Ạli ibn Abu Ṭalib, a woman whom God had permitted to live until that time."[2]

Nevertheless, owing to numerous other reports that had come to the Caliph's ears about the disloyalty of the Imam, Ạli Naḳi was kept a prisoner at Samarra. This town was at first called *al-Askar* (the army), because Mu'tasim had built it as a canton-

[1] Mas'udi, *op. cit.*, pp. 379-382 ; Kulaini, *op. cit.*, p. 206. ; and Majlisi, *op. cit.*, p. 100.

[2] Mas'udi, *op. cit.*, p. 383 ; cf. *Khulasatu'l-Akhbár*, ch. xxxviii, miracle No. 5.

ment city outside Baghdad, and consequently the Imam Ạli Naḳi has sometimes been designated as "al-Askarí," on account of the twenty years he spent as a prisoner in the city of the army.

The miracles that his friends and acquaintances have related are for the most part reminiscent of his life in Samarra. Abu'l-Hashim, Ja'farí, reported that on one occasion he saw a group of people approaching Samarra from Medina, and that the Imam Ạli Naḳi had come out of the city to meet them. He rode a horse with a gold-embroidered saddlecloth, and at a particular point on the desert he dismounted and seated himself on the sand. Abu'l-Hashim took advantage of this opportunity to acquaint him with his dire financial needs, and the Imam answered, "Do not distress yourself, for I will relieve your anxieties." He then thrust his blessed hand into the ground and gave him a handful of sand and stone, saying, "This will be enough for you." Abu'l-Hashim protested, but notwithstanding, he kept what the Imam had given him, and when he examined it some time afterwards, he found it was yellow gold, which he took to an assayer, who said that he had never tested finer gold in his life. It proved to be enough for Abu'l-Hashim's expenses for a long time.

One time his friend Muhammad ibn Khazib was riding with him and told him to make his horse go faster. The Imam replied, "You will be in chains in prison before me," and sure enough, in but four days' time Muhammad ibn Khazib was chained in prison and was put to death a few days afterwards.

A group of slaves that belonged to Mutawakkil recognised the Imam Ạli Naḳi in the presence of the Caliph, and went and prostrated themselves before him, kissing his hands and feet. Mutawakkil afterwards asked Bultán, who had charge of these slaves, "What was this the slaves did?" Bultán said that he himself did not understand it, so the Caliph asked the slaves, "Why did you do this?" They answered, "Because this is the man who comes to the sea every year and teaches us religion. He is the *wasi* (representative) of the last prophet of the age, and we have seen him do many miracles." When the Caliph heard this, he said to Bultán, " Kill those slaves." Bultán further relates, " I killed them and buried them. When night came I decided to go to the Imam, so I arose and hastened to him to explain the matter. A servant at the door told me the Imam was seeking me, so I accompanied him to the *andarun* (private family apartment), where I found the Imam seated. He said to me, ' How are the slaves ? ' I said, ' I killed them all.' ' You killed them all ? ' he asked. ' Yes,' I replied, ' I swear that I did.' Then he asked, ' Do you want to see them ? ' ' Yes,' I said, ' but I tell you that I have killed them and buried them.' He then motioned that I should go further within the *anderun*. I did so, and there I saw all the slaves. They were sitting at ease and eating fruit." The writer of the *Khulasatu'l-Akhbár* observes, " This tradition appears in two or three books, but God is the one to determine whether it is true."[1]

These traditions would suggest, however, that for the most part the Imam Ali Naki was allowed considerable personal freedom in his life at Samarra—to meet his friends, to go in and out of the city on horseback, and to sit in the presence of the Caliph. He also had his own house, but he was closely watched by spies. It is said that Mutawakkil finally gave orders for his execution. " In open durbar he ordered his chamberlain to bring the Imam to his presence, and summoned four servants with naked swords to stand ready when the order was given to slay him. When the Imam left the hall of audience, the four servants stood by the door with drawn swords, but instead of striking him they threw away the swords, and fell at his feet and humbly saluted him. Mutawakkil inquired the cause of such strange conduct. They said that they saw near the Imam a person with a drawn sword who said : ' If you give any trouble to the Imam I will slay you all,' so they dared not obey the Caliph's order to slay him. Hence it is said that by divine aid the life of the Imam was saved.

" After a while Mutawakkil became very ill with a boil, which was so bad that he could neither sit nor rise. The royal

[1] *Khulasatu'l-Akhbár, op. cit.*, miracles Nos. 2, 3, and 4.

physicians wished to lance it, but the patient did not agree. Other remedies failed. Then Mutawakkil's mother sent secretly to the Imam for advice. He recommended a plaster which was made from the dung of goats. When the prescription was read the assembled doctors laughed and said it was useless, but Fatḥ ibn Khaḳán recommended that it should be tried. This was done and the boil at once burst and the patient was cured."[1]

The Caliph Mutawakkil was himself killed in the year A.D. 861 by the Turkish mercenaries who had come to control the affairs of Baghdad, and particularly to dominate the Caliphs at Samarra. His son Muntasir died a year later, and his successor Musta'in ruled only three years until his death in 865. But the Imam Ạli Naḳi still lived on as an honoured prisoner in Samarra. "His high qualities are duly set forth by Shi'ah historians. Allowing for the fulsome flattery which characterizes their accounts of the Imam, it does appear that he was a good-tempered, quiet man, who all his days suffered much from Mutawakkil's hatred, and under it all preserved his dignity and exhibited his patience."[2]

Yaḳubi says that he "died mysteriously on the twenty-sixth or twenty-seventh of Jamadí al-Akhir, 254 A.H. (868), and that al-Mu'tass sent for his brother Ahmad ibn al-Mutawakkil, who prayed for him in the quarter known as the district of Abu Ahmad, but when many people gathered and there was great tumult and crying, the bier was taken to his house and he was buried there in the courtyard. He had reached the age of forty years, and he left two sons, Ḥasan and Ja'far."[3]

[1] Sell, *Ithna Ạshariyya*, Madras, *C.L.S.*, 1925, p. 44; and *Khulasatu'l-Akhbár*, *op. cit.*, miracle No. 21.
[2] Sell, *op. cit.*, p. 47.
[3] Yaḳubi, *Tarikh*, edit. Houtsma, Vol. II, p. 614; and Mas'udi, *op. cit.*, p. 379.

CHAPTER XX

THE ELEVENTH IMAM, HASAN AL-ASKARI

THERE is doubt as to whether the eleventh Imam, Hasan al-Askari, was born in Medina or in Samarra, in the year 230 A.H., or one or two years later. Kulaini says he was born in 232, but has not committed himself in regard to the birth-place.[1] Majlisi has cited varying opinions of ancient authorities in the twelfth volume of his voluminous *Baharu'l-Anvár* (Oceans of Lights), without throwing any special light on the subject.[2] We know, however, that it was not until 234 A.H. that the Imam Ạli Naḳi was taken as a prisoner to Samarra, so that up until that time the family home was in Medina, where it would seem more probable that the boy was born. As in the case of quite the majority of the imams, his mother was a slave girl, who was honoured, after bearing children to her master, with the special title Umm Walad (mother of offspring). Her own name was Hadith, though there are some who say that she was called *Susan*, or *Ghazala*, or *Salil*, or *Haribta*. He himself acquired the titles *a-Sámat* (the Silent), *al-Hádí* (the Guide), *ar-Rafiḳ* (the Friend), *az-Zakí* (the Just), and *an-Naḳi* (the Pure). But the designation he usually received, indicating his residence in the "army town," was *al-Askari*. His patronymic was Abu Muhammad. The unsophisticated reader of Persian or Arabic books may at times be amused at the way the biographers frequently employ the patronymic in describing the doings of little boys, in such expressions as "When the father of Muhammad was two years old."

However, at that very time, when Abu Muhammad was two years old (or possibly three or four), his father, the Imam Ạli

[1] Kulaini, *Usulu'l-Káfi*, p. 208.

[2] Majlisi, *Baharu'l-Anwár*, xii, p. 122. Cf. Ibn Khallikan's brief notice, edit. Bulak, i, p. 147.

Naḳi (cf. ch. xviii) was suspected of being involved in plots against the Caliph Mutawakkil and was brought to Samarra as a prisoner. As he was allowed to live in his own house, the family were also permitted to come to Samarra. There the boy grew up and gave most of his time to study. In addition to the ordinary studies required of Muhammadan boys in the Ḳoran and the *Shari'at* he may have occupied himself somewhat with languages, for in later years one of the remarkable things that was observed about him was that he could talk Hindi with the pilgrims from India, Turkish with the Turks, and Persian with the Persians.[1] He and his father and his grandfather were each spoken of at times as "Ibn Riḍa," for there was a large sect of the Shi'ites, the Waḳifiyya, who contended that the imamate stopped with Ạli ar-Riḍa and who were thus unwilling to concede that it was continued through his descendants.

One of the miracles related about Hasan al-Askari is that in his early childhood he fell into a well and the women of the household cried out in despair and ran to report the accident to his father, who was busy saying his prayers. The father was unruffled, as the account runs, and assured them that the boy would be all right. He went deliberately to the well, and behold, the child was seen gaily playing on the top of the water, and more than that, the water rose quickly to the surface so that he was rescued with ease.[2]

When he was seventeen or eighteen years old, during the caliphate of Musta'in, he is said to have had the satisfaction of riding a high-spirited mule that belonged to the Caliph. It was rumoured that the Caliph fully expected that the mule would kill him, but much to his surprise, the Imam showed complete ability to master the animal.

An interesting story is told of the great pains his father took to procure for his son a Christian slave girl. He entrusted this important matter to his friend Bashar ibn Sulaiman. First he wrote a letter in the "script of Rum" and sealed it with his own

[1] *Khulasatu'l-Akhbár*, ch. xxxix, miracle No. 17.
[2] *Ibid.*, *op. cit.*, miracle No. 19.

noble seal. He placed the letter in a red purse, with 220 dinars, and then said to his friend, "Take this and go to Baghdad. Go to the ferry at the river when the boats from Syria are being unloaded. When you observe that most of the buyers of the female slaves are the agents of the Beni Ạbbas, and that there are only a few of the young Arabs making purchases, spend that whole day on the look-out for a shipowner whose name is Amr ibn Yezid. Observe when he exhibits a slave girl who will wear two silk garments to protect her from being seen or handled by the buyers. You will hear her call out in the language of Rum, 'Even if you have wealth and the glory of Solomon the son of David, I can never have affection for you, so take care lest you waste your money.' And if a buyer approaches her she will say, 'Cursed be the man who unveils my eyebrow!' Her owner will then protest, 'But what recourse have I, I am compelled to sell you?' You will then hear the slave answer, 'Why this haste, let me choose my purchaser, that my heart may accept him in confidence and gratitude.'

"You are to go, then, O Bashar, and tell Amr ibn Yezid that you have a letter, written in the script of Rum by a certain nobleman, and that this letter shows his kindness, appreciation, and liberality. You must give the letter to the slave to read, that she may discern from it the character of the man who desires to buy her."

Bashar reported later, "When I carried out these instructions, and gave the girl the letter, she was not able to keep from crying as she read it. Then she said to Amr ibn Yezid, 'Sell me to the writer of this letter, for if you refuse I will surely kill myself.' I therefore talked over the price with Amr until we agreed on the 220 dinars my master had given me. When I had paid the money, and received the girl, she came with me without protest. In fact she was laughing and very happy. And in her excitement she took the letter of the Imam Ạli Naḳi from her pocket and kissed it, and put it on her eyes and her eyebrows, and rubbed it on her face and her body. I told her I was amazed that she should act this way when as yet she did not know the writer. She answered, 'May the offspring of the Prophet dispel your doubts!' Afterwards she gave me the following account of herself:

"'I am a princess, the granddaughter of the Emperor of Rum. My mother was a descendant of the disciple Thimun (Simon), the vicegerent (wasí) of Jesus. My grandfather, the Emperor, was anxious to marry me to his nephew. I was thirteen years old. At his castle he gathered a great assembly, including 300 monks and hermits, 700 of the nobility, and 4,000 of the officials of the army and the landed gentry. He had had a special throne made, which was inlaid with jewels. It stood in the court of the castle and was approached by forty steps. On that throne he had his nephew seated in state, and round about the throne there were images standing. Christian priests were there to pay him honour. They opened the Injíl (New Testament, literally "gospel") and the supports of the throne gave way and all the images fell. My cousin also fell down with his throne, and he fainted. All the great officials and the gentry were overcome with fear, and said, 'O King, preserve us from witnessing this ill-fated day, for this sort of a thing is a proof of the decline and disappearance of the Christian religion.' At this my grandfather was exceedingly angry, and commanded that the pillars of the throne should again be made firm, and that the images should be put back in their places, and that my unfortunate cousin should be brought forth once more for his wedding. But again the same thing happened, and this time the people were so terrified that they scattered in all directions. My grandfather fell himself and it was in sorrow and chagrin that he arose and went to his private quarters.

"'One night after this I saw a dream, in which Jesus appeared with his disciples at the place where the throne had been erected. There they built a pulpit of light, and behold, Muhammad, peace be upon him and his family, and his *wasí* (Ạli), and all his exalted descendants had come into the castle. Jesus went forward to embrace Muhammad, who said, "O Spirit of God, I have come to seek the daughter of your *wasí*, Thimun, for my son Hasan al-Askari." Jesus looked to Thimun (who was among the disciples), and said, " Nobility and glory has come to you in this opportunity to unite your mercy with that of the family of Muhammad." To this Thimun assented, and all of them ascended the pulpit of light, while Muhammad conducted the wedding service. After the dream, when I awoke I was afraid, and dared not repeat the story of what I had seen for fear that my father or my brother would kill me. While I kept the secret, love for Hasan al-Askari found its place in my heart and constrained me to give up drinking wine and I did not want to eat. Consequently I grew thin and ill. My father consulted every doctor in the city in vain. Finally he said to me, " O you who have seen a light, is there some desire in your heart that I might satisfy ? " I answered, " The doors of pleasure are closed for me, however, if you set free the Moslem prisoners, it is possible that Jesus and his mother may help me." My father granted my request, and after that I took a little food and felt better. A few days passed and I had another vision, when Fatima and Zahra and Maryam came to me and explained that the Imam Hasan al-Askari could not come to me unless I should become a Muhammadan and declare, *There is no god but God, and Muhammad is the Apostle of God.* This I accepted, and after that every night I saw Hasan al-Askari in a vision.' "

" But how did you come to fall among the prisoners ? " Bashar asked her. She replied, " The Imam Hasan told me that my father was planning to send an army against the Moslems, and that I should disguise myself and some of my women and arrange to go along with that army. I did this, and before long some of the Moslem guards captured us, and now you see how it has turned out."

Bashar has related that when they reached Samarra he went to the Imam Ạli Naḳi, who received them gladly. The Imam asked the girl if he should give her ten thousand dinars or a bit of good news. When she chose the latter he informed her that she was to be given to his son Hasan, as she had seen in her dreams, and that she was to be the mother of the one who was to cause justice to reign upon the earth. She was then committed to the

Imam Ali Naḳi's sister, Hakimah (or Halimah), who was to look after her instruction in the customs of Islam.

Such is the account of the purchase of Narjis Khatun (Madame Narcissus) that Majlisi has given at somewhat greater length from Shaikh Tusi.[1] There is no description of a wedding, however, for after all she was but a slave girl, who had been bought and paid for, and all that remained was for the father to hand her over to his son. The aunt, Hakimah, relates how she dressed up the girl and sent her to Hasan al-Askari. " For a few days," she said, " I had them together in my house, and then I sent them both to my brother's house. And it was about that time that my brother was taken from the world, and Hasan al-Askari took his place as the Imam."[2]

After the death of the Imam Ali Naḳi, the Caliph Mu'tazz had one of his Turkish guards, Shaḡí al-Kab, take Hasan al-Askari to Baghdad, where he was kept in prison during the short reign of the succeeding caliph, al-Muktadi. Most of his prison experiences, however, were in the time of the next caliph, al-Mu'tamid, who is represented in the special Shi'ite book that has been written in memory of Hasan al-Askari[3] as his particular oppressor. Sometimes he was denied water for his ceremonial ablutions. Once he was taken where the lions were kept, and was pushed inside the enclosure. He was not afraid, they say, but patted the animals and spread his prayer cloth on the ground and began to pray, while the lions stood around him in a circle, and the officer in charge ran to tell the Caliph to come and watch what was happening.

According to the *Aḳa'id ush-Shi'ah*,[4] he had no legal wife, and the one of his concubines who was the mother of his son Muhammad al-Ḳa'im, was Narjis Khatun, who was the daughter of Yashu'á, the son of the Emperor of Rúm. His only children were the son and the daughter she bore him.

The suggestion has been made that slaves were given pet names,

[1] Majlisi, *Baharu'l-Anwár*, Vol. XIII (Persian translation), p. 4.
[2] Majlisi, *op. cit.*, p. 7.
[3] *Al-Askari*, p. 30 ff. Cf. Sell, *Ithna Ashariyya*, p. 49.
[4] *Aḳa'id ush-Shi'ah*, Bk. IV, ch. ii.

such as *Narjis* (narcissus), *Susan* (lily), and *Khamt* (fragrant milk). Perhaps the idea has poetic value, but the fact seems to be that these names were rather those in common use among the Christian peoples from whom the slave girls were captured. The story that Narjis Khatun was a princess may be but a fiction to enhance the nobility of the twelfth imam, but it is well within the range of probability that she was indeed a slave who had been taken from somewhere in the Byzantine empire, and who had been sold into that type of slavery that provided concubines for the harems of the gentry in Moslem cities. Wavell has called attention to the fact that this sort of slave traffic was still being carried on in Mecca in 1912.[1]

While the Imam Hasan al-Askari was a prisoner, there was a severe drought with a consequent famine in Baghdad. A Christian priest was said to have lifted up his hands toward heaven and to have prayed, with the result that rain fell. The Caliph was concerned lest for this reason the people would forsake Islam. When the Imam was consulted he said that if the people would gather in one place he would remove their doubts. He was allowed to leave his prison and to go before the people, to whom he said, "When the priest prays, seize his hand!" They did this and found that the priest was holding in his hand a bone, which the Imam declared was from the body of some prophet of God, "for when a prophet's bone was lifted up that way, the clouds would come and rain would fall." In this way he succeeded in removing the doubts of the people, and in recognition of his services the Caliph allowed him to return to his home in Samarra.[2]

It is related also that once the Imam was accosted by a beggar who swore that he had absolutely nothing on which to live. The Imam rebuked him, as he declared, for swearing to a lie. He then gave him 100 dinars on the understanding that hereafter he was not to swear to a falsehood. "And for doing

[1] Wavell, *A Modern Pilgrim in Mecca*, p. 142. On the question of the names of slave girls, see Friedlander, *J.A.O.S.*, Vol. 29, p. 54.
[2] *Khulasatu'l-Akhbár*, *op. cit.*, miracles 14; and Sell, *op. cit.*, p. 50.

so on this occasion," the Imam admonished him, "you will be greatly in need of the 200 dinars you now have hidden in your house, and you will not be able to find them." The beggar afterwards testified that the time came when he wanted exactly this amount, which was what he had hidden, but he discovered that his worthless son had stolen it and gone away.

Another story is related by a man who said he had gone to see the Imam Hasan al-Askari, and while he was seated in his presence, he suddenly remembered that he had fastened fifty dinars in the sleeve of his coat, but when he felt to see if it was there, he failed to find it and feared that he had dropped it. The Imam saw his confusion and said to him, "Do not worry, it fell in your brother's house and he is keeping it for you." When he returned, as the Imam had said, his brother had it and gave it to him.[1]

One of the Imam's visitors said that when he had seated himself, the Imam said to him, "Look under your feet, for you are sitting on a carpet on which many of the prophets and apostles and imams have sat." He sat there thinking to himself, "Would that I could see this carpet!" Reading his thoughts, the Imam said, "Come near to me." He went closer and the Imam drew his blessed hand across his face so as to give him supernatural discernment. Then he saw the carpet, on which the Imam pointed out the footprints of Adam, Abel, Seth, and Noah; of Kedar, the son of Ishmael and the progenitor of the Arabians; of Ezra, Enoch, Methusaleh, Hud, Abraham and Lot; of Isaac, Joseph, Jacob, Moses, David, and Solomon; then of Khizr, Daniel, Elisha, and Alexander the Great; and finally of Abdu'l-Muṭṭalib, of Abdu'l-Manaf, of Muhammad, of Ạli, of the several Imams who were his descendants, and of the Mahdi himself. After this remarkable experience, the visitor relates, "the Imam told me to close my eyes, and after I did so, I found that I had returned to my former situation and could no longer perceive the carpet."[2]

[1] *Ibid., op. cit.,* miracles Nos. 12 and 20.
[2] *Ibid., o . cit.,* miracle No. 24.

During the last four or five years that the Imam Hasan al-Askari lived, his chief annoyance from the Caliph was the restriction of the payment of the "one-fifth," which was a tax on particular products and which went to a charity fund from which many of the descendants of the Prophet were accustomed to receive assistance. In the early days the income from the garden of Fadak, which had once belonged to the Prophet Muhammad, had been set aside by Omar II for the Prophet's descendants, but later caliphs had taken this also for the state treasury.

It was in 260 A.H. (873), by a general agreement of the authorities, that the eleventh imam, Abu Muḥammad Ḥasan al-Askari died in his own house in Samarra, where he was buried in the same place with his father.[1] The people's handbooks say that he died from "the poison of Mu'tamid al-Ạbbasí."[2]

[1] Mas'udi, *Muruju'l-Dhahab*, Vol. VIII, p. 40; and Majlisi, *Baharu'l-Anwár*, Vol. XII, p. 140.
[2] *Tadhkiratu'l-A'imma*, p. 158; and the *Aḳa'id ush-Shi'ah*, Bk. IV, ch. ii.

CHAPTER XXI

THE HIDDEN IMAM, WHO IS EXPECTED TO RETURN

FOR the Sunnites the " Mahdi " stands for " an eschatological individual in the future," of whom " the Prophet gave good tidings that he would come in the End of Time."[1] The word means the one who is absolutely guided by God, and it is in this sense that he is regarded as worthy to guide others. The term that occurs in the Ḳoran, however, is not *al-mahdi*, the one guided, but the active participle, *al-hádí*, the guide (Surahs xxii, 53; and xxv, 33). In the first reference it is declared that " God is surely the Guider of those who believe," and the second reference states, " But thy Lord is a sufficient guide and helper." It is obvious that these references are not in themselves sufficient to justify the expectation of the coming of the " Mahdi," but they have been subsequently utilized as a background for an elaborate premillennial hope, which is based on traditions that have been summarized as follows[2]:

" The world will not come to an end," said the Prophet Muḥammad, " until a man of my tribe and of my name shall be master of Arabia."

" When you see black ensigns coming from the direction of Khorasan, then join them, for the Imam of God will be with the standards, whose name is *al-Mahdi*."

" The *Mahdi* will be descended from me, he will be a man with an open countenance and with a high nose. He will fill the earth with equity and with justice, even as it has been filled with tyranny and oppression, and he will reign over the earth seven years."

" Quarrelling and disputation shall exist amongst men, and then shall a man of the people of al-Madínah come forth, and shall go from al-Madínah to Mekkah, and the people of Mekkah shall

[1] Macdonald, *Encyclopædia of Islam*, Vol. III, p. 112.

[2] Hughes, *Dictionary of Islam*, p. 305, translated from the *Mishkátu'l-Maṣábih*, Bk. XXIII, ch. 3.

make him Imám. Then shall the ruler of Syria send an army against the *Mahdi*, but the Syrian army shall perish by an earthquake near Badá', between al-Madínah and Mekkah. And when the people shall see this, the Abdál will come from Syria, and also a multitude from al-Iráq. After this an enemy to the *Mahdi* shall arise from the Quraish tribe, whose uncles shall be of the tribe of Kalb, and this man shall send an army against the *Mahdi*. The *Mahdi* shall rule according to the example of your Prophet, and shall give strength and stability to Islam. He shall reign for seven years and then die."

"There shall be much rain in the days of the *Mahdi* and the inhabitants both of heaven and earth shall be pleased with him. Men's lives shall pass so pleasantly, that they will wish even the dead were alive again."

It is very probable that the dismal failure of the Muhammadan Empire to attain to equity and justice during the period of the Umayyad caliphate (41-132 A.H.) may have had something to do with the rise of the tradition that one absolutely guided by God would come in the End of Time. Very early indeed, in 66 A.H., after the killing of Ạli and of Husain, and after the prolonged horrors of civil strife, the term *mahdi* had been applied to Muhammad, the son of Ạli by the Hanifite woman. He was called "*al-mahdi ibn al-wasí*" (the legatee, i.e., Ạli), and when he died and was buried on Mount Raḍwá, the sect that had followed him began looking for his return from this mountain. Thus he came to be the "expected Mahdi."[1] It is noteworthy that this use of the term, which may be said to be known to history, was nearly two hundred years before the compilation of any of the standard books of traditions, so that there was ample time for the hopes of pious Moslems to crystallize into ever more definite eschatological beliefs. At the same time the very fact that the Ḳoran did not warrant any such hopes made it all the more necessary that they should be confirmed by appropriate and reassuring traditions.[2]

Ibn Khaldun, however, has thrown doubt on the validity of these traditions, for he called attention to the fact that they are not included in the great works of Bukharí or Muslim, and he

[1] Macdonald, *op. cit.*, p. 112.
[2] Wensinck, *A Handbook of Early Muhammadan Traditions*, p. 130.

questioned the right of Tirmidhí and of Abu Dáúd to rely on the authority of Ạsim, for as he pointed out, on the testimony of several of his contemporaries, "all the Ạsims have had bad memories." Accordingly, on account of the indefiniteness of the Ḳoranic statements and the untrustworthy character of the pertinent traditions, the Sunnite systematic theologians have not required belief in the coming of the *Mahdi* in their creeds. Nevertheless, Ibn Khaldun recognised the prevalence of this expectation as a popular belief among the Sunnites, for he wrote: "It has been commonly accepted among the masses of the people of Islam, as the ages have passed, that there must needs appear in the End of Time a man of the family of Muhammad who will aid the Faith and make justice triumph, that the Muslims will follow him, and that he will reign over the Muslim kingdoms and be called *al-Mahdi*."[1]

For the Shi'ite theologians, on the other hand, the expectation of the coming of the Mahdi is an essential belief. They maintain that the terms in the Ḳoran that express the idea of divine guidance should be referred scrupulously to the Imams, and they give special emphasis to the verse which says, "And among those whom we have created are a people who guide others with truth, and in accordance therewith act justly" (Surah vii, 180). Kulaini and others of the Shi'ite teachers have asserted, on the basis of traditions from the Imam Ja'far a -Ṣadiḳ and from the Imam Baḳír, that the word *ummat* (people) signifies the *a'imma* (the Imams) of the family of Muḥammad, and there is a tradition that Ạli said, "This people will be divided into seventy-three sects, seventy-two of which will be in Jahannam (Hell), and but one in Bahisht (Heaven), and it is only that one sect that God referred to in this text."[2] Many verses in the Ḳoran refer directly to the resurrection judgment (al-Ḳiyáma),[3] and the reference to the "one standing" in judgment, in the verse, "Who is it

[1] Ibn Khaldun, *Muḳaddima*, ed. Quatremere, ii, p. 142 ff. Cf. translation by Macdonald, *op. cit.*, p. 113, and by Guillaume, *The Traditions of Islam*, pp. 89-93.

[2] Majlisi, *Hayatu'l-Qulub*, iii, section 32, p. 290.

[3] Macdonald, *Encyclopædia of Islam*, Vol. II, p. 1048.

then that is standing over every soul to mark its actions?" (Surah xiii, 33), is believed to be to the *Mahdi*.[1]

But with the Shi'ites also the Ḳoran has not been regarded as sufficiently explicit, and what is lacking has been supplied in the traditions. According to a clear statement by Majlisi,[2] the Prophet Muhammad is related to have said:

"O ye people! I am the Prophet and Ạli is my heir, and from us will descend *al-Mahdi*, the seal (i.e., the last) of the Imams, who will conquer all religions and take vengeance on the wicked. He will take fortresses and destroy them, and slay every tribe of idolaters, and he will avenge the deaths of the martyrs of God. He will be the champion of the Faith, and a drawer of water at the fountain of divine knowledge. He will reward merit and requite every fool according to his folly. He will be the approved and chosen of God, and the heir of all knowledge. He will be valiant in doing right and the one to whom the Most High has entrusted Islam. . . . O ye people, I have explained to you, and Ạli also will make you understand it."

In the Shi'ite hope, however, both in the hearts of the multitude and in the declarations of the theologians, the coming of the Mahdi is identified with the *radj'a* (return) of the Hidden Imam. There are accordingly three salient points to consider, first, to inquire what may be known about the Twelfth and Last Imam before the time of his concealment (ghaibat); second, to indicate from the best authorities what the doctrine of his concealment is; and third, to describe the nature of the Shi'ite expectation of his return.

The Twelfth Imam, who is called the Master of the Age, is said to have been born in Samarra in 255 or 256 A.H. This would have been four or five years before the death of his father, the Imam Hasan al-Askarí. We observe that what is related about the child is scrupulously adapted to what was expected of the Mahdi, and this fact in itself throws suspicion on the traditions that afford the only evidence of his life. Over two hundred years before his time the Prophet had declared, or so we are told,

[1] R. Strothmann, *Encyclopædia of Islam*, art. "al-Ḳá'im," Vol. II, p. 642; and Majlisi, *op. cit.*, iii, section 35.
[2] Majlisi, *Hayatu'l-Qulub*, Merrick's translation of Vol. II, p. 342; and Hughes, *Dictionary of Islam*, p. 305.

that "his name shall be my name, his patronymic will also be mine, and his titles will be al-Mahdi (the One Guided), al-Hujjat (the Proof), al-Muntazar (the One Awaited), and aṣ-Ṣahibu'l-Zamán (the Master of the Age). We are not therefore greatly surprised to find that these names are repeatedly ascribed to him in the traditions.[1]

The son of one of his father's head servants has related: "When he was born the Imam Hasan al-Askarí called for my father and told him that ten thousand *raṭl* (about one thousand *man*) of bread, and ten thousand *raṭl* of meat should be given in charity to the Beni Hashim and others, and that many sheep should be killed. This was for the *ákíḳa*," which was a sacrifice that had been customary from pre-Islamic times on the seventh day after the birth of a child. Also two of the Imam Hasan al-Askarí's slave girls, Nísím and Máríya, have related that when His Excellency al-Ká'im was born, he knelt at once and raised his forefingers in witness towards heaven, sneezed, and said: "Praise to God the Lord of the Worlds, and salutation to Muhammad and his Family!" Then they said that he continued speaking, and said, "The oppressors thought that the Proof of God would disappear, but if I get the opportunity for speech there will be no further doubt about God." Nísím has also related that one night when she went to attend the child, she sneezed, and the boy said, "By the command of God! I am very glad. Do you want me to tell you what is indicated in your sneeze?" When she assented, he said, "You are safe from death for three days."

According to the report of his aunt Halimah, when the boy was born he exclaimed, "I testify that there is no God but God, and that my grandfather (a good many generations removed) was the Apostle of God, and that my father was the Amiru'l-Mu'minín and the Friend of God." Then he counted the Imams one by one until he came to himself, when he said, "O God, fulfil my covenant, perfect my service, vindicate my authority,

[1] Ibn Babawaihi (d. 381 A.H.), *Kamalu'd-Dín*, Teheran 1307 A.H., p. 240; and Majlisi, *Haḳu'l-Yaḳín*, p. 146.

and fill the earth with righteousness and justice." The aunt related that then the Imam Hasan al-Asharí called her to bring the boy to him, and when she picked him up she found that he was already circumcised, and that the birth cord had been cut and his navel was clean, and that on his right arm was written, "Truth has appeared and folly has vanished, surely folly is destined to perish."

When the Imam Hasan al-Askarí received the child, according to Halimah's account, he fondled him for a while and the boy conversed with his father in fluent Arabic, in praise of God and the Imamate, when a flock of birds came and hovered close to his head. The Imam Hasan al-Askarí called to one of these birds and said, "Take this infant and nurture him well, and bring him to us every forty days." The bird took him and flew off into the sky. The Imam repeated the command to the rest of the birds and they also flew after him. The Imam remarked, "I have committed you to the one to whom Moses' mother entrusted him." Then his mother, Narjis Khatún, began to cry. The Imam rebuked her and said, "Be quiet, he will not take milk, but they will shortly bring him back to you, just as in the case of Moses, whom they restored to his mother." Halimah relates that then she asked, "What bird was this to which you committed him?" The Imam answered, "This was the Holy Spirit, the guardian of the Imams, to make them worthy messengers from God, to protect them from sin, and to equip them with learning." Halimah went on to say that afterwards, when forty days had passed, she went to see her brother and she saw the child walking about the house. At this she expressed her surprise, but she was assured by her brother that such a child would make the growth in a month that might be expected of ordinary children in a year. For he said that while in the womb the Imams are known to speak, to read the Ḳoran, and to worship their Preserver. He said that while they are still in their infancy, the angels instruct them, for they descend to their service each morning and evening.

Ḥalimah went to see her brother every forty days until a few days before his death. And on that occasion she met a fully grown man whom she failed to recognize as her nephew, but her brother assured her that he was indeed his son, born of Narjis and none other, and that he was to be his successor in the imamate as he himself expected soon to depart from the world. "Therefore," he said, "accept his word and obey his commands." It was only a few days after that that her brother died, and she saw the Master of the Age every morning and evening, and he answered whatever she asked, and often told her beforehand just what she wanted to know.[1]

It was near the time of the death of his father that the boy, who was called Muḥammad, is said to have been designated as the Imam. A certain Isma'íl has reported: "I visited the Imam Hasan in his final illness, and I sat beside him. He said to Ạḳíd, his servant, 'Prepare for me a brew of gum-mastic,'[2] and directly the mother of the Master of the Age brought the bowl and put it into the hand of Hasan Askarí. But when he tried to drink, his hand trembled so that the bowl struck his teeth. He set it aside and said to Ạḳíd, 'Go into that room and have the child who is praying there come to me.' Ạḳíd said, 'When I entered the room I saw a child saying his prayers, with his forefingers raised to heaven. When I saluted him he *lightened* his prayer (namázra sabuk kard) and said, 'Salaam.' When he finished his prayer, I said, 'My Master commands you to come to him.' Then his mother came and took his hand and brought him to his father. When he came before his father the noble child's complexion was luminous, his hair curly, and his teeth showing (as he smiled). When the dying Imam looked upon him he wept and said, 'O Master of your own household, give me a drink, for I go to my Preserver.' The child took the bowl

[1] Majlisi, *Baharu'l-Anwár*, Vol. 13, Persian translation, pp. 2-4; and *Haḳu'l-Yaḳín*, p. 146 ff.; and Ibn Babawaihi, *op. cit.*, p. 240. Cf. Mas'udi, *Ithbát al-Wasíya li Ạli b. Abi Ṭalib*, pp. 195-200.

[2] "The lentisk or mastic plant (μαστίχη) is indigenous to the Mediterranean coast region from Syria to Spain. . . . During the 15th, 16th and 17th centuries mastic enjoyed a high reputation as a medicine, and formed an ingredient in a large number of medical compounds; but its use in medicine is now obsolete, and it is chiefly employed for making varnish" (*Encyclopædia Britannica*, 11th edit., Vol. XVII).

of gum-mastic water (ábi maṣṭakí), touched it to his lips in prayer, and gave it to his father. When he drank it, he said, 'Make me ready for prayer.' So the Master of the Age took a towel and gave his father the ceremonial ablution, and anointed his head and his feet. The dying Imam then declared, 'O my dear child, you are the Master of the Age, you are the Mahdi, you are the Proof of God on earth, my child, my *wasí* (representative), and, as my offspring, you are *m-h-m-d* (Muḥammad), my good son, a child of the Apostle, the last of the Imams, pure and virtuous. The Apostle of God has informed the people about you. He has mentioned your name and your patronymic. This is the covenant of my fathers that has come down to me'— and at that moment the Imam died." Such is the story that Isma'íl heard from the servant of Ạḳíd, and which is repeated in many popular books on the authority of Shaikh Tusí.[1]

It was apparently at about this time that the boy disappeared, or went "into concealment." According to the *Jannatu'l-Khulud*,[2] "he disappeared in his own home, which he had inherited from his father, in Samarra, in a cellar (sardáb) in that house which had several steps leading to it. It was the place where he and his father used to conceal themselves from the annoyance of the wicked when they wished to perform their devotions. There is great reward to the one who visits him and his father at this place. At the time of his disappearance he was six, or seven, or nine years of age, plus several months and some days, according to differences in the records." The *Aḳa'id ush-Shi'ah* (Mishkát iv) makes no mention of the manner in which he disappeared, but observes that the statement that "the Imam has not yet been born is a mistake and the statement that he was born and died during the lifetime of his father is also a mistake, so therefore it is necessary to believe that he has been born and that he is alive, *but in concealment,* and that by God's will he shall appear at the End of Time."

While it is the general Shi'ite opinion of the present day,

[1] Majlisi, *Haḳu'l-Yaḳin* p. 146 ff.; and Ibn Babawaihi, *op. cit.*, p. 240.
[2] *Jannatu'l-Khulud,* table xix.

which is in accord with the older authorities, that it was in Samarra that he disappeared, yet in the seventh or eighth century of the Moslem era (approximately four hundred years after the event), it was sometimes said that it was in Hilla. Ibn Khaldun and Ibn Khallikan and Ibn Batuta evidently had this impression,[1] and Ibn Khaldun states that "when imprisoned with his mother, he entered a sort of well or pit in the house that his family occupied at Hilla, and there he disappeared, but he is to come forth at the end of the age to fill the earth with justice."

The opinion that, if he lived at all, he was mysteriously lost very close to the time of his father's death, is confirmed by the fact that the traditions attribute miraculous reappearances to him immediately in connection with his father's funeral and to defend his own rights at the time of the distribution of the property. We are informed, for example, that when his uncle, the "false Ja'far," was about to say the prayer at the Imam Hasan's funeral, "a fair child, with curly hair, and shining teeth" appeared and seized his uncle's cloak and insisted that he himself should offer the prayer. And a few days later a company of pilgrims came from Ḳum to visit the Imam who they found was dead. They inquired for his successor, and were told by some of the Shi'ites that his brother, Ja'far, had taken his place. They said they would accept him if he would prove himself by telling them their several names and indicating how much money they had. While Ja'far was protesting against this examination, a servant of the boy Ḳa'im appeared, saying that his master had sent him to say that they had certain particular names and a definite amount of money. Accordingly they sent the servant to tell his master that they accepted him. And when Ja'far had laid false claim to the inheritance, the Master of the Age appeared at the side of the house and said, "Why do you lay claim to my rights?" Ja'far could but turn pale and keep silence. His Excellency then disappeared, and Ja'far hunted

[1] Ibn Khaldun, *Muḳaddima*, edit. Quatremere, i, p. 359; and Ibn Khallikan, trans. de Slane, ii, p. 581; and Ibn Batuta, edit. and trans. C. Defremery and R. B. Sanquinetti, ii, 98. Cf. *Encyclopædia of Religion and Ethics*, Vol. VIII, p. 338, which shows that Shahrastani (ed. Cureton, p. 128) and the Tarikh-i-Guzidah (ed. Brown, p. 208) do not connect the Mahdi with Hilla.

everywhere but could find no signs of him. The grandmother of the Imam Hasan appeared and ordered that he should be buried in that house. Ja'far interfered and said, "This is my house, do not bury him here." Again the Master of the Age appeared and said, "O Ja'far, is this your house?" And at once he departed and they saw him no more.[1]

The traditions are full of instances when he was manifested to believers, after prayer or in time of need. But for a period of about seventy years he was represented on earth by *wakíls*, i.e., by agents or advocates. The first of these was Ụthmán ibn Sa'íd. When Ụthmán died he was succeeded by his son, Abu Ja'far, who in turn designated Abu'l-Ḳasim ibn Ruh, who appointed Abu'l-Hasan Samarrí. When the latter was about to die they urged him to designate someone in his place, but he refused, and replied, "Now the matter is with God."[2] Accordingly the period when the Hidden Imam was represented by his *wakíls* is known as the "Lesser Concealment," and this period extended, it is said, from A.D. 869-940. Since that time the Shi'ite Mahdi or the Hidden Imam has been in the "Great Concealment," and he is not expected to return until just before the End of Time.

The doctrine of his *ghaiba*, or concealment, declares simply that he has been withdrawn by God from the eyes of men, that his life has been miraculously prolonged, that he has been seen from time to time, has been in correspondence with others, and maintains a control over the fortunes of his people.[3] An interesting illustration of the way the people have been encouraged to seek the assistance of the Hidden Imam is found in the practice of sending him short letters. In the manual in which he sets forth the many duties and privileges of pilgrims, Majlisi has given an accepted form for a short letter in Arabic, which anyone can write or have written and sent to the Master of the Age. It may be placed on the tombs of any of the Imams, or it may be

[1] Majlisi, *Haḳu'l-Yaḳin*, pp. 152 and 146.
[2] Ibn Babawaihi, *Kamalu'd-Din*, p. 241. Cf. Majlisi, *Baharu'l-Anwar*, Persian trans., Vol. XIII, p. 8.
[3] Macdonald, *Encyclopædia of Islam*, art. "Ghaiba," Vol. II, p. 135.

fastened and sealed, and covered with clean earth, and cast into the sea or into a deep well. In any case it will reach the Hidden Imam and he will give it his personal attention.[1]

It is, however, in portraying the nature of the return (raj'a) of the Hidden Imam that the Shi'ite traditionists are at their best. In the elaboration of the doctrine of the return of the Hidden Imam special emphasis is given to the following verses in the Ḳoran (Surah xxviii. 2-6):

"We will recite to thee portions of the History of Moses and Pharaoh with truth, for *the teaching* of the faithful.

"Now Pharaoh lifted himself up in the earth, and divided his people into parties: one portion of them he brought low—He slew their male children, and let their females only live; for he was one of those who wrought disorders.

"And we were minded to shew favour to those who were brought low in the land, and to make them spiritual chiefs (imams) and to make them *Pharaoh's* heirs.

"And to establish them in the land; and to make Pharaoh and Haman and their hosts the eyewitnesses of what they dreaded from them.

"And we said by revelation to the mother of Moses, 'Give him suck; and if thou fearest for him, launch him on the sea; and fear not, neither fret; for we will restore him to thee, and make him one of the apostles.'"

When asked for his interpretation of this passage the Imam Zainu'l-Abidín is said to have replied: "I swear by the truth of God who surely sent Muḥammad, that the good are we People of the Household and our followers, like Moses and his followers, whereas our enemies and their partisans are like Pharaoh and his followers."[2] Majlisi's own succinct statement of the doctrine of the return is that "on the Day of Judgment, in the time of His Excellency the 'One Standing,' a great assembly of the good, who have been very good, and of the evil who have been very bad, will return to the world. The bad will return for retribution and suffering here on earth, and to see much more glory given to the People of the Household of the Apostle than that which they have

[1] Majlisi, *Tofatu'z-Za'irin*, p. 396.
[2] Majlisi, *Hayatu'l-Qulub*, Vol. III, sect. 35, p. 303.

denied them. The return of these evil ones is that they may undergo particularly severe punishment. Other people will remain in their graves until the final resurrection. There are many traditions to confirm the teaching that only those will return at the time of return (raj'a) who have either been especially distinguished for their faith or for their unbelief, whereas the rest of mankind will remain in their own state."[1] Thus the return is represented as a preliminary judgment, in which the Hidden Imam and his followers will be vindicated, and those who have refused to give them their rightful place of leadership will suffer just retribution. For example, among the first to come back to earth will be Husain ibn Ạli, with his followers, and at the same time will come the wicked Yezid ibn Muawiyya, with his supporters, and against them all Husain and his army will take summary vengeance.[2]

In discussing the question of the return of believers, a distinction has been made between those who have been killed by violence and those who have died a natural death. The Imam Riḍa is said to have pronounced that "Whatever believer dies a natural death in this life will be killed at the time of the return, and likewise whatever believer is killed in this life will die a natural death at the time of the return. . . . Hence one who is killed by the sword has no advantage over one who dies under the bedcovers, for the one must come back to drink the cup of death and the other must return to be killed." The prophets who have been killed are to return according to the Imam Baḳir, and are to be established in their homes, to eat food, to marry, and to live as God wishes, enjoying their lives, and after that they will die among their own people.[3]

When Ạli reappears on earth he will have the staff of Moses and the ring of Solomon. He will meet his companions by the Euphrates, near Kufa, and they will go forth to fight Satan, who will be at the head of an army of all of those who have followed him

[1] Majlisi, *Haḳu'l-Yaḳin*, p. 160; and *Baharu'l-Anwár*, Persian trans., Vol. XIII, p. 335 ff.
[2] Majlisi, *Baharu'l-Anwár*, Persian trans., Vol. XIII, p. 341.
[3] *Ibid.*, p. 336.

from the time of Adam until that day. Then there shall occur a battle such as never happened before. And the forces of the Amiru'l-Muminín will indeed be forced back a hundred paces, until the feet of some of them are in the river. At that time a cloud will arise in the sky, and in front of this will come a host of angels, led by Muḥammad, the Apostle of God, armed with a spear of light. But when Satan sees Muḥammad, he and his hosts will give way. Muḥammad will kill him with his gleaming spear and all of his almost innumerable army will be destroyed.[1]

One of the strangest characters who is expected to return is Ṣá'if ibn Ṣá'id, or as some say the son of the sorcerer Shiḳḳ. The Prophet Muḥammad's encounter with him, in company with Ụmar and others of his Companions, in a place called Rahtun, is related by al-Bukhári and Ahmad ibn Hanbal and Tirmidhi,[2] and like the Shi'ite traditionists, supposedly on the authority of the Prophet,[3] they usually identify this Ṣá'if ibn Ṣá'id with *al-masíḥ ad-Dajjál* (the false Christ) who is expected to return before the Mahdi. A popular and modern book in Persian (Teheran, 1328 A.H.), called the *Nuru'l-Anwár* or *Light of Lights*, describes this Ibn Ṣá'id as he was known in real life and shows how he is expected to reappear.[4]

Muḥammad went with several of his Companions to the house where it was understood that Ṣá'if lived. Ụmar knocked at the door, and an old woman came and admitted them to the outer court of the house. Muḥammad had heard that he was regarded by the Jews as a prophet and thought that he would test him by asking him about two of the surahs in the Ḳoran (Nos. 61 and 87). When they entered the house they saw him fanning himself, and that he was getting bigger with each stroke of the fan. He was talking with everybody. The Prophet Muḥammad commanded him to witness to the Unity of God and to his Apostleship (cf. Bukhári, *Ṣaḥíḥ*, 23 : 80), but he refused and said, " You are

[1] Majlisi, *Haḳu'l-Yaḳín*, p. 160.
[2] Bukhárí, *Ṣaḥíḥ*, ed. Leyden, 23 : 80 ; Ahmad ibn Hanbal, *Musnad*, Cairo, 1313, Vol. I, pp. 380, 457 ; Tirmidhí, *Ṣaḥíḥ*, ed. Cairo, 1292, 31 : 63. See further references in Wensinck, *Handbook of Early Muhammadan Traditions*, p. 103.
[3] Bukhárí, *op. cit.*, 96 : 23 ; and Ahmad ibn Hanbal, *Musnad*, Vol. III, pp. 79 and 97.
[4] *Nuru'l-Anwár*, a compilation by Ali Asghar Burujurdi, publ. Teheran, 1328 ḍ.H., p. 126 ff.

no more of an Apostle than I am," and afterwards he claimed to be God. The Prophet therefore gave up what he had in mind because of the aversion that he felt toward him. But at once Ṣá'if repeated rapidly the surahs Muḥammad had been thinking of, at which the Prophet exclaimed, "May God kill you!" Then Ụmar drew his sword, without the permission of the Apostle, and struck the head of Ṣá'if a terrific blow, which had, however, no effect, except that the sword returned on Ụmar's own head with such force that his head was cut open, so that four fingers could be inserted, and the blood ran all down his face. The Apostle remarked, "You are not able to kill him, for you cannot alter what God has permitted," but at the same time he put his blessed hand on the head of Ụmar and the wound was healed at once.

The Apostle then started towards Medina, and Ṣá'if leisurely put on his sandals and took his staff and started to follow him. When the people saw this, however, they were ready to mob him, but he ran away towards a mountain, and placed a huge stone between himself and his pursuers. Then the Prophet came to that mountain and raised his hands in prayer, saying aloud, "O God, stop the wickedness of this tyrant!" Immediately a great bird descended from the sky and seized the accursed Ṣá'if in its talons and bore him to the sea of Tabaristán (the Caspian Sea) and cast him on an island where he has since been imprisoned.

In some of the books it is written that God has imprisoned him, along with the ass that he rode, on an island that is more than two hundred miles square, and although God fills that island every day with green pasture, and supplies it abundantly with water, yet the monstrous ass is never satisfied.

Tamím al-Darí[1] related to the Apostle: "We were thirty men in a ship, and our ship was adrift for a month, until at last we reached an island, where we saw an ass that was so huge that on looking at him from the front you could not see his tail. He had the head of a camel and a human face. His back was like that of a cow, and spotted. We swore we had never seen such an animal. The beast called out, 'ad-Dajjál who rides me is bigger than I am!' We asked, 'Where is he?' The ass replied, 'He is in this castle.' We entered the castle and saw a veritable giant there. He had one eye blinded, but the other eye shone like a star in his forehead (Ibn Babawaihi, *Kamalu'd-Din*, p. 291), and from his eyebrow there were six hairs that stood out like a spear, and on his forehead was written *al-káfír* (the infidel). His feet were fastened with chains, and his hands were in a yoke that was bound to his neck. When he saw me he

[1] Ahmad ibn Hanbal, *Musnad*, vi, p. 373 ff.; Tirmidhí, *Ṣaḥíḥ*, 31 : 65; and Tayalisi, *Musnad*, No. 1646.

recognized me and asked if I knew Muḥammad. I said, 'Which Muḥammad?' He said, 'The Prophet of Arabia, who was born in Mecca and fled to Medina.'"

It is this Jewish contemporary of the Prophet Muḥammad that the traditions represent as the Anti-Christ who is to come forth as one of the signs of the approach of the End of Time. He is to appear in the Jewish quarter of Isfahan or in Kufa or in Khorasan.[1] In many ways he will attract the thoughtless to follow him. Even the ass that he will ride will have hairs like musical instruments that will vibrate beautifully in the wind, to interest people; and instead of ordinary dung, the mysterious animal will drop dates that will deceive the young.

The literal meaning of the name Dajjál is a "Deceiver" and it is probable that this name for a repulsive character in an old Arab myth, was used by Muḥammad to express his contempt for Ṣá'if ibn Ṣá'id, so that thus both the man and the myth have survived in the evolution of the story of the coming of the expected Anti-Christ. The Shi'ites quote many sayings of the Imams about the signs of the coming of ad-Dajjál. Ạli is said to have foretold that there would first be a widespread falling away from faithfulness in prayer and from the obligations of the Law, that there would be much deceit and laxity of all kinds, with undue freedom between men and women, when women would affect the attire of men, and ride on horseback like men.[2]

When ad-Dajjál shall return and gather a horde of followers, he will approach Jerusalem, where the Hidden Imam will have appeared to mobilize the Faithful. Then suddenly, at a place called Afiḳ, the true Christ will descend from Heaven, each hand resting on the shoulder of an angel. The Christ will go first and kill ad-Dajjál, and after he has wiped off the blood from his lance, he will come to Jerusalem and join in worship behind the Imam and show himself a true Muḥammadan. This he will demonstrate by killing swine and breaking crosses, destroying synagogues and churches, and by killing all the Christians who refuse to

[1] *Encyclopædia of Islam*, Vol. I, p. 886.
[2] Ibn Babawaihi, *Kamalu'd-Dín*, p. 290.

believe in him in his new rôle. For " after he has killed the false Messiah (al-masíḥ al-da*djdj*ál) not one of the People of Scripture will be left who does not believe in him, so that the community (milla) will become one, the community of Islam. Then will come universal security of man and beast and Jesus will remain for forty years; thereafter he will die and the Muslims will hold funeral service for him and bury him (at Medina, it is universally accepted, beside Muḥammad, in a vacant space between Abu Bakr and Ụmar)."[1]

[1] Macdonald, *Encyclopædia of Islam*, Vol. II, p. 525. Cf. Ḳoran, Rodwell's translation, iv, 157; and the commentary of al-Baidawi, edit. Fleischer, ii, 241.

CHAPTER XXII

SAMARRA, THE CITY OF THE LAST IMAMS

IN the year A.D. 836, after two years' experience with factional strife in Baghdad, the Caliph Mu'tasim departed with his Turkish army to Samarra, "which he founded and made his residence and military camp."[1] There eight caliphs lived in the short period of fifty-six years.[2] The distance of Samarra from Baghdad is sixty miles, and according to the road book of Ibn Rustah (A.D. 903), there were ninety-nine stages of twelve miles each between Surra-man-raa and Mecca.[3] This name, Surra-man-raa (He who sees it rejoices), is said to have been given by Mu'tasim himself, when, for approximately £2,000, he purchased as a site for his new city a garden that had been developed by a Christian monastery. The Caliph's happy Arabic pun was based on the Aramaic name, Sâmarrâ, which was a town in the immediate vicinity from the times before the Arab conquest. The general district, however, was known as Ṭirhán.[4] Thus the site chosen was an attractive garden spot in a fertile valley of the Tigris, and there the Caliph built his new capital, which became known as "the second city of the Caliphs of the Beni Hashim." A main avenue, with many residences, ran along the river bank. In the garden of the monastery he built his royal palace, known as the Dáru'l-Ạmma, and the monastery itself became his Treasury.

A Friday Mosque, the walls of which are still standing, was built by Mu'tasim very close to the quarter of the city that was set aside for the army. Mustawfi informs us further that "he

[1] Dinawari, *Akhbar aṭ-Ṭiwal,* ed. Guirgass, p. 396.
[2] Ya'ḳubi (A.D. 891), *Kitab al-Buldán,* ed. de Goeje, p. 255; and Mustawfi, *Nuzhatu'l-Qulub,* Eng. trans. Le Strange, p. 40.
[3] Ibn Rustah, *Kitáb al-A'lák an-Nafísa,* ed. de Goeje, p. 180.
[4] Ya'ḳubi, *op. cit.,* p. 255; and Le Strange, *Lands of the Eastern Caliphate,* pp. 53, 54.

THE WALLS OF THE ANCIENT MOSQUE OF MUSTASIM, AND THE MODERN CITY OF SAMARRAH IN THE BACKGROUND

Facing p. 243]

[Royal Air Force Official—Crown Copyright Reserved

built a Minaret for the Mosque, 170 ells in height, with a gangway (to ascend it, that went up) outside, and no Minaret after this fashion was ever built by anyone before his time."[1] This minaret, which is shown in the foreground of the accompanying photograph, is so large that a man on horseback is said to be able to ascend its so-called gangway. The same thing is claimed for the similar minaret in the Mosque of Tulun, which may have been modelled after it.[2]

But the Turkish mercenaries, on whom Mu'tasim and his sons and grandsons relied, soon became the true masters of the situation. While they cherished their position as guardians of the caliphs, whom they permitted to live in luxury and security, nevertheless they so exploited their own opportunities for gain, through cruelty and oppression, that in matters of internal administration the authority of the Muḥammadan Empire sank to a low ebb. This was at a time, however, according to Dinawari, when there were more victories for the troops than during any preceding caliphate.[3]

In Samarra the caliphs busied themselves building palace after palace, on both sides of the river, and at a cost that Yaḳut estimated as 204 million dirhems, which would not be less than eight million sterling.[4] A great cypress tree is celebrated in the *Shah Nameh* as having sprung from a branch brought by Zoroaster from Paradise. It is said to have stood at the village of Kishmar, near Turshíz, and to have been planted by Zoroaster in memory of the conversion of King Gushtasp to the Magian religion. "Such too was its power that earthquakes, which frequently devastated all the neighbouring districts, never did any harm in Kishmar. According to Ḳazvini, the Caliph Mutawakkil in 247 (861) caused this mighty cypress to be felled, and then transported it across all Persia, in places carried on camels, to be used for beams in his new palace at Samarra. This was done in spite of the grief and protests of all the Guebres,

[1] Mustawfi, *op. cit.*, p. 49.
[2] *Encyclopædia Britannica*, 11th edit., Vol. II, p. 424.
[3] Dinawari, *op. cit.*, p. 396.
[4] Le Strange, *op. cit.*, p. 55.

but when the cypress arrived on the banks of the Tigris, Mutawakkil was dead, having been murdered by his son."[1] Mustawfi, who wrote in the fourteenth century, and with Shi'ite sympathies, mentions how the Caliph Mutawakkil enlarged Samarra, and in particular, how " he built a magnificent Kiosk, greater than which never existed in the lands of Irán, and gave it the title of the Ja'fariyyah (his name being Ja'far). But evil fortune—brought down on him in that he had laid in ruins the tomb of the Imam Husayn, son of Ạli (at Kerbala), and furthermore had prevented people from making their visitation to the same—decreed that, shortly after his death, his Kiosk should be demolished, so that no trace of it now remains. Indeed, of Samarra itself, at the present time, only a restricted portion is inhabited."[2]

The restricted portion that was still inhabited in the fourteenth century was approximately the same as the modern Samarra, and was a part of the " Camp of Mu'tasim." Here the Imams, Ạli Naḳi and his son, Hasan, had been allowed to live, and hence they were called the Askariyain, or the " dwellers in the Camp." It was here also that both of them were buried.[3] The modern Samarra is only a few paces removed from the walls of the old Friday Mosque, which agrees with Mustawfi's observation that " in front of the mosque stands the tomb of the Imam Ạli an-Nakí, grandson of the Imam Ạli ar-Riḍa ; and also of his son, the Imam Ḥasan al-Ạskarí." That the city of the Caliphs was much more extensive is indicated by the modern observation that " the ground plan of the many barracks, palaces and gardens can be very plainly seen by anyone flying over the site in an aeroplane."[4] The historical topography of the ephemeral capital of the Caliphs as outlined by the Arab geographers, Ya'ḳubi and Yaḳut, has been investigated recently by archeologists, so that the location of the principal streets and of many of the palaces has

[1] *Ibid.*, p. 355.
[2] Mustawfi, *op. cit.*, p. 49.
[3] It is interesting to observe that Shahrastání (ed. Cureton, p. 128) makes the statement that the Imám Ạli Naḳi is buried at Ḳumm, but this is probably an error. Cf. Mustawfi, *op. cit.*, p. 49; and Herzfeld, *Ency. Islam*, art. " Ạskar Sámarrá."
[4] *Historical Mesopotamia*, a Guide Book published by the *Baghdad Times*, Baghdad, 1922, p. 51.

been determined. Also the findings have proved to be of special value to students of Muslim art, for they are representative of the period when the civilization of the Abbasid caliphate was "shedding its lustre over the world."[1]

It was in the part of Samarra that still remains that the Imam Mahdi—Muḥammad ibn Hasan al-Ạskarí—is said to have disappeared from human sight. Mustawfi says this happened in 264 (878) at Samarra.[2] The fact that the Shi'ite community was permitted to have its headquarters after the fall of the Buyids in the near-by city of Hilla, from which place they conducted their negotiations at the time of the invasion of Khulagu Khan, gave rise to the tradition that the Hidden Imam would reappear in that town. This accounts for the confusion of the traveller, Ibn Batuta (A.D. 1355), who found shrines dedicated to the last Imam, both in Hilla and Samarra. The "mosque of the last Imam" in Hilla marks the place of his expected reappearance, but the place of his disappearance is at Samarra. At Hilla, Ibn Batuta found that the mosque had an extended veil of silk stretched across its entrance, and it was a practice for the people "to come daily, armed to the number of a hundred, to the door of this mosque, bringing with them a beast saddled and bridled, a great number of persons also with drums and trumpets, and to say: 'Come forth, Lord of the Age, for tyranny and baseness now abounds; this then is the time for thy egress, that, by thy means, God may divide between truth and falsehood.' They wait till night and then return to their homes." Samarra itself was at that time in ruins, though Ibn Batuta mentions that "there had been a *mashhad* in it, dedicated to the last Imam by the Ráfiza."[3] It may have been owing to the fact that the place was in ruins that pains were not taken to ascertain that the *mashhad* was the "place of witness" in memory of the Imams, Ạli Naḳi

[1] *Ency. Islam,* art. "Samarra," with references to the investigations of E. Herzfeld.

[2] Mustawfi, *op. cit.,* p. 47.

[3] The reference is to the Rawafiz. Sayyid Murtaḍa remarks in the *Alamu'l-Huda* (ch. xix), "The Second Division of Islam call themselves 'the followers,' the Shi'ites, but their adversaries call them 'the abandoners,' the Rawafiz." For a full discussion of this name, see article by Dr. Freidlander, *J.A.O.S.,* Vol. xxix, pp. 137-159.

and Hasan al-Ạskarí, and that a different spot near by was highly regarded as the place where the last Imam disappeared.[1]

From the point of view of present-day Shi'ites, the modern city of Samarra is of outstanding importance on account of its two shrines, both of which have in recent years been kept in excellent repair. It is the Shrine of the Ạskariyain that has the golden dome, which was presented by Naṣr al-Din Sháh and completed under Muzaffer al-Dín Shah in the year 1905.[2] Beneath it there are four graves, those of the two Imams, Ạli Naḳi and his son, Hasan al-Ạskarí, and those of two illustrious women who are associated with them in the traditions. One of these is Halimah, the sister of the Imam Ạli Naḳi, who has related at length the circumstances of the birth of the Hidden Imam, and the other is Narjis Khatun, the Christian slave who is said to have been the mother of this boy, who disappeared when he was five (or nine) years old. The second shrine marks the place where it is considered that the Hidden Imam went into concealment. It has a dome that is distinguished for the soft and delicate design that is worked out in blue tiles, and beneath it is the *sardáb* (a cellar or pit) where the young Imam is said to have disappeared. Visitors may enter this pit by a flight of steps.

The Pilgrims' Guide Book gives directions for visiting each of these Samarra shrines.[3] "When you wish to visit the tombs of the Imams, Ạli Naḳi and of Hasan al-Ạskarí, you should first bathe, and then go before their graves. If it is not practicable for you to do this (i.e., if there is danger involved in your doing so), you should make a gesture of salutation before the lattice (in front of the shrine), when you are in line with the sepulchre, and then repeat the prayer of salutation." After repeating the prescribed form of salutation, you are "to put forth effort in your prayer on behalf of yourself, and for your father and your mother, and to make whatever other petition you wish. If you are able

[1] Ibn Batuta, ed. Paris, ii, p. 98; *ibid.*, trans. Lee, ch. viii, p. 48; De Herbelot, *Ann. Mosl.*, tom. iii, p. 716; and the *Encyclopædia of Religion and Ethics*, art. "Mahdi," Vol. III, p. 338.

[2] Dr. Herzfeld was apparently misinformed and considered that the golden dome is over the *sardáb*. Cf. *Ency. Islám*, art. "Ạskar Sámarrá."

[3] Majlisi, *Tofatu's-Zá'irín*, pp. 335 and 356 ff.

to go close to the tombs, do so, and make two prostrations in prayer, and whatever prayer it is your desire to make will surely be answered." Attention is called to the fact that the authorities have mentioned also in their books that it is advisable to visit also the tomb of the mother of the Sahibu'l-Amr, Narjis Khatun. "Also the tomb of Halimah Khatun, the daughter of the Imam Muḥammad Taḳi, is in this sacred shrine (beneath the golden dome), and the prayer of visitation must be made at her grave also, for she was honoured by the Imams in a high degree, and both during the lifetime of the Imam Hasan al-Ạskarí and afterwards, she visited the Sahibu'l-Ạmr. She was present, indeed, at the time of his birth, so that she served four Imams." It is especially recommended that visits to the tombs of the Ạskariyain should be made on their birthdays and on the days commemorative of their death.

At the pit, or *sardáb*, a prayer of salutation is made to the Hidden Imam, who is addressed as the Caliph of God, the Representative of those sent in the past, the Guardian of the secrets of the two worlds, the Last Gift of God, the Door of Approach to God, the Light of God that will never be extinguished, and the Proof of God for all beings on earth and in the heavens. Then follows the following Confession of Faith:

"I bear witness that thou art the Proof of God for the living and the dead, that thine army is to be victorious, thy friends to be saved and thine enemies to suffer. Thou art the keeper of all learning, the revealer of all that is hidden, the demonstrator of all truth, and the frustrator of all folly. I rejoice that thou art my Imam, my Guide, my Leader, my Master. I seek no other in thy stead and accept no master in thy place.

"I bear witness that thou art the established truth, that there can be no mistake or doubt, and that God's promise of thy coming is sure. But I am dismayed at thy tarrying so long, and do not have patience to wait for the distant time. It is not surprising that some have denied thee. I am waiting, however, for the day of thy coming. Thou art an Intercessor who will not be questioned and a Master who will not be taken away. God has kept thee for the assistance of the Faith, a protection for believers and a punishment for infidels and heretics.

"I bear witness that it is by thy favour that our actions will be approved, our works made pure, and our merits multiplied. Whosoever comes to thy friendship and acknowledges thee as the Imam, surely his works will be accepted, his word believed, his good deeds made many, and his sins blotted out. But whosoever rejects thy friendship and denies thee, or substitutes another for thee, surely God will send him face first into the Fire, without taking the trouble to weigh his good works.

"I testify to the existence of God, to the existence of the angels, and to thy existence, O my Leader. In this my faith is sincere, the same in my heart as in my words, the same in secret as in public, and to this thou art my witness.

"This is the covenant that God has commanded between me and thee. If the time is prolonged and my life is continued, my assurance, my friendship, my trust, my certainty, surely all will increase. I will be waiting for thy appearance, and for the Holy War along with thee. It is for this that I am ready to forfeit my life, my property, my son, my wife—all indeed which God's favour has granted me—they are all in thy hands and are for thee to give or to deny. O my Leader, if I am living on the bright day of thy coming, with its glistening standard, then am I thy servant to command. May I have opportunity for martyrdom before thee! And, O my Leader, if I should die before thy coming, grant me thy intercession, and that of thy pure fathers, before God on High, that God may allow me to appear again before thee at the time of thy coming, that I may follow thee and satisfy my heart against thine enemies.

"O my Leader, I come as a sinner, as one who is ashamed and afraid when he thinks of the punishments to come from the Sovereign of the Universe; but I have trusted in thy intercession, and have referred all to thy leadership, that I may be forgiven from sin, that my faults may be overlooked, and my mistakes pardoned. I beseech thee for thy intercession, O my Leader, to help me to accomplish my desire. Ask God to forgive my sins, for I have grasped the life-line from thy hand."

The pilgrim is then instructed as to the right procedure on entering the *sardáb*, where the Imam disappeared. He is to stand between the two doors, to grasp one of the doors with his hands, "and to cough like one asking to enter," and to say slowly and from the heart, "In the name of God the Merciful and Forgiving." There in the court of the *sardáb* he should repeat two raḳats of prayer, after which he should say:

"God is great, there is no God but God! God is great, all praise be unto God! Praise be unto him who has guided us to know his friends and to recognize his enemies. Praise be unto him who has assisted us to make this pilgrimage to our Imam, and who did not appoint us to be of those who were enemies to Ạli, or of those who considered Ạli to be God, or of those who attributed all human actions to God or to Ạli, or of those who were scornfully disobedient to Islam. Peace be upon the Friend of God, the son of God's friends, the one treasured for the honour of God's friends and for the confusion of his enemies. . . .

"O God, as thou hast led my heart to remember him, so make my sword ready and notable in his service. If I am to die first, grant him authority in thy Caliphate for the death of those who oppose him. Cause me to rise from the dead at the time when he appears, to come out from my tomb with my grave clothes, that I may fight in the Holy War before his face, in the ranks of those whom thou hast chosen in the Book: 'Surely Allah loves those who fight in His way in ranks as if they were a firm and compact wall' (Ḳoran 61, 4).

"O God, Thou hast lengthened the period of our waiting! Those who oppose are ridiculing us, and further waiting is a sore trial. Show us the face of Thy blessed Friend during our time, or after we have died. O God, as I trust thee that I will return, hear my cry, hear my cry, hear my cry!

"O Master of the Age, I have left all friends for thee! I have left my native land to visit thee! Concealing my action from those of my home town, I have sought that thou mightest be my intercessor before my Sovereign and thy Sovereign, and before thy fathers, who are also my friends. Be thou my good fortune, and as thy bounty is ample, send good to me."

Such is the faith and hope of "the Twelvers" (ithná ạshara), the Shi'ites who believe in a series of twelve Imams, and who say that the Imamate passed from Ạli to his two sons, Ḥasan and Ḥusain; from Ḥusain to his son, Ạli Zain al-Ạbidín, to his son, Muḥammad al-Baḳir, to his son, Ja'far as-Ṣadiḳ, to his son Musa al-Kazim, to his son, Ạli ar-Riḍa, to his son, Muḥammad al-Taḳi, to his son, Ạli an-Naḳi, and to his son, Ḥasan al-Ạskarí; and finally, on the evidence of traditions that are not easily confirmed, to Muḥammad al-Mahdi, "who disappeared and will come again at the end of time to announce the last judgment and to fill the earth with justice."[1]

[1] *Ency. Islam,* art. "Ithna Ạshariya."

CHAPTER XXIII

THE FOUR AGENTS OF THE HIDDEN IMAM

WE are told that the birth of the twelfth and last Imam occurred on the eighth of the month, Sha'bán, in the year 256/869, and that "his agent (wakíl) was Uthman ibn Sá'íd, who left his authority to his son, Abu Ja'far Muḥammad, who left it to Abu'l-Kasim ibn Ruh, who left it to Abu'l-Hasan Ali ibn Muhammad Samarrí."[1] The tenth and the eleventh Imams had regarded Uthman ibn Sá'íd as their private secretary and treasurer, and they had both considered him thoroughly reliable. What he said on their behalf was the same as if they had said it. At times the Imam Hasan Askarí addressed him in public as the "agent for the property of God," for which property he was to give a receipt when he accepted it on behalf of the Imam.

A company of forty leading Shi'ites called upon Hasan Askarí shortly before his death to learn who was to be his successor as the Proof of God on earth. He retired from the group for about an hour, when he returned with a beautiful child in his arms. He explained that this child was the one who was to succeed him, but that after that day they would not see the child until he was considerably older. "In the meantime," he said, "you are to accept what Uthman ibn Sá'íd says, as he is the representative of your Imam." It is further related that Hasan Askarí said of him, "He is my agent (wakíl), and his son, Muḥammad, is the agent of my son, Muḥammad." It was he therefore who washed the body of Hasan Askarí and anointed it for burial and placed it in the grave.

When he was asked if he had seen Hasan Askarí's son, who was

[1] Majlisi, *Bahâru'l-Anwár*, Persian trans., Vol. XIII, p. 139.

supposed to have been born near the time of his father's death Ụthman ibn Sá'íd broke down weeping, and said: "Yes, it is true, I saw him and his neck was like this," and he made a gesture to indicate that the boy had an enormous neck. But he would not reveal the name of the child, for he said that if his name should be mentioned his enemies would begin searching for him.

The grave of Ụthman ibn Sá'íd is said to be in Baghdad at the Shári'-al-Maydán, in the mosque near the city gate. In 408 A.H. there was an entrance to the tomb room from a small door in the prayer niche of the mosque, but thirty-two years later this wall was destroyed and the tomb was left in the open court where it could be visited by anyone.[1]

The second agent, Abu Ja'far Muhammad ibn Uthman, was designated by the written will of his father to succeed him as the representative of the Hidden Imam. He washed his father's body and attended to the funeral rites. There was unanimity among the Shi'ites of Iraḳ in according to him the authority his father had exercised. He is said to have had several books on the Law which he had inherited from his father and which his father had received from the Imams. During the period that he served as his agent, he took an oath that the Master of the Age was present among the pilgrims of Mecca every year and that he sees them although they fail to see him.

As a sign of Abu Ja'far's supernatural intuition it is related that one of his friends found him inscribing a verse from the Ḳoran on a slab of stone, and in the margins he was cutting the names of the Imams. His friend asked him what he was doing. "It is for my grave," he said, and then he told this man when he expected to die. To others he expressed the same opinion, and the traditions say that his prediction proved to be true. After he had served the Imams, visible and invisible, for about fifty years, he died in the year 305/917. He was buried beside the grave of his mother, on the roadside at the Kufa Gate, at the place where his house had stood, and which is now in the midst of the desert.[2]

[1] *Ibid., op. cit.*, p. 130 ff. [2] *Ibid., op. cit.*, p. 132 ff.

While there were about ten men in Baghdad with whom Abu Ja'far had shared his responsibility as the recognised leader of the Shi'ite community, men who helped him in the administration of affairs, his most trusted associate was Abu Ḳasim Husain ibn Ruh. He allowed him to do for him much the same kind of work that his own father had done for the Imam Hasan Askarí and before he died he designated Abu Ḳasim to take his place as the representative of the Hidden Imam. He became therefore *the third agent.*

Abu Ja'far's daughter, Umm Kulthum, has related as follows: "Husain ibn Ruh was my father's agent for many years. He looked after the property and conveyed his secret messages to the chief men of the Shi'ites. He was also most zealous in the service of my father, who trusted him implicitly, for he even told him what occurred between himself and his slave girls." Although her father had another friend and loyal patron, Abu Ja'far ibn Admad, he saw fit to choose Husain ibn Ruh to be his successor and no objections were raised.

The traditionists say that he was esteemed by both the Shi'ites and the Sunnís as a most learned man. He was admired especially for his shrewdness in dissimulation. In a discussion in the presence of the Caliph Muḳtadir, one of those present made the remark, "After the Prophet of God, the greatest of all creation was Abu Bakr, then Umar and then Ạli." Another objected, "But Ạli was greater than Umar." This led to much talking, and after a while Abu Ḳasim remarked, "Those who follow the *ijma* (agreement) say that Abu Bakr took precedence over them all, and that after him is Fárúḳ (the Discerner, i.e., Ụmar), and after him is Ụthman, Dhu'l-Nurín (the Possessor of Lights), and after him is Ạli, who is the *waṣí* (executor) of the Prophet. This agrees with the traditions and this is what seems to me to be right." But the spectators were surprised at what he said. And the Sunnís who were present jubilantly congratulated him and carried him on their shoulders as they ridiculed and abused those who had considered him among the Rafiḍah (the Repudiators of Abu Bakr and Ụmar). But the Shi'ite narrator says that when he heard Husain ibn Ruh's careful statement, he found great difficulty in concealing his laughter, even though he drew his sleeve across his mouth, and to avoid further embarrassment he left the room. But as he departed he caught the eye of Husain ibn Ruh, and an hour or so later he received a call from this eminent personage and they enjoyed the joke together.

That he was gifted with persuasive tact is evidenced by the tradition that ten men went to see him about a matter in which nine of them were his opponents. At first they were bitter in denouncing his attitude, but at the end of the interview they had not only come to agree with him but had been much impressed by his patience and gracious consideration.

On one occasion his opinion was asked concerning the practice of temporary marriage. Now the word ordinarily used to express this relationship is *mutá*, which means "enjoyment." According to Shi'ite law, "Marriage, like other contracts, requires declaration and acceptance for its constitution; and both must be expressed in such a manner as to demonstrate intention, without any sort of ambiguity. The words appropriate to the declaration are *zuwwujtoku* and *ankuhtoku*, both signifying, 'I have married thee.' With regard to the word *muttuátoku*, which signifies, 'I have bestowed on thee' or 'given thee the enjoyment,' there is some doubt of its being legally sufficient; but the opinion which is in favour of its legality has been generally preferred."[1] According to the Hanifites this word *mutá*, or any of its derivatives, is not sufficient to make a marriage legally binding. Among the Sunnites such temporary marriage is looked upon with extreme disfavour, and the fact that it is permitted by the Shi'ites[2] is a point of frequent criticism.

For this reason Abu Ḳasim was asked to explain, "Why is temporary marriage with a virgin looked upon with disfavour?" He replied, "The Prophet has declared that modesty is part of faith. When you take a girl in temporary marriage, to have pleasure with her, you spoil her modesty and injure her faith."

[1] Baillie, *A Digest of Muhammadan Law*, Vol. II, p. 2.
[2] aṭ-Ṭusi, *Istibsár*, Vol. II, p. 76.

When one of those present asked him, "But if anyone does this, has he committed adultery?" the representative of the Imam replied, "No, I wouldn't say that."

It is said that once he sent a book of regulations and admonitions to a number of learned Shi'ites at Ḳumm. They gave the book their approval, except that the specified tithe to be paid at the time of the feast of breaking the fast was listed at only half as much as they thought it should be.

Abu Ḳasim ibn Ruh died in 326 A.H., and again on the testimony of Umm Kulthum, the daughter of Abu Ja'far, it is recorded that the grave of Abu Ḳasim ibn Ruh is near the house of Ạli ibn Ahmad Nubakhtí, at a point beyond the Shawk bridge and towards the city gate. Majlisi calls special attention to the propriety of Shi'ite pilgrims also visiting the tomb of Abu Ḳasim ibn Ruh.[1]

The *fourth agent* was Abu'l-Hasan Ạli ibn Muhammad Samarrí. Seventy years had passed since the death of the Imam Hasan Askarí, and notwithstanding the devoted expectation of the Shi'ite community, the Hidden Imam had not appeared. In these two generations those who had known the Imam personally had died. In the rugged path of dissimulation a mere remnant of the Shi'ite community had survived, and that through a period of political and social turmoil when the faith of all the people languished. Oppression and injustice had become so rife upon the earth that many felt that surely the long expected Imam must come. For not only was the small Shi'ite community divided and downtrodden but the prestige of the empire of Islam had suffered from the repeated raids of border tribes and the Muslim armies had suffered serious losses in the continued warfare with the Byzantines.

For in the very same year that the Imam Hasan Askarí died, the Caliph al-Muhtadi, the good Caliph, perished, after torture, a victim to the resentment of his Turkish chiefs. The reign of his successor, al-Mu'tamid, brought a series of dire calamities. First the Zanj entered Basrah, where they are said to have killed

[1] Majlisi, *op. cit.*, p. 136 ff. Cf. *Tofatu'z-Záirín*, p. 423.

three hundred thousand in one day, and to have swept across Persian Iraḳ like a scourge. They carried death and destruction wherever they went. Their leader was Ạli al-Khabíth, who claimed to have been sent by God, and who was bent on destroying all the people who refused to accept him and his mission. He had a pulpit set up at his headquarters and there he openly reviled the heroes of Islam. He took special delight in dishonouring the Alide women, letting them be sold for a mere pittance, and allowing his followers to hold them in abject slavery. Finally, after he had spread terror for four years, he was killed and his head was brought to Baghdad on a spear, and the people gave themselves over to a day of public rejoicing.[1]

But in the meantime the cities had been stricken with plague, and earthquakes were added to complete the horror. In the remaining years of the reign of Mu'tamid, until 279/892, the empire was torn with civil strife, and at the same time strained to the utmost in the desperate but ever indecisive war with the Byzantines. And of the next Caliph, al-Mu'tadid, it is written, "dissensions were lulled during his days through the excessive dread he inspired."[2] Since he inspired such fear on account of the number of people he arbitrarily put to death, and because he succeeded in restoring the power of the house of Ạbbas, he was called aṣ-Ṣaffah the Second, in memory of the great "shedder of blood" who was the founder of the Ạbbasid dynasty.

A few years later there occurred the widespread and somewhat mysterious rise of the Karmatians, who in the year 317/929 slaughtered the pilgrims at Mecca and carried away the Black Stone from the Kaaba. As part of a general movement for social reform and justice, controlled by the Isma'ilíya, who had founded the Fatimid dynasty in Egypt and Syria, they exploited the Ạlíd legitimist tradition in a grand conspiracy, which spread rapidly throughout the empire.[3] And about the same time the Dailamites, a warlike people from the mountainous region of

[1] as-Suyuti, *History of the Caliphs*, pp. 376-383.
[2] *Ibid., op. cit.*, p. 386.
[3] *Encyclopædia of Islam*, Vol. II, p. 767.

Gilán, and who had furnished mercenaries to the armies of the Caliphs, captured Isfahan and were making rapid headway in Mesopotamia.

The fourth agent of the Hidden Imam, therefore, had come upon evil times. He may have felt that the years that had passed since the time of the last Imams had been so filled with oppression, bloodshed and iniquity that the Imam himself must certainly appear. Or he may have been thoroughly disillusioned and have felt the insignificance and unreality of his position as the accredited agent of the supposed Imam. In any event, at the time of his death, when he was urged to name his successor, he gave an answer that has come down in history, "The matter is now with God." He refused therefore to name anyone to succeed him, so that from the year he died, 329/940, the Hidden Imam has had no visible representative on earth. The period of the Lesser Concealment, extending from 256-329 A.H., was finished, and the almost one thousand years that have passed since then are part of the Greater Concealment. The grave of the last "agent" is on the Sháría Khalbakhi near the canal Nahrábi.[1]

[1] Majlisi, *Baháru'l-Anwár*, Persian trans., Vol. XIII, p. 138.

CHAPTER XXIV

PILGRIMAGES TO THE GRAVES OF IMAMZADEHS

IMAMZADEHS are descendants of an Imam, whether they be the immediate children or whether their descent is through several generations. Majlisi remarks that it is doubtful if there are any traditions from the Imams that can be cited as giving authority for pilgrimages to the tombs of all of their children, but "it is a custom that has been sanctioned by the learned doctors of faith, and with due allowance for uncertainties, the visit to each of their tombs is advisable on account of their evident connection with the Imams and the probability that visiting their tombs may be a means of blessing."[1]

Ḳumm

Traditions are recorded, however, in support of the pilgrimage to the distinguished mausoleum of Fatima at Ḳumm. She has been called Ma'ṣumah, the innocent. She was a daughter of the Imam Musa Kazim, and a sister of the Imam Ạli Riḍa. Ḳumm was a city in Persian Irak that was recognised as a Shi'ite centre. It is said that when the sister of the Imam Riḍa was on her way to join her brother in Khorasan, she had halted in Ḳumm. There she took ill and died. There are some who say she was poisoned.[2]

Mustawfi found Ḳumm in ruins when he visited it in the fourteenth century. While he makes no mention of the tomb of Fatima, he observes that the population were Shi'ites of the sect that followed the Twelve Imams.[3] However, Ibn Babawaihi (A.D. 991) related the tradition that Sa'd ibn Sa'd asked the Imam

[1] Majlisi, *Tofatu'z-Za'irin*, p. 420.
[2] Le Strange, *Lands of the Eastern Caliphate*, p. 209.
[3] Mustawfi, *Nuzhatu'l-Ḳulub*, ed. Le Strange, p. 67; English trans., p. 71.

Riḍa concerning the pilgrimage to the tomb of his sister, the daughter of Musa ibn Ja'far, and the Imam Riḍa replied, " Who ever visits her will go to Heaven."[1] Other traditions to the same effect are related by Majlisi, from both the Imam Riḍa and from his son the Imam Muhammad Taḳi, in the instructions he gives for the pilgrimage to her tomb. " When you arrive at her grave," he says, " stand opposite the head and repeat thirty-four times ' God is Great,' and thirty-three times ' Praise be to God,' and also say thirty-three times ' God be exalted.' " Then after invoking peace upon Adam, Noah, Abraham, Moses, Jesus, and Muhammad, upon Ạli and Fatima and Hasan, and Husain and all the Imams, the devout pilgrim is to salute Fatima, the daughter of Musa ibn Ja'far, and in his prayer he is to trace her ancestry on back through the line of her father's predecessors.[2]

There is another tomb in Ḳumm where they have built a sepulchre, with a large stone that indicates that it marks the graves of Ạli ibn Ja'far aṣ-Ṣadiḳ and of Muhammad ibn Musa. The date of the placing of this stone was about four hundred years before the time of Majlisi, i.e., about A.D. 1300, which would suggest that it was placed there at the time of an attempted restoration of the Shrine after the Mongol conquest. But Majlisi takes pains to add that " while there is no doubt of the distinction of Ali ibn Ja'far, yet it has not been proved that this is his grave, for in various books of biography and elsewhere, it is shown that he did not come to this region. It is generally considered that he was buried in the valley of Ụraiḍ (near Medina), and since the inscription on that old tomb is so clear, perhaps it is better to make the pilgrimage to him there."

The present town of Ḳumm, a walled city that one enters through a typical Persian gateway that is decorated with ornamental tiles, owes its importance to the fact that Shah Ạbbas, the great Safawíd, took special pains to encourage pilgrimages to the shrines lying within Persian territory, that less money might be carried out of the country. It is for this reason also that the

[1] Ibn Babawaihi, *Uyunu'l-Akhbar*, ch. 68 (p. 371).
[2] Majlisi, *op. cit.*, p. 420 ; and *Miftahu'l-Janán*, the Key of Paradise, p. 425.

later rulers of the Safawid dynasty are buried at Ḳumm, and the shrine itself is a striking example of the architecture of that period.

Shah Abdu'l-Azim

One of the best known shrines in Persia is the tomb of the imamzadeh Shah Abdu'l-Azim. He was only four generations removed from the Imam Hasan and was distinguished as a traditionist, a scholar, an ascetic, and a saint. He was also a personal companion of the Imam Muhammad Taḳi and of his son the Imam Ạli Naḳi, both of whom he served with the greatest devotion and self-sacrifice.

His tomb was outside the city of Ray. But at the time of the Mongol invasion Ray was totally destroyed, and the remnants of the population gathered in the village of Ṭihrán, which in later years became the capital of modern Persia, Teheran. The proximity of the shrine of Shah Abdu'l-Azim to the capital city has doubtless given it exaggerated importance in recent years, but there is nevertheless sufficient mention of it in the older books to show that it has long been recognised as a place of pilgrimage.

The story is that Shah Abdu'l-Azim fled from the Caliph and came secretly to Ray, where he was in hiding in a pit in the house of a Shi'ite. He spent most of his time in worship, for during the day he fasted and at night he would rise for prayer. It was discovered that he went secretly at night to visit the tomb which now lies opposite his own. There is a road between the two. He said that this was the tomb of a man from the descendants of the Imam Musa Kazim. As he spent so much of his time there, gradually the people of Ray came to know about it. Before long one of them claimed to have seen the Apostle of God in a dream, and that the Apostle had said, " A man from my descendants shall be taken from Lords' Street and they shall bury him near an apple tree in the garden of Abdu'l-Jabbár ibn Abdu'l-Wahháb." The man who had seen the dream went at once to the owner of this garden and made an effort to buy it.

But in his conversation he learned that the owner of the garden had also seen the same dream and had already dedicated the garden to the descendants of the Prophet and as a cemetery for other Shi'ites.

It was at about this time that Abdu'l-Azim, who lived on Lords' Street, became ill and died. When they stripped him to bathe his body before burial, in his pocket they found a note of identification, in which he had written, "I am Abu'l-Ghasim Abdu'l-Azim, the son of Abdulla ibn Ạli, the son of Hasan ibn Zaid, the son of the Imam Hasan ibn Ạli ibn Abu Ṭalib." [1]

There is a tradition that when a man went from Ray to see the Imam Ạli Naḳi in Medina, the Imam asked him, "Where have you been?" He answered, "I have been to visit the grave of the Imam Husain at Kerbala." To this the Imam Ạli Naḳi replied, "If you had visited Abdu'l-Azim, whose tomb is near your home, you would have gained the same advantage as one who has visited the Imam Husain."[2]

The prescribed prayer for this pilgrimage includes the following petition, "I ask that thou wilt intercede for the redemption of my neck, and the neck of my father, and the necks of my brothers, and of all the believers, men and women, from the Fire and for entrance into Heaven with thy followers."[3] The first and for many years the only railroad in Persia was the line five miles long that runs from Teheran to the shrine of Shah Abdu'l-Azim, which is a most popular sanctuary for devoted believers to visit on Fridays. And near this tomb is a grave that is considered to be that of Hamza, a descendant of the Imam Musa. Majlisi thought it was probably the tomb that Abdu'l-Azim was accustomed to visit secretly, and he therefore advised pilgrims to also make the visit of salutation to the tomb of Hamza.

[1] He is wrongly identified by Le Strange with Husain ibn Ạli ar-Riḍa (*op. cit.*, p. 217), who is buried, according to Mustawfi, in Kazwin (Nuzhatu'l-Ḳulub, English trans., p. 64). This mistake is corrected, however, in a note in the same author's translation of Mustawfi, showing that according to the *Haft Iqlím* the saint commonly called Abdu'l-Azím, whose shrine is still the most popular sanctuary of Teheran, "was the son of Hasan (son of Zaid, son of Hasan, son of the Caliph Ạli), who was Amir of Medina, in the time of the Caliph Mansur, and who died at Ray."

[2] Majlisi, *op. cit.*, p. 422.

[3] Majlisi, *Miftahu'l-Janán*, p. 430.

Ardabil in Adherbaijan

It has been claimed that Shaikh Safiyyu'd-Din (d. 735/1334) of Ardabil, from whom the Ṣafawi kings traced their descent, was himself a descendant of the Imam Musa Kazim. He was twenty-two generations removed, however, and the line included five Muhammads without further designation, so his character as an imamzadeh may at least be doubtful. Nevertheless, as a saint in his own right, he was most highly esteemed and influential. Ardabil was the first capital of the Ṣafawids, and many of the earlier rulers of the dynasty are buried there at the shrine of Shaikh Ṣafí, who was described by one of his contemporaries as "His Holiness the Pole of the Heaven of Truth, the Swimmer in the Oceans of the Law, the Pacer in the Hippodrome of the Path, the Shaikh of Islam and of the Muslims, the Proof of such as attain the Goal, the Exemplar of the Bench of Purity, and the Rose-tree of the Garden of Fidelity." His life and teachings, with special emphasis on his *karámát* (spiritual gifts), were described in a book of 216,000 words that was written by his follower Tawakkul ibn Isma'íl, who has come to be known as Ibnu'l-Bazzáz. This huge book is called the *Ṣafwatuṣ-Ṣafa*, "The Best Things of the Chosen Ones." It was lithographed in Bombay in 1329/1911, and has been described and outlined by Professor Browne.[1]

Ardabil is a town of great historic interest, for at the time of the Muslim conquest of Persia the Umaiyads made Ardabil the capital of Adherbaijan. It has an elevation of nearly 5,000 ft., and among the mountains that seem to virtually surround it is the lofty extinct volcano, Mount Sawalán. This mountain town continued to be the administrative centre of the province of Adharbaijan until shortly before the Mongol conquest. Yaḳut says that in 617/1220 it was "a very populous town." When the Mongols came, however, the town was almost completely destroyed and the Muslim population were ruthlessly massacred. But in the fourteenth century, under the successors of Shaikh Ṣafí,

[1] Browne, *Persian Literature in Modern Times*, p. 33 ff.

"there arose in Ardabil a kind of theocratic state, the military power of which depended on the descendants of the Turkish slaves manumitted by Shaikh Ṣadr al-Ḍin, the so-called Ḳizil-Básh (Redheads)."[1] The rulers in this state were hereditary spiritual instructors,[2] descendants of Shaikh Ṣafi, and in the sixteenth century Isma'íl, the sixth in descent, became the founder of the celebrated Safawid dynasty of Persian Shahs. It was Shah Isma'íl I who made Shi'ite Islam the official religion of Persia, and as he and his immediate successors are buried in Ardabil, in the courtyard of the mausoleum of Shaikh Ṣafí, the continued significance of this shrine to Shi'ite pilgrims can be readily appreciated. When the Russians sacked the place in 1827 they took away the library of Shaikh Ṣafí and it is now part of the Imperial Library of Leningrad. Earthquakes have also damaged the buildings. Even the non-Muslim visitor who goes to the Shrine in the early morning when there are not many Shi'ite pilgrims there who might protest, or who gets permission from the Department of Public Instruction, may enter the long room containing the tombs of several of the Ṣafawid Shahs and see there several interesting stone tablets, valuable carpets, and a collection of old Persian and Chinese porcelain.

Shah Tahmasp (1524-1576) mentions in his diary a visit he made to the Shrine at Ardabil at a time when he was in doubt as to the outcome of a particular battle in his long continued warfare with Turkey. "There I made the pledge with twelve candles as had been commanded (by Ạli, whom he had seen in a dream), along with other offerings that I determined myself. I visited the tombs of the great saints, I prayed in the courtyard of the Shrine, and then I slept at the tomb of Shaik Haidar (the father of Shah Isma'il I). Here it was that Shaikh Safiyyu'd-Din appeared to me in a dream and declared: 'After twenty days your affair will be either *zuhúr* (appearance) or *khurúj* (departure).' I was uncertain which of these two words he used, but when I awoke I said to myself, If it is *zuhúr*, perhaps it refers to the Imam,

[1] *Encyclopædia of Islam*, art. "Ardabíl."
[2] Sir T. Wolseley Haig, *Encyclopædia of Islam*, art. "Ṣafawíds."

T

the Deliverer to be sent by God and the Established Representative of the House of Muhammad, but if it is the other word, *khurúj*, well what would that mean?"[1]

Graves of other Imamzadehs

Majlisi remarks that "in all the cities there are many tombs attributed to imamzadehs and other relations of the Imams. The graves of some of them, however, are not marked, and in case of others there is nothing in particular that is known of their lives. It is advisable to visit all of them whose tombs have been identified. Honour shown to them is equivalent to honouring the Imams. While no separate instructions are given for these pilgrimages, it is well that their tombs should be visited in the same manner as those of other believers. If a distinction is made in the mode of addressing them let the salutation to them be the same as to the Imams, with whatever words flow to the tongue to show them honour. Any written salutations that the learned doctors have included in books are also acceptable."[2]

There is a shrine on the site of the old town of Kuchan in Khorasan that is in memory of Ibrahim, who was one of the sons of the Imam Riḍa,[3] and the fact that this town was destroyed by an earthquake in 1895, with considerable damage to the Shrine, was explained to me by the naive village people who are living there now in vineyards. They said that it happened that the Imamzadeh Ibrahim had gone to visit his father in Mashhad on the night of the earthquake, and thus the place had been left without his protection. Otherwise such a disaster would not have occurred.

Another Imamzadeh, Muhammad ibn Muhammad ibn Zaid ibn Imam Zainu'l-Abidín, is buried in a garden outside Nishapur. There his grave is marked by a mausoleum which has a dome that is noted for its beautiful tile designs. It is said to have been repaired by Shah Ṣafi in 1041/1631. It is in a niche in a building

[1] D. C. Phillpott, "Memoirs of Shah Ṭahmásq," *Bib. Indica*, No. 1319, p. 38.
[2] Majlisi, *Tofatu'z-Za'irín*, p. 423.
[3] Muhammad Taḳi Khan, Hakím, *Ganj-i-Dánish*, ed. 1305/1887, p. 371.

that adjoins this Shrine that the traveller may see the exceedingly unpretentious tomb of the Persian poet Umar Khayyám. Every Friday, and on religious feast days, scores of visitors go out from Nishapur to this garden. Most of them know little about Umar Khayyám. They go out to this Shrine to seek the intercession of the descendant of the Imam. In their prayers they tell him their personal needs and their fears, their misfortunes and their diseases in this life, with the hope that he may use his influence to help them. They plead with him also to intercede for their forgiveness and happiness after death. Surely he would do this much for them, since they have taken the trouble to come and honour him by saying their prayers at his grave—for honouring him is honouring the Imams, and honouring the Imams is honouring God.

CHAPTER XXV

MINOR PLACES OF SHI'ITE PILGRIMAGE

IN spite of the boasted monotheism of the Ḳoran, the Muhammadan peoples have retained many animistic customs and one of the most vital phases of the religious life of the common people in nearly all Muslim countries is the veneration they pay to the graves of saints. In both these matters the theologians and traditionists have followed the tide of public opinion. Honour is paid by the Shi'ites, not only to the grave of the Prophet at Medina and to the graves of the Imams and their descendants, and to the place where the Hidden Imam disappeared and to the graves of his four agents, but there are many other sacred places that pilgrims are advised to visit. The people have come to have their local saints, whose graves or other relics they visit with the hope that the respective saints will thereby be pleased and will intercede for them, that they may have health and prosperity.

Stones with the Footprints of Imams

"Among the miracles (mu'djizát) popularly attributed to Muḥammad was the fact that when he trod on a rock, his foot sank into the stone and left its impress there. . . . The most famous of these footprints is that in the Masdjid al-Aḳṣá, at Jerusalem, on the rock from which Muhammad mounted Buráḳ for his journey to heaven."[1] Similar footprints that are attributed to Muhammad are pointed out in Damascus, in Cairo, in Constantinople, and in India "such slabs of stone are found all over the country." In Persia, however, it has been more in harmony with the genius of Shi'ite Islam to attribute the supposed footprints on such stones to particular ones of the Imams. Not

[1] T. W. Arnold, *Encyclopædia of Islam*, art. "Ḳadam Sharíf."

far from Nishapur, and on the road to Mashhad, there is an old fortified village on the top of a hill, at the foot of which there is a beautiful shrine that lies half hidden among trees. Beneath the blue dome of this shrine a stone is kept that bears the huge impress, supposedly, of the foot of the Imam Riḍa. Pilgrims who travel to Mashhad in the modern way, by motor-lorry, almost always insist that the driver should stop in Ḳadamgah (the place of the footprint) to enable them to visit this shrine. We read of a similar place in Adharabaiján, in a village called Jiwaldar, where there is another *ḳadamgah,* and where the imamzadeh Sayyid Amir Admad is said to be buried.[1]

The Graves of Companions of the Prophet

Majlisi has recommended that the pilgrimage salutation should be made also at the graves of Companions of the Prophet who gave their support to the Shi'ite cause, especially in the case of those whose outstanding merit is recognised. Among these is Salman the Persian, who suggested to Muḥammad the digging of a moat for the defence of Medina, and who, in his later years, so identified himself with the life of the common people by the simplicity of his habits that he has become the subject of many popular legends. Many Shi'ites visit his tomb on their return from Kerbala, for it is located at the village of Asbandur, in the region of al-Madain. There are other authorities who say that he was buried in the environs of Isfahan.[2]

The tomb of Abu Dhar is also regarded as worthy of a pilgrimage, for he was the third person to profess his belief in the Apostle, and he went to Persia as a missionary for the new faith. He is particularly remembered on account of his truthfulness, for it is related that the Prophet himself once said: "The sky never cast its shadow upon anyone, and the earth never received anyone who was more truthful than Abu Dhar." He was also absolutely fearless, and it is said that it was because he had openly reproached the Caliph Uthman that he was banished to a place at

[1] Fursat Shirázi, *Athdru'l-Ajam,* ed. 1314 A.H., p. 245.
[2] Donaldson, "Salman the Persian, *Moslem World,* Vol XIX, p. 351.

a distance of four days' march from Medina, a village called Rabdhi, where he died in the year 34 A.H.[1]

Others of the loyal Companions of the Prophet and supporters of the rights of Ali whose tombs are to be visited if possible are al-Mikdad, who died in Egypt and who is buried in Medina[2]; Ammár ibn Yásír, with whom the Prophet entered into the covenant of brotherhood, and of whom he declared, "Ammár was always ready in battle, showing his manhood and receiving many wounds"[3]; Idí ibn Hatim, who was noted for his generosity and his zeal for Islam, and who served "at the stirrup of Ali"[4]; Jabir ibn Abdulla, who was one of the helpers of Ali, and who outlived all the other Companions[5]; Hudhaifa ibn al-Yamán, who was killed with his father and his brother in the battle of Uhud, and who was buried in Medina[6]; Hujr ibn Idí, who had become a Muslim in his childhood and who fought with Ali in the Battle of the Camel and also at Siffín[7]; and finally Kanbar, who is mentioned as the faithful "freedman" of Ali.[8] All of these Majlisi has given special mention and advises that their graves be visited.[9]

The Graves of Scholars, Poets, and Saints

It is said that the tombs of great Shi'ite scholars and traditionists should be visited whenever possible. Such men are Shaikh Mufid and Sayyid Murtada, who were the teachers of the famous traditionist at-Tusi, and who were buried in Baghdad.[10] The tomb of Shaikh Tusi is at Najaf, though as his name indicates he came from Tus in distant Khorasan. The lawyer-theologian Aláma Hillí, whose name shows he was from Hilla, was another

[1] Fursat Shirázi, *op. cit.*, p. 77; and Ibn Sa'd, *Tabakat*, IV, ii, pp. 161-174.
[2] Ibn Sa'd, *op. cit.*, III, i., pp. 114, 115.
[3] *Ibid.*, VI, p. 7; and *Athǽru'l-Ajam*, p. 74.
[4] *Ibid.*, VI, p. 13; and *Athǽru'l-Ajam*, p. 73.
[5] *Ibid.*, III, ii, p. 114; and *Athǽru'l-Ajam*, p. 73.
[6] *Ibid.*, VI, 8, and VII, 64.
[7] *Ibid.*, VI, 151-154; and *Encyclopædia of Islam*, art. "Hudjr."
[8] *Ibid.*, VI, 165; and Yakubi, *Taríkh*, ii, pp. 250, 253.
[9] Majlisi, *Tofatu'z-Za'irín*, p. 423.
[10] Muhammad ibn Sulaiman Tanukábuni, *Kisasu'l-Ulama*, Nos. 97, 98, 90. Cf. Browne, *Persian Literature in Modern Times*, pp. 405, 449.

man of ability and distinction in the Baghdad school. His able service is recognized and his tomb also should be visited.[1] As Majlisi has observed, many scholars and traditionists were buried in Ḳumm. Among those whose graves should be visited are Ạli ibn Babawaihi, Muhammad ibn Ḳalawaihi, Ḳuṭb Rawandi, Zakariyyah ibn Adam, Zakariyyah ibn Idris, and Adam ibn Ishaḳ.[2]

The possible advantage of poets also as mediators is not overlooked. A few years ago the writer saw eight blind men, all of them aged, who were sitting patiently at the tomb of Shaikh Abdulla Ansárí, which is in a garden that lies outside the city of Herat, in Afghanistan. It was Ansárí who gave the following counsel to beware of selfish introspection[3]:

" Great shame it is to deem of high degree
Thyself, or over others reckon thee :
Strive to be like the pupil of thine eye—
To see all else, but not thyself to see."

In another of the gardens of Herat, rich with beautiful pine trees, is the white marble tomb of the versatile Mulla Nuru'd-Din Ạbdu'r-Rahmán Jámí, who was buried there the same year Columbus discovered America. A tree was growing right up from the grave, which is not infrequent at the tombs of poets, and is not inappropriate for the man who said, " Life is a very splendid robe : its fault is brevity." It was he also who said, " O Jámí, close thy mouth from speech in this garden, for there the song of the nightingale and the shriek of the raven are one." And one wondered, as he watched the visitors gazing upon the tomb, how many of them were familiar with what Professor Browne called Jámí's prayer for spiritual enlightenment[4]:

" My God, my God ! Save us from preoccupation with trifles, and show us the reality of things as they are ! Withdraw from

[1] *Kiṣaṣu'l-Ulama*, No. 88 ; Browne, *op. cit.*, p. 406 ; and the English translation of al-Hilli's *Al'Bábu'l-Ḥádí Ạshar*, by Rev. William M. Miller, Oriental Translation Fund, Vol. XXIX.
[2] Majlisi, *Tofatu'z-Za'irín*, p. 422.
[3] Browne, *Literary History of Persia*, ii, p. 260.
[4] Browne, *Persian Literature under Tartar Dominion*, pp. 547, 548.

the eyes of our understanding the veil of heedlessness, and show us everything as it truly is! Display not to us Not-Being in the guise of Being, and place not a veil of Not-Being over the beauty of Being. Make these phenomenal forms a Mirror of the Effulgences of Thy Beauty, not a cause of veiling and remoteness, and cause these phantasmal pictures to become the means of our knowledge and vision, not a cause of ignorance and blindness. All our deprivation and banishment is from ourselves, leave us not with ourselves, but grant us deliverance from ourselves, and vouchsafe us knowledge of Thyself!"

There is another Jámí, the saint Shiháb-ud-Din Ahmad, who is buried in his home town, the large village of Jám in Khorasan. At his grave also there is a wide-spreading tree that affords restful shade to many visitors. Timur came to this shrine in the fourteenth century, and the traveller Ibn Batutah, who visited it about the same time, reported that most of the land appeared to belong to descendants of the saint. At the present time the town itself is known as Turbat-i-Shaikh Jámí, or the place where Shaikh Jámí is buried.[1]

Pilgrimages by Proxy.

Specifications are given by Majlisi for pilgrimages to be made by proxy (nayábat). "Understand," he says, "that the merit of a pilgrimage to any of the Apostles of God, or to any of the Imams, may be bestowed upon the holy spirit of any of them, or *may be bequeathed to the spirit of any one of the believers*, and through them the pilgrimage can be made *by proxy*." In explanation of this statement he cited the following traditions[2]:

Dawud ibn Ṣarma said to the Imam Ạli Naḳi, "I visited your father and I gave the merit of the visit to you." The Imam replied, "There is great reward and merit for you from God, and praise and honour from us." There is a tradition also that the Imam Ạli Naḳi sent a person to the *ḥa'ír* (pool or swamp) where the Imam Husain is said to be buried, "to make the pilgrimage and prayer for him."

[1] Le Strange, *Lands of the Eastern Caliphate*, p. 357.
[2] Majlisi, *op. cit.*, p. 423; and Ibn Babawaihi, *Kamalu'd-Din*, p. 241; and Majlisi, *Baharu'l-Anwár*, Persian translation of Vol. 13, p. 8.

The Imam Musa is reported to have said, "When you visit the enlightened tomb of the Apostle of God, and have finished the ritual of the pilgrimage, you should pray with two prostrations and take your stand by the head of the Apostle of God. Then say: 'Peace be unto thee, O Prophet of God, from my father, my mother, my wife, my son, and from all the people of my town—and their freedmen and their slaves, white and black.' Then when you return it will be right for you to tell each person from your town, 'I was your proxy on the pilgrimage.'"

Another witness relates that he asked several of the Imams, "If in the case of a man who made two prostrations of prayer, or fasted for a whole day, or who went on the pilgrimage to Mecca, or who made the pilgrimage to the tomb of the Apostle of God, or to the shrine of one of the pure Imams, and bestowed the merit of his action on his father and his mother, or on his believing brothers, is that merit genuine and will it count?" The answer was that the merit is genuine, and that it accrues to the person himself without being diminished by what he has bestowed upon the others.

Definite instructions for the pilgrimage by proxy are given by Shaikh Ṭusi as follows: "Anyone who goes on a pilgrimage as a proxy for a believing brother should say (after he has performed his ablutions and attended to the necessary requirements of the pilgrimage), 'O God, keep me from weariness or illness or disorder or weakness, and reward ——— the son of ——— for this pilgrimage, and reward me for completing it.' And after he has made the pilgrimage, at the end he should say, 'Peace be on thee, O my Master, from ——— the son of ———, I have come to thee as a pilgrim on his account, so intercede for him with thy Lord.'" Then he may offer any prayer he wishes on his account, or he may employ the set prayer that was written by Shaikh Ṭusi to meet this situation.[1]

[1] *Ibid.*, *op. cit.*, pp. 418-420.

CHAPTER XXVI

THE RISE OF THE BUWAIHIDS

IN the Muhammadan conquest of Persia, frontier posts were established south of the Caspian Sea on the line represented by Zanján, Ḳazvín, Ray, and Damghán. The region lying north of this line and extending to the shores of the Caspian is included in the modern Gilán and Mazandarán. With its marshes and wooded mountains it had been like an impenetrable jungle that had continued for many years to be the refuge of tribes of Guebres and pagans. By the tenth century, however, all this district, made up of the small provinces of Ṭabaristán, Jurján and Ḳúmis, was included in the province of Ḍaylam.[1] The Daylamites were at that time most prominent and influential, for from among them had sprung the remarkable family of the Buwaihids, who had succeeded in establishing their authority throughout western Persia and were the recognised dictators to the Caliphs for more than a century.

It was by recruiting Ḍaylamites along with Turks for the huge armies of mercenaries that fought for the Caliphs against the Byzantines that Islam had first won its way among these peoples. Later on there was a Muhammadan governor of Ṭabaristan, Náṣiru'l-Haḳḳ Abu Muhammad, and through his influence "a large number of fire-worshippers were converted to Islam in Daylam."[2] Mas'udi mentions the missionary work that was done for Islam by Hasan ibn Ạli Utrush. He had spent many years in Daylam, where he found that the "people were entirely unbelievers, either Magians or pagans, and he called them to the Most High God, and they listened and became

[1] Le Strange, *Lands of the Eastern Caliphate*, p. 173.
[2] T. W. Arnold, *The Preaching of Islam*, p. 210.

Muslims." He built places of worship for them, and in 301 A.H., with the assistance of his Daylamite followers, he led the Ạlíd uprising that drove the "Blacks," or Ạbbasids, out of the Daylamite country.[1]

Thus it was that various military leaders, chiefs in their own districts, and who had become converts to Islam, found opportunity for advancement in the service of neighbouring Muslim rulers. At the same time it should not be forgotten that their friendly contacts had been with Shi'ites, and consequently they had become convinced of the righteousness of the cause of the persecuted house of Ạli. The friendship of these mountain chieftains, newly converted to Islam, proved to be of inestimable value, for it was during the one hundred and twenty-five years of the supremacy of the Buwaihids that the Shi'ite traditions were compiled and their distinctive doctrines were formulated. But strange as it may seem there is but little known about the origin of this Daylamite family.

The story that is recorded by Ibn Ṭiḳṭaḳa in the *El Fachri* reads more like a tradition of little historical value. He says that concerning the founding of the (Buwaihid) dynasty, Shariyár ibn Rustam, ad-Daylamí, has related the following story: "Abu Shuja' Buwaih was a true friend of mine in his early life, and one day I went to him when his wife had died. She was the mother of his three sons who afterwards ruled the country. They were Ạli and Hasan and Ahmad. Abu Shuja' Buwaih had been most devoted to his wife. I managed to console him and quieted his trouble, and brought him to my house and prepared food for him. There I called his three sons and we were explaining the matter to them, when a man walked past the gate, a man who was regarded as a great astrologer, an interpreter of dreams, and a writer of charms and talismans. Abu Shuja' summoned him and said to him, 'Yesterday I saw a dream, will you explain it to me? I dreamt that a great fire started from my loins and that the flame grew very long and kept extend-

[1] Mas'udi, *Muruju'l-Dhahab*, Vol. VIII, p. 280, and Vol. IX, pp. 4-6; also Goldziher, *Muhammedanische Studien*, Part I, p. 59; and T. W. Arnold, *op. cit.*, p. 210.

ing until it reached the sky. Then it opened and divided into three parts, and from these parts were born a number of other parts, and the world itself was hidden by these flames.' Then the astrologer said, 'This is a most significant dream and one which I will not interpret for less compensation than a robe of honour and a horse.' But Buwaih said to him, 'I swear that I have no other clothes than what are on my body, and if I give you these I will be naked.' The astrologer said, 'Then ten dinár?' Buwaih said, 'I swear that I do not have two dinár, so how could I give you ten?' He promised him something, however, and the astrologer explained that the dream signified that he would have three sons who would rule the earth and those who dwell upon it, and that their fame would ascend to the vaulted heaven, as this fire had done, and that there would be born to them a company of powerful kings, just as he had seen the flames spring forth from the separate parts of the fire. But Buwaih protested, 'You should be ashamed to ridicule us this way, for I am but a poor man, and afflicted, and my sons are these simple, poverty-stricken men, how is it that they will be kings?' The astrologer said, 'Tell me the exact time of the birth of each of your sons.' Buwaih told him this. The astrologer began to look in his astrolabe and in his almanacks, and he arose and took the hand of Ạli, and said, 'I swear that he is the one who will rule the provinces.' He then took the hand of Hasan and said, 'And this one will rule after him.' But Abu Shuja' Buwaih was enraged and called out to his sons, 'Slap him, for he has insolently been making fun of us!' They slapped him, therefore, and we laughed at him. But the astrologer only said, 'There is no harm done, for you will recall this when you are in your kingdom.' Abu Shuja' gave him ten darhams and he went away.'[1]

About as much as can be determined about the Buwaihid family is that they were in the military service of the dominant Daylamite prince of the time, Mardáwíj ibn Ziyár, who, in a grand raid, had made himself the independent ruler of Ṭabaristán and Jurján, occupied Isfahán and Hamadan, and in the year

[1] Ibn Ṭiktaḳá, *El-Fachri*, ed. Ahlwardt, p. 324 ff.

A.D. 931 had pushed on to the Mesopotamian frontier.[1] The sons of Abu Shuja' Buwaih were among his most valiant chiefs, to whom he doubtless owed much of the dashing brilliancy of his campaign. Accordingly he made one of them, Abu'l-Hasan Ạli, the governor of an important and well fortified town south-east of Hamadan that was called Karaj (or Karah). But the young warrior had no sooner established himself there when he pressed on, apparently on his own authority, and took Isfahán. Mardáwíj is said to have been fearful concerning the young Buwaihid's rapid advance and ordered that Isfahán should be restored to the Caliph. At this rebuff the Buwaihid chief was indignant, and immediately broke off further relations with his patron and continued to carry on his depredations and conquests. In a series of rapid raids he and his brothers captured so many important places that in a very short time Ạli was governing Fars, Hasan was dominating Medina, and Ahmad had conquered Kirman. Ahmad then made a further campaign to the West, and in A.D. 945 "he entered Baghdad, and the Caliph Mustakfi had to create him *Amir al-Umara* and gave him the honorific title of Mu'izz ad-Dawla (the Strengthener of the Empire). At the same time Ạli and Hasan received the titles *Ịmád ad-Dawla* (the Support of the Empire) and *Rukn ad-Dawla* (the Pillar of the Empire) respectively, and similar pompous titles were henceforth the usual appellation of the Buwaihid rulers."[2]

In regard to the way the Caliphs gave these high-sounding titles, al-Biruni made an interesting comment: "When the Beni-Ạbbas had decorated their assistants, friends and enemies indiscriminately, with vain titles, compounded with the word *Dawla* (that is 'empire,' such as Helper of the Empire, Sword of the Empire, etc.), the empire perished; for in this they went beyond all reasonable limits. This went on so long that those who were especially attached to their court claimed something like a distinction between themselves and the others. Thereupon the Caliphs bestowed double titles. But then also the others

1 Stanley Lane-Poole, *Muhammadan Dynasties*, p. 136; and Mas'udi, Vol. IX, p. 10 ff.

2 *Encyclopædia of Islam*, art. "Buyids."

wanted the same titles and knew how to carry their point by bribery. Now it became necessary a second time to create a distinction between this class and those who were directly attached to their court, so the Caliphs bestowed triple titles, adding besides the title of Shahinshah. In this way the matter became utterly opposed to common sense, and clumsy to the highest degree, so that he who mentions them gets tired before he has scarcely commenced, he who writes them loses his time writing, and he who addresses them runs the risk of missing the time for prayer."[1]

It was not long after Ahmad ibn Buwaih, or the Mu'izz ad-Dawla, had made himself master of Baghdad, until he had the Caliph Mustakfi blinded. It is said that he thus disqualified him to rule because he feared the possible return of the Turks who had fled to Mosul, but the immediate provocation on which he justified the act was a reception that the chief lady of the Caliph's *ḥarím* had given to the officers of the Turkish and Daylamite mercenaries who were still in Baghdad. This was construed as an effort to influence them against the conqueror to whom they had surrendered.[2] Accordingly, a few days later, when the Caliph was giving a reception to a foreign ambassador, when the Mu'izz ad-Dawla arrived he showed his apparent obeisance by kissing the Caliph's hand. As he withdrew two of his officers came forward to give the Caliph the same greeting, but instead, as they took the Caliph's hand " they pulled him from his throne and threw him on the ground and dragged him by his turban, and the Daylamites thronged through the palace into the *ḥarím* and plundered it until nothing was left therein."[3] The Buwaihid dictator returned to his own palace, whither the humiliated Caliph was driven on foot through the streets. There he was deposed from his exalted office and his eyes were seared over with a hot iron. Such was the vengeance of the first Buwaihid, as awe-inspiring as it was precipitate.

[1] Sachau, *Chronology of Ancient Nations*, p. 129.
[2] Muir, *The Caliphate, Rise, Decline and Fall*, p. 575.
[3] As-Suyuti, *History of the Caliphs*, p. 417; and T. W. Arnold, *The Caliphate*, p. 62.

Although the deposed Caliph's cousin was appointed to succeed him, hereafter, for the next hundred years, the Caliphs were to exercise only nominal authority, and that only at the bidding and with the approval of their Buwaihid masters. Moreover there was grim irony in the fact that the Buwaihids and their Daylamite supporters were Shi'ites who only tolerated the Caliphate as an administrative convenience in governing their Sunnite subjects. The suggestion was made to the Mu'izz ad-Dawla that he appoint a member of an Ạlid family to the Caliphate, but " one of his friends dissuaded him, urging that at present he was under a Caliph whom both he and his adherents would readily kill if he ordered his death ; whereas if he appointed to the Caliphate an Ạlid whose title was acknowledged to be valid by both him and his followers, the latter would refuse to kill the Caliph if ordered to do so."[1]

One of the greatest innovations introduced by the Mu'izz ad-Dawla was the custom of public mourning during the first ten days of Muḥarram.[2] This order was given in A.D. 963, that there might be an annual commemoration of the tragic death of the Imam Husain (chapters vii and viii). The practice has continued as the most distinctive and most widely known of all Shi'ite customs ; and in connection with the public parade on the tenth day of Muharram to show their loyalty to the house of Ạli, the mourners have resorted to a great variety of spectacular and gruesome ways of shedding their blood and mutilating their bodies.

The most celebrated ruler of the Buwaihids was not one of the original three brothers. Four years after the capture of Baghdad, Ạli, the *Ịmád ad-Dawla*, died and was succeeded by his brother Hasan's son, who was known by the title *Ạḍud ad-Dawla*, the Arm of the Empire. For thirty years, A.D. 949-982, he exercised an arbitrary authority in Fárs, Irák, Ahwáz, and Kirmán. In the history of Persia he is mentioned frequently and with great praise for the encouragement he gave to poets and scholars.

[1] Zaydan, *Umayyads and Ạbbasids*, p. 275, from Ibn Athir, viii, p. 177.
[2] Browne, *Persian Literature in Modern Times*, p. 31.

The Shi'ites regard him as their great benefactor, who contributed magnificently to the restoration of their sacred shrines, the building of mosques, and the endowment of schools for religious education. At one time he commanded that the Caliph's name should be omitted from the public prayers in the mosques on Fridays for a period of two months. But again, when he was at the height of his power, as the acknowledged ruler of the provinces from the Caspian to the Persian Gulf, and from Isfahan to Damascus, we read of his accepting the most exalted honours he could imagine from the Caliph. The Caliph gave him whatever he demanded of the insignia of royal rank—the robe of honour, the jewelled crown, the banner of the Commander-in-Chief, and the banner of the Heir Apparent. At times it looked very much as though he was about to take the Caliphate itself, for he went so far as to require that the Caliph permit his name to be mentioned in the Friday prayers in the mosques.

To quote Professor Arnold, " The infliction of such humiliations on the Caliph is in striking contrast with the honour and reverence paid to him, whenever it was politic to bring him forward, as the supreme head of the faith. In the very year after the Ạdud ad-Dawla had extorted the privileges above-mentioned, an ambassador was sent to Baghdad in 980 by the Fáṭimid Caliph of Egypt, Ạzíz bi'lláhi. He was received with impressive ceremonial: the troops were drawn up in serried ranks, and the nobles and officers of the state were arranged in order of their dignity in the place of audience, but the Caliph was invisible behind a curtain. When Ạdud ad-Dawla received permission to approach, the curtain was raised, and the spectators could see the Caliph seated on a high throne surrounded by a hundred guards in magnificent apparel and with drawn swords. Before him was placed one of the most sacred relics in Islam—the Qur'án of the Caliph Ụthman; on his shoulders hung the mantle of the Prophet; in his hands he held the staff of the Prophet, and he was girt with the sword of the 'Apostle of God.' Ạdud ad-Dawla kissed the ground before this spectacle of imposing majesty, and the Egyptian envoy, awe-struck, asked him:

'What is this? Is this God Almighty?' Aḍud ad-Dawla answered: 'This is the Khalifa of God upon earth,' and he continued to move forward, seven times kissing the ground before the Caliph. Then Ṭá'i' (the Caliph) ordered one of his attendants to lead him up to the foot of the throne. Aḍud ad-Dawla continued to make a show of reverence before such unapproachable and impressive majesty, and the Caliph had to say to him: 'Draw near,' before he would come forward and kiss the Caliph's foot. Ṭá'i' stretched out his right hand to him and bade him be seated. Aḍud ad-Dawla humbly asked to be excused, and only after repeated injunctions would he consent to sit down in the place assigned to him, after first reverently kissing it. After this elaborate ceremony, Ṭá'i' said: 'I entrust to you the charge of my subjects whom God has committed to me in the East and in the West, and the administration of all their concerns, with the exception of what appertains to my personal and private property. Do you therefore assume charge of them?' Aḍud ad-Dawla answered, 'May God aid me in obedience and service to our Lord, the Commander of the Faithful.' This solemn farce ended with the bestowal of seven robes of honour upon Aḍud ad-Dawla, who kissed the ground on the presentation of each, and then took his leave, followed by all the rest of the great assembly."[1]

The Turkish generals, who had dominated the Caliphs for many years before, were effectively succeeded by the Buwaihids, who reduced the Caliphate to a mere figure-head. During their reign, however, there was continued literary activity. Each of the several contemporary dynasties, all virtually independent of the Caliph, had its own circle of grammarians, poets and theologians. The outstanding poets were Mutanabbi and Tha'álibí, who were known throughout the empire, but we find mention of the fervent Shi'ite bard, Ibn al-Hajjaj, who is said to have expressed the desire in his will that his body should be laid at the feet of the Imam Musa at Kazimain. And the Daylamite poet, Mihyar ibn Marzuya, employed his art in the expression

[1] T. W. Arnold, *The Caliphate*, pp. 65-67.

of his Shi'ite opinions in a way that so displeased the Sunnites, that one of them, recalling that Mihyár had originally been a Zoroastrian, exclaimed, "Mihyár, when you were converted, all you did was to shift from one corner of Hell into another."[1]

Three eminent Arab geographers also belonged to this period, Iṣṭakhrí, Ibn Hawḳal, and Muḳaddasi, all of whom were familiar with Baghdad. But the most distinguished of all the writers of this period was the celebrated historian, Mas'udi, who has included in his *Muruju'l-Dhahab* (*Prairies of Gold*) an excellent contemporary account of the way the Daylamites came suddenly into power.[2] Mas'udi was himself a Shi'ite and it is probable that we are indebted to the sympathetic Buwaihid dynasty for the freedom of his narratives about the Caliphs up until A.D. 947.

[1] Huart, *A History of Arabic Literature*, New York, 1903, p. 86.
[2] Mas'udi, *Muruju'l-Dhahab*, Vol. IX, pp. 1-34.

CHAPTER XXVII

THE EARLIEST COLLECTIONS OF SHI'ITE TRADITIONS

SIGNIFICANT effects of political changes on the development of the Ḥadith literature are easily traced throughout the course of Muslim history. It is noteworthy in the first place that there are no existing compilations of Muḥammadan traditions, whether Sunnite or Shi'ite, that date as far back as the Umayyad caliphate. Málik ibn Anas is the only one of the early writers who was born during that period, and the last forty-five years of his life, the years of his literary activity, were lived under the authority of the Ạbbasids.

He was one of a group of Ạlids who had given their oath of allegiance to Al-Mansur. They had done this under compulsion, and afterwards, in A.D. 762, they wished to declare themselves in favour of Muḥammad ibn Ạbdulla. Málik ibn Anas, who was the founder of the earliest school of Muḥammadan law, ventured to make the decision that an oath given under compulsion was not binding, and for so doing, in spite of whatever authority he could cite from the traditions, he was publicly flogged. The experience taught him the lesson that even a chief justice must recognize existing political authority, for after his whipping he continued to figure in the public life of Medina for thirty-three years, and during the last year of his life the Caliph Harún ar-Rashíd attended his classes. While his interest in collecting traditions was for the sake of their bearing on questions of jurisprudence, and the *Muwaṭṭa* is not one of the six canonical collections, notwithstanding this limited objective it was necessary for him to scrupulously regard the wishes of those who were in political authority.

Nevertheless, there are traditions included in the canonical collections that have been handed down from Umayyad times.

The tragedy at Kerbala had made such an impression on the minds of the people that travelling story-tellers and poets who sympathized with the house of Ạli had to be considered by the unpopular rulers in Damascus. Of these poets in Umayyad times, there were men like al-Kuthayyir, who had allied himself with the Kaisanís, who were favourably received at Damascus, and who were kept under the very influential shadow of the court; but there were others like Ferazdaḳ, "a pious and fervent Moslem, entirely devoted to the Prophet's family, and with it all a cynic and a libertine," who wrote verses to foster the cause of Zain al-Ạbidín that so offended the Caliph Sulaiman that he committed him to the dungeon.[1] Likewise those who occupied themselves in collecting and narrating traditions soon found that they had to reckon with severe state censorship. For, as Professor Guillaume has pointed out, "Tabari states that Mu'áwiya I ordered that all ḥadith favourable to the house of Ạli be suppressed, and that the glories of the family of Ụthman be extolled. The Umayyad hand is perhaps most clearly seen in the traditions which were forged to emphasize the sanctity of Jerusalem *vis-à-vis* Mecca and Medina."[2] Reference to Wensinck's *Handbook of Early Muḥammadan Tradition,* under such heads as "Ụthman" or "Jerusalem," will reveal the nature of this propaganda. And al-Zuhri has definitely stated concerning the Umayyads, "these princes have compelled us to write ḥadith."[3]

Aḥmad ibn Ḥanbal (d. 241 A.H.), who is generally remembered for his resistance to the Mu'tazilite teaching, in so much that he was scourged by the order of the Caliph Mu'tasim because he would not affirm that the Ḳoran was created, compiled a vast and most inclusive collection of traditions which has not been expurgated so as to entirely please the Ạbbasids. It includes traditions of obviously Syrian origin that are favourable to the Umayyads, as well as a very great many exceedingly detailed records that support the claims of the Shi'ites. The collections

[1] Huart, *Arabic Literature*, p. 51.
[2] Guillaume, *The Traditions of Islam*, p. 47. Cf. Tabari, ii, p. 112.
[3] *Idem, op. cit.*, p. 50.

of Bukhari and Muslim are different in both these respects, for "the compilation of the canonical collections (al-Bukhári, Muslim, Abú Dá'úd, al-Tirmidhí, al-Nasá'í and Ibn Mádja) dates from the time when the Ạbbasids were firmly in the saddle, and by this time systematic efforts had been made to extirpate the memory of the predecessors of the reigning house. We know that the names of the Umayyads were even removed from public monuments."[1]

Dominant public opinion was always a most influential factor in determining what traditions were to be circulated, as is evidenced by the experience of al-Nasá'í in Damascus. He had come from Khorasan and had lived in old Cairo until A.D. 914, when he went to Damascus with a collection of traditions that were favourable to Ạli. The people whom he was addressing in the mosque, however, were not disposed to tolerate any such statements, and they suddenly became an angry mob and literally trampled him under foot. Some of his friends saved him from being immediately killed and got him out of the city, but at Ramla, in Palestine, he died from the severe injuries he had received in Damascus.[2] But in many parts of the empire traditions favourable to the house of Ạli, and making heroes of members of his family who were martyrs, were accepted without protest during the early days of the Ạbbasid caliphate. The last of the forty-six chapters in the *Saḥiḥu'l-Tirmidhí* is devoted to the "Virtues of the Household of the Prophet," and there are numerous traditions in praise of Ạli that are on the tongues of pious Shi'ites at the present day that can be found in the great works of the six canonical writers.[3]

There was a vast difference, however, when under the Buwaihid dictators the tide of politics turned against the Ạbbasids and in favour of the Shi'ites. We find that the Imams were exalted beyond the range of any ordinary imagination, that both the

[1] *Idem, op. cit.*, p. 37.
[2] Huart, *op. cit.*, p. 221.
[3] Suyuti, *Táríkhu'l-Khulafá*, trans. Jarrett, p. 172 ff.; Tirmidhí, *Saḥiḥ*, ii, p. 308 ff.; and Wensinck, *Handbook of Early Muhammadan Traditions*, under the headings "Ạli," "Hasan," "Husain," etc.

Umayyads and the Abbasids were anathematized, and that new collections of traditions were systematically compiled. It was the first time in the history of Islam that the Shi'ites had had the advantage of a sympathetic dynasty, and the large number of books on religious subjects that were written and circulated during the Buwaihid period (A.D. 932-1055) shows how eagerly the oppressed ones, who had schooled themselves in dissimulation, now seized the opportunity to make effective use of their new freedom.

The list of Shi'ite writers on questions of tradition and jurisprudence that is given by Brockelmann is under two headings: the writers of the Zaidite sect, and the Persian Shi'ites.[1] It is the latter who are more important for the study of the doctrine of the Imamate and whose great literary activity at this time gave rise to the standard collections of Shi'ite traditions, though it is not without interest to observe that the large community of Zaidites in the Yemen were working along similar lines.[2] A considerable amount of information is available in regard to the outstanding traditionists of this period among the Persian Shi'ites in the *Fihrist* or "Index," by aṭ-Ṭusi, in the *Kiṣaṣu'l-Ulamá* or *Tales of the Divines*, by Muḥammad ibn Sulaiman of Tanukabun, and in the *Fihrist*, by Ibnu'l-Nadím. The fact of most significance is that in this Buwaihid period there were "three Muḥammads" who wrote "the four books" which are still considered as the standard collections of traditions from the Shi'ite point of view.

KULAINI.[3] The first and most highly esteemed of these

[1] Brockelmann, *Geschichte de Arabischen Litteratur*, Vol. I, p. 187, and p. 404 ff.

[2] Huart (*op. cit.*, p. 241) observes that "in the province of the Yemen, the Zaidite sect, which had taken possession of that country in the second century of the Hegira, and is still dominant there, reckoned among its teachers: al-Ḳasim ibn Ibrahím al-Hasaní, who died in 860; his grandson, al-Hadí Ilá'l-Ḥaḳḳ (He who guides to the truth) Abu'l-Husain Yaḥyá (859-910); another descendant of his, al-Mahdí Lidínillah (He who is guided towards the religion of God) al-Husain ibn al-Ḳasim, who died in 1013; and the Imam al-Mu'ayyad-Gillah Aḥmad ibn al-Ḥusain (944-1020). The works of these writers, formerly unknown to European students, have been brought back from Yemen by Herr Glaser, and are now in the Berlin Library."

[3] The *Ḳiṣaṣu'l-Ụlamá* (No. 96, p. 307), says that the name Kulaini should be pronounced as here indicated and not "Kalini," as it appears in the Ḳamus.

great traditionists is Muḥammad ibn Yaḳub al-Kulaini, who wrote the *Kafi fi Ịlm ad-Dín,* "A Compendium of the Science of Religion." It is a large book that contains over sixteen thousand traditions, which are classified: as *saḥiḥ* or Certified, 5,072; as *ḥasan* or Good, 144; as *muthaḳat* or Authoritative, 1,116; as *ḳawí* or Strong, 302; and as *za'af* or Duplications, 9,485. The edition lithographed in Teheran in 1307 A.H. is in two volumes; chapters i-vii being included in the first volume, which is called the *Usulu'l-Káfi,* or the "Roots of the Compendium"; while the second volume, including chapters viii-xxx, is called the *Furu'l-Káfi,* or the "Branches of the Compendium." It took al-Kulaini twenty years to write the Káfi, and in recognition of his diligence in collecting the traditions he was called Thiḳat al-Islam (the "Trustworthy Authority of Islam"). When he died in Baghdad in 329 or 328 A.H. (A.D. 939), he was buried at Kufa. As there was a saying that the bodies of saints and highly honoured men of the faith were preserved from corruption after death, his grave is said to have been opened to see whether this saying was true. The report is that he was found in his grave clothes, unchanged in any way, and lying with a little child that had been buried with him. For this reason a place of prayer was built over his tomb.[1]

AṢ-ṢADUḲ or AL-ḲUMMI.[2] The second of the great Shi'ite traditionists was Muḥammad ibn Ạli ibn al-Ḥusain ibn Musa ibn Babuwaihi (d. A.D. 991), and who was known as aṣ-Ṣaduḳ or as al-Ḳummi. He is sometimes difficult to distinguish from his father, who was also a writer of religious books and who was called all the names that his son bore except Muḥammad. His father died in 329 A.H., which was ten years before the close of what is called the Lesser Occultation of the Twelfth Imam. The story is told of a conversation his father is said to have had with Abu Ḳasim Ḥusain ibn Ruh, who was the third of the four agents of the Hidden Imam during that period of seventy-three years (256-339 A.H.). He said that he had asked

[1] *Ibid.*, p. 307. Cf. Tuṣi, *Fihrist,* No. 709.
[2] *Ibid.*, No. 94, pp. 300-307; and Tusi, *Fihrist,* No. 661.

the Imam's agent a number of questions, and when he left his presence he wrote a letter which he gave to Ạli ibn Ja'far ibn Aswad to deliver to him. In the letter he urged that the request that he might have a son would be brought to the notice of the Imam of the Age. After three days he received an answer from Abu Ḳasim, saying, "We have prayed for it." Subsequently the prayer appeared to have been more than answered, for as he said, "God gave me two sons, Muḥammad and Ḥusain." Aṣ-Ṣaduḳ therefore always maintained that he was born on account of the prayers of the Imam of the Age. However this may be his birth occurred in Khorasan, where his father had gone on a pilgrimage to the shrine of the Imam Riḍa. In 355 A.H., twenty-six years after the death of his father, he came to Baghdad, where he took advantage of the freedom that prevailed during the Buwaihid supremacy and carried on most arduous literary work for about thirty years. During this time he is said to have written three hundred treatises. One hundred and ninety of these works are named in the *Kiṣaṣu'l-Ulama* on the authority of an-Najjáshí in the *Kitábu'r-Rijál*. The *Kamal ad-Dín*, "The Perfection of Religion," begins with Adam and extends through sixty-two chapters to the signs of the return of the Imam of the Age. This book he is said to have written at the command of the Imam himself, whom he saw and with whom he conversed in a dream at Mecca. But his great work on the traditions as they form a basis for Muhammadan law, the title of which Professor Browne has translated as "Every Man His Own Lawyer" (man lá yahḍuruhu'l-faḳíh), is one of "the four books" and includes 4,496 traditions. The edition of this book that was lithographed in Persia in 1326 A.H. is unusually clear. While it has no index, the pages are numbered and the names of the various books, with their secondary subjects, are plainly indicated.

AṬ-ṬUSI.[1] The third of the three traditionists of this early period was Muḥammad ibn Hasan aṭ-Ṭusi. He also had come to Baghdad from Khorasan. The authority of the Shi'ite faith is

[1] *Ibid.*, No. 100, pp. 319-321; and Tusi, *Fihrist*, No. 620.

said to have been greatly advanced by his influence, for at times he had as many as three hundred students in his class. Both his friends and his opponents recognized his outstanding ability. He was exceedingly versatile and wrote on almost all the subjects included in Muslim learning, for he had had the advantage of having studied with Shaikh Mufíd and Sayyid Murtaḍa and other scholars. The first of these teachers was so highly esteemed that eighty thousand people are said to have gathered in the public square in Baghdad at the time of his funeral.[1] And Sayyid Murtaḍa, known as the *Alamu'l-Huda*, was an imamzadeh, the great-great-grandson of the Imam Musa Kazim, and was the recognized leader of the Shi'ite community in Baghdad. Rumour has it that the Caliph had agreed with Sayyid Murtaḍa to include the Shi'ites as a fifth division in the Ijma', calling them the Ja'farí, and ranking them with the Shafi'í, the Hanafí, the Malikí, and the Ḥanbalí, so that they would no longer have to resort to dissimulation (taḳiyya). But the sum agreed upon for this concession was two hundred thousand tomans and Sayyid Murtaḍa could only raise half that amount.[2]

Aṭ-Tusi was born in 385 A.H. at Ṭus in Khorasan and came to Baghdad when he was twenty-three years of age. In his later life he left Baghdad and went to live in Najaf. This was because he lived for twelve years after the overthrow of the Buwaihid dynasty and he had been burned out in Baghdad. It was thought that this burning of his house was the work of opponents who had complained against him to the Caliph. Their complaint had been that in one of his books he had cursed the Companions of the Prophet, in something he had written about "the early oppressors being accursed." He was called before the Caliph to explain, but denied that he had ever had any such intention, saying, "O Commander of the Faithful, the first oppressor was Cain the murderer of Abel. He it was who thus started murder among mankind." The second reference he said was to Ḳaidar ibn

[1] *Ibid.*, No. 97, pp. 307-314; and Tusi, *Fihrist*, No. 685.
[2] *Ibid.*, No. 98, pp. 314-317.

Salaf, the third to the murderer of Yahya ibn Zakharia, and the fourth to Ibn Muljam the murderer of Ạli. Thus his ready memory had enabled him to make an apt reply and the charge against him had been dismissed. It was not long afterwards, however, that he died at Najaf at the age of seventy-five, in the year 460 A.H.

In addition to numerous books on the principles of belief, on worship, on questions of the law, and on biography, he wrote the *Fihrist* or " Index " of Shi'ite books to which reference has been made. But the books for which he is best known are the remaining two of " the four books." The first of these is the *Tahdhíb al-Ahkám*, a " Correcting of Judgments," which has been lithographed in Persia in two volumes in 1316-1317 A.H. The second of these two books is the *Istibsár*, or an " Examination of the Differences in Traditions." The best text is the one lithographed in Lucknow in two volumes, with a comprehensive table of contents at the beginning of each volume.

The fact that these four standard collections of Shi'ite traditions were not made until the Buwaihid period, A.D. 932-1055, whereas the canonical Sunnite collections were completed a full generation before the beginning of that period, is fully compensated for by the Shi'ite doctrine of the infallibility of the Imams. For whereas the Sunnite traditionists have to trace the *isnád* of each separate tradition back through seven or eight generations, covering a period of approximately two hundred years, until they arrive at the testimony of a contemporary of the Prophet, the Shi'ite traditionists need only ascribe a statement through three or four creditable witnesses to one of the Imams and trace it to his predecessors as far back as they desire. Through the Imams they had a main line back to the Prophet himself.

The first volume of Kulaini's *Káfi fi Ịlm ad-Dín*, known as the *Usulu'l-Kafi*, or " Roots of the Compendium," stands out from the other books as primarily a work on theology. The titles of its seven chapters are not included in the works of aṣ-Ṣaduḳ (Ibn Babuwaihi) or of aṭ-Ṭusi, but with one exception they are found in the works of one or more of the canonical books of the Sunnites, as appears in the following table of contents.

The one exception is naturally the chapter on *al-Hujjat,* "the Proof" of the right of the Imams.

Contents of the *Usulu'l-Káfi.*

1. *Faḍlu'l-Ịlm* (p. 5), the "Value of Learning."
   Cf. Bukhari, Bk. 3; Muslim, Bk. 47; Tirmidhi, 39.
2. *Tawhíd* (p. 12), the "Unity of God."
   Cf. Bukhari, Bk. 97.
3. *Hujjat* (p. 58), the "Proof" of the right of the Imams.
4. *Imán wa'l-Kufr* (p. 231), "Faith and Unbelief."
   Cf. Bukhari, Bk. 2; Muslim, Bk. 1; and Tirmidhi, Bk. 38.
5. *Faḍlu'd-Du'á* (p. 392), the "Value of Prayer."
   Cf. Muslim, Bk. 48; and Nasá'í, Bk. 50.
6. *Faḍlu'l-Koran* (p. 440), the "Value of the Ḳoran."
   Cf. Bukhari, Bk. 66; and Dárimí, Bk. 23.
7. *Kitabu'l-Ịshrat* (p. 454), the "Book on Society."
   Cf. Nasá'í, Bk. 36.

The remaining books in this group of the earliest collections of Shi'ite traditions may be seen at once to be so similar in their contents that they can be reduced to an approximate Harmony. If the chapter headings of the *Furu'l-Káfi,* which consists of parts ii and iii of Kulaini's *Káfi fi Ịlm ad-Dín,* are taken as a basic outline, it will be evident how readily the tables of contents from the other books fall into place for easy comparison. The page numbers that are given are those of the lithographed texts that have been mentioned in this chapter, and which are in common use by present day Shi'ite lawyers and divines in Persia.

A Brief Harmony of Early Shi'ite Traditions.

	Kulaini (Káfi)	Ṣuduk (Faḳíh)	Ṭusi (Tahdhíb)	Ṭusi (Istibsár)
Ṭahára .. .. .. Ceremonial Purity.	ii— 2	1	i— 1	i— 1
Ḥaiḍ .. .. .. Menses.	ii— 22	..	..	i— 64

	Kulaini (Káfi)	Ṣuduḳ (Faḳíh)	Ṭusi (Tahdhíb)	Ṭusi (Istibsár)
Janá'iz .. .. .. Corpses.	ii— 31	..	..	i— 98
Ṣalát .. .. .. Prayer.	ii— 73	39	i—134	i—110
Zakát .. .. .. Alms.	ii—139	114	i—216	ii— 2
Ṣiyám .. .. .. Fasts.	ii—177	126	i—262	ii— 36
Ḥajj .. .. .. Pilgrimage to Mecca.	ii—214	151	i—315	ii— 76
(Mazár) Shrines to visit.	ii—314	220	ii— 2	..
Jihád .. .. .. Religious War.	ii—327	..	ii— 41	iii— 2
Ma'ishat .. .. .. Livelihood.	ii—345	268	ii— 98	iii— 28
(Tijárat) Commerce. ..	ii—402	274	ii—119	iii— 40
Khums (wa'l-Ḥuḳuḳ) .. The one fifth and other taxes.	ii—423	234	..	..
Nikáh .. .. .. Marriage.	iii— 2	311	ii—183	iii— 73
Ạkíḳa .. .. .. Shaving hair of infant as sacrifice.	iii— 82	..	..	..
Ṭaláḳ .. .. .. Divorce.	iii— 96	337	ii—195	iii—134
Itḳ (pl. Ụtuḳ) .. .. Manumission. (Tadbír), by bequest. (Kitábat), by ransom.	iii—133	262	ii—253	iii—199
Ṣaid .. .. .. Hunting.	iii—140	299	ii—283	iii—227
Aṭ'ima .. .. .. Victuals.	iii—150	..	..	iii—243
Ashriba .. .. .. Beverages.	iii—185	..	..	iii—243
Zay wa't-Taḥammul .. Fate and Resignation.	iii—202	..	..	..
Dawá'-i-Jinn .. .. A Remedy for Jinn.	iii—228	..	..	..
Waṣáyá .. .. .. Wills.	iii—234	401	ii—322	iii—253
Mawárith .. .. .. Inheritances.	iii—254	421	ii—346	iii—268
Ḥudúd .. .. .. Boundaries.	iii—285	362	ii—389	iii—296
Díyát .. .. .. Compensation for Murder.	iii—315	375	ii—432	iii—327
Shahádát .. .. .. Testimonies.	iii—348	246	..	iii— 8
Ḳaḍá' wa'l-Ahkám .. Judgments and Decisions.	iii—357	237	ii— 68	iii— 22
Aimán wa'n-Nuzur wa'l-Kaffárát .. .. Faith and Vows and Penance.	iii—366	307	ii—270	iii—217

CHAPTER XXVIII

LATER SHI'ITE SCHOLARS AND THEOLOGIANS

THE central Asian peoples whose young men were employed as mercenaries to fight in Muslim armies gradually adopted the religion of their patrons. However, in the instances when they came in hordes and as conquerors, while they also adopted Islam, they preferred generally the opposite sect to that professed by the particular Muslim rulers they displaced. For example, the Shi'ite Buwaihids ousted the Sunnite Turks, and the Sunnite Seljuks came from Bukhara and overwhelmed the Buwaihids. Then came the irresistible invasion of the Mongols, with their inclination to favour the Shi'ites, and they were in turn followed by the Timurids, whose preference was for the Sunnites. In the beginning of the sixteenth century, accordingly, when the Safavid dynasty came into power, they made Shi'ite Islam the established religion within their domains. This later movement, however, was not due to an invasion, but was rather a union of Persian tribes to resist the further depredation and exploitation of their country by foreign peoples, and the enthusiasm of the Safavids for the Shi'ite faith was in full agreement with their distinctively Persian traditions and prejudices.

During the long periods of Sunnite supremacy the Shi'ite theologians had been driven to cover, for they took refuge in their doctrine of dissimulation (taḳiya). But whenever the political and military dominance of the rival sect was destroyed, though it were by a foreign foe, then the Shi'ites came to light, and looking upon the invaders as God-sent deliverers, they eagerly curried favour and used every opportunity to write books to justify their faith. We have shown in the previous chapter how the early collections of Shi'ite traditions were compiled in the reign of the Buwaihids, and it is the object of the present chapter to indicate conspicuous revivals in the writing of Shi'ite theological literature that occurred, first during the period of the supremacy of the Mongols, and afterwards under the Safavids.

The fall of the Buwaihids that followed the rise of the Seljuks brought to an end all preferential treatment for the Shi'ites. The new dynasty, which had sprung from a horde of Turkomans that had abandoned the Kirghiz steppes to settle in the region of Bukhara, were staunch Sunnites. They were capable administrators, who managed the military affairs of their empire thoroughly; and they were also interested in all manner of public works, and did much to encourage Arabic scholarship. But they looked upon the Shi'ites as enemies to the State, and the Nizamu'l-Mulk, their greatest patron of literature and science, has devoted sixty-seven pages in his *Siyasat-Nama*, or "Treatise on the Art of Government," to denouncing the Shi'ite heretics.[1] Consequently, almost the only Shi'ite theologian of importance in the twelfth century was Shaikh Ṭabarsi, who gave up his more public work of teaching in Mashhad and retired to the quiet town of Sabzewar, where, after he was sixty years of age, he wrote his famous commentary on the Ḳoran, the *Kitáb al-Jami' al-Jawami' fi Tafsír al-Koran.*[2]

It was the period of the Crusades, and it was against these Seljuks, who were but recently removed from the simple life of the desert and the mountains, tribes of natural fighters and firm believers, "unspoilt by town life and civilized indifference to religion," that the Crusaders had to contend.[3] The Shi'ites of the period resorted to dissimulation, but many of them also were recruited in the armies and were scattered in all parts of the empire. It is recorded that a certain Shaikh Ạli of Herat claimed that a manuscript that he had written concerning pilgrimages to the Shi'ite shrines had "been taken from him by the King of England, when engaged in the Crusades."[4] The usual type of Shi'ites,

[1] Browne, *Literary History of Persia*, ii, pp. 214-216. Cf. *Siásset Nameh, Traité de Gouvernement*, edit. Schefer, Paris, 1891.

[2] Brockelmann, ii, p. 404 ff.; and the *Ḳiṣaṣu'l-Ulama*, No. 110, p. 227.

[3] Stanley Lane-Poole, *Muhammadan Dynasties*, p. 150.

[4] Ibn Batuta, *Travels*, trans. Lee, preface, p. xv; and Le Strange, *Palestine under the Moslems*, p. 316.

however, that the Crusaders came to know were either subjects of the heterodox Fatimid dynasty, who had maintained themselves in Egypt, or they were those who belonged to the sect of Isma'ilis who were known as the "Assassins," and whose exploits have made Alamut a place of renown.[1] It is likely that there were Shi'ites of other sects also who fought in the Muslim armies in the Crusades, for even to-day we read of heretic villages in Asia Minor whose people desire to avoid all intercourse with the Sunnites with whom they are surrounded.[2] There are also Ạliví Turks who are still living in Asia Minor and who are described as "pitiably simple, ignorant and despised, and therefore secretive, deceptive, and cunning." The fact that they recognize twelve Imams, and look upon Ạli as a divine incarnation, would suggest that they owe their origin, not to the Ismá'ílís, but to the Ạli Ilahís, of the *ghulat* (erroneous) order of Shi'ites, who considered Ạli as divine.[3]

Whatever may have been the extent of the Shi'ite participation in the Crusades, these campaigns to the West, under Seljuk commanders, were scarcely over when "the Mongol armies, divided into several immense brigades, swept over Khwarizm, Khorasan, and Afghanistan, on the one hand; and on the other, over Adherbaijan, Georgia, and southern Russia, whilst a third division continued the reduction of China."[4] When at length the great new empire was divided among the sons of Chingiz Khan, Persia fell to the lot of Húlágú, who ruled, with his successors the Il-khans of Persia, for nearly a century.

Great Shi'ite Scholars under the Mongols.

Among the Shi'ite theological writers who flourished during the period of the Mongols were several exceedingly interesting

[1] "Un grande maitre des assassins au temps de Salidin," by M. Stan. Guyard, in the *Journal Asiatique*, Series 7, Vol. IX; and General Sykes, *History of Persia*, ii, pp. 109-110.

[2] Sir William Ramsay, "The Intermixture of Races in Asia Minor," in the *Proceedings of the British Academy*, Vol. VII, pp. 3-4.

[3] "Alevi Turks of Asia Minor," by Rev. G. E. White, in the *Contemporary Review*, November, 1913.

[4] Stanley Lane-Poole, *op. cit.*, p. 204.

men. First mention may be given to the philosopher, astrologer and theologian, Nasíru'd-Dín aṭ-Ṭusi (d. 672/1274). At the time of the Mongol invasion of Gilán he was a prisoner of the Ismá'ílí chief, Ruknu'd-Dín, at Maimundiz, and when that stronghold fell, he was one of the party of men of distinction who went with Ruknu'd-Dín to surrender to Húlágú Khan. The Mongol ruler received him kindly and made him one of his closest friends. When Baghdad was taken it was Nasíru'd-Dín who persuaded him not to hesitate to kill the Caliph Musta'ṣim. Afterwards, at Maragha, he ventured to suggest, since he had been made Húlágú's *wazir*, that the victorious chieftain should not be content with merely works of destruction. The Mongol saw the point and commissioned him to build a great observatory on a hill north of Maragha. Twelve years were required to complete this work, and in connection with it he compiled astronomical tables that were published after the death of Húlágú, under the title Zíj ul Ilkhaní, that " showed an error of forty minutes in the position of the Sun at the beginning of the year as calculated by previous tables."

Nasír ad-Dín was blessed with an inclination to be scientific. In his eagerness to show that " events do not cause panic when they can be foretold," he arranged, with the knowledge of Húlágú Khan, to roll a metal bowl down a hill in such a manner as to make a terrific noise and to thoroughly frighten the soldiers who were taken by surprise, whereas those who understood were merely amused.[1]

He gathered together a tremendous library, to which he made large acquisitions at the time of the sacking of Baghdad. In Persian he wrote a short book on Ethics, the *Akhlák-i-Náṣirí*, which is still taught in the Persian government schools. In this book, according to Bar-Hebraeus, " he collected all the dicta of Plato and Aristotle on practical Philosophy, confirming the opinions of the ancients and solving the doubts of the moderns and the criticisms advanced by them in their writings."[2] His

[1] Howarth, *History of the Mongols*, iii, p. 137-139.
[2] Browne, *op. cit.*, iii, p. 18.

chief work in Arabic is the *Tajrídu'l-Aḳá'id*, or "Analysis of Beliefs," which is mainly devoted to scholastic philosophy, and for which the *Kiṣáṣu'l-Ulama* mentions several commentaries.[1]

The story has been told that once when he went to Shiraz, the poet Sa'di came to see him. Nasíru'd-Dín took him to task for having written, "It would have been right if the sky had rained blood upon the earth, in lamentation for Musta'ṣim, the *Amiru'l-Muminín*." Sa'di's protest that he had so written only in dissimulation (taḳiya) was met with the answer, "When we had killed the Abbasid Musta'ṣim, from fear of whom did you dissimulate?" Sa'di had no answer, and Nasíru'd-Dín ordered him to be bastinadoed. He was so severely beaten, as the story goes, that his body was covered with the broken rods. They took him then upon their shoulders and carried him off to his house, and he lived for only seven or eight days. Some say that at the time he was one hundred and ten years of age.[2]

There is a long prayer that is commonly used in salutations to the twelve Imams which is included in the official prayer manuals, and which is said to have been written by Nasíru'd-Dín Ṭusi, after it had been revealed to him in a dream by Muhammad. In writing it out, however, he found he had forgotten a part of it, so he slept again and once more Muhammad appeared and repeated for him what he had forgotten.[3]

Another of the influential Shi'ite writers during the period of the Mongols was *Najmu'd-Dín Ja'far ibn Yaḥya* (d. 726/1325). He was the author of the *Sharáyi'ul-Islam*, a book on Muhammadan jurisprudence which is one of the principal sources that is used in the outstanding European work that treats of the Law of the Shi'ites, i.e., "Droit Musulman: Recueil de Lois concernant les Musulmans Schyites," by M. Amédée Querry. It is said that when Najmu'd-Dín was a young man he showed ability in writing poetry, but his father assured him that poets were under a curse and that he would not be able to reconcile

[1] *Kiṣaṣu'l-Ulama*, No. 90, p. 297 (edit. lithographed, 1290 A.H.).
[2] *Ibid.*, No. 90, p. 291.
[3] *Ibid.*, No. 90, p. 286.

his necessary conduct as a poet with a devout life, and that accordingly he had better be a lawyer.[1]

The leading systematic theologian of the Mongol period was *Hasan ibn Yusuf ibn Ạli ibnu'l-Muṭahhar al-Hilli* (d. 726/1325). On his mother's side he was a nephew of Najmu'd-Dín, who has just been mentioned, and he is generally spoken of as the Allláma-i-Hilli, or the "Sage of Hilla." Hilla was for a long time the recognized centre of the Shi'ites when Sunnite rulers were in authority in Baghdad. He travelled from place to place, studied for a while with Nasíru'd-Dín Ṭusi, and worked constantly as a student and as a writer. The mass of work that he was able to turn off was a marvel to all who knew him. Of the seventy-five of his books that are named in the Ḳiṣaṣu'l-Ụlama,[2] a similar list to that in the *Amal al-Amil*, the following major works may be mentioned[3]:

1. *Kashf al-Yaḳín fí Faḍá'l Amír al-Mu'minín*, which treats of the virtues of Ạli ibn Abu Ṭalib.
2. *Minhádj al-Ṣaláḥ fi 'khtiṣár al-Misbáh*, which is a work on prayer and religious obligations.
3. *Minhádj al-Karáma fí Ma'rifat al-Imáma*, a treatise on the nature of the Imamate. It is in ten chapters, but an eleventh chapter has been added, *al-Bábu 'l-Ḥádí Ạshar*, on "The Principles of Shi'ite Theology," for which an English translation has been recently published by the Royal Asiatic Society.[4]
4. *Minhadj al-Yaḳín fí Uṣúl al-Din*, which explains the fundamental principles of the Shi'ah creed.
5. *Tadhkirat al-Fuḳahá'*, which is a work in three volumes on Shi'ite jurisprudence.

The Allláma-i-Ḥilli lived to be seventy-seven years of age, having maintained his reputation in many controversies as a great

[1] *Ibid.*, No. 89, p. 283. Cf. Browne, *op. cit.*, p. 405.
[2] *Ibid.*, No. 100, pp. 320-321.
[3] *Encyclopædia of Islam*, ii, p. 277.
[4] *Oriental Translation Fund*, N.S., Vol. XXIX, trans. by Rev. William M. Miller, of Meshed, Persia.

jurist and theologian, and when he died his body was taken to Mashhad for burial.

When the empire of the Il-Khans in Persia and Mesopotamia literally disintegrated, owing to the jealousies and animosities of rival families, for approximately one hundred and fifty years, i.e., from 1349 until the rise of the Safavids in 1502, this whole region was under the unstable government of contending tribal states. But finally, far in the north-west corner of Persia, in the mountainous province of Adherbaijan, a horn of deliverance was raised up in an old town that had been a provincial capital in the days of the early Abbasids, the town of Ardebil. This distant town lay at a strategic point in the road system that had been established by the Mongols to the western frontiers, and here it was that a religious movement, of tremendous significance for Persia, started through the influence of an aged saint. The saint was Safiyyu'd-Dín, who was a five-year-old boy when Húlágú Khan first came to Persia. It was claimed that he was a descendant of the Imam Musa Kazim (see chapter xxiv), and when he died in A.D. 1334, at the age of eighty-five, he was buried at Ardebil. His influence continued long after his death, for not only was his tomb regarded as a shrine and sanctuary, but his successors for three generations were semi-official saints for the whole region of Adherbaijan. In the fourth generation the scion of his house, Shaikh Haydar, "added the role of warrior to the profession of saint."[1] He was himself soon put to death, but his son, Ismá'íl, whose mother was Martha the daughter of Uzun Hasan, the "Tall Hasan" who was the Turkoman king of Armenia, began when he was nineteen years of age to preach aggressively the Shi'ah faith. At first he had scarcely more than a dozen followers, but he soon gathered together a fighting band of three hundred men. He made rapid headway in his raids in Persia, until he raised an army of sufficient size and captured Tabriz, when he boldly declared himself to be the *Grand Sophi* of Persia. The name *Sophi* was not from the Greek *sophos*, "wisdom," but was from a Persian word meaning "wool" or

[1] Stanley Lane-Poole, *op. cit.*, p. 275.

"cotton," and the reference was to the cap with twelve different coloured knots which he and his men wore to distinguish themselves as the followers of the Twelve Imams. As the cap itself was red, the troops of the *Grand Sophi* came to be known as the Ḳizil Bash, or "Red Heads."[1] It was Ismá'il, the *Grand Sophi*, therefore, who united seven powerful Persian tribes and established the distinctly Shi'ite dynasty of the Safavíds.

Among these tribes, with the sanctuary of Ardebil as a centre, strong Shi'ite teaching had, in the course of several generations, gained the necessary momentum to make these conquests possible. The war cry was, "Allah! Allah! wa Ạli Wali Allah!" The whole movement was bitterly intolerant, so much so in fact that Shah Ismá'íl issued a proclamation demanding the public cursing of the first three Caliphs, and declaring that the Shi'ah faith was to be *the only acceptable creed*. But hereafter, as Don Juan was proud to observe, "We have therefore now finally done with all these foreign kings, or Caliphs, whether Arabs or Turkomans or Ottomans, who in long past times and seasons have held rule over the lands of Persia."[2]

In the long consecutive rule of the Safavids (1502-1736), who were avowedly and aggressively Shi'ites, theological colleges were founded and shrines in the cities of pilgrimage were restored throughout Persia and Mesopotamia. Every encouragement was given to writers who endeavoured to lead the people back from the teachings of numerous sects to a sincere following of the Twelve Imams. In consequence of this national commitment to a widespread campaign of religious education, we have voluminous writings by theologians who lived during the sixteenth and seventeenth centuries. Professor Browne has already given a list of the principal ones of these writers, with brief observations about them from the *Kiṣaṣu'l-Ulama* and the Rawḍatu'l-Jannat.[3] The theologians of the Safavid period that are included in this

[1] *Relaciones* of Don Juan of Persia, trans. Le Strange, pp. 107-111. Cf. Krusinski, *Revolution of Persia*, Du Cerseau, Vol. I, p. 4.
[2] *Ibid.*, p. 100.
[3] Browne, *op. cit.*, iv, pp. 406-411.

list are mentioned here with a few additional particulars from the first of these sources.

Theologians of the Safavid Period

Nuru'd-Dín Ạli Ạbdu'l-Ạli (No. 84),[1] was known as the Muḥaḳḳiḳ-i-Thani, or the "Second Investigator." Among his books were the *Jámi'u'l-Maḳaṣid,* a commentary in six volumes on the *Kawáhid* of the Ạllâma-i-Hilli, and the *Risálat-i-Ja'fariyya,* which he wrote while he was still in Khorasan. In Persia he was highly esteemed and was particularly honoured by Shah Ṭahmasp I. The date of his death was 940/1533.

Aḥmad ibn Muḥammad (No. 83) was called the "Saint of Ardebil" and is remembered for his successful intervention on behalf of others with Shah Ạbbas the Great. In praise of his piety it was said that for a period of forty years he was not known "to stretch out his legs in sleep." The story is related that once in the courtyard of the shrine at Najaf he lowered a bucket into a well, and when he drew it up it was full of gold, which he threw back into the well and said, "O Lord, Ahmad asked thee for water and not for gold." He was accustomed to wear a tremendously large turban, and when he would go out into the street for a walk, and meet a man perchance who was poor and naked, he would tear off two or three yards of this turban for him. After having repeated this several times he would return with only a few inches of his turban left. One of his best known books was the *Majma'u'l-Ká'ida wa'l-Burhán,* which is a commentary on the *Irshád* of the Ạllâma-i-Hilli. Another book that he is said to have written, *Haḳiḳatu'sh-Shi'at,* has been attributed by some to Majlisi, but the writer of the *Kiṣaṣu'l-Ulama* insists that it belongs to Aḥmad ibn Muḥammad himself, who died in 993/1585.

Mir Muḥammad Baḳir-i-Damád (No. 77) was the grandson of the *Muḥaḳḳiḳ-i-Thani,* and he also was highly favoured by Shah Ạbbas. His best known book is the *Ṣirátu'l-Mustaḳim*

[1] The number in parenthesis indicates the order in which each writer is mentioned in the *Ḳiṣaṣu'l-Ulama.*

(" The Straight Path "). It is related that Shah Ạbbas urged him to ascertain how bees make wax and honey, so he had a house of glass prepared and put the bees in it so that they could be watched. They first darkened the glass house and then proceeded to build their hives and make their honey. As a writer Mir Ḍamád was regarded as somewhat obscure and technical, for Mulla Ṣadru'l-Ḍín claimed that he had seen him in a dream and that he took occasion to say to him, " People have been accusing me of heresy, whereas my beliefs are practically the same as yours were." And the ghost of Mir Ḍamád replied, " The reason is that I wrote on the subjects of philosophy in such a way as to be beyond the understanding of the clergy, and so that only philosophers could sense them at all, whereas you have put these things plainly in everyday language, and any ordinary schoolmaster who sees your writings can understand them and accuse you of heresy." The *Kiṣaṣu'l-Ulama* names some six or seven other books that he wrote which were commentaries and expositions of scholastic philosophy. He died in the year 1041/1631.

Shaikh Muḥammad Baha'u'd-Dín al-Ạmilí (No. 37) wrote the *Jami'-i-Ạbbasí,* a popular manual of Shi'ite Law in Persian, of which an exceptionally clear text was lithographed in Isfahán in 1329 A.H. His collection of anecdotes in Arabic, the *Kashkul* or " Alms-bowl," has been printed at Bulaḳ and also lithographed in Persia. Two of his poems are well known, one the *Nán u Ḥalwá* (" Bread and Sweetmeats ") and the other, *Shír u Shakar* (" Milk and Sugar "). Mention is made of his arrival one night in Isfahan, and he got to thinking of the condition of that city, on account of the extensive wine business there, and said to his servants, " Let us leave, for God will send punishment upon this city and we also will be burned." The servants therefore got his baggage loaded and he mounted his mule and left the city. But before morning he again fell to thinking of the true state of Isfahan, and he turned to his servants and said, " Let us return, for there are several thousand devout worshippers, a great crowd, praying at night, and this assembly calls me back." He was a determined Shi'ite, who insisted on his right to curse Ụthman. At the age of seventy-eight he died in 1031/1622, and is said to be buried at Mashhad.

Muḥammad ibn Murtaḍa, from Káshán, was known as Mullá Muḥsin-i-Faiḍ (No. 76), and is described as more of a mystic and a philosopher than a theologian. He wrote the *Abwabu'l-Jinán* ("Gates of Paradise"). To the western reader it is interesting to find the story that a foreign representative came to the Court of Shah Ạbbas, with the request from his sovereign that he be allowed to carry on religious discussions with the scholars in Persia, and suggesting that if he should be convinced of the right of Islam he would become a Muslim, and that otherwise they should become Christians. He had gotten the reputation of being able to tell what men held in their hands. Mullá Muḥsin was the chairman (sar ámad) of the meeting that was called, and he opened the discussion by asking the foreign envoy why his sovereign had not sent a scholar to interview them instead of an ignoramus. The foreigner replied, "You will not thus escape your agreement with me, but take something in your hand and I will tell you what you hold." Accordingly Mullá Muḥsin took in his hand a rosary of beads that were made from the sacred clay of the tomb of Husain. The envoy was seen to be in the sea of deep meditation, and Mullá Muhsin asked, "Why are you hesitating?" He answered, "It is not that I am perplexed, but according to my way of thinking you have in your hand a piece of the earth of Paradise, and what I have been thinking of is how it could happen that a piece of the earth of Paradise should be in your hand." Mullá Muḥsin said, "You have spoken the truth, that I have in my hand a piece of the earth of Paradise, a rosary that is from the purified tomb of one born from the daughter of our Prophet, one who is an Imam, so it seems that the truth of our religion and the futility of your faith is apparent." And it is said the foreigner accepted Islam.

He gave it as his opinion that singing was permissible, and was seen reverently kneeling in his garden while a slave girl sang to him, and he wept. He is represented as in some respects exceedingly simple minded, for once he dropped his penknife in the bazaar and about a year afterwards he remembered having done so and wanted to send someone to get it. When he was told that it could scarcely be found after so long a time, he remarked, " The people are Muhammadans, how is it that anyone would take my knife without my permission ? " Nevertheless he is said to have written more than two hundred books and treatises, the titles of sixty-seven of which are given in the *Kiṣaṣu'l-Ulama*. He died in 1091 /1680.

Mir Abu'l-Kasim Findariskí is mentioned in the *Kiṣaṣu'l-Ulama* along with Shaikh Baha'ud-Ḍín (No. 37). He was from Astarabád in Mazandarán. When he was in India one of the rulers there asked him why he cursed Mu'áwiya. He replied with the question, " If the army of Ạli was fighting with the army of Mu'áwiya, on which side would you be ? " The Sultan answered, " With the army of Ạli." Again he asked, " If Ạli should say to you, smite the neck of Mu'áwiya, what would you do ? " " I would smite him," said the Sultan. " Well then," said Findariskí, " if you acknowledge that killing him would be permissible, then surely cursing him is allowed."

It was commonly believed that the body of Findariskí had the quality of turning metals to gold, i.e., when iron or copper or brass were rubbed on his body they would turn to gold. Accordingly when he died there were Indians who knew of this who were eager to dig up his corpse and take it to their own country, so for this reason his grave was bound firmly in cement.

It is said that Shah Ạbbas regarded him highly but disapproved of the way he had of mingling with the lowest orders of society, and especially of his attending cock-fights. He died in Isfahan about 1050 /1640.

Mullá Ṣadru'd-Dín Muḥammad ibn Ibrahim is included in the *Kiṣaṣu'l-Ulama* along with Mullá Muḥsin (No. 76). He has been considered " the greatest philosopher of modern times in Persia." It was perhaps for this reason that he was usually at odds with the orthodox Shi'ite theologians, and that his largest influence was principally with the Shaikhi School. He went from Shiraz to Isfahan, where he studied with Shaikh Bahau'd-Dín and afterwards with Mir Dámád, from both of whom he received the licence to teach. He was in business for a while, however, in the vicinity of Ḳum. Seven different times he went to Mecca, and it was on his return from the last of these pilgrimages that he died in Basra. It was probably about 1050/1640.

Among the books of Mullá Sadrá was a commentary on the *Kafí* of Kulaini in three volumes, and his two best known works on theology are the *Asfár-i-Arba'a*, or "Four Books," and the *Shawahidu'r-Rububíyya*, or "Evidences of Divinity." In addition to these were various commentaries on particular portions of the Ḳoran, notes on Avicenna's *Shifá*, etc.[1]

Ạbdu'r-Razzáḳ-i-Láhijí had studied with Mullá Ṣadrá. He wrote two well-known books in Persian, the *Sar-máya-i-Imán* ("Substance of Belief") and the *Gawhar-i-Murád* ("Pearl of Desire"). In common with Shaikh Tabarsi, he is said to have held the strange belief in a relation between the sound of words and their "essential meaning,"—that having heard the sound one should be able to sense the meaning.

Mullá Muḥammad Taḳí-i-Majlisí (No. 36) devoted himself to gathering and arranging a great number of traditions, from every possible source, during the Safavíd period. He was thought to have had Ṣúfí tendencies, but this may very well have been due to his association with all sorts of people in his work of collecting traditions. The story is told of how he took a liking to one of his pupils, Akhúnd Mulla Muḥammad Salih, who was not properly clothed. After he had supplied him with shoes and clothing, he saw that the boy was desirous of getting married, so he took him into the women's apartments of his own home and showed him his daughters and told him to take his choice. The boy did so, and after that he studied in Mulla Muḥammad Taḳí's own library (No. 34). According to the *Rawḍátu'l-Jannát* he died in 1070/1659.

Mullá Muḥammad Báḳir-i-Majlisí (No. 33) was the last and the greatest theologian of the Safavid period. Thorough and diligent

[1] Browne, *op. cit.*, pp. 427-432.

as a scholar, he has the distinction also of having perceived that the masses should be reached in their own language. While his monumental work on the traditions is in Arabic, the *Bihāru'l-Anwār* (" Oceans of Light "), he managed to put the bulk of that vast amount of material about the Prophet and the Imams into a series of readable manuals in Persian. His remarkable success in thus making the sources of the Shi'ah faith intelligible to the people of Persia in their own language has made him undoubtedly the most influential of all the Shi'ah theologians. He died in 1111/1699.

In addition to his famous *Ḥaḳu'l-Yaḳīn* (" The Real Truth "), which is reported to have been instrumental at the time when it was written in converting seventy thousand Sunnites to " the true faith," the following is a list of others of his well-known books in Persian:

Ạynu'l-Ḥayāt (" The Fountain of Life ").
Mishkatu'l-Anwār (" The Lamp of Lights ").
Ḥilyatu'l-Muttaḳīn (" The Ornament of the Pious ").
Ḥayatu'l-Kulub (" Life of Hearts ").
Tuḥfatu'z-Za'irīn (" The Pilgrim's Present ").
Jala'u'l-Uyun (" The Clearing of the Eyes ").
Zadu'l-Ma'ad (" Provision for the Hereafter ").
Tadhkiratu'l-A'immeh (" Record of the Imams ").

CHAPTER XXIX

THE DOCTRINE OF THE IMAMATE

THE main issue that Majlisi had to face, when the Safavid dynasty was encouraging Shi'ite theologians to think through their distinctive doctrines and to write books for the religious instruction of the people, was the question as to whether an Imam was really necessary. The theory had caused division in Islam and much bloodshed, and sober minds were ready to seriously consider whether as a matter of fact it was essential to the faith. A clear statement of the "historic imamate," showing how the question of succession repeatedly gave rise to new sects, has been given by Ibn Khaldun, and the various sects have been minutely described by Shahrastani.[1] It is impossible, however, to appreciate the fervour of a Shi'ite theologian, who is convinced of the absolute importance of this subject, except by following his own arguments. To this end, therefore, the theological considerations that are set forth by Majlisi to establish the necessity of the Imamate are here translated.[2]

[1] Ibn Khaldun, "Prolegomena," in *Extraits des Manuscrits de la Bibliotheque Imperiale*, Arabic text, Vol. XVI, Part II, p. 355 ; *Traduction*, Vol. XIX, p. 400. See English translation of this section by present writer in *The Moslem World*, Vol. XXI, No. 1. Cf. Shahrastani, *Religious and Philosophical Sects*, ed. Cureton, pp. 108-145 ; also Ibn Hazm, *The Heterodoxies of the Shi'ites*, trans. Friedlander, *J.A.O.S.*, Vols. 28 and 29.

[2] Majlisi, *Hayatu'l-Ḳulub* (Life of Hearts), Vol. III, pp. 1-23. This is a most useful book of 345 pages, but without an index or a table of contents and with only two chapters. The first chapter, on "The Necessity for the Existence of an Imam," treats the subject from a theological point of view, and is divided into the following nine sections : (1) Concerning the Necessity for the Imamate—and showing that no time is without an Imam ; (2) The Sinlessness of the Imams ; (3) The Imamate on the Authority of God and the Apostle—and that each Imam must appoint his successor ; (4) The Necessity of Recognizing the Imams ; (5) To Deny One Imam is to Deny Them All ; (6) The Necessity of Obeying the Imams ; (7) Guidance and Salvation is only through the Imams ; (8) The Two Precious Trusts, the Ḳoran and the Household ; and (9) Concerning the Designation of the Several Imams. The second chapter, entitled "Verses from the Ḳoran That Are Interpreted as Referring to the Imamate," is of a strictly exegetical nature. It occupies 259 pages of the book and is divided into forty-three sections. It would be difficult to find anywhere a clearer or more comprehensive outline of the distinctly Shi'ite interpretations of the Ḳoran than is here afforded.

The Necessity of the Imamate

" It should be understood that there is disagreement among scholars on this question of the appointment of the Imams. Was their appointment necessary after the end of *the period of prophecy* ? If we say it was necessary, do we mean that it was a necessity for God himself or rather for the Imams ? Or, in either case, is it to be considered as a rational necessity, a belief that reason itself demands, or is it proved merely by the traditions ?

" All the recognized Shi'ite scholars hold that the appointment of the Imams was an actual necessity for God himself, and that this is demonstrable both by reason and by the traditions. The Ash'arites, the Sunnites and the writers of their traditions, and some of the Mutazilites, believed that the appointment of the Imams was a matter that depended on the wish of mankind, and that it was not a rational necessity but rested merely on traditions. One group of the Mu'tazilites taught that the appointment of Imams was allowable on the condition that it could be accomplished without employing force.[1]

" The word *imám* means an Example or Leader, and when used at the time of prayer it generally signifies the prayer-leader ; but in the literary sense, when the word *imám* is used, the reference is to a person who has come from God to be the *caliph* or *ná'ib* (representative) of His Highness the Possessor of the Apostleship (i.e., Muḥammad), and there are times when the word is used to designate the Prophet himself. Several traditions suggest that the degree of Imam is higher even than that of Prophet, for it was after God had given the rank of Prophet to Abraham that he said, ' Truly I appoint you as a Leader (*imám*) of men ' (Ḳoran, ii. 118). Some authorities have said that an *imám* is a person appointed of God to be a ruler in matters of religion and of state, much like a prophet, only a prophet speaks from God without the mediation of any man, whereas an *imám* speaks by the mediation of a prophet.

[1] Goldziher, *Vorlesungen*, ch. iii, sect. 5.

(*Majlisi's opinion.*) "This distinction is hard to establish because many of the prophets were obedient to the five specially distinguished ones and taught mankind their law.[1] And numerous traditions show that our Imams acquired learning from God directly through the Holy Spirit. In the traditions several differences are indicated between a prophet and an *imám* which we hope to explain later. And in honour of Muḥammad, since he is the *seal of the prophets*, the use of the simple term prophet (nabí) is not considered to be sufficiently comprehensive. . . . Evidently whatever advantage lay in the person of the Prophet is also to be attributed to the person of the Imam—all that pertains to warding off evil, to guarding law, to restraining men from violence and oppression and all kinds of disobedience, and even the divine necessity for the appointment of the succeeding Imam.

"For the necessity of the existence of the *imám* there are many proofs to be found in such books as the *Sháfi* of Sayyid Murtaḍa and the *Talkhis* of Shaikh Ṭusi. We will now give several of these proofs.

1. *From the Kindness of God.* "We must presume that kindness is one of God's characteristics, for obviously God will do that which is best in behalf of his servants; for reason demands that we should consider that the works of the Merciful and the Eternal are distinguished by wisdom and expediency. Whenever the best, which is the preferred and the most convenient, is not prohibited, then the refusal of it, or the changing of it without advantage would be unworthy of the All Powerful, the Rich, and the Merciful. Since the necessity of giving the best is established, kindness also must be shown to be necessary to God, for kindness is among the commands that are capable of human attainment, on account of the ease with which it can be exercised. It is understood, of course, that God's kindness would not be carried so far as to cause injury or harm, and that the real ground of merit or of censure would rest on the intention of the action.

[1] The *Ulu'l-Azm* (Possessors of Constancy) are said to have included Noah, Abraham, David, Joseph, Job, Moses, Jesus, and Muhammad (Cf. Hughes *Dictionary of Islam*, p. 650), but the five most distinguished ones were Noah, Abraham, Moses, Jesus and Muhammad.

Those who have written on what reason considers to be good or bad, and on the necessity of the best, are agreed that kindness *must* be conceived as a divine attribute, for the reason that we observe that the duties of worshippers have many advantages and profits, both in this world and the next. . . . And it would seem also to be clear that kindness is responsible for the existence of the Imám, for ordinary intelligence leads people, whenever they are organized as a people, to have someone to restrain them from rebellion and corruption and violence and oppression, to withhold them from various forms of disobedience, and to establish them in faithfulness, in the forms of worship, in practices of justice, and in habits of civility. For it is in this way that the conduct of peoples becomes regular and orderly, and that they approach the best and forsake the base.

2. *The Guardian of the Law.* " The second proof lies in the necessity of a guardian for the Law of the Apostle, to protect it from change or misinterpretation, and from additions or subtractions. The verses of the Ḳoran are stated briefly and most of the commands are not obvious. An authoritative interpreter from God is needed, therefore, to make the legal deductions or conclusions from the Ḳoran. This is opposed to the opinion of Ụmar, for at the time when the Apostle was about to die, and asked for a pen and ink that he might write a declaration for the nations, so that they should never be lost, Ụmar objected and said, ' Surely the man talks nonsense, sufficient for us is the Book of God ! ' This was from Ụmar, the Accursed, who did not know the interpretation of a single verse of the Ḳoran, and on every matter on which he had difficulty, either he or his friend, Abu Bakir, went secretly to Ạli. The Sunnites themselves have related that seventy times Ụmar said, ' Without Ạli, Ụmar would have been destroyed.'

" And indeed, if the Book of God had been enough, then why are there so many differences among those who follow it ? For example, there is the verse, ' You are the one making afraid and the one leading every people,' in which case ' the one leading ' refers to the same person as ' the one making afraid.' Others, however, have said that the meaning is, 'You are the one who makes afraid the unbelievers and the base, and for everyone there is a leader.' In this case the one declaration is made dependent upon the other, and furnishes a proof text that no epoch is left without its *imám* or leader. . . . In the *Basa'ir al-Daraját* it is related that the Imam Baḳir said that the Apostle of God is 'the one making afraid,' and that after him, in every age, 'there is a leader among us who guides mankind towards that which the Apostle of God has revealed; that the leader who followed the Apostle was Ạli ibn Abu Ṭalib, with the *imáms* who came after him, each following the other until the Judgment Day.' Ibn Babuwaihi had recorded in the *Kamálu'd-Dín*, also, that when explaining the verse, 'To every people a leader,' Muḥammad Bakir said, 'The reference is to the Imam, for in every time there must be a leader for the people among whom the Imam lives.'

"Another example where explanation is required is the verse, 'And now have we caused our word to come unto them that they may be warned' (Rodwell, Surah xxviii. v. 51). The majority of commentators explain this as meaning that God gave them verses, following one after another, and likewise incidents, and exhortations, and prohibitions, and counsels, and parables, so that they would comprehend good and evil. But there are many traditions that have come down from the Household of the Prophet that indicate that the real point of this verse is that *the Imams were to come following one after another*. . . .

"Ibn Babuwaihi (Ṣuduḳ) has recorded in both the *Majalis* and the *Kamalu'd-Dín* that the Imam Zain al-Ạbidín said: 'We are the leaders of the Muḥammadans and the Proofs of God among all men, and through us, on the Day of Judgment, the Shi'ites will approach Paradise with their faces and hands and feet pure white, as though they had been washed with light. As the leaders of the faithful we will save the people of the Earth from the wrath of God. As long as the stars are the guards of the sky, the angels also have no fear of the Judgment, for as long as we are on the Earth the Judgment will not come and punishment will not occur.

But when we shall be taken from the Earth, this will be a sign of its destruction and of the death of all those dwelling upon it. When the stars fall from their places, this will be a sign of the end of the heavens and of the scattering of the angels.' And he said again, 'We are those through whose blessing God maintains the heavens, that they should not fall upon the Earth except by his permission at the day of Judgment. It is *by our blessing* that God maintains the heavens, that they do not fall and destroy their inhabitants; and it is *by our blessing* that God sends the rains and shows forth his mercy, and brings forth the bounties of the Earth. For if there were no Imam on Earth to represent us, verily the Earth itself would collapse, with all those who dwell upon it.'

"So we see that the Imam declared that from the time when God created Adam the Earth would never be without God's Proof or Representative, either as an evident and public proof, or concealed and hidden. In any event the Earth shall never be without God's witness until the Judgment Day. For if there should be no *Proof of God* upon the Earth, there would be no worship of God, for the way of worship men learn from him (the imám), as he is the one who directs men in worship.

3. *Advantages from the Imam in Concealment.* "When the Imam Zainu'l-Abidín was asked, 'How could men profit from a Proof of God that was concealed and hidden from them?' he replied, 'They would profit in the same way they do from the Sun when it is concealed by a cloud.' From this it is evident that even in the time of his concealment, the grace and blessing of the Imam reaches the Earth. If there should be mistakes among the uninformed, he will guide them in ways they will perceive, and yet they will not know it was he. And there are many times when his concealment works for the blessing of the majority of men. For God knows that if the Imam should come, the majority of mankind would not accept him. And in the personal presence of the Imam the obligations that would fall upon men would be more difficult, such as fighting in the *jihád* (holy war) against those opposing the Faith. There are many

times when unseeing eyes and blind hearts have not the strength to look upon the light of the Imam, just as lots do not have the strength to look upon the light of the Sun. Kings and nobles, also, during the concealment of the Imam, have faith in his coming, but when he shall actually come and reduce the noble and the poor to one level, many will not be able to endure this and will disbelieve. For when Ạli, the Amiru'l-Mu'minín, was distributing rewards, he treated Talha and Zubair in the same way as a slave he had freed but the day before, and it was this that caused them to forsake him.

"In considering the favour of the Imam during the time of his concealment, it is enough to observe that belief *in his being* and *in his imamate* should be accepted as necessary and as meriting the highest reward. Sayyid Murtaḍa, in the *Sháfí*, has given several answers to the statement that a concealed imam can be of no profit to mankind. The *first* is that all the time there is the expectation that the Imam will appear, and this expectation in itself makes for abstinence from numerous sins. There is this difference at least between the non-existence of an imam and simply his concealment. The *second* answer is that the Most High has by his grace given the Imam, and the reason he is concealed is on account of his enemies among men. The situation is similar to that of the Prophet in Mecca, when the unbelieving Ḳuraish prevented men from coming to him, especially when he was in the ravine of Abu Ṭalib with others of the Beni Hashim. During the time he was in exile, and up until the time when he appeared as a Prophet in Medina, there can be no doubt that his status was that of a Prophet and was always advantageous to men. The *third* answer is that it is perfectly possible that God knows that there are friends of the Imam during his concealment who would deny him if he appeared, so that his appearance would thus become a reason for their loss of faith. The *fourth* answer is that it is not at all necessary that all should profit equally. It might be that a select number would see him and be thus advantaged, just as they say that there is a city where the descendants of the Imam live and that the Imam will go to that city. Although the people of the city may not see him, yet they will utter their requests to him, as it were behind a curtain.

"After mentioning these considerations, Sayyid Murtaḍa goes on to say that the profit or advantage that comes to the people from the Imam cannot be completed except by several commands from God, commands that must first be accepted and obeyed. These commands have come down through the Imams and must be obeyed. God's part has been to send the Imams, and to make them able to discharge the duties of their Imamate—in their learning, in the Law, and in the sufficiency of the Proofs that they are Imams—but it is necessary for them on their part to execute the commands of God. The Imam's task, therefore, is to accept these obligations and to arrange to carry them out. What we need to do in reference to the Imamate is to assist the Imams to fulfil their tasks, and to overthrow whatever stands between us and them, that we may obey them and serve them and carry out their orders.

4. *Analogy from the Mind, the Imam of the Senses.* "Both Kulaini and Ibn Babuwaihi (Ṣuduḳ) tell the story of an illustration that was used by Hisham ibn Salim, who was one of the most learned supporters of the Imam Ja'far aṣ-Ṣadiḳ. Hisham said to the Imam, 'I had heard about the reputation for scholarship that was enjoyed by Amru ibn Ubaid (a Sufi scholar among the Sunnites), and that he was teaching at Basra. But I did not like his conceit. So I went to Basra, and since I arrived on Friday I went at once to the *masjid* or place of prayer. There I saw that a large crowd had assembled about Amru. He had a coarse, black, woollen scarf bound about his waist, and another scarf of the same kind over his shoulder. The people were asking him questions. I forced my way into the midst of them and sat down. Then I said, "O learned scholar, I am a stranger and I have a question to ask, if you will permit me?" He consented. I asked, "Do you have eyes?" He replied, "My son, what sort of a question is this?" I said, "This is my question." He said, "Ask whatever you wish, even though it be foolish." Then I repeated, "Have you eyes?" He said, "Yes." I asked,

" What do you see with them ? " He said, " Colours and people." I said, " Have you a nose ? " He said, " Yes." I asked, " What do you do with it ? " He said, " I smell smells." I asked, " Have you a mouth ? " He said, " Yes." I asked, " What do you do with it ? " He said, " With it I speak." I said, " Have you ears ? " He said, " Yes." I asked, " What do you do with them ? " He said, " With them I hear sounds." I asked, " Have you hands ? " He said, " Yes." I asked, " What do you do with them ? " He said, " I pick up things." I said, " Have you a mind (literally a heart) ? " He said, " Yes." I asked, " What do you do with it ? " He said, " I reason out what the senses tell me." I said, " Are the senses not enough, and are they not independent of the mind ? " He said, " No, they are not enough, and they are not independent of the mind, even though they should all be in health." And he continued, " My son, when these senses are doubtful as to something they have smelled or heard or tasted or touched, they refer to the mind, which gives assurance and banishes doubt." Then I said, " So God has made the mind the governor of the body, to banish the doubts of the senses ? " He said, " Yes." Then I remarked, " O Abu Marwan, so the Lord of the Worlds has not left your members and senses without an *imám* or guide to explain what he desires and to banish their doubts. Can we think, therefore, that he has left all creation in confusion and has not given mankind an *imám* in order that they may take their doubts and uncertainties to him, that he may guide them to the truth and set them free from doubt ? " When I said this he was silent and did not answer. But he favoured me by coming and asking me, " Are you not Hisham ? " I said, " No." Then he asked, " Where do you come from ? " I said, " I come from Kufa." Then he exclaimed, " Of course you are Hisham ! " and he seized me and led me forward to sit with him, and said nothing until I arose.'

5. *Man a Little Universe* (Majlisi's statement). " Man is a little universe which is a prototype of the great universe, as was said by Ạli, the Amiru'l-Mu'minín : ' Do you think that you are a small thing ? Know that the universe is wound up and hidden

in you.' For the bones in the body are similar to mountains, and the flesh is like the soil; the little and the large veins are like streams of water; the head, the centre of power and reason, which is the noblest part of the body, is like the sky, which holds the stars that give their light to the earth; the power of the brain, which is given to the whole body, is like the light of the stars which is given to the Earth; and as there are rulers and kings on the Earth, and some are more powerful and more esteemed than others, so the supreme ruler of the body is the speaking spirit which rules the heart. As on Earth the compass points to the North, so (when facing the East), the heart, which is the reason for the life of the body, is to the North. And as kings have viziers to regulate the affairs of state, so the liver functions for the whole body. And as the land casts off its surplus to be washed into the sea, so also the human body throws off what it does not need."

Another section from the same source may be translated to show the nature of the orthodox Shi'ite conception of divine authority for the Imamate.[1]

The Imamate on the Authority of God and the Apostle

"The Imamate is on the authority of God and the Apostle and is not to be determined by the agreement or choice of men. It is necessary for each Imam to appoint his successor. . . . The Ạbbasids said that the Imamate may be either by appointment or by inheritance, and all the Sunnites say that it may be either by appointment or by choice, i.e., by the agreement of those in responsibility. But reasonable proofs that the right of the Imamate is based solely on divine appointment are numerous.

"1. Since the Imam must be free from sin, and sinlessness is a state which only God can know, therefore the appointment must lie with God, for he alone knows who is sinless.

"2. In observing the course of human history and development, those who are reflective will readily understand that whenever a people do not have a governor who is strong and a ruler

[1] Majlisi, *op. cit.*, Vol. III, p. 35ff.

who is severe—someone to restrain them from injustice and anger, someone to prevent them from following their own lusts or doing things that are forbidden—the majority of that people will resort to brute force, and will misappropriate property, etc. There will be much useless killing, and for this reason all kinds of corruption and many disturbances, so that mankind will rapidly deteriorate. This can not be God's will, for we read, ' For God is not pleased with corruption.' We are justified in assuming that God will be disposed to take away or prevent corruption. But this can only be accomplished in any age when the authority of the government is given into the hands of one who seeks the way of public advantage and the salvation of the people. He will look after the laws and be concerned about the general welfare of mankind in this world, as well as the prospects in the next world. Such a person is the Imam. And if for any particular age the Most High should not appoint an Imam, then God would appear as being willing that corruption should continue, whereas corruption is deplorable and cannot be reconciled with the will of God.

" 3. It is established both by reason and by tradition that the favour and grace of the Most High is unlimited towards his servants, for He guides them in the right way and directs them to that which is advantageous in this world and the next. For in several places in the Ḳoran it is said, ' and God is kind to his servants,' and one of the proofs of the perfection of his kindness and the unlimited nature of his favour towards all of his servants is that in arranging even the little things in their affairs he has not been neglectful. For example, the method of removing the hair and of trimming the moustache, the manner of entering and leaving the toilet, the way of cleansing with water or with stone, and directions in sexual matters—all such little things have been explicitly provided for by the words of the Apostle, the Possessor of Kindness and Learning, who has set forth in detail these things for his servants, so that all may understand.

" Now surely the appointment of the vicegerent or representative of the Apostle, the one to guard the Law and teach the Faith to men, the one to protect the people from evil and from those opposing them, surely this is more imperative than the little things that have been mentioned. Since God did not deem these little things as beneath his notice, how can we imagine that he would ignore anything so absolutely necessary as the chief need of the Faith? It is clear, therefore, that the appointment of the caliph or representative, the one to command all peoples, has been determined, and that God must have sent a revelation to the Apostle concerning the Imams. And all Muslims agree in this, that other than Ạli, the Amiru'l-Muminín, the caliphs were not so appointed. Ạli, therefore, must be the one recognized as having the appointment of the Apostle.

"4. The fourth proof is in accord with the belief of the Sunnites that it was God's practice, from the time of Adam to the time of Muḥammad, that the prophets should not leave this world until they had appointed their successors. Besides this, it was the custom of the Apostle, whenever he went out from Medina for a few days, whether for battle or otherwise, to designate someone to exercise authority in his place. He did this when he went to Mecca. He did the same thing for every town or village where there was a group of believers, and also when he appointed commanders for the army. He did not leave these matters to the choice of the people, but he himself sought the command of the Most High before making such appointments. Accordingly, in this situation of the utmost importance, involving laws and commands for the followers of Islam until the Judgment Day, can we conceive that the Apostle would have been neglectful of this, or that he would have left it to the choice of the people?

"5. The fifth proof is that the office of the Imam is like that of the Prophet in that each has the function of complete authority over all the followers of the Faith in matters of religion and of the state. The people themselves are incapable of judging who is worthy for this responsible office. With all the various opinions that they would have, if we assume that they might make this choice, it could only be according to their limited understanding and changing purpose, and it would not be for the common welfare or in harmony with the wisdom of God. Each one would vote according to his personal advantage. Such a procedure might be put into effect by a mere rule of force, and could be reconciled with the requirements of an autocratic and oppressive kingdom, but it would not be a suitable way to determine the Imamate or to direct a government that is based on Law. It is as unreasonable to think that the people would be able to choose the Imams as it would be to imagine that they are capable of choosing their Prophets, which would manifestly be impossible. Another remarkable thing is this, that if a King dismisses the governor of a city and does not appoint anyone in his place, or if the head man of the village leaves the village and does not appoint anyone in his stead to oversee the affairs of the village, but on the contrary leaves everything to the choice of the people, how is it that people who claim that it is not necessary that God and the Apostle should appoint the Imams would most severely censure such a King or such a head man of a village ? Can conduct of this sort be unbecoming on the part of a King or a head man of a village, and yet be regarded as acceptable and perfectly worthy of God and the Apostle ? There are those, however, who say that the Apostle left the world and did not leave a successor in his place, but that he left the choice of the Imam to the people.

"6. On the assumption that the people should be free from all personal prejudices, and should not have vain desires of their own, but should give themselves entirely to the work of choosing the Imam, nevertheless, since they would all be subject to mistakes, it is altogether possible that their choice might be a mistaken one, and that they would reject the right and choose the wrong. For we are aware that in the choice of Kings and Sultans and other prominent men, it often happens that for a time they are esteemed to be trustworthy and capable and deserving, but it afterwards turns out that they are the very opposite.

"7. If we assume further that the choice of the people should prove to be correct, notwithstanding, it is perfectly evident that the Knower of Secrets knows better as to who is best qualified for each and every work. It is more appropriate for God himself to exercise this choice. For if God should have the superior knowledge and yet should not make the choice himself but assign it to others there are grave difficulties involved, for this would be a case of God's preferring an expedient which would not be the best, a mistake which we cannot attribute to the All Powerful and the All Wise.

"8. If the Imamate were to be determined by the choice of the people there would be two probable consequences. In the first place their choice might well be a mistake, and since God would know beforehand that they would make this mistake, i.e., in spite of his knowledge and power and wisdom he would commit the direction of the Faith and Practice of the Muslims to an assembly that would be certain to make mistakes and to choose an unjust governor—surely this would be exceedingly unsatisfactory, a procedure in fact that we could not attribute to a wise God. And in the second place, if God should know that they would choose a good Imam, yet the recognition of this Imam, the duty of making him known to the people in general, the task of getting people to obey, the necessity of frustrating opposition and suppressing jealousies—all this would be unspeakably difficult for the people to accomplish, whereas for God himself it would be exceedingly easy. Hence we are bound to consider that to give work of such difficulty to others, and to thus force upon the people in their weakness a matter that would involve all this trouble, would be absolutely unworthy of God the Most High, of whom it is said, 'God wisheth you ease, but wisheth not your discomfort" (Ḳoran ii. v. 131).

"In summing up what has been said, it is clear that after the matter of prophecy itself our faith has had no other such real need as for an Imam. Muslims have required of God no other such favour as the existence of an Imam, for if there were no Imam, in a short time there would be no influence left in the Faith and it would disappear entirely. Without an Imam the faith and condition of Muslims everywhere would be left incomplete and in disorder. If God, therefore, had not appointed the Imam, if God had not sanctioned the Imamate, it would have been the same as withdrawing the influence of his Prophet from the world, and in that case both the Faith and God's favour would have been incomplete. Whoever says that this is the case most certainly gives the lie to the Ḳoran and to the Prophet of God, the Merciful, and to deny the truth of the Ḳoran and the Prophet is infidelity."

CHAPTER XXX

THE "SINLESSNESS" OF THE PROPHETS AND THE IMAMS

THE number of prophets that God has sent in past times is usually estimated by Muḥammadans as 124,000, but the majority of these are minor prophets of whom little is known. The *Ạḳa'idu'sh-Shi'ah*, the "Beliefs of the Shi'ites," contains a statement that has been conveniently summarized by Professor Browne:

"The number of the true prophets antecedent to Muḥammad, the seal of the prophets and the last of them, is variously stated, as from 140 to 124,000. It is necessary to believe that these, whatever their number, were true and immaculate (ma'sum), that is, that during the whole of their lives they were guilty of no sin, major or minor; that they all enunciated the same essential truths; and that the revelations which they received were essentially identical, though in detail the later abrogate the earlier, to wit, the Ḳoran the Gospel, and the Gospel the Pentateuch. These three, together, with the Psalms of David and the Books of Abraham, are the principal 'scriptures,' but the total number of revealed books is estimated by some as 104 and by others as 124. Of the prophets sent to all mankind, four were Syrian, i.e., Adam, Seth, Enoch (or Idris), and Noah; five were Arabs, i.e., Hud, Salih, Shuayb, Isma'il and Muḥammad; and the remainder were of the children of Israel. The five great prophets are called the *Ulu'l-Ạzm,* including Noah, Abraham, Moses, Jesus, and Muḥammad."[1]

The theologians of the Shi'ites are practically in agreement concerning the doctrine of the sinlessness of the Prophets and the Imams. In the statement in which Majlisi treats of the two together, he says:

"They are to be considered free from all sins, great or small. No sort of sin can be attributed to them, no oversight or forgetfulness, and no mistakes in interpretation. Neither are they to be

[1] Browne, *Persian Literature in Modern Times,* p. 288.

thought of as having sinned before the time of their being appointed prophets, not even in their childhood. No one has objected to this doctrine except Ibn Babuwaihi and Shaikh Muḥammad ibn Walid, who have maintained that God could allow them to forget something now and then, either for his own purpose, or when it was something that was in no way essential to their service. But all agree that belief in the sinlessness of the prophets is one of the necessary beliefs of the Shi'ah faith."[1]

Nine proofs are given which are stated briefly as follows:

1. If the prophets have been sent to be obeyed they must surely be without sin.
2. It is not possible to think of it being necessary to obey a prophet in some things and not in others.
3. If a prophet sins, then you must obey him, for if you deny him you trouble him, and to trouble a prophet is forbidden: "Those who trouble God and His Apostle have been cursed by God in this life and hereafter."
4. If a prophet sins it is necessary for the hearers of his testimony to refuse it.
5. If a prophet should sin, then his status ought to be lower than that of ordinary men.
6. If a prophet should sin, he would deserve rebuke, and the curse and punishment of God.
7. Prophets command men to obey God, so if they themselves do not obey God they are condemned by this verse: "Do you command men to do good and forget your own souls? Although you read the Book of God, do you not stop to think about it?"
8. Since Shaitán said to God: "By your glory, I swear that I will cause all to be lost except those pure ones of your servants," so if the prophets should sin, they are among those whom Shaitán has caused to be lost, and not among the pure ones of God's servants.
9. If the prophets are sinners, then they should be reckoned among the evildoers, and God has said, "My covenant and the Imamate will not come to evildoers."

While in the above statement Majlisi had primarily in mind the doctrine of the sinlessness of the prophets, in the third volume of his *Hayátu'l-Kulub*, which is devoted to showing the significance

[1] Majlisi, *Hayatu'l-Kulub*, Vol. I, pp. 11-12. This book is in three volumes, (1) The Prophets before Muḥammad, (2) The Life of Muḥammad (see English translation of this volume by Merrick, entitled *The Life and Religion of Muḥammad*, Boston, 1850), and (3) The Imamate.

of the Imamate, the belief in the sinlessness of the Imams is also laid down as fundamental:

"Know that all Shi'ah scholars are agreed that the Imam is free from all sins, whether great or small, from the beginning of his life until the end, and whether intentional or accidental. No one has objected to this teaching except Ibn Babuwaihi and his teacher, Muḥammad ibn Walid. They considered that it was permissible to believe that before his appointment to the Imamate it was possible that a man should make mistakes. For example, he might slip up in his prayers, or in the observance of some of the forms of worship or commands of the faith, but we are not to think that he would make any mistakes in explaining the commands of the faith, for in this they also do not allow the possibility of any sort of error. All the sects of the Shi'ites, except the Isma'ilís, are united in this, however, that they recognize no limitations to the sinlessness of the Imams."[1]

The verse in the Ḳoran which is deemed the most important to prove the necessity of believing in the sinlessness of the Imam is that which was revealed to Abraham, "For I have appointed you as a leader (imam) for mankind. Abraham then inquired, 'And those who come after me?' To this God answered, 'My covenant does not come to evildoers'" (Surah ii. 118).

"Now we know," says Majlisi, "that every sinner is cruel and the oppressor even of his own soul," and the explanation of Ibn Babuwaihi in the *Kisal* is quoted in interpreting this passage: "It is not to be supposed that anyone should have the right of an *Imam* who was an idol worshipper, or one who for one moment would associate a partner with God, even though he should eventually become a Muslim. 'Force' is to be understood (in the evil sense) as the *placing of something in the wrong place*, and the greatest instance of it is the assumption of a partner for God. This is clear from what the Most High has said, 'For the joining of Gods with God is the great impurity.' Also we could not consider that the Imamate belonged to anyone who had done that which was forbidden, whether the offence were great or small, even though he should afterwards repent, for the command to scourge another cannot be allowed to one who himself deserves scourging. The Imam, therefore, *must* be sinless.

"The sinlessness of an Imam cannot be known, however, unless he has received divine appointment and has been designated to his

[1] Majlisi, *op. cit.*, iii, p. 23 ff.

office by the word of his Prophet. It is not something to be noted in his external appearance, something that can be seen, like black or white or such qualities. Sinlessness is rather a hidden virtue which can be recognized only by announcement from God, who knows all that is concealed."

To elaborate and further explain the doctrine, various traditions are assembled. Hisham ibn Hakam, who was a favourite young scholar among the Shi'ites in the time of the Imam Ja'far aṣ-Ṣadiḳ, was asked, "Is the Imam sinless?" He said, "Yes." He was then asked, "How can you know that he is sinless?" To this he replied more at length, "All sin has four varieties, not five—greed, envy, anger and lust. The Imam can have none of these. He can have no reason to be greedy, for the whole world is under his seal (this reference is to Solomon's powerful ring), and he is the guardian of the treasury of Islam. He cannot be envious, for envy is something that one has toward a superior, whereas the Imam has no superiors. Also he cannot show anger for any carnal reason, but only in the service of God, when he may be called upon to punish others so that those who oppose him should not succeed in obstructing the commands of the Most High, for mercy of course should not be allowed to be an obstacle to the advancement of the faith. Likewise he cannot seek the lust and pleasure of this world, as his preference and love is for the world to come. In much the same way as this world is the object of our love, he looks to the next world; and have you ever seen anyone who has abandoned a beautiful face for an ugly one? Or have you ever seen anyone refuse delicious food for something bitter, or soft clothing for coarse, or an everlasting reward for merely temporary advantages?"

When the fourth Imam, Zainu'l-Adidín, was asked, "What meaning does sinlessness have?" he answered, "Sinlessness is that quality which enables a man to seize firmly the strong 'life-line' from God, i.e., the Ḳoran, so that the Imam and the Ḳoran are never to be separated until the Judgment Day. The Imam will direct men to the Ḳoran and the Ḳoran will direct them to the Imam. For this is the meaning of the word of God, 'Verily this Ḳoran guideth to what is most upright' (Surah xvii. 9), namely, that this Ḳoran directs men to a people who are the most upright of all peoples, and to a way which is the straightest of all ways—which refers to the way of obedience to the true Imams."

At this point Majlisi adds the personal comment, "The explanation of sinlessness as the seizing of the 'life-line' from God, is either that God guards the Imam from sin by his devotion to the Ḳoran, or the meaning may be that God has made him devoted to the Ḳoran, so that he may fulfil in his conduct whatever is in the Ḳoran, and know the meaning of all its contents."

In as much as it is universally believed among Muslims that every person has two recording angels, literally "illustrious writers," it is interesting to observe that there is a tradition in the *Kanz al-Fawayid*, cited from a man called Karajakí, which asserts that the Apostle of God said that the angel Gabriel had informed him that the recording angels of Ạli had declared that from the day they were appointed to associate with him until the present time they had never written any sin against him. Approximately, the same statement is made also on the authority of Amr ibn Yasir, i.e., that the Apostle of God had said that the two angels who recorded the works of Ạli had boasted over the other recording angels of their good fortune in being appointed to associate with him, for he had never committed any act that deserved punishment from God.

Psychological Explanations

In the same connection Majlisi endeavours to correct what he considers as mistaken ideas of the doctrine of sinlessness which would make it a *necessary* characteristic of the prophets and the Imams: "Know that those who accept the doctrine of sinlessness have been in error at times in regard to the point as to whether a sinless man has the *power* to commit a sinful act. Some of those who say that he is not able to do so claim that there is some special quality in his body or in his soul which has the effect of making it impossible for him to be involved in sin. Others have said that the *condition* of sinlessness involves in itself the power to be obedient and to refrain from sin. Most theologians, however, agree that the Imam does have the power to commit sin. Some of them have interpreted *ísma,* or immunity from sin or error, as a command which God gives his servant, a favour bestowed upon him, in order to lead him to obedience, and that it is in this way that he does not become involved in sin. There is the restriction, nevertheless, that he is not to be regarded as constrained or compelled by force. Others have said that sinlessness is a *habit of the soul*, by reason of which the person will not fall into sin. Still others have said that it is a gracious gift from God to his servant, so that he will not give up his obedience or commit any act of sin. In this gift there are four things, first, that his soul or his body should have some special characteristic worthy of being a habit and strong enough to forbid transgression ; second, that a special knowledge comes to him to enable him to perceive evils in sin and foresee its consequences, as well as to appreciate the advantages and profits in obedience ; third, that there is constant repetition of this knowledge by means of revelation from God ; and fourth, that he is continuously admonished by God concerning that which is forbidden and that which it is best that he should not do ; with the consequence that he is able to know what is right. Whenever he is tempted to do something that is not required, then God gives him specific warning. And he knows that God will not neglect to lead him to do that which is necessary and to avoid that which is obviously wrong. Accordingly, whenever these four qualifications characterize any one person, he would then be regarded as sinless. He has the capacity, however, to commit sin at any time, for otherwise he would not be entitled to any credit for avoiding sin and there would be no merit attained by his righteousness, and he would have no sense of obligation. Sinlessness in that sense would be meaningless, as the traditions show.

" Also, we may observe that sinlessness would not be a desirable state if it is construed to mean that by oppressing others one could become sinless (which refers to the assertion that an imamate established by force could be recognized). The essential meaning of the term is that a man, by the power of reason, by strength and worthiness of mind, by persistence in prayer and fasting, and by the guidance and help of the Most High, will thus arrive at a state where he will always be thinking about pleasing God. He will set aside entirely those desires and motives that are peculiarly his own, and will reach the place where he will not desire anything except the will of God; when he will fulfil this tradition, 'Through me he hears and sees and walks.' In this way it becomes impossible for him to abandon obedience to God or to commit sin—not even the minor offences.

"He becomes like one who stands before a King, always ready with perfect love and affection, good-will and gratitude, to serve him with the utmost veneration and fear, and who recognizes that the King manifests the greatest favour towards him. And he himself has the utmost love for the King. Thus it becomes impossible for him to do anything against the King's will, however easily it might be accomplished. One reason for this is his excessive love, for the lover is under the necessity of serving the beloved. A second reason is his sense of shame, for with such devotion he would be ashamed to do anything in the absence of the King that he would not do in his presence. In the third place he would have a kind of fear and anxiety, lest on account of the very special nature of the favour he had enjoyed from the King, who had given him so much power and authority, he might do something displeasing and that would thus deserve and probably receive the utmost punishment. What a punishment it would be for one who had enjoyed such love and honour to see that he had fallen in the esteem of his Sovereign. Evidently the one so favoured would find the actual committing of sin impossible, but not, however, in such a way as to make his merit compulsory. For compulsion occurs where the choice and will of men is not given opportunity, whereas in the case we are considering, the power of choice and will is in no way restricted, since he is free to do as sinners do if he wishes. For example, he can drink intoxicating liquor if he wants to.

"Again, it is related on the authority of the Imams, that prophets and apostles are of four degrees: (1) there is the prophet who does not prophesy to others; who sees visions in his sleep and hears the voices of angels, but when he is awake he does not see the angels, he has not been chosen, however, as a prophet for others and there is some other one who is his *imám* or guide. For example, there was Lot, for whom Abraham was the *imám*. And (2), there is the prophet who sees visions in his sleep, and who hears voices and sees the angels, but who is definitely sent to lead a group of men, be they few or many—as God has said regarding Jonah (Surah xxxvii. 147), 'And we sent him to a hundred thousand persons, or even more,'—and yet there was another who was the *imám* for him. And (3), there is the prophet who sees visions and hears the voices of angels, and who is himself an *imám* for others. For example, Abraham was a prophet but not an *imám* until God said (Surah ii. 118), 'For I have appointed you an *imám* for mankind.' But when Abraham asked about his offspring God said, 'My covenant embraces not the evildoers,' i.e., those who worship idols or graven images.

"Salabí has related from the Imam Ja'far aṣ-Ṣadiḳ that God has indicated the purity of those of the Household from uncleanness, i.e., from doubt and sin, in the 'verse of the purification,' in which he said, 'For God only desireth to put away filthiness from you as his Household, and with a cleansing to cleanse you' (Surah xxxiii. 33). And Muḥammad ibn Ạbbas and Ibn Mahiyar in his Commentary, have related from the Imam Ṣadiḳ that 'the Most High does not abandon us, for if he would abandon us to ourselves, then we, like other men, would be in sin and error.' But God has said in regard to us, 'Pray until I give you salvation.'"

At this point in his argument Majlisi undertakes to reply to objections that have been offered. "You must understand," he says, "that the Shi'ah theologians are all in agreement as to the freedom of the Imams from any kind of sin. Notwithstanding, in many of the prayers there are expressions that mention the sin of the Imams. In some of the traditions, also, there are cases where we are apt to think that the Imams have committed sins. These can all be explained, however, in one or other of several ways. (1) Sometimes there are instances of their not having done *the preferred things* and of their having done what was not the best to do. These failures they have spoken of as sins. And there are inconsequential matters that the Imams have spoken of as sins in that they considered them unworthy of their exalted rank and of the rest of their actions. It has been observed that usually their desires are fixed on God and his service, and their thoughts are bound to exalted things, so that when occasionally they descend from these heights, and busy themselves in eating or drinking or in sexual matters, things that are inconsequential, sometimes they call these acts sinful and ask forgiveness for them. As an illustration, have you not observed how most servants, if they happen to be occupied in such personal things when their master appears, instinctively ask to be forgiven as though they had done wrong? (2) When they do particular things in their association with mankind, acting for their benefit and guidance, as they have been commanded by the Most High, they afterwards return to the place of devotion and nearness and communion with God. This privilege of communion is more precious to them than the other, and they may speak of themselves as erring in the other, and ask for pardon and sometimes weep. Notwithstanding that this association with men has been by the command of God, and recognizing that this is a matter that is beyond proper illustration, yet it is very much as though a King should assign some of his most intimate associates to a particular service, and for this purpose they should have to go away from the King's presence, and we can see how on their return they might speak of themselves as though they had been at fault for their absence from their place of devotion and affection. (3) Since their knowledge and skill and purity is from the kindness and grace of God—for if this were not the case it would be possible that they should commit all sorts of sin—when they consider this fact they acknowledge God's grace and their own unworthiness. The significance of this is the same as though they were to say, 'If sinlessness were not from Thee, I would surely commit sin; and if it were not for Thy help, I would certainly do great wrong.'

(4) Remembering that the knowledge of God is not something that can be fully attained, and that the prophets and the apostles and the Imams are always making progress in their perfections, and advancing higher and nearer to God, consequently, every hour, in fact every minute, they are in varying degrees of fellowship with God and of knowledge of His truth. A previous degree of attainment may be recognized as lower, and the worship that was in place at that point may afterwards be considered inferior, so that they may think of themselves as having at that time been deficient, and for this reason they may ask to be pardoned. Or perhaps it refers to something like this, as when the Apostle said, 'I ask pardon every day seventy times.'[1] (5) Since the knowledge of God that the Imams have is so vast, and the blessings they receive are so numerous, and they put forth such exertions in their obedience and worship, they do not consider themselves worthy before God and regard their obedience as imperfect and consider that they have shortcomings for which they ask forgiveness.

"Thus in addition to the first explanation, which is given by most theologians, I have added such other explanations as have occurred to me, and anyone who has tasted a drop of the wine of love will accept them all. 'He to whom God shall not give light, no light at all hath he' (Ḳoran, Surah xxiv. 40). And Ibn Babuwaihi has remarked in his statement of beliefs that our belief in the prophets and the apostles and the Imams is that they are free and pure from every stain, and that no sin, whether great or small, can be attributed to them; for they do not disobey God in anything which God has commanded, and they do what he has directed, and anyone who refuses to grant them this quality of sinlessness has certainly not known them. Our belief is that they are endowed with perfection in conduct and learning, from the beginning of their works until the end of their lives, and on no condition are they in any way to be considered as imperfect or ignorant or transgressing."

[1] Goldziher, *Vorlesungen*, ch. v, sect. ix, note 4, where Ạli ibn Kárí, in the *Sharḥ al-Fiḳh al-Akhbár*, gives the tradition that the Prophet said, "My heart is often sad and I ask pardon from God a hundred times a day."

CHAPTER XXXI

THE ORIGIN OF THE ISLAMIC DOGMA OF "SINLESSNESS"

SINCE the belief in the sinlessness of the prophets and of their successors, the Imams, is fundamental in Shi'ite Islam, it is important to inquire into its origin and development. It did not come by way of the canonical Jewish scriptures, for even a cursory study of the Old Testament shows clearly that the authority of the Jewish prophets was not attributed to their sinlessness, but on the contrary, the sins of the prophets are freely recorded as matters of fact. Adam, Noah, Abraham, Job, Moses, David, Solomon, Isaiah and Ezra can all be readily shown to have been sinners by the Bible records, and in several places, as it happens, by their own confession.

Likewise, if the New Testament is examined, it is easily seen that the writers of the gospels and the epistles attribute the status or quality of sinlessness only to Jesus. Those who first believed on him accepted him as the expected Messiah, and it was as the Christ and not as a prophet that he came to be regarded as sinless. Neither the disciples nor the apostles are represented in the New Testament as sinless or inerrant, and no doctrine of the sinlessness of the prophets is developed in their writings; for the verse (Luke xv. 8) that refers in parable to the "ninety and nine righteous who need no repentance" is to be regarded as a recognition of Pharasaical pretensions rather than an acknowledgment that there actually are any such persons.

The suggestion has been made that the idea of attributing sinlessness to the prophets may have come into Islam from the influence of particular ones of the Jewish apocryphal books.[1] Reference is made to the "Prayer of Manasses." Manasseh,

[1] Tisdall, *Religion of the Crescent*, Appendix.

the King of Judah (695-641 B.C.), had seduced Judah and the inhabitants of Jerusalem, but when he was taken captive by one of the armies of Esarhaddon and brought in fetters to Babylon, he "humbled himself greatly before the God of his fathers." His prayer of repentance is not given by the chronicler (2 Chron. xxxiii), though mention is made in a verse that may be a later interpolation of its being written in the *History of the Seers*. The "Prayer of Manasses" that is included in the Apocrypha is thought to have been written as late as the time of Christ, and in this brief prayer we find what I believe is the earliest Jewish statement of a doctrine of the sinlessness, not so much of the prophets, but of the patriarchs. For the writer of this prayer declares, "Thou therefore, O Lord, that art the God of the Just, hast not appointed repentance to the Just, to Abraham, and Isaac, and Jacob, which have not sinned against thee; but thou hast appointed repentance unto me that am a sinner."[1] The "Testament of Abraham" also speaks of Abraham as being without sin.[2] In so much as it is a fact that the Ḳoran itself, as well as earlier and later Muḥammadan theology, was greatly influenced by apocryphal stories and teachings, it is not impossible that they may have had something to do with the development of the Muḥammadan doctrine of the sinlessness of the prophets, but it is the writer's belief that there was another factor that may be regarded as demonstrably a more potent and more immediate cause.

But before undertaking to develop the thesis that the Islamic dogma of the "sinlessness" of the prophets is a direct outgrowth or corollary of the Shi'ite doctrine of the Imamate, it is of the utmost importance to observe that the sinlessness of the prophets is not supported by the Ḳoran. In its references to Adam and to Moses and to David, for example, we find statements regarding their sins. Adam was banished from Paradise for disobedience to God. It is true that the Devil is made responsible to some

[1] Apocrypha, *Prayer of Manasses*. Cf. Hastings' *Dictionary of the Bible*, art. "Sin," with reference to Weber, *Jud. Theol.*, pp. 32 and 54.
[2] *Testament of Abraham*, Eng. trans., *S.P.C.K.*, p. 88.

extent for the fall of Adam and Eve, but at the same time they were punished for their transgression :

" And we said, ' O Adam ! dwell thou and thy wife in the Garden and eat ye plentifully from wherever ye list ; but to this tree come not nigh, lest ye become the transgressors.' But Shaitan made them slip from it, and caused their banishment from the place where they were. And we said, ' Get ye down, the one of you an enemy to the other ; and there shall be for you in the Earth a dwelling place, and a provision for a time.' " (Surah ii. 35-36.)

In the acknowledgment of their fault, also, Adam and Eve are represented as using the same expression in the Arabic as that used by God in warning them :

" O our Lord, with ourselves we have *dealt unjustly* : if thou forgive us not and have not pity on us, we shall surely be of those who perish " (Surah vii. 22).

The Ḳoran also mentions that Moses killed a man and fled to the people of Midian, and that he afterwards confessed :

" ' This is the work of Shaitan ; for he is an enemy, a manifest misleader.' Then he said, ' O my Lord, I have sinned to my own hurt, forgive me.' So God forgave him, for he is the Forgiving, the Merciful " (Surah xxviii. 21-25).

The account in the Ḳoran of David's sin (Surah xxxviii, 21-25), shows that two pleaders came to David with a case for him to judge, the one charging the other with having taken his one ewe when he already had ninety-nine ewes of his own. David pronounces judgment, after which follows the statement : " And David was sure that we had tried him, so he sought the protection of his Lord, and he fell down, bowing time after time to him " (verse 24).

In connection with these statements in the Ḳoran about the sins of Adam and Moses and David, a comparison of some of the words and expressions that are used in describing other characters whose sins are freely admitted would not be out of place. In the following references the expressions in italic type are used also by the prophets in acknowledging their sins :

1. (Surah xxix, 38-39) " And Corah and Pharaoh and Haman. With proofs of his mission did Moses come to them, and *they behaved proudly on the Earth*: but us they could not outstrip. For everyone *did we seize in his sin*. Against some of them did we send a stone-charged wind: some of them did the terrible cry of Gabriel surprise: for some of them we cleaved the Earth: and some of them we drowned. And it was not God who would deal wrongly by them, but *they wronged themselves*."
2. (Surah iv, 67) " We have not sent any apostle but to be obeyed, if God so will: but if they, after they *have sinned to their own hurt* by unbelief, come to see thee and ask pardon of God, and the Apostle ask pardon for them, they shall surely find that God is he who turneth unto man, Merciful.

In addition to the fact that the Ḳoran neither states nor confirms the doctrine of the sinlessness of the prophets, it is significant to observe that in the earliest Muhammadan apologetic literature *versus* Christianity, particularly in two such presentations of orthodox Muslim beliefs that date from the third century after the Hegira, this doctrine is not enunciated. The first of these records is a brief letter that was written by Abdullah ibn Isma'il, the Hashimite, to Abdu'l Masih ibn Ishaḳ al-Kindi.[1] This letter dates from the reign of the Caliph Mamun (A.D. 813-833). Although the writer's express purpose was to convince his friend of the truth of the claims of Islam, this letter makes no reference whatever to the teaching of the sinlessness of the prophets. In the reply, also, which is known as the " Apology of al-Kindi," notwithstanding the fact that much space is devoted to setting forth reasons for refusing to consider Muḥammad as a true prophet, the doctrine of the sinlessness of the prophets is not referred to, either directly or by implication. Likewise in the similar doctrinal statement that dates from the caliphate of Mutawakkil (A.D. 847-861), the *Kitábu'd-Dín wa'd-Dawlah*, or " The Book of Religion and Empire,"[2] there is no discussion whatever of this

[1] T. W. Arnold, *The Preaching of Islam*, Appendix I; also the *Apology of al-Kindi*, translated by Sir William Muir.

[2] *Kitabu'd-Dín wa'd-Dawlah*, or *The Book of Religion and Empire*, trans. Mingana, London, 1926, Introduction.

doctrine. The author of this book, Ạli Tabari, was himself a convert from Christianity, and while he comments on the variation of Muḥammad's teaching and practice from the rules of the *Taurát* (Old Testament books of Law) and the *Injíl* (New Testament), he makes no statement that suggests that a doctrine of the sinlessness of the prophets had been developed in Islam in the course of controversy with the Christians.

Historically considered, it is more probable that the teaching of the sinlessness of the prophets in Islam owes both its origin and its acquired importance to the development of the theology of the Shi'ites. In order to establish the claims of the Imams, as over against the claims of the Sunnite Caliphs, the discontented Shi'ites evolved the doctrine of the sinlessness of the Imams, and of the prophets also, in so much as they acted as Imams or as guides for mankind, and whom God made it necessary for men to obey. In the way the Shi'ite theologians state the proofs for this belief we see also the influence of the rationalistic type of argument that characterized the Mu'tazilites.[1] In the elaboration of the doctrine great stress is laid repeatedly on God's saying to Abraham (Surah ii, 118), "For I have appointed you as a leader (imám) for mankind." Another verse that is associated with this in the proof of the sinlessness of the prophet-imams is: "O Believers, if any bad man come to you with news, clear it up at once, lest through ignorance ye harm others, and speedily have to repent of what ye have done" (Surah xlix. 6). The query is, How could God require men to obey Abraham if Abraham was a sinner? And Majlisi asks, "How could any reasoning mind accept the teaching that the imám or guide of mankind should himself be one of the sons of Hell, for the Most High has appointed Hell as the place for the unrighteous, according to the verse, 'And for those who transgress, their abode is the fire'" (Surah xxxii. 20). "The scholars of the Sunnites," he says, "who do not accept the doctrine of the sinlessness of the Imams are those who also fail to see that cruelty and corruption should disqualify an Imam, and this is the reason they have been able to accept

[1] Goldziher, *Vorlesungen*, ch. v, sect. 5.

the guidance or *imamate* of the Umayyad Caliphs and the Ạbbasid Caliphs, with all the oppression and vice that they manifested."[1]

Heredity also, without the divine appointment, is deemed insufficient. The son of an Imam must have been particularly designated by his father in order that his appointment may have the divine sanction. If in addition a prediction concerning him has been made by his grandfather the case is strengthened, and traditions are not wanting to show that some of the Imams have anticipated their successors for several generations. But the all important deduction from their divine appointment is their sinlessness, for as in the case of Abraham, so with Ạli and his successors, God would surely not thus appoint them to be Imams, to be obeyed by mankind, if they were transgressors. Having gone so far, and with such an obviously useful purpose to serve, it is not difficult to see how the dogma developed that Muḥammad and all the prophets *must have been* without sin.

The growth of this doctrine among the Shi'ites took place, as the traditions clearly indicate, during the time of the historic Imamate, i.e., in the period between the death of Muḥammad and the disappearance of the Twelfth Imam. According to Majlisi, Kulaini and Shaikh Mufid both attribute to the Imam Ja'far aṣ-Ṣadiḳ (d. A.D. 765) the interpretation of Surah ii. 18 that shows that Abraham *must have been* sinless in order to be appointed by God as an Imam, adding that it was evident "that the foolish cannot be the leaders of the righteous." As Kulaini and Shaikh Mufid and Ibn Babuwaihi Ṣuduḳ belonged to the group of Shi'ite traditionists who lived during the time of the Buwaihid supremacy, it is clear that the doctrine of the sinlessness of the prophets and the Imams was at that time fully developed in the Shi'ite community. For this statement there is further

[1] Majlisi, *Hayatu'l-Ḳulub*, III, ch. i, sect. 2. Mullah Said al-Dín, a Sunnite, is quoted in this connection as having said, "The Imamate or Caliphate is dependent upon might or conquest. If anyone becomes Imam through might and conquest, and another comes to conquer and subdue him, the one conquered is dismissed, and the victor becomes the *imám*." And Majlisi exclaims, "Surely this is shallow doctrine!"

evidence in the *Tabsiratu'l-Awwam* or "Consideration of the Common People," the early work in Persian on Comparative Religion that was written by Sayyid Murtaḍa, the Alam al-Huda, during the same period. For this useful writer openly ridiculed the Sunnites for holding the contrary belief.

The doctrine of *iṣma* was not mentioned in the Canonical Hadith (Wensinck, "The Muslim Creed," p. 217). It was stated as an orthodox belief, however, as early as the latter part of the tenth century in the Fiḳh Akbar II, not long after Kulaini (Káfí, i, 98) had included it in traditions from the Imams. There is question, however, as to how rapidly it was accepted in the Sunnite community, for as late as al-Ghazzali (d. A.D. 1111), we find an expression of what would seem to be a contrary opinion:

"The proof of the invariable necessity of repentance in all cases is that no one of mankind is free from bodily sin. The prophets also were not free from it, for the Ḳoran and the Traditions mention the sins of the prophets, together with their repentance and weeping for them. For in case a man should be free from bodily sin, he would not be free from sins in his heart. And if in any way he should be free from sins in his heart, still he would not be free from the suggestions of Shaitan, which bring in scattering thoughts which distract a man from thinking of God. If indeed he should be free from the suggestions of Shaitan, he would still not be free from neglect and imperfection in his knowledge of God, both as to his attributes and his works. All this means deficiency and there are causes for it. The way to get rid of these causes is to be occupied with things opposite to them, and thus return from one way to an entirely different way. In this sense the meaning of repentance is 'returning.' It is inconceivable that anyone should be free from the deficiency that makes it necessary, for sin is a fact in the experience of every man. The Prophet, peace be upon him, has said, 'There is a covering of sin on my heart until I have asked God's forgiveness seventy times during the day and night.' And for this confession the Most High honoured him when He said, 'May God forgive your former and your latter sins.' Therefore, if this was true of the Prophet, what must be the condition of others?"[1]

But about a century later than al-Ghazzali there lived among the Sunnites the influential writer Fakhr ad-Din ar-Rázi (d. A.D. 1210). As Dr. Goldziher has pointed out, he "was one of the most zealous advocates of the doctrine of the sinlessness of the Prophets. Besides treating the subject in the appropriate places in his Commentary on the Ḳoran, he wrote a separate book, entitled *Ịsmatu'l-Anbiya* or the 'Sinlessness of the Prophets,' in which he took up each prophet mentioned, giving his explanations and references and disproving other opinions with copious argument."[2] Like his famous predecessor al-Ghazzali he was one of the Shafi'ís, and also like al-Ghazzali he was strongly influenced by the devotional methods of speculative thinking that characterized the Súfis, who, like the Mu'tazilites of earlier times, were a transmitting medium for the exchange of ideas between the Sunnites and the Shi'ites. Usually whatever the one main group has learned from the other has come through either the Súfis or the Mu'tazilites. For example, the famous Súfi al-Shárani who lived more than two centuries before ar-Rázi, wrote that the Prophet could see behind him as well as in front of him, could see in the dark, could change his own height, and that his body never cast a shadow for it was full of light. Such conceptions are attributed to ideas the Shi'ites had formed very early in regard to their Imams, to whom the Prophet must of course not be inferior,[3] and which, as we have seen, have been continually influenced by the underlying conception of the 'light of Muḥammad.'[4]

It was due to the writings of ar-Rázi, therefore, that the present dogma of the sinlessness of the prophets was finally included in the Ijma', or general agreement, of the Sunnite theologians. The contribution of the Mu'tazilites was the distinction between the 'great' and the 'little' sins. According to ar-Rázi most

[1] Ghazzali, *Ihya Ụlum ad-Dín*, Part IV, pp. 5-6.
[2] Goldziher, *Der Islam*, iii, p. 238. Cf. Brockelmann, i, p. 507, No. 14.
[3] *Idem, Vorlesungen*, ch. v, sect. 9.
[4] See chapter xii; also art. "Incarnation," in the *Encyclopædia of Religion and Ethics*.

of the Mu'tazilites taught that it was not permissible to consider that the prophets should intentionally commit 'great' sins, but they might intend the 'little' ones, on the condition that they should be inconsequential and not be loathsome or base.

In the accepted creed of al-Faḍali, who ranks as a modern Sunnite theologian, some six hundred years later than ar-Rázi, we read that the "Forty-third article of belief which it is necessary to accept is the trustworthiness of the apostles, that is, their being preserved from falling into things forbidden or disliked."[1] The creed of an-Nasafi, who died two generations before ar-Rázi, contains merely the statement that "a great sin (kabira) does not exclude the creature who believes from the Belief (imán) and does not make him an unbeliever,"[2] which is the connection in which the Mu'tazilite distinction between sins was first and more generally accepted. But an-Nasafi makes no declaration whatever about the sinlessness of the prophets.

It is interesting to observe that in the detailed instruction that is given for inflection in reading the Ḳoran, "after reading the verse 'Adam disobeyed his Lord and went astray' (Surah xx. 119), the reader should not pause but quickly pass on to the following words, 'Afterwards His Lord chose him for himself and was turned towards him.' The idea is, that as Adam was one of the Anbiyá-úlú'l-Ạzm, the six chief prophets, the stress should be laid on God's forgiveness of his fault and not on his disobedience."[3] Thus even Adam may be qualified to share in the *necessary* sinlessness of the prophets and the Imams.[4]

[1] MacDonald, *Development of Muslim Theology, Jurisprudence and Constitutional Theory*, p. 347.

[2] *Idem, op. cit.*, p. 311.

[3] Sell, *Faith of Islam*, p. 377.

[4] In his recent article in the *Encyclopædia of Islam* on "Isma," Dr. Goldziher observes that the Sunnite theologians differ as to the extent of the immunity of the prophets from error and sin, for questions arise "as to whether the immunity existed before or only after the prophetic calling, and as to whether it is from all kinds of sin or only applies to minor slips. It is applied in unlimited fashion to Muḥammad only, in oppostion to his own judgment. Among Sunni authorities Fakhr ad-Dín ar-Rázi in particular extends the *isma* (immunity from sin and error) to all prophets in the highest degree." The philosopher and physician Ibn Sina (d. A.D. 1037) accepted the statement that the prophets "are in no way subject to error or forgetfulness" (Goldziher, *Vorlesungen*, ch. v, sect. 9, note 1, with reference to *Die* Metaphysik Avicennas, trans. by M. Horten, pp. 88 and 19). *Cf.* T. Andrae, *Die Person Muhammeds*, pp. 124-134.

CHAPTER XXXII

THE PROPHETS AND THE IMAMS AS MEDIATORS

THE doctrine that the prophets are mediators before God in behalf of their followers was developed very early after the death of Muḥammad. That it was not the intention of Muḥammad to teach that he or the prophets would have this responsibility is suggested, however, by the verse in the Ḳoran which says: "No soul shall labour but for itself; and no burdened one shall bear another's burden" (Surah vi. 164), which indicates a belief in individual responsibility before God. We find also that Muḥammad ridiculed the Jews for the way they trusted complacently that their punishment would be mitigated because of their prophet's mediation or by virtue of their privileges as people of the Covenant:

"Hast thou not marked those who have received a portion of the Scriptures, when they are summoned to the Book of God (the Ḳoran), that it may settle their differences? Then did a part of them turn back, and withdrew far off. This—because they said, 'The fire shall by no means touch us, but for certain days'—their own devices have deceived them in their religion" (Surah iii. 22-23).

On the last sentence in this passage al-Baidawi comments, "that the fire would not touch them, except for a few days, or *that their fathers, the prophets, would mediate for them*, or that the Most High had promised Jacob that he would not punish his children beyond the stipulations of the Covenant." The following verse in the Ḳoran reads, "But how, when we shall assemble them together for the day of (which) *whose coming* there is no doubt, and when every soul shall be paid what it hath earned, and they shall not be wronged?" (Surah iii. 24).

In modern Islam, however, both the Sunnite and the Shi'ite

accept the intercession of Muḥammad on the Day of Judgment as a necessary belief. "And it must be believed that he (Muḥammad) will make intercession (shafa'a) on the day of Resurrection in the midst of the Judgment, when we shall stand and long to depart, even though it be into the Fire. Then he shall intercede that they may depart from the Station (mawqif), and this intercession belongs to him only."[1] Ample ground for this authoritative declaration of al-Fadali's is found in the traditions, where there are numerous references that show both that intercession was one of Muḥammad's prerogatives in contradistinction to the prophets and that it is a function that is exercised likewise by other prophets and martyrs and individual members of the Muslim community.[2] It is said in fact that "seventy thousand will enter Paradise through the intercession of one member of the community."

One of the traditions that shows the far-reaching necessity of the intercession of Muḥammad is as follows:[3]

"It is recorded that when Adam was punished and sent into the world on account of his sin, he repented of his sins with weeping and sorrow, but his repentance was not accepted, until at length he took Muḥammad, the Apostle of God, *for his mediator*, saying, 'O God, forgive my sins for Muḥammad's sake!' God asked him, 'Whence knowest thou Muḥammad?' Adam replied, 'At the time when thou didst create me, the foot of the Throne was straight opposite my sight, and I beheld written upon it: There is no God but Allah; Muḥammad is the Apostle of Allah. Then I knew that the dearest and noblest of beings in thy sight is Muḥammad, whose name Thou hast joined close to thine own name. After this the voice came, 'O Adam, know thou that one of thy offspring is the last of the prophets: I have created thee that thou shouldst be a residuary portion of him.' It is said that on the same day Adam was commanded by God to assume the surname Abu Muḥammad (i.e., father of Muḥammad)."

Professor Hurgronjl has given a brief statement of the typical

[1] MacDonald, *Muslim Theology*, p. 349, quoting al-Fadali, Arabic text, Cairo, 1315 A.H., with commentary by al-Baijurí.
[2] Wensinck, *A Handbook of Early Muhammadan Traditions*, under "Intercession."
[3] Koelle, *Muhammad and Muhammadanism*, p. 335.

Muhammadan point of view when they attempt to reconcile their belief in the prophets as mediators with apparently contradictory verses in the Ḳoran.[1] "Allah gives to each one his due. The actions of his creatures are all accurately written down, and when Judgment comes the book is opened; moreover, every creature carries the list of his own deeds and misdeeds; the debit and credit sides are carefully weighed against each other in the divine scales, and many witnesses are heard before judgment is pronounced. Allah, however, is clement and merciful; he gladly forgives those sinners who have believed in him, who have sincerely accepted Islam, that is to say: who have acknowledged his absolute authority and have believed the message of the Prophet sent to them. These prophets have the privilege of acting as mediators on behalf of their followers, not in the sense of redeemers, but as advocates who receive gracious hearing."

Among the Shi'ites the idea of mediation or intercession has been carried much farther, particularly in regard to Ḥusain. For on the tenth of the month of Muharram, in memory of his martyrdom at Kerbala, it is customary for men and boys to endure voluntary suffering, and to spatter their white garments with blood from self-inflicted wounds. "Unable to believe that their Imam was conquered and killed against his will the Shi'a have made the whole tragedy a predestined case of vicarious sacrifice. Ḥusain is foretold as a victim in the cause of Islam. 'He shall die for the sake of my people,' says Muḥammad of his grandson, according to these legends, and the 'Passion Play' is full of allusions to Husain's redemptive work and voluntary sacrifice of his body for the sins of the Muslim world. Husain himself knows, when only a child, the destiny that lies before him. 'All rational creatures,' he says, 'men and Jinn, who inhabit the present and future worlds, are sunk in sin, and have but one Ḥusain to save them'; and when Ạli speaks mournfully of the woes that shall come upon his family, Ḥusain answers, 'Father, there is no occasion to call these things trials, since all refer to the salvation of our sinful followers. Thou, Hasan and I,

[1] Hurgronje, *Lectures on Muhammadanism*, p. 56.

together with our mother the Virgin, will accept sufferings according to the best of our ability.' Standing by the grave of Muḥammad, before departing on the fatal journey to Kerbala, Ḥusain says, ' How can I forget thy people, since I am going to offer myself voluntarily for their sakes ? ' and Muḥammad tells him he has taken off from his heart the burden of grief he had for the future state of mankind ; and Ḥusain departs with this speech, which savours of Sufism : ' I have found behind this veil what my heart has sought after for years. Now I am made free. I have washed my hands of life. I have girded myself to do the will of God.' And so throughout the journey and on the field of battle, he and all those about him are continually referring to this voluntary expiation of the sins of his people ; and he dies with this thought, in meek compliance with the will of God, and will awake at the Resurrection with the intercessory power he has purchased with his blood.

" Without the introduction of this important element of self-sacrifice to idealize the character of Ḥusain, the unvarnished tale might not call forth the intense sympathy with which it is received among the Shi'a. When Ḥusain has been represented as a self-renouncing redeemer of men, and his sufferings voluntarily undergone out of love for mankind, the tragedy wears a new interest and gains a wider influence. The Persian sects have always shown a leaning towards asceticism and the renouncing of self—or what they fancied such—and this sacrifice of Ḥusain immediately appealed to their predisposition. But more than this ; the story of a life surrendered for others' sake, the sad devotedness of Ḥusain, stir a feeling that exists in every heart—a certain admiration for self-denial which the most selfish men feel—a sort of admiration for high ideals of conduct which has a corner in the most unromantic heart. It is the sorrowful resignedness, the willing yet tortured self-dedication of the martyr, that touches. One may see in it a Christian side to Islam. In the dry severity of the Arabian faith there is too little of the self-giving love which renounces all, even life itself, for the sake of others ; there is more of the stiff-necked pharasaical pride which holds up its righteous head on its assured way to the pleasures of Paradise. The death of Ḥusain, as idealized by after ages, fills up this want in Islam; it is the womanly against the masculine, the Christian as opposed to the Jewish, element that this story supplies to the religion of Muḥammad."[1]

With Muḥammad as the special mediator for the community of Islam, and with Ḥusain as the "self-renouncing redeemer," it is easy to see how the present widespread reliance on the intercession of saints and martyrs has come as an altogether natural sequence. Strange as it may seem in the light of the rigid logic of the early faith, it is no more extraordinary, perhaps, nor less natural to a highly imaginative people, than the changed attitude that came to prevail towards Muḥammad. The fact is that both of these developments are astounding to anyone who studies them in their wider significance. Muḥammad wanted to be an ordinary son of man, but later biographers have represented him as "the incarnation of Divine Light": and as Dr. Hurgronje has pointed out, "the intercession of saints has become indispensable to the community of Muḥammad, who, according to Tradition, cursed the Jews and Christians because they worshipped the shrines of their prophets. Almost every Moslem village has its patron saint; every country has its national saints; every province of human life has its own human rulers, who are intermediate between the Creator and the common mortals."[2]

While this observation is particularly applicable to the Shi'ite community of Islam, in that prophets, martyrs, saints and mystic poets are popularly considered as possible mediators or advocates with God for their friends, yet in the systematic writings of Shi'ite theologians it is noteworthy that this general belief in intercessors has been modified and restricted by the central principle that the Imams are the true guides. In the following section from the Hayátu'l-Ḳulub,[3] Majlisi makes it very clear that the true intercessors for mankind are the Imams.

[1] Stanley Lane-Poole, *Studies in a Mosque*, p. 218 ff.
[2] Hurgronje, *op. cit.*, p. 85.
[3] Majlisi, *Hayatu'l-Ḳulub*, III, ch. i, sect. 7.

Guidance and Salvation is only through the Imams.

" The Imams are the mediators between God and mankind. Except by their intercession it is impossible for men to avoid the punishment of God.

" Ibn Babuwaihi has recorded that the Imam Ṣadiḳ related, ' Our responsibility on behalf of mankind is great indeed, for if we call upon them to accept us they will not do so, and if we let them go their way they will not find other guides.' Likewise the same traditionist remarks that the Apostle of God said to Ạli, ' There are three things that I swear to be true. The first is that you and your descendants are mediators for mankind, as they will not be able to know God except through your introduction. The second is that you are to present to God those who may enter Paradise, i.e., those who recognize you and those whom you recognise. The third is that you are the absolute mediators, for those who will go to Hell will only be those who do not recognize you and whom you do not recognize.'

" It is said also that the Imam Hasan Askarí wrote a letter in which he said, ' God, by his favour and mercy, has put obligations upon you, not because of his own need of anything, but altogether out of his mercy, because there is no other God for you. God's object has been for you to be able to distinguish between good and evil, and that he should make trial of your desires, so that your purposes should be pure, that you may advance in his mercy and that your situation in Paradise may be prosperous. This is why he has required of you the ceremonial circumambulation of the Kaaba, when you wear the *ihrám* ; and has made necessary for you fixed prayers, the giving of an appointed portion to the poor, fasting, and friendship for those of the Household. This friendship is like a door before you, leading you to your duties—a door that has its key within it. For if it had not been for Muḥammad and his descendants, you would still have been helplessly scattered among the four-footed beasts and would not have comprehended any of your duties. Are you able to enter a city except through its gate? Accordingly, God has so favoured you that after the coming of your Prophet, the Imams came with authority to lead you. For on the day at Ghadir Khum God said, " This day have I perfected your religion for you, and have filled up the measure of my favours upon you, and it is my pleasure that Islam be your religion " (Surah v. 5). And the Prophet went on to explain, " I have made obligatory for you and your friends several duties. What you have is permitted to you, your wives and your property, and what you eat and drink, and that God should remember you and give you blessing bountifully, so that it will be evident who obeys God in secret." And again God has said, "Say: For this I ask no wage of you, save the love of my kin" (Surah xliii. 22). Accordingly you should understand that whoever withholds his gift really withholds something from his own soul, for the advantage would be for himself, as God is independent of your help, whereas you are poor and needy in relation to God. Therefore, after truth has been revealed to you, do what you think best. "But God will behold your work, and so will his Apostle, and the faithful" (Surah ix. 106). Your return will be to him who knows all things, whether evident or secret. He will give word concerning what you have done. A favourable end awaits those who are pious, "and praise be to God, the Lord of the Worlds" (Surah xxxvii. 182).'

"It is related also from the Imam Baḳir that the Apostle said, 'O Ạli, when the day of Judgment comes, we will sit, you and I, with Gabriel at the Sirát (the rope bridge going to Paradise), and no one will be able to pass this bridge unless he has a permit, showing that he is not deserving of Hell and that he has been friendly to you.'

"And Shaikh Ṭusi has called attention to a statement from the Imam Sadiḳ, who said, 'We are mediators between you and the Most High.' And from the Imam Ḥusain he has related that the Apostle said to the Amiru'l-Mu'minín, 'O Ạli, you and your followers are in Paradise.'

"And Shaikh Tabarsi gives the testimony of a man from Basra who came and said to the Imam Baḳir, 'Hasan al-Basri teaches that those who hide learning even the people of Hell will rebuke and torture.' The Imam answered, 'If this were the case, then the believers from the household of Pharaoh would have been destroyed, for God has said concerning them, "And a man of the family of Pharaoh who was a believer but hid his faith" (Surah xl. 29). Learning was always hidden and secret, from the day when God sent Noah as a prophet. So Hasan al-Basri has the choice to go to the right or to the left. For my part, I swear before God that learning can only be attained from the Household of the Prophet, peace be upon them.' And the Imam Baḳir went on to say, 'We have a great burden on behalf of mankind. If we call them to God they will not accept our invitation, whereas if we leave them to themselves they will have no guidance.'

"Also it is related in a credible tradition that the Imam Baḳir said, 'Through us God should be worshipped and may be known, and through us mankind may know God's unity, and that Muḥammad is the mediator of God, who intercedes with God for men.' Again it is said that he declared, 'Whoever calls upon God through our mediation is saved, and whoever calls upon

God through others is not only destroyed himself but is the means of destroying others.' "

This fundamental belief of Shi'ite Muḥammadans in the Imams as mediators is easily illustrated from the official prayers that are appointed for use when visiting their shrines. One of these prayers, which is written so as to be applicable to any or all of the Imams, and which is therefore called the *Ziarat-i-Jami'a*, or "Prayer of Visitation for All," is here quoted, with Majlisi's introductory remark[1]:

"By this prayer, which is appropriate for each and every Imam, their help may be sought, needs may be made known to them, and blessings may be solicited. When the Imam Riḍa, the eighth Imam, was asked how the pilgrim should pray at the tomb of his father, the Imam Musa, he replied: 'You must pray in the mosques which are in the neighbourhood of his tomb, and it is sufficient to use the following prayer in behalf of every Imam:

I

"Peace be to the friends of the Chosen Ones of God;
Peace be to the Trusted and Favoured of God;
Peace be to the Helpers and Representatives of God;
Peace be to the places where God has been made known;
Peace be to the places where God is remembered.

Peace be to those who have revealed God's commands;
Peace be to those who call upon God;
Peace be to those who obey what God has approved;
Peace be to the tested followers of God's will.
Peace be to those who are Proofs for God (the Imams);
Peace be upon their friends, for they are the friends of God;
As likewise their enemies are the enemies of God.
Those who have known them have surely known God;
And those ignorant of them are ignorant of God.
Those who take them by the hand, and commit themselves to them,
Have given their hands to God:
But those who abandon them have truly abandoned God.

"I bear witness before God that I am loyal to whoever is loyal to Thee, and I am ready to fight those who are not loyal to Thee.

[1] *Idem, Tuḥfatu'z-Za'irin*, p. 360 ff.

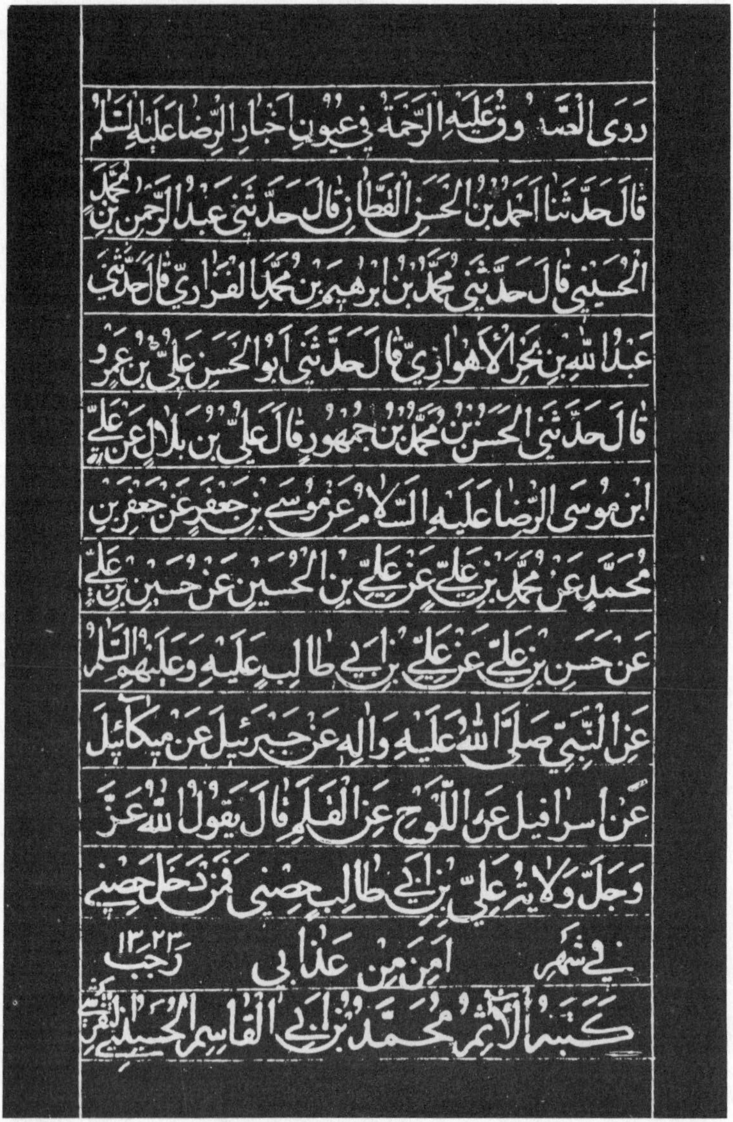
روى الصدوق عليه الرحمة في عيون اخبار الرضا عليه السلام
قال حدثنا احمد بن الحسن القطان قال حدثني عبد الرحمن بن محمد
الحسيني قال حدثني محمد بن ابرهيم بن محمد الفزاري قال حدثني
عبد الله بن بحر الاهوازي قال حدثني ابو الحسن علي بن عمرو
قال حدثني الحسن بن محمد بن جمهور قال علي بن بلال عن علي
ابن موسى الرضا عليه السلام عن موسى بن جعفر عن جعفر بن
محمد عن محمد بن علي عن علي بن الحسين عن حسين بن علي
عن حسن بن علي عن علي بن ابي طالب عليه وعليهم السلام
عن النبي صلى الله عليه وآله عن جبرئيل عن ميكائيل
عن اسرافيل عن اللوح عن القلم قال يقول الله عز
وجل ولاية علي بن ابي طالب حصني فمن دخل حصني
امن من عذابي في شهر رجب ١٣٢٣
كتبه الآثم محمد بن ابي القاسم الحسيني

"The Friendship of Ali is my Stronghold"

[*Facing p.* 347

TRANSLATION

The Friendship of Ạli is my Stronghold

Aṣ-Ṣuduḳ, mercy be upon him, has related in the Ụyuni Akhbári'r-Riḍa, unto him be peace, thāt Aḥmad ibn al-Hasan al-Ḳaṭṭán said, Abdu'r-Rahmán ibn Muḥammad al-Husainí said to me, Muḥammad ibn Ibrahim ibn Muḥammad al-Fuzárí said to me, Abdulla ibn Bakhr al-Huwárí said to me, Abu'l Ḥasan Ạli ibn Ạmr said to me, al-Ḥasan ibn Muḥammad ibn Juhúr said to me, that Ạli ibn Balál said, *on the authority of Ạli ibn Musa ar-Ri'da*, peace be upon him, from Musa ibn Ja'far, from Ja'far ibn Muḥammad, from Muḥammad ibn Ạli, from Ạli ibn al-Ḥusain, from Ḥusain ibn Ali, from Ạli ibn Abu Ṭalib, upon him and upon them be peace, *from the Prophet*, the favour of God be upon him and his family, from Jibra'íl, from Miká'il, from Isráfíl, from the Tablet (al-lauh) and Pen (al-ḳalam) (of Divine decrees), *that God the Most High said:* "The friendship of Ạli is my stronghold, and whoever enters my stronghold is safe from my punishment."

Dated in the month Rajab, 1323 A.H.

"The unrighteous Muḥammad ibn Abu'l-Ghasim al-Husainí has written it."

I have faith in Thy works that are manifest, in those also that are hidden, and in Thy purposes. I give all to Thee. May God curse all the enemies of Muḥammad, whether Men or Jinns, from the first to the last. I pray God for their destruction, but peace be upon the Prophet and his successors."

A second prayer for the use of pilgrims to the shrines of any of the Imams is attributed by Ibn Babawaihi to the Imam Ạli Naḳí. Someone asked him, " O descendant of the Prophet of God, teach me the good and perfect word, that I may repeat it whenever I visit the tomb of any of the Imams." He replied, " When you enter the court of one of these tombs, stand and say :

' I bear witness that there is no God but the one God, and he has no partner ; and I bear witness that Muḥammad, blessing be upon him and his descendants, is the servant of God and was sent by Him.' "

The Imam then added these instructions, " It is necessary that you should have bathed, and when you enter the court and see the tomb, stand and repeat thirty times, ' God is great.' Proceed, then pause and repeat again thirty times, ' God is great.' Afterwards you may go close to the tomb and repeat forty times, ' God is great,' when the one hundredth time will have been completed. Then pray as follows :

' Peace be upon thee, O ye of the Household of the Prophet, of the place of the Prophet, the place frequented by the angels, where revelation was given, where mercy was shown, where learning is kept and wisdom is complete ; the place of guidance and where forgiveness is perfect. You are the Lords of all Bounty, the Elements of all Goodness, the Pillars of Virtue, the Governors of the Servants of God, the Supporters of the Cities, the Doors of the Faith, the Trusted of God, the Progeny of the Prophets, the Choicest of Those Sent, the Descendants of the Best of God's Creation—may the mercy and blessing of God be upon you.

' Peace be upon the true Imams, upon the Lights in Darkness, upon the Manifestations of Piety, the possessors of Reason, the Masters of Sagacity, the Caves of Refuge, the Heirs of the Prophets, the Exalted Examples (from God), those who summon men to goodness, who are the Proofs of God upon the Earth, at the beginning and at the end—may the mercy and blessing of God be upon you.

'I testify that there is no God but the one God, and He has no partner. He has given witness to himself, and so have the angels and the learned of those whom he has created borne witness to Him. There is no God except the God who is mighty and wise, and I bear witness that Muḥammad is his servant, the Chosen servant, and the Apostle who has pleased Him, and whom He sent with the true Faith, that he should make it prevail over all religions (Surah xlviii. 28), notwithstanding the opposition of those who associate partners with God.

'I bear witness that you are indeed the Imams, who indicate the true way, the ones who have found Guidance, who are Sinless, the Noble, the Near to God, the Pious, the Upright, the Elect, the Obedient to God, who are firm adherents to His commands. You are those who fulfil His will, and who are saved by His goodness, for God chose to impart His learning to you, chose you to understand what is not revealed – to know His secrets; and God has appointed you to exercise His authority, and has made you victorious by His guidance. He has given you His own proof, his Light, and has helped you with His Spirit. He has designated you to be His Representatives, His Caliphs on the Earth; His Proofs for His creatures; Helpers of the Faith; Guardians of His mysteries; the Repositories of His learning; the Trusted with His wisdom; the Interpreters of His revelation; the Supporters of His unity; the Witnesses for His creation; the Standards for His servants; the Minarets for His cities; and the Proofs of His way. God has chosen to keep you from errors and rebellion. He has kept you from pollution and impurity (Surah xxxiii. 33). Therefore you have exalted God's glory and have dignified His name and praised His goodness. You have constantly thought on Him and have kept his covenant. In your obedience to Him you have received counsel in your outer and your inner lives. Thus you have summoned men to God by wisdom and good preaching (Surah xvi. 126). You have given your lives to please Him and have endured what has happened to you for His sake. You have established the Prayers and the Alms, have commanded the good and forbidden the evil, and you have conducted for God the kind of holy war that needs to be carried on.' "[1]

When the pilgrim has finished his prayers at the appointed places in the shrine of an Imam and is ready to say "Farewell," he should pray as follows:

"Peace be upon thee, the peace invoked by those who say farewell, not wishing you evil, not depreciating you, and not with

[1] *Idem, op. cit.*, p. 363.

envy: may the mercy and blessing of God be upon thee, O Household of the Prophet, for He is the Glorious and the Accepted. Peace be upon thee, the peace of the friend that does not desert thee or change His attitude towards thee; who does not try to offer anything to thee, and who does not approach thee indirectly, and who does not come reluctantly. May God not let this visit to thee be my last, this coming to the place of your martyrdom, the place of your burial. Peace be unto thee, and may God include me among your adherents and cause me to arrive at the Hauḍ-i-Kawthar (the "Pond of Abundance" in Muḥammad's Paradise), and appoint me among your followers. May *you cause God to be pleased with me and give me a place in your bounty*. Let me live at the time of your returning and have part in your government. Accept my efforts on your behalf, and may *my sins be forgiven because of your intercession*. Overlook my faults by your friendship and grant me progress by your favour. Let me attain nobility through obedience to thee, and become dear to God through your guidance. Appoint me among those whose hearts are changed and saved. Grant that I may prosper, and that forgiven and favoured, having found grace in God's goodness, having been fortunate in receiving the best of things that are attained by pilgrims who are your friends, your Shi'ah followers—grant that I may have something worthwhile to bring. May God appoint for me the opportunity to make the pilgrimage again, and the opportunity to return to eternal life by true purposes—by faith, by discipline, by humility. And may God grant that I may have daily food that is plentiful and permitted and clean.

"O God, do not decree that this is to be my last pilgrimage. But *wilt thou keep the Imams reminded of me*, and send blessing upon them, and make necessary the forgiveness of my sins. And may I enjoy that mercy and goodness and blessing—self-control, salvation, light, faith and high favour—such as Thou hast appointed for those who are their friends, those of whom Thou hast required obedience to the Imams, those who are eager to make pilgrimages to their tombs, and those who are near to thee and to them."

And then, as he prays directly for the Imams, the pilgrim becomes himself an intercessor on behalf of the several members of the Prophet's family:

"My father, my mother, my life and all that I have are dedicated to thee. Keep me in your regard and cherish me among your followers. Let me profit by your intercession and mention me before your Preserver. O God, grant Thy blessing to

Muḥammad and his Family, and cause my greeting to reach their spirits and their bodies. Peace be upon him and upon all the Imams, with God's blessing and mercy. And may the mercy of God be upon the Prophet and his Family, peace and great mercy, for surely God is enough, and what a sufficiency ! "

After giving this prayer, Majlisi adds as a personal observation that " this is the best of the general prayers of pilgrimage, both in its text and its authority, and it should be read at every feast of mourning and on every visit to a sacred tomb."[1]

It is important, however, to note that the twelve Imams are not to be regarded merely as possible mediators before God on behalf of those who trust in them, but they are considered to be the only advocates whose intercession will prove efficacious. To make this point unmistakably clear, Majlisi sets forth in a special section—

The Necessity of Recognizing the Imams [2]

" There is no excuse for abandoning the true Imams, and whoever dies without knowing the imam of his time, dies in unbelief and disobedience. Be assured that among the Shi'ites the acknowledgment of the Imam is one of the required tenets of the faith. If one denies the Imam, in the judgments that come in the end he will be declared an unbeliever. In most of the judgments on this earth, those who abandon the Imams are treated as belonging to the Muslim community, except those who are the positive enemies of the people of the Household, such as the Kharijís, who must be judged as unbelievers also on this Earth. But by some traditions it is maintained that at the time when there is no true imam in visible power, favour may be shown to those who are tolerated as Muslims, so that in association with them the Shi'ites may not have difficulty. But after the appearance of a government with true authority, and the coming of the Twelfth Imam, a judgment will certainly be pronounced upon them that they have been guilty of absolute unbelief. The belief of the majority of the Shi'ite theologians is that with the exception

[1] *Idem, op. cit.*, p. 369.
[2] *Idem, Hayatu'l-Ḳulub*, III, ch. i, p. 45 ff.

of the simple-minded among those rejecting the Imams, they shall, like other unbelievers, remain in Hell for ever.

"A few writers maintain, that after a very long time indeed, there is some hope that they may be delivered. The simple-minded include those who through weakness of reason are unable to distinguish between right and wrong. There is no proof of their responsibility. They are such unfortunates as those who have been born and brought up in the *harem* of a Sunnite king, who have not heard of differences in belief; or in case they have heard, who have had no one to show them the truth of the Imamate. For them there is hope of salvation at last. My own opinion is that except for the simple-minded there is no hope of salvation whatever for those who deny the Imams, but their lot is everlasting punishment. For both the Sunnites and the Shi'ites have a tradition that the Apostle said, 'Whoever dies and does not know the Imam of his own time, dies in the state of ignorance in which men died before the appointment of the Prophet of God,' i.e., those who died in unbelief or in ignorance of the tenets of the faith. Some of the scholars of the Sunnites say that the meaning of the expression 'imam-i-zamaniyya' is the Ḳoran, but every reasoning man knows that, while it is possible to refer this to the Book, still that is not its obvious meaning. The significance of the word *zamaniyya* (of the time) makes this evident, namely, that every time has its *imam*, whereas the Ḳoran is for all the times. Others say that the expression refers to the Apostle, but this may be answered in the same way, for no one would call an imam who died 'the imam of the time,' so evidently the true idea is that in every time there should be an imam whom men might know. With the exception of the Shi'ites, however, there are no Moslems who teach that there is an imam for every time and that no time is without its imam. . . . Kulainí and Na'maní have related traditions from Abu Basir, who said that he asked the Imam Riḍa about this verse, 'Who is more surely lost than he who follows his desires without guidance from God.' The Imam replied that the person referred to was anyone who held his faith according to his own thought, without following any of the imams sent by God. . . . Ali ibn Ibrahim and Ibn Babuwaihi and others have related on good authority from the Imam Baqir that God does not excuse, on the Judgment Day, anyone who says, 'O Preserver, I did not know that the children of Fatima were Thy representatives among mankind, and for all the Shi'ites. Then this verse was quoted (Surah xxxix. 54), 'Say: O my servants who have transgressed to your own hurt, despair not of God's mercy, for all sins doth God forgive. Gracious, merciful is He!' But the Imam's point was that the Shi'ites are those who deserve the forgiveness of their sins, not others of mankind, for the others are to remain in Hell for ever.

"Himyari has related from the Imam Riḍa that whoever desires that there should be no separation or curtain between himself and God, and trusts the mercy of God, and believes that God intends to have mercy upon him, his course of action is to love the Household of Muḥammad and not be at enmity with them, but rather to follow the imam of the time from among them. Whoever does this will always be depending on the mercy and generosity of God, and God's intention to have mercy upon him will not be thwarted. (Here several additional traditions are omitted.)

"Accordingly we see that the knowledge of God is explained as meaning the knowledge of the *imam*, for it is impossible to know God except through knowing the Imam. Otherwise men might think of God as one who would create mankind and then leave them helpless, not appointing any imam for them, and hence they would not esteem God as kind and generous. . . .

"Kulainí and Barqí and Na'maní have all related from the Imam Baqir that whoever worships God with the sort of worship that involves great exertion and bodily fatigue, but who does not believe in the righteous Imam, who by God's favour is sinless, then his worship cannot be accepted, for his efforts are not worthy in the sight of God. He is therefore but one of those who are lost and bewildered. He is like a sheep who has lost both his shepherd and his flock, and is wandering hither and yon all day. As darkness came on he thought he saw his flock and their shepherd and went and joined them for the night. But when the shepherd was ready to take them out to pasture the next morning, the sheep saw that it was not his own shepherd at all, so he again became a wanderer, seeking his own flock and his own shepherd. Then he saw another flock and wanted to join it. The shepherd of that flock called him, seeing that he was a wanderer, seeking his own flock and his own shepherd. But again he was disappointed, for it was not his shepherd, to lead him to his own pasture and to bring him to his own fold at night. He was a wanderer again, when a wolf came and found him, and took advantage of his being alone and ate him. Such is the man who wakes to find that he does not have an Imam. He finds himself a wanderer, and if he continues in this state he will die the death of an unbeliever."

The Covenant Agreement

The Imam who is spoken of as the Master of the Age (sahib al-zaman) is the Twelfth Imam, Muḥammad ibn Askarí, who is considered to have disappeared in about the year 260 A.H., but who still lives in concealment. He, therefore, is the *imam-i-zamaniyyah* (the imam of the time or age) whom all loyal Shi'ites must acknowledge. "By a trustworthy tradition from the sixth Imam, Ja'far as-Ṣadiḳ," Majlisi observes in the *Tuhfatu'z-Za'irín*, "it is said that whoever repeats the following pledge or covenant for forty mornings will be among the established companions of the Imams, and if he should die before the appearance of the Twelfth Imam, God will cause him to rise from the grave and to minister to the Imam at the time of his coming. For every word that he repeats of this creed, God will give him one thousand degrees of merit and will forgive one thousand of his sins.

"O God, Thou who art the Master of the Great Light, and the Master of the Exalted Throne, and the Preserver of the Swollen Sea (Ḳoran lii. 6), and the Sender of the Taurat and the Injil and the Zabur, and Master of the Shade and the Sun-light, Thou who art the one sending down the great Ḳoran, the Master of the Nearer Angels (i.e., Gabriel, Michael, Azrail and Israfil), and the

Master of the Prophets and of the Apostles; O God, I pray towards Thy generous face, Thy light-giving countenance, Thy Kingdom is of old, O thou Living and Eternal; I beseech Thee by Thy name, which hath enlightened the Heaven and the Earth, by Thy name which hath ordered all things at the beginning and at the end; O Thou who wert living before other life, O Thou who wilt live after all life, when there shall be no life; O Lord, Thou giver of life to the dead and who dost decree death to the living, O Thou living God, there is no God besides Thee.

"O God, bless our Master the Imam, our Guide and Leader, the one who serves Thee, peace be upon him and his pure feathers, and upon all the believers, male and female, in the East and the West, among the hills and on the plains, on the land and on the sea. For myself and on the part of my parents, I wish blessing upon the Ornament of the Throne of God, upon the Ink of His Scripture, and in the measure I estimate his Knowledge, let him see the exaltation of his Book.

"O God, I renew my covenant through the Imam this morning, and for the time my life continues, as a covenant and agreement and promise through him, and as my sacred obligation. I will not avoid it or break it. O God, keep me among his friends and companions and defenders, those to arrive quickly at his service and to meet his needs, those who carry out his commands, those who resist opposition to Thee, those who anticipate Thy will and find their opportunity for martyrdom in his behalf.

"O God, if only death stands between me and the Imam, the death that Thou hast decreed for Thy servants as inevitable, then deliver me from my grave—arrayed in my grave clothes, my sword evident, my naked lance in my hand, myself in readiness to answer the summons of my leader, in commands immediate and remote.

"O God, show me his good face, as pleasing as the new moon, that he may look upon me for the healing of my eyes and that he may hasten his coming; and do Thou facilitate his coming, and prepare his way, that his staff may guide me: and foster his rule and strengthen his arm. O God, through him restore Thy cities, and through him revive Thy servants, for Thou hast promised and Thy promise is secure. 'But corruption has appeared on the land and the sea on account of what the hands of men have wrought' (Ḳoran xxx. 41, edit. Muḥammad 'Ạli).

"And manifest to us, O God, Thy Representative, the descendant of the daughter of Thy Prophet, the namesake of Thy Apostle, that he may overthrow all that is vain and worthless and establish the truth for those who are worthy. O God, appoint him as a place of refuge for Thy oppressed servants, a helping friend to those who have no friends but Thee, that he may hasten the fulfilment of what has been neglected from the requirements of Thy word; and make him a champion of the standard of Thy faith and of the saying of Thy Prophet, may the mercy of God be upon him and his successors. And, O God, guard him within Thine own fortress from the evil of those who oppose him. And, O God, make Thy Prophet to rejoice at the sight of him and of those who obey his call. O God, be merciful to the helpless, and take away grief and sorrow from this people by granting his presence, and hasten his appearance. 'They, forsooth, regard that day as distant, but we see it nigh' (Ḳoran lxx. 6-7). So may it be, by Thy mercy, O Thou Most Merciful of all who have mercy."

CHAPTER XXXIII

THE RISE OF RELATED SECTS IN MODERN TIMES

THE doctrine of the "hidden Imam," which was first asserted by dissenting factions among the early Shi'ites, was later developed and widely preached by the Isma'ilís. Isma'il was the son of the Imam Ja'far aṣ-Ṣadiḳ who had been designated to succeed his father in the Imamate, but who, according to his opponents at least, had been deprived of his designation on account of his habit of getting intoxicated. There was a more unanswerable argument, however, in that he died before his father, and the Imam Ja'far aṣ-Ṣadiḳ therefore made a second designation in favour of Musa Kazim. But in his Shi'ah community there was a discontented element, who soon came to be known as the Isma'ilís, and who considered that the Imamate had been determined as the right of Isma'il and must therefore continue through his line; and consequently, after his death, it should fall to his son Muḥammad. There was difference of opinion among them as to whether Isma'il himself or his son Muḥammad should be regarded as the seventh and the last visible Imam. They agreed, however, that there were only seven, and for this reason they were called the "Seveners" in distinction from the "Twelvers." Afterwards they had a series of seven "concealed Imams," whom the very nature of their existence makes it impossible to place clearly in history. But the Isma'ilí books give them the names Isma'il, Muḥammad, Aḥmad, Abdulla, Aḥmad, Ḥusain, and Ạbdulla, and they are all regarded as descendants of the Imam Ja'far aṣ-Ṣadiḳ through his son Isma'il.

The Isma'ilís were also primarily responsible for the extensive development among Islamic peoples of the idea of periodic manifestations of the world intellect. They began with the great prophets, Noah, Abraham, Moses, Jesus and Muḥammad, to whom they added also Isma'il and his son Muḥammad to make a series of seven *naṭiḳ* or " speakers." The Imams, beginning with Ali and following the regular line to the sixth, the Imam Ja'far aṣ-Ṣadiḳ, could also be completed to the number of seven if they considered either Isma'il or his son Muḥammad as the seventh. The long intervals between Noah and Abraham and Moses and Jesus and Muḥammad were filled up likewise, each with its respective series of seven " speakers." Possibly the neo-Platonic doctrine of the emanation of ideas had something to do with this, though it has a striking resemblance also to the more poetic and theologically more useful conception of the " light of Muḥammad." We read, however, that " the guiding thought of the Isma'ilian sect was the self-perfection of the divine revelation through the progressive manifestation of the great world intellect."[1]

When the twelfth Imam of the orthodox Shi'ites disappeared in about 260 A.H. (A.D. 874), this doctrine of the " hidden Imam " that had been developed by the Seveners was appropriated by the Twelvers. In the subsequent history of Shi'ite Islam there was diligent study of the nature of this concealment of the "Imam of the Age." The generally accepted teaching is that there have been two periods of concealment, the first being known as the Lesser Occultation and the second as the Greater Occultation. During the first period it is considered that the Imam did not leave himself without his appointed witnesses within the Shi'ite community, for at this time (A.D. 874-941) there were four successive *wakils* or representatives. (See chapters xxi and xxiii.)

The following century saw the rise of the Buwaihids to political power and their persistent efforts to unite and strengthen the Shi'ite community—rebuilding their shrines and compiling their traditions, and giving substantial encouragement to their scholars and theologians—yet during all this century of a better general outlook for their community, the expected Imam did not appear. Another century passed, in which their Buwaihid protectors were overthrown, but the Imam continued to remain in the " Great

[1] Goldziher, *Vorlesungen*, ch. vi, 10; trans. Arin, p. 228.

Concealment." A third century passed, a century characterized by oppression, rebellion and dynasties of slaves, but the Imam they prayed for failed to come. And these were the centuries of the Crusades, in which the "people of the Household" participated, but they had no "guidance." On the side of Islam the authority to command in the Holy War was with Saracens and the heretical Fatimids as they repelled the invading armies of the nominally Christian peoples of Europe. Yet the Imam delayed his coming, and even greater calamity fell upon the peoples of Islam. For early in the fourth century after the last of the *wakils*, the thirteenth century of the Christian era, invading hordes of Mongols came down into Persia, killing and destroying with unmitigated cruelty, and yet in spite of all the ruin and suffering, the longed-for "Master of the Age" did not appear. And as late even as the beginning of the sixteenth century, at the time of the rise of the priest-kings in Adherbaijan, the new dynasty of the Safawids, the only communication with the hidden Imam was in dreams that these kings claimed to have seen.

But toward the close of the eighteenth century there arose a school of heterodox Shi'ite theologians that was known as the "Shaikhís." They were first a group of devotees who gathered around Shaikh Aḥmad Ahsai, who lived from about 1741 until 1826. Shaikh Aḥmad had come from Ahsa in the province of Bahrein, and he first attracted attention as a teacher of religion and philosophy during his residence in the pilgrimage cities of Kerbala and Najaf. There he saw the people, who were his own people, living in an atmosphere of mourning and despair, and yet they were constantly praying for the return of the Imam, "their own shepherd to lead them to their own pasture." Shaikh Aḥmad then went up on to the plateau in Persia, where, after he had visited Kermanshah and Teheran, he made his residence in Yezd. For twelve years he lived in Yezd, though during this time he made several pilgrimages to Mecca. He made a visit also to Háji Mulla Muḥammad Taḳi of Kazvin, who was at that time the outstanding champion of the sternest kind of Shi'ite orthodoxy. It was after this visit that he was officially pronounced a heretic.[1] He was then seventy-five years old and he left Kazvin to make another pilgrimage to Mecca, but when he was two or three stages from Medina, at a place called Haddé, he fell ill and died on the 28th of June, 1826.[2]

Professor Browne, in his account of the Shaikhís,[3] has shown why it was that Shaikh Aḥmad was looked upon as unsound in his teaching. " He believed that the body of man was compounded of parts derived from each of the nine heavens and the four elements; that the grosser elemental part perished irrevocably at death; and that only the more subtle celestial portion would appear at the resurrection. This subtle body he named the *huwarḳilyá* body (a name supposed to be of Greek origin), which was believed to be similar in substance to the forms in the " world of similitudes " (*alam-i-mithal*). Similarly, he denied that the Prophet's material body had, on the occasion of his night journey to heaven (mi'ráj), moved from the spot where it lay in a trance or sleep. He was much given to fasts, vigils, and austerities, and *believed himself to be under the special guidance of the Imams,* especially, as it would appear, of the Imam Ja'far aṣ-Ṣadiḳ. He regarded the Imams as creative forces, quoting in support of this view the expression, ' God, the Best of Creators ' (Ḳoran xxiii. 14), ' for,' said he, ' if God be the *best* of creators, he cannot be the sole creator.' He also adduced in support of this view the tradition wherein the following words are attributed to Ạli: ' I am the Creator of the heavens and the earth.' He even went so far as to assert that in reciting the opening chapter of the Ḳoran the worshipper should fix his thoughts on Ạli as he repeats the words, ' Thee do we worship.' "

In the *Ḳiṣaṣu'l-Ụlama* the following works of Shaikh Aḥmad are mentioned: a *Commentary on the Ziyárat-i-Jámi'a* (four volumes); *Answers to Questions*; a *Commentary on the Ạrshiyya of Mulla Ṣadrá*; a *Commentary on the Mash ir of Mulla Ṣadrá*; a *Commentary on the Tabṣira-i-Ạlláma*; and the *Fawá'id with Commentary.*

[1] *Ḳiṣaṣu'l-Ulama,* p. 20.
[2] A. L. M. Nicolas, *Essai sur le Cheikhisme,* Part I, p. 60.
[3] Browne, *Episode of the Bab,* pp. 234-244.

The second outstanding leader of the Shaikhís was Háji Sayyid Kazim, of Resht (d. A.D. 1844). His home as a boy was at Ardebil, near the venerated tomb of Shaikh Safá ud-Dín Isḥaḳ, the mystic teacher who was said to have been a descendant of the Imam Musa Kazim and who was the esteemed ancestor of the Safawid dynasty. Sayyid Kazim was only twelve years old when one night there at Ardebil he had a vision in which one of the Imams seemed to communicate to him that he should go and study with Shaikh Aḥmad Ahsai, who was then living at Yezd. He went accordingly to Yezd, where he remained as a student and close associate with Shaikh Aḥmad until his honoured teacher died, when he was himself unanimously recognized as the leader of the Shaikhí school. For the following seventeen years he continued to disseminate the Shaikhí doctrines, devoting himself mainly to writing. It was before he was fifty years old, however, that he took sick suddenly in Baghdad and died without having chosen any successor. Of his numerous writings, one hundred and twenty-three separate works are mentioned in the *Essai sur le Cheikhisme*, by A. L. M. Nicolas.[1]

The following brief outline of the teachings of the Shaikhís is based on a recent article by Cl. Huart in the *Encyclopædia of Islam*[2]:

Principal Beliefs of the Shaikhís.

They protested against the ill-considered acceptance of an immoderate number of traditions.

They regarded the twelve Imams as " the effective cause of creation, being the scene of the manifestation of the divine will, and the interpreters of God's desire. If they had not existed God would not have created anything; they are therefore the ultimate cause of creation. . . . God can only be understood through the intermediary of the Imams."

They asserted that man possesses two bodies: the first is formed of temporal elements and is like a robe that dissolves in the grave; whereas the second subsists as a subtle body that belongs to the invisible world. It is this second body which is resurrected on this Earth and then goes to Paradise or to Hell.

[1] A. L. M. Nicolas, *op. cit.*, Part II, pp. 32-36.
[2] Cl. Huart, " Shaikhís," in the *Encyclopædia of Islam*, Vol. IV, p. 279.

They maintained that knowledge is of two kinds: the first is *essential,* and has no connection with contingencies; but the second is *created,* and the Imams are the *gates* to this knowledge. They insisted that it was not possible for known things to be eternal. The term *ịlm-i-imkání,* or the "knowledge of possibility," they considered to be applicable to beings before their existence, and they applied the term *ịlm-i-akwání,* or "knowledge of beings," to all things that exist. But the command (*amr*) to exist must necessarily precede the thing created (*khalk*).

After the death of Háji Sayyid Kazim the Shaikhís were anxiously awaiting the appearance of someone to assume the leadership of the party. A number of them went together to the mosque of Kufa, where the twelfth Imam is expected by many to reappear. There they sought for guidance in the choice of their spiritual director. While they devoted themselves to fasting and to prayer that their new leader should be revealed, one of their most influential men is said to have been led to go to Shiraz in order to confer with a certain Mirza Ạli Muḥammad, whom he had previously known at Kerbala. The question as to whether Mirza Ạli Muḥammad might not be the chosen leader was in his mind. While he visited him at Shiraz he was favourably impressed by a commentary he had written on the Surah of Joseph, and after a few days' further consideration, he announced publicly that it was his personal belief that Mirza Ạli Muḥammad was indeed the *báb* or "Gate" of communication with the absent Imam. Thus the conviction of the Shaikhís, that there must be some visible form of present-day revelation from the "hidden Imam," took a very significant form.

The figure of the *báb* or "Gate" goes back to one of the oldest and most important of the traditions of the Shi'ites. It is related that the Prophet said, "I am the *city* of knowledge and Ạli is the *gate* thereof."[1] It was a matter therefore of the greatest consequence both religiously and politically, when Mirza Ạli Muḥammad was thought to have been designated as the "Gate." Those who protested against what they regarded as his intolerable presumption soon had him brought before a company of the

[1] Tirmidhi, *Saḥih* 46, 20; cf. Goldsack, *Selections from Muhammadan Traditions,* p. 15.

leading Shi'ite theologians in Tabriz, and there they questioned him as to the meaning of his pretensions. He courageously stood his ground, however, for when he was asked to explain what he meant by the term *báb*, he replied, " It is the same as in the holy tradition, ' I am the city of knowledge and Ạli is the *báb* or gate thereof.' "

The boldness of his developed doctrine may be clearly shown by a brief quotation from the Persian book of the Bábís that is called the Beyán, and which was composed by Mirza Ạli Muḥammad during his imprisonment in Mákù :

Wahid ii, ch. i.—" God commanded in his own speech, ' Whose book is the Ḳoran ? ' All believers said to Him, ' It is the book of God.' Afterwards it was asked, ' Is any difference seen between the Furḳan (i.e., the Ḳoran) and the Beyán ? ' The spiritually minded answered, ' No, by God, all is from our Lord,' ' and none are mentioned but those endowed with discernment.' Then the Lord of the World revealed, ' That Word is by the tongue of Muḥammad the Apostle of God, and this is my Word by the tongue of the Person of the Seven Letters, the Gate of God.' "

Wahid ii, ch. iv.—" For God hath assimilated refuge in himself to refuge in His Apostle, and refuge in His Apostle to refuge in His executors (i.e., the Imams), and refuge (in His executors to refuge) in the Gates (Abwab or Bábs) of His executors. . . . For refuge in the Apostle is identical with refuge in God, and refuge in the Imams is identical with refuge in the Apostle, and refuge in the Gates is identical with refuge in the Imams."

In the claims that were made by the Shaikhís for Mirza Ạli Muḥammad, we easily recognise that they were a group in the Shi'ite community that had grown tired of the ever prolonged Greater Concealment. Over nine hundred years had passed since the close of the period of the Lesser Concealment, since the death of the last *wakíl*, and in their support of Mirza Ạli Muḥammad the Shaikhís were virtually enunciating another period, when the expected Imam should be visibly represented again, but this time by a " Báb " instead of by a " Wakíl."

But as Professor Browne has pointed out,[1] not all the Shaikhís accepted the new doctrine. There was Háji Muḥammad Karim

[1] Browne, *op. cit.*, p. 241.

Khan of Kirman, with a considerable number of followers, who would not admit the pretensions of the so-called "Báb," and hence the old Shaikhí school was divided into the "New Shaikhís" and the "Bábís." The characteristic doctrine of the "New Shaikhís" was the "Fourth Support." The five "supports" or fundamentals of the orthodox Shi'ites are (1) the Unity of God, (2) the Justice of God, (3) the authority of the Prophet, (4) the Imamate, and (5) the Resurrection. The Shaikhís reduced these to three, by regarding the Justice of God and the Resurrection as being included in the authority of the Prophet. To the remaining three, therefore, they added what they called the "Fourth Support," which was "that there must always be amongst the Shi'ites some one perfect man, capable of serving as a channel of grace between the absent Imam and his people." It has been generally considered that Háji Muḥammad Karim Khan looked upon himself as the "Fourth Support," the one perfect man amongst the Shi'ites, and it appears that he was so regarded by his followers.

The other faction, however, the Bábís, made use of the fact that Mirza Ạli Muḥammad came before the public just about one thousand years after the disappearance of the twelfth Imam. According to the Shi'ite expectation, this twelfth Imam was to return as the Mahdi. That was what all of them had been waiting for, and among the numerous prognostications about his coming there was a saying that he would appear at "the end of the first millennium." Mirza Ạli Muḥammad, therefore, declared himself to be, not only the Báb or Gate, a claim which others had made before him,[1] but, with a background of marked Isma'ili influence and definite Shaikhí teaching, he went on to affirm that he was "the point of manifestation" of the spirit to the world. As Moses and Jesus and other prophets had come in the past, as manifestations of tle same spirit, so it was that he came now.

In his preaching also he was in daring opposition to the orthodox Shi'ite mullahs. He interpreted the Ḳoran largely in an allegorical

[1] *Idem, op. cit.*, p. 229, with reference to Von Kremer, *Herrschenden Ideen des Islams*, p. 209.

sense and gave little weight to its laws in regard to ceremonial purity. He found other meanings, for example, for the divine Judgment, for Paradise, for Hell, and for the Resurrection. As Dr. Goldziher has observed, he held that "the Resurrection is every new periodic manifestation of the divine spirit in relation to a preceding one. The latter comes to new life through its successor. This is the meaning of the 'meeting with God,' as the future life is designated in the Ḳoran."[1] In this same connection Dr. Goldziher has also pointed out that Mirza Ạli Muḥammad taught the brotherhood of all mankind; that he was desirous of raising women from their low position to a state of equality with man; that he undertook to set forth a nobler conception of marriage, based on the function of the family; and that he sought a general reform of education. His disposition to give attention to combinations of letters according to their numerical values, attaching particular importance to the number *nineteen*, was neither original nor surprising, but rather in keeping with a common tendency among Persian writers. As the new "Báb," after a thousand years of the complete concealment of the Imam, he did not teach that the channel of revelation would be closed again at his death, but that the same divine spirit would continue to be manifested.

In so much as the official religion of Persia was orthodox Shi'ite Islam, the claims of the "Báb" were regarded as dangerous. Mirza Muḥammad Ạli and his followers were consequently persecuted and proscribed, until finally, in A.D.1850, he himself was put to death. Those of his followers who managed to escape took refuge in Adrianople, where they were under the protection of the Turkish Sultan. There it was that Baha-Ullah declared himself to be the "more perfect manifestation" that was proclaimed by his master, and through which the master's work was to be raised to a higher level.

At this point, however, another division occurred, for a group of the Bábís followed one of the Báb's disciples who was known as *Subb-i-Ezal* (Dawn of Eternity), who established his head-

[1] Goldziher, *Vorlesungen*, ch. vi, sect. 10.

quarters in Fumagista, Cyprus, and who proposed to carry on the work of the Báb in the form given to it by his master.

The more influential group were the followers of Baha Ullah (" Splendour of God "), who was born in 1817, and died of fever in 1892. In 1844, when Mirza Ạli Muḥammad first announced his mission, Baha Ullah was but twenty-seven years of age. He is said to have accepted the doctrine of the Bábís before he met the Báb, but he soon became one of the outstanding disciples and was recognized by the majority as their master's successor. He taught that the Báb was the *ḳa'im*, " the one who rises," and that he himself was the *ḳayyum*, " the permanent one." In the course of his teaching the designation he preferred for himself was the *mazhar* or *manzar*, the " revelation " of God, in which he said the beauty of God was to be seen as in a mirror. He was himself " the beauty of Allah," whose face shines between the heavens and the Earth as a precious, polished pearl. Through him alone, he said, the *being* of God can be known, whose *emanation* he is. In 1852, as one of his followers attempted to take the life of Nasiru'd-Ḍín Shah, Baha Ullah was exiled to Baghdad. He went afterwards with a company of his followers to Constantinople, then to Adrianople, and finally to Akka, where he lived and carried on his work from 1868 until his death. In Akka he worked out a system of doctrine which was radically different from that of the followers of the Ḳoran, and that was also not restricted to the beliefs of those who accepted the Beyan. The principal one of his written works was called the *Kitab-i-Aḳdas* or " The Most Holy Book," and for this book he claimed divine origin. The translations of the Bible that were beginning to be circulated at the time in Muḥammadan lands were commonly designated as the " Holy Scripture," the *Kitáb-i-Muḳaddas*.

Baha Ullah sought to evolve from Islam and from the Beyan and from the special revelations he claimed to receive " a larger conception of a world religion which was to unite mankind in a religious brotherhood." In his political teachings he professed cosmopolitanism, and he held that no preference should be given to him who loves his country, but rather to him who loves the world. In this sense he regarded himself as the manifestation of the world spirit to all mankind and sent epistles to rulers of Europe and Asia, and "to the Kings of America and the Chiefs of the Republic." In his letter to Napoleon III, he predicted the empire's downfall four years before Sedan. With a world mission in view, he commanded his followers to prepare themselves, by the study of foreign languages, for the mission of apostles to the world.

As has been suggested, in his teaching the ethical and social factors were emphasized. War was strictly forbidden, and the use of weapons was allowed only "in case of need." Slavery was also forbidden, and the equality of all men was taught as the nucleus of his new gospel. As to marriage, he regarded monogamy as the ideal, but he permitted bigamy. He recognized divorce and allowed remarriage, on the condition that the separated parties had not married again, which is exactly opposite to the provision in the law of Islam. But the *shari'at* ("Law") of Islam he regarded as completely superseded, and he introduced also new forms for prayer and ritual. Bodily cleanliness he ordained as a religious duty and condemned the continued toleration of unclean bathing places. He recognized no professional spiritual rank, and claimed that those who were true religious teachers should work without compensation. Civil law, he said, was necessary on the ground that man must be guarded from his own barbarity.

That Baha Ullah was indeed a man of keen judgment and receptive to higher ideals of social ethics is obvious, and as has been pointed out, some of his principles are admittedly an echo of Christianity. But in his fundamental positions it must be remembered that he professed to be leading a system of faith and thought that had its origin in the expectation of the return of the Shi'ite Twelfth Imam. However much may have been included by his eclectic method in the further development of his doctrines, his authority depended on the pretensions of the Báb, who found his opportunity in the restlessness of the Shaikhís for the return of the Imam. But in so much as the established Shi'ite religion of Persia did not allow individual freedom of conscience, or even freedom for the discussion of religious subjects, Baha Ullah was compelled to spend his life agitating his reforms from outside the bounds of his native country.

Abbas Effendi, the son of Baha Ullah, was called *Abd al-Baha* (the slave of Baha) and also *Ghuṣn Azam* (the great branch), and he succeeded in carrying the views of his father to a still more comprehensive development. He was born in 1841 and died in 1921, and by the modifications he also introduced, the teachings of his father are made to conform still more nearly in some respects to the intellectual thought of the Occident. He made a wide use also of the books of the Old and the New Testaments. Considerable publicity was given to the whole movement by the fact that a certain Dr. Khayrullah, who was one of the ardent admirers and followers of Abbas Effendi, made a tour of the United States in 1912 to lecture in his behalf. Professor Browne's book, *The Bábí Religion,*[1] shows the letter that Dr. Khayrullah persuaded a number of Americans to write to the "Great Branch," and also contains a translation of the shorthand notes that were taken of the lectures.

"According to a Bahai statement, Abd al-Baha (or Abbas Effendi) had covenanted in his will that after his passing there would be a continued and perpetual centre of guidance for the Cause, a Guardian, the office to be hereditary. . . . Abd al-Baha appointed his eldest grandson, Shogli Effendi, to be the first of this line of Guardians. Shogli Effendi descends on his mother's side from Baha Ullah through Abd al-Baha, and on his father's side from a collateral branch of the family of the Báb."[2] The pamphlet by Mr. Remey, from which the above statement is quoted, contains also a translation of the supposed will of Abbas Effendi, and it is not without interest to observe how similar the discussion of the right of succession of the various Bahai leaders is to the old question of the designation of the successive Imams.

It will be evident to any careful student of Islam in Persia

[1] Browne, *The Babi Religion,* pp. 119-141.

[2] Remey, *A Series of Twelve Articles Introductory to the Study of the Bahai Teachings.*

that the teachings of the Shaikhís and the Bábís, the Ezelís and the Bahais have all had their origin in the long Shi'ite expectation of the return of the Twelfth Imam. The efforts put forth by these several sects, one after another, have been movements of groups that were not contented to go on giving their formal testimony to the Imams of the past. Especially in their closer contact with modern civilization, eager and inquiring minds in Persia have been anxiously seeking to find for themselves and their people some vital, present-day knowledge of God. But notwithstanding, the great bulk of the population are still looking to the golden domes over the tombs of the Imams and frequently repeat the following creed or testimony as a summary of their officially adopted hope and faith:

"I testify, O my Leader, in thy presence, that there is no God but God; that He is One and has no partner. And I testify that Muḥammad was his Servant and Apostle, and that Muḥammad was the only worthy 'friend' of God. I testify also that Ạli was the Commander of the Faithful, the Manifestation of God; and that Ḥasan was God's Manifestation; and that Ḥusain was God's Manifestation; and that Ạli the son of Ḥusain was God's Manifestation; and that Muḥammad, the son of Ali, was God's Manifestation; and that Ja'far, the son of Muḥammad, was God's Manifestation; and that Musa, the son of Ja'far, was God's Manifestation; and that Ạli, the son of Musa, was God's Manifestation; and that Muḥammad, the son of Ạli, was God's Manifestation; and that Ạli, the son of Muḥammad, was God's Manifestation; and that Hasan, the son of Ạli, was God's Manifestation. And above all I witness that thou (O hidden Imam, the Master of the Age), art a Manifestation of God."[1]

[1] Majlisi, *Tuḥfatu'z-Za'irin*, p. 235.

CLASSIFIED BIBLIOGRAPHY

I. ARABIC SOURCES AND TRANSLATIONS

(*a*) Ḳoran and Commentaries

Fluegel, G., *Coranus arabice*, Leipzig, 1834, and reprinted.

— *Concordantiæ Corani Arabicæ*, Leipzig, 1842.

Sale, G., *The Koran*, with a " Preliminary Discourse," London, 1734, and frequently reprinted.

Kasimirski, M., *Le Koran*, Paris, 1840.

Rodwell, J. M., *The Koran*, London and Hertford, 1861.

Palmer, E. H., *The Qur'an*, Oxford, 1900.

Noeldeke, T., *Geschichte des Qorans*, Leipzig, 1909–19. *Cf.* " Koran," Ency. Brit., 11th ed.

Maulvi Muhammad Ali, " *The Holy Qur-an*," Arabic text with English translation and commentary, 2nd ed., 1920.

Baidawi (1286), *Anwar al-tanzil wa-asrar al-ta'wíl*, ed. Fleischer, 1846–48.

Tabari, Abu Ja'far (922), *Tafsir*, 30 vols., Cairo, 1901.

Zamakhshari (1143), *Kashshaf*, Boulaḳ, 1864.

Razi, Fakru'd-Din (1209), *Al-Tafsír al-Kabir*, 8 vols., Cairo, 1890.

Ṭabarsi, Fazl b. Hasan (1138), Majma'u'l-Ụlùmi'l-Ḳoran, 10 vols. (of special importance for Shi'ite exegesis).

(*b*) Historians

Ibn Kutaiba (889), *Uyunu'l-Akhbár*, 4 vols., Cairo, 1925–1930.

Baladhuri (892), *Kitábu Futúḥi'l-Buldán*, ed. de Goeje, Leyden, 1866.

Dinawari, Abu Hanifa (895), *Kitáb al-Akhbar al-Ṭiwál*, Book of Long Histories, ed. Kratchkovsky and Guirgass, 1912.

Al-Ya'Ḳubi, Ibn Wadhih (about 900), *Historiæ*, ed. Houtsma, Leyden, 1883.

Tabari, Abu Ja'far (922), *Tarikhu'l-Rusul wa'-Muluk*, " Annals of the Apostles and the Kings," ed. de Goeje, 15 vols., 1879–1901.

MAS'UDI, ALI B. HUSAIN (956), *Murúju'l-Dhahab* (Prairies d'Or), ed. Barbier de Meynard, 9 vols., 1861 ; and *Kitabu'l-Tanbíh wa'l-Ishráf* (" Book of Admonition and Rescension ") ed. de Goeje, Leyden, 1894.

BIRUNI (1048), *Chronology of Ancient Nations*, edited and translated in English by M. Sachau, London, 1879.

IBNU'L-ATHIR (1234), *Kitábu'l-Kámil fi'l-Taríkh,*" The Perfect Book of Chronicles," 14 vols., Leyden, 1851–1876.

IBNU'L-TIKTAKA, *Al-Fakhri* (written 1302), ed. Ahlwardt, Gotha, 1860.

IBN KHALDUN (1406), *Muḳaddima*, Arabic text and French translation in " Notices et Extraits," Vols. XVI–XXI.

MAKRIZI (1442), *Itti'áz al-Ḥunafá' bi-Akhbár al-A'imma wa'l-Khulafá*, ed. Hugo Bunz, Leipzig, 1909.

AS-SUYUTI (1505), *History of the Caliphs*, trans. Jarrett, Calcutta, 1881.

(*c*) COLLECTIONS OF TRADITIONS

(1)—*Sunnite*

MALIK IBN ANAS (795), *al-Muwaṭṭa'*, " The Smoothed Path," printed with al-Żurḳání's commentary, 4 vols., Cairo, 1862.

ṬAYALISI (819), *Musnad*, 1 vol., Haidarabad, 1321 (1903).

WAKIDI (822), *Kitáb al-Magházi*, trans. by J. Wellhausen, " Muhammad in Medina," Berlin, 1882, 1 vol.

IBN HISHAM (883), *Sira*, ed. by Weil, Gottingen, 1860.

IBN SA'D (844), *Ṭabaḳát*, ed. Sachau, Leyden, 1904–1908.

IBN HANBAL, AHMAD (855), *Musnad*, 6 vols., Cairo, 1895.

AL-DARIMI (869), *Musnad*, lithographed on margin of *al-Muntaḳá min Akhbár al-Muṣṭafá* (by Ibn Taimiya), Dihli, 1919.

AL-BUKHARI (870), *Sahíh*, ed. Krehl and Juynbool, Leyden, 1862–1868 and 1907–1908.

MUSLIM (874), *Sahíh*, 2 vols., Bulaḳ, 1873.

IBN MADJA (886), *Sunan*, 1 vol., Lucknow, 1897 ; 2 vols., Cairo, 1895.

ABU DA'UD (888), *Sunan*, 2 vols., Cairo, 1875.

TIRMIDHI (892), *Sahíh*, 2 vols., Cairo, 1875.

NASA'I (915), *Sunan*, 2 vols., Cairo, 1894.

RIFA'I, *Asru'l-Ma'mun*, 3 vols., Cairo, 1928.

(2)—*Shi'ite*

ZAID IBN 'ALI (712), *Majmú' al-Fikh*, ed. by E. Griffini," Corpus Juris di Zaid ibn Ali," 1 vol., Milano, 1919.

KULAINI, MUHAMMAD IBN. YA'KUB (939), *Kafi fi Ilm ad-Dín*, "A Compendium of the Science of Religion," lithographed, 2 vols., Teheran, 1889.

IBN BABAWAIHI, AL-KUMMI or AS-SADUK (991), *Man lá yahdurul-Fakíh*, "Every man his own lawyer," lithographed in Persia, 1908; and *Kamál ad-Dín* (The Perfection of Religion), lith. in Teheran, 1883; *Uyunu'l-Akhbari'r-Rida* (Sources of the Traditions of ar-Rida), lith. in Persia, 1858.

AT-TUSI, MUHAMMAD B. HASAN (1076), *Tahdhíb al-Akhám*, "Correcting of Judgments," lithographed in Persia, 1899; *Istibsár*, "Examination of the Differences in Traditions," lith. in Lucknow.

MAS'UDI, ALI B. AL-HUSAIN (956), *Ithbát al-Waṣíya i-Ali b. Abi Talib*, 1 vol. Teh., 1902.

SAYYID RAZI, ABU'L-HASAN MUHAMMAD B. MUSA (1073), *Nahju'l-Balágha*, The Open Road of Eloquence (containing discourses attributed to Ali), lithographed in Meshed, 1892.

MAJLISI, MUHAMMAD BAKIR (1699)—*Bihár al-Anwár*, "Oceans of Lights," lithographed in Persia, 24 vols.

AMILI, MUHAMMAD B. MUHAMMAD, *Ithna Ashariyya*, The Sect of the Twelve Imams, written in Meshed, 1657, and lith. in Teheran, not dated.

NAJMU'D-DIN JA'FAR, MUHAKKIK-I-AWWAL (1860), *Sharáyiu'l-Islam*, ed. Abdu'l-Ibrahim, 1882. Cf. translation by A. Querry, *Droit musulman recueil de lois concernant les musulmans Schyites*, 2 vols., Paris, 1871.

SHAIKH MUHAMMAD JA'FAR, *Urjatu'l-Ahmadiyya*, 1907.

(*d*) GEOGRAPHERS AND TRAVELLERS

IBN ROSTEH (9th cent.), *Kitáb al-A'lák an-Nafísa*, ed. de Goeje, "Bib. Geog. Arab.", Vol. VII, 2nd ed., Leyden, 1892.

YA'KUBI (9th cent.), *Kitábu'l-Buldán*, ed. de Goeje, "Bib. Geog. Arab.", Vol. VII, Leyden, 1892.

YAKUT (1229), *Mu'jam al-Buldán*, ed. Wustenfeld, 6 vols., Leipzig, 1866. Cf. trans. by C. Barbier de Meynard. (Paris, 1861), *Dictionnaire geographique, historique et litteraire de la Perse et des Countrees adjacentes.*

IBN JUBAYR (1217), *Travels*, Wright's text, ed. de Goeje. "Gibb Memorial" series, Vol. V., 1907.

(*e*) Biography and Bibliography

Al-Nadim, Muhammad b. Ishaq (995), *Kitáb al-Fihrist,* "Index." ed. G. Fluegel, 1871–2.

Al-Tusi, Muhammad b. Hasan (1067), *Fihrist,* "Index" of Shi'ite writers and their books. Bibliotheca Indica, Calcutta, 1853.

Yaqut (1229), *Dictionary of Learned Men*, ed. by D. S. Margoliouth "Gibb Memorial" series, Vol. VI, in 7 parts, 1910-1925.

Ibn Khallikan (1282), *Biographical Dictionary*, trans. de Slane, 4 vols., 1842–71. Arabic text, Bulak, 1284 A.H.

Al-Khawnsari, *Rawḍátu'l-Jannát* (written 1869–70), lithographed in Teheran, 1888.

(*f*) Comparative Religion

Al-Baghdadi, Abu Mansur (d. shortly after 1037), *Kitáb al-farḳ baina'l-Firáḳ*, Cairo, 1910.

Ibn-Hazm (d. 1064), "The Heterodoxies of the Shi'ites," trans. by Friedlander, with copious notes, J.A.O.S., Vol. XXIX.

Al-Ghazzali (1111), *Iḫya Ulum ad-Dín,* "Revivication of the Religious Sciences," edited and translated by M. L. Gautier; also printed in Cairo, 4 vols., 1289 A.H.

Shahrastani (1153), *Kitábu'l-Milál wa'l-Niḥál,* "The Book of Religions and Sects," ed. Cureton, 1846, and reprinted in 1923. *Cf.* German trans. Haarbrucher, Halle, 1850.

Allama-i-Hilli (1326), *Al-Rábu'l-Ḥádí Ạshar,* "A Treatise on the Principles of Shi'ite Theology," trans. by William McE. Miller, 1928. "Oriental Translation Fund," Vol. XIX; *Minhāj al-Karāma fī Ma'rifat al-Imāma*, a treatise on the nature of the Imamate, Teheran (1880); *Kashf al-Ya ḳīn fī Fadā'l Amiru'l-Mu'minīn,* which treats of the virtues of Ạli b. Abu Talib, Teheran, 1880.

II. PERSIAN BOOKS AND TRANSLATIONS

(*a*) The Ḳoran.—Persian Versions and Commentaries

Basiru'l-Mulk prepared the best Persian translation of the Ḳoran that is available. It was lithographed in Teheran in 1896, has the Arabic and Persian texts on opposite pages, and has also a Kashfu'l-Ayát, or Concordance.

KAJURANI, HAJI MUHAMMAD HUSAIN, has published the Ḳoran with a Persian interlinear translation, and with a Concordance. It was lithographed in Teheran in 1923.

MULLA FATHULLA, KASHANI (1579), *Tafsíru-l-Kabír, Musamma bi Munhaju'l-Ṣádiḳin,* " The Great Commentary, called the Plain Path of the Truthful," written in 1574, lithographed in Persia, 3 vols., 1892.

(*b*) MEMOIRS OF THE IMAMS IN PERSIAN

MULLA FATHULLA (1579), wrote a Persian translation of al-Razi's *Nahju'l-Balaghat* (Speeches of Ạli the Fourth Caliph and the First Imam), Teheran, 1858.

MIRKHOND, MUHAMMAD B. KHAVENSHAH (1498), *Rauzatu's-Safa,* trans. Rehatsek, Part I, Vols. I and II, Oriental Translation Fund, 1891.

SHAIKH-I-BAHA'I (1622), *Jami'-i-Ạbbasi,* lithographed in Teheran, 1910. A translation of selected traditions bearing on the Muhammadan law.

MAJLISI, MULLA MUHAMMAD BAKIR (1699), *Tadhkiratu'l-A'imma,* Memoirs of the Imams, lithographed in Persia, 1913.

JA'FAR SHARIF, *Ḳanún-i-Islám,* trans. Herklots, 1832.

MULLA NORUZ ALI, *Tufatu'r-Riḍáwiyah,* The Gift through the Imam Riḍa, lithographed in Persia, 1871.

SAYYID MUHAMMAD MAHDI, *Khulasatu'l-Akhbár,* lithographed in Kerbala, 1879.

HAJI MIRZA AKASI, *Aḳáidu'sh-Shi'a,* Beliefs of the Shi'a, lithographed in Meshed, 1879.

MUDARIS, MULLA MUHAMMAD RIDA IMAMI, *Jannatu'l-Khulud,* " Perpetual Gardens," written in 1713, is a tabular Index to the lives of the Prophets and the Imams. Lithographed in Teheran, 1841.

(*c*) SHI' TE APOLOGETICS, PRAYERS AND PILGRIMAGES

HUSAIN WA'IZ-I-KASHIFI (1504), *Rauḍatu'l-Shuhadá,* or Garden of Martyrs, lithographed in Lahore, 1870.

MAJLISI, MULLA MUHAMMAD BAKIR (1699), *Mishkatu'l-Anwár,* " The Niche for Lights," lithographed in Tabriz, 1863.

— *Zadu'l-Ma'ád,* " Provision for the Hereafter," a manual for prayer and fasting, lith. Bombay.

— *Tuḥfatu'z-Zá'irín,* " The Pilgrims' Present," Teheran, 1857.

— *Hilyatu'l-Muttaḳín*, "The Ornament of the Pious," lith. in Persia, 1859.

— *Haḳḳu'l-Yaḳín*, "Certain Truth," compiled 1698, printed in Teheran, 1825.

— *Hayátu'l-Qulúb*, "Life of Hearts," 3 vols. (Prophets, Muhammad, the Imamate), lith. in Persia, 1909, 1906, and 1867 respectively. *Cf.* translation of Vol. II by James L. Merrick, *The Life and Religion of Muhammad*, Boston, 1850.

Burujurdi, Ali Asghar (time of Násiru'd-Din Shah, d. 1896), *Núru'l-Anwár*, "The Light of Lights," lith. in Persia, 1910.

Mazandarani, Agha Muhammad Sahih, *Maṭárihu'l-Anzár*, "Places for Regard," lith. Bombay, 1870.

Rahmatullah (time of Muzaffaru'd-Din Shah), *Miftáh al-Jannán*, "The Key to Paradise," lith. in Teheran, 1920.

(*d*) History, Geography and Travel

Nizamu'l-mulk (1092), *Siyásat Namah*, ed. C. Schafer, Ecole des langues orientale vivantes, Sirie 3, Vol. VII.

Al-Rawandi, *Ráhatu's-Sudur*, composed 1203 A.D., Persian text, ed. Muhammad Iqbal, "Gibb Memorial Series," 1921.

Hamdulla Mustawfi Kazvini, *Nuzhatu'l-Qulúb* (1340), ed. and trans. by G. le Strange, "Gibb Memorial Series," Vol. XXIII, 1, 2 (1915 and 1919).

Phillott, D. C., *Memoirs of Shah Tahmasp*, Bib. Indica, No. 1319.

Nasir-i-Khusraw, *Safar Namah*, Paris, 1881.

Mirza Muhsin Kashmiri, *Dabistan al-Mazahib*, "School of Sects," Bombay, 1875. *Cf.* translation by Shea and Troyer, London, 1843.

Sharif'd-Din Ali Yezdi, *Zafar Namah*, or A History of Timur, 2 vols., Calcutta, 1887–88.

Muhammad Hasan Khan, *Matla'u'sh-Shems*, "The Rising Place of the Sun," 3 vols., lith. in Teheran, 1885.

Muhammad Taki Khan, Hakim, *Ganj-i-Dánish*, A Treasure of Learning, lith. in Teheran, 1887.

Fursat Shirazi, *Athάru'l-Ajam*, Ancient Remains in Persia, lith. in Bombay, 1896.

(*e*) Biography and Bibliography

Faridu'l-Din 'Attar (1230 a.d.), *Tadhkiratu'l-Awliya*, "Memoirs of the Saints," ed. Nicholson, London, 1907.

Dawlatshah (1495), *Tadhkiratu'sh-Shu'ara*, "Memoirs of the Poets," ed. E. G. Browne, London, 1901.

Shushtari, Sayyid Nurulla al-Marashi (1611), *Majálisu'l-Mu'minín*, "Assemblies of Believers," compiled 1582, lith. in Persia, 1866.

Tanukabuni, Muhammad b. Sulaiman, *Qisasu'l-'Ulama*, "Stories of the Doctors," written 1873, lith. in Persia, 1890, along with the *Tabṣiratu'l-Awam* by Sayyid Murtaḍa.

Abdu'l-Aziz, Jawahiru'l-Kalam, *Atharu'l-Shiati'l-Imamiyya*, The (Literary) Remains of the Imami Shi'ites (planned in 20 parts), Part IV, biographical, having been printed in Teheran, 1929.

Asadi, Mirza Muhammad Wali Khan, Mutawalli Bashi, *Fihrist-i-Kutub-i-Kitáb Khanahyi Mubarak-i-Asitán-i-ḳudsi Raḍawi*, Catalogue of the Blessed Library of the Holy Shrine of the Imam Riḍa (at Meshed), printed in Meshed in 3 vols., 1927.

(*f*) Comparative Religion

Sayyid Murtada, The Alamu'l-Huda (1044), *Tabsiratu'l-Awam*, "Consideration of the Common People," lith. in Persia along with the Qisasu'l-'Ulama, 1890.

Muhammad Taki Mustawfi, Kashani (1879), *Násikhu'l-Tawáríkh*, "The Abrogator of Histories," in 13 vols., lith. in Teheran, 1888 to 1897. The first vol. of this work is representative of current Shi'ite beliefs about other religions.

III. ENGLISH, AMERICAN AND EUROPEAN AUTHORITIES

(*a*) Muhammad and the Ḳoran

Weil, W. G., *Das Leben Mohammed's*, translated from Ibn Hisham, 2 vols., Stuttgart, 1864.

Wellhausen, J., *Muhammad in Medina*, selected and translated from Wákidí, Berlin, 1882.

Koelle, *Muhammad and Muhammadanism*, 1889.

MARGOLIOUTH, D. S., *Mohammed and the Rise of Islam*, "Heroes of the Nations" series, London and New York, 1905.

MUIR, SIR W., *Life of Mahomet*, Edinburgh, 1923.

SYED AMEER ALI, *The Spirit of Islam*, London, 1922.

STANTON, H. W., *The Teaching of the Koran*, London, 1920.

BLAIR, Rev. JOHN C., *The Sources of Islam*, Madras, 1925.

BELL, R., *The Origin of Islam in its Christian Environment*, London, 1926.

(*b*) ISLAMIC HISTORY AND CIVILIZATION

WELLHAUSEN, JULIUS, *Die religioes-politischen Oppositions partien im alten Islam*, Berlin, 1901.

WEIL, G., *Geschichte der Chalifen*, 3 vols., Mannheim, 1846–61.

PELLY, SIR LEWIS, *The Miracle Play of Hasan and Husain*, 2 vols., London, 1879.

MUIR, SIR W., *The Caliphate, its Rise, Decline, and Fall*, 2nd ed., London, 1924.

G. VON VLOTEN, *Zur Abbasiden Geschichte*, ZDMG., lii.

GOLDZIHER, I., *Muhammedanische Studien*, 2 vols., Halle, 1888–90.

MULER, AUGUST, *Der Islam in Morgenland und Abendland*, 2 vols., Berlin, 1885–87.

MALCOLM, SIR JOHN, *History of Persia*, 2 vols., London, 1829.

CAUSSIN DE PERCEVAL, *Essai sur l'histoire des Arabes avant l'Islamisme*, 3 vols., Paris, 1847–48.

NOLDEKE, TH., *Geschichte der Perser und Araber zur Zeit der Sassaniden*, trans. from the Annals of Tabari, Leyden, 1879.

SMITH, W. R., *Kinship and Marriage in Early Arabia*, 2nd ed., London, 1903.

ARNOLD, T. W., *The Caliphate*, Oxford, 1924.

GIBB, H. A. R., *Arabic Literature: An Introduction*, London, 1926.

NICHOLSON, R. A., *A Literary History of the Arabs*, 2nd ed., 1930.

BROWNE, E. G., *A Literary History of Persia*, 4 vols., London, 1908–1924.

ARNOLD, T. W., *The Preaching of Islam*, 2nd ed., London, 1913.

HUART, C., *Histoire des Arabes*, 2 vols., Paris, 1912.

LANE-POOLE, STANLEY, *The Muhammadan Dynasties*, 2nd ed., 1925.

LANE, E. W., *Arabian Society in the Middle Ages*, London, 1883.

LE STRANGE, G., *Baghdad during the Abbasid Caliphate*, Cambridge, 1905.

— *Palestine under the Moslems*, London, 1890.

MARGOLIOUTH, D. S., *Umayyads and Abbasids*, being a trans. of Part IV of Zaydan's *History of Islamic Civilization*, Gibb Memorial series, Vol. IV.

BUKHSH, S. KHUDA, *Contributions to the History of Islamic Civilizations*, translated from A. von Kremer's *Culturgeschichtliche Streifzuge auf dem Gebiete des Islams*, Calcutta, 1905 and 1929.

HOWARTH, *History of the Mongols*, particularly Vols. III and IV, London, 1888 and 1927.

SYKES, GENERAL SIR PERCY, *History of Persia*, 2 vols., London, 1915.

GUYARD, M. STANISLAS, *Un Grand Maitre des Assassins au temps de Saladin*, in the Journal Asiatique, Paris, 1877.

GILMAN, *The Saracens*, in the "Story of the Nations" series, New York, 1896.

FINLAY, GEORGE, *History of the Byzantine Empire*, "Everyman's Library," ed. 1913.

LANE, E. W., *Manners and Customs of the Modern Egyptians*, ed. "Everyman's Library."

LAMMENS, H., *Fátima et les filles de Mahomet*, Rome, 1912.

PALMER. E. H., *Haroun al-Raschid, Caliph of Baghdad*, London, 1881.

BLOCHET, E., *La Conquète des Etats Nestoriens de l'Asie centrale par les Schi'ites et les Influences Chretienne et Bouddhique dans le dogme Islamique*, Paris, 1926.

(c) TRADITIONS, BELIEFS AND LEGAL SYSTEMS

BAILLIE, *A Digest of Muhammadan Law*, 2 vols., London, 1869; particularly the second volume, "Imameea."

GARCIN DE TASSY, *L'Islamisme*, Paris, 1874.

BROWNE, E. G., *A Traveller's Narrative written to illustrate the Episode of the Bab*, Cambridge, 1891.

— *Materials for the Study of the Babi Religion*, London, 1918.

CANON SELL, *Faith of Islam*, 2nd ed., London, 1896.

BLOCHET, E., *Le Messianisme dans l'Heterodoxie Musulmane*, Paris, 1903.

DE BOER, T. J., *The History of Philosophy in Islam*, trans. by E. R. Jones, London, 1903.

GOLDZIHER, I., *Das Prinzip der Taḳiya im Islam*, ZDMG., lx, 1906.

NICOLAS, A. L. M., *Essai sur le Cheikhisme*, Paris, 1910.

MACDONALD, D. B., *The Religious Attitude and Life in Islam*, Chicago, 1909.

— *Development of Muslim Theology, Jurisprudence, and Constitutional Theory*, New York, edition, 1926.

NICHOLSON, R. A., *The Mystics of Islam*, London, 1914.

— *Studies in Islamic Mysticism*, Cambridge, 1921.

HURGRONJE, C. SNOUCK, *Muhammedanism*, American lectures, 1916.

GOLDZIHER, I., *Vorlesungen uber den Islam*, 2nd ed. 1925, and French trans., *Le dogme et la loi de l'Islam*, by F. Arin, 1920.

CANON SELL, *Ithna Ạshariyya*, or The Twelve Shi'ah Imams, Madras, 1923.

GOLDSACK, WILLIAM, *Selections from Muhammadan Traditions: translated from the Arabic*, Madras, 1923.

GUILLAUME, W., *The Traditions of Islam*, Oxford, 1924.

WENSINCK, A. J., *A Handbook of Early Muhammadan Tradition*, Leyden, 1927.

LAMMENS, H., *L'Islam, croyances et institutions*, 1926; English translation by E. Denison Ross, London, 1929.

(*d*) GEOGRAPHERS AND TRAVELLERS

HERZFELD, E., *Samarra. Aufnahmen und Untersuchungen zur Islamischen Archæologie*, Berlin, 1907.

NOLDEKE, A., *Das Heiligtum al-Husains zu Kerbalá*, Berlin, 1909.

DOUGHTY, C. M., *Travels in Arabia Deserta*, 2 vols., Cambrdge, 1888, new ed., 1921.

FRASER, JAMES B., *Journey into Khorasan*, London, 1825.

SYKES, GENERAL SIR PERCY, *The Glory of the Shi'ah World*, London, 1910.

LE STRANGE, G., *The Lands of the Eastern Caliphate*, Cambridge, 1905.

BURTON, SIR R. F., *Personal Narrative of a Pilgrimage to al-Medinah and Meccah*, 2 vols., London, Memorial ed., 1893.

RUTTER, ELDON, *The Holy Cities of Arabia*, London, 1928.

LE STRANGE, G., *Don Juan of Persia, a Shi'ah Catholic*, London, 1926.

IBN BATTUTA, *Travels in Asia and Africa*, 1325–1354, translated and selected by H. A. R. Gibb, London, 1929.

CLAVIJO, *Embassy to Tamerlane*, 1403–1406, translated from the Spanish by Le Strange, London, 1928.

HAKLUYT, *The Principal Voyages of the English Nation*, edition "Everyman's Library."

MARCO POLO, *Travels*, ed. "Everyman's Library," 1921.

CHARDIN, SIR JOHN, *Travels in Persia*, Argonaut Press, 1927.

(*e*) WORKS OF GENERAL REFERENCE

HUGHES, T. B., *A Dictionary of Islam*, London, 1885.

BROCKELMANN, CARL, *Geschichte der Arabischen Litteratur*, 2 vols., Weimar, 1898–1902.

HUART, CLEMENT, *Litterature Arabe*, 4th ed., Paris, 1923; and English trans., *A History of Arabic Literature*, London, 1903.

PHANMULLER, *Handbuch de Islam Literatur*, Leipzig, 1923.

LANE, E. W., *Arabic-English Lexicon*, London, 1863–93.

WORTABET and PORTER, *Arabic-English Dictionary*, 3rd ed., Beyrout, 1913.

ZWEMER, SAMUEL M., editor, *The Moslem World*, New York, 1911—

MASSIGNON, *Annuaire du monde Musulman*, Paris, 1923—

The Encyclopædia Britannica, Cambridge, 11th ed. with supplementary, Volumes XXX–XXXII, 1922.

The Encyclopædia of Religion and Ethics, edited by J. Hastings, Edinburgh, 1908–1921, especially useful with Index volume, 1926.

The Encyclopædia of Islam, Leyden, 1913—

(*f*) COMPARATIVE RELIGION

VON KREMER, A., *Geschichte de herrschenden Ideen des Islams*, Leipzig, 1868.

GOLDZIHER, I., *Beitrage sur literatur gezchechte der Shi'a und der sunnitichen Polemik,* Academie der Wissenschaften, 1874.

FRIEDLANDER, *Abdullah b. Saba, Der Begrunder der Shi'a und sein judischer Ursprung,* Leipzig, 1909.

MUIR, SIR WILLIAM, *The Apology of Al-Kindy, written at the court of al-Mamún,* London, 1882.

NOLDEKE, *Zur Ausbreitung der Schiitismus,* in "Der Islam," 1923.

SHAIKH MUHAMMAD IQBAL, *The Development of Metaphysics in Persia,* London, 1908.

ALI TABARI, *The Book of Religion and Empire,* trans. by A. Mingana from MS. 631 in the John Rylands Library, London, 1922. The defence dates from the Caliphate of al-Muttawakil, 847–861 A.D.

GUILLAUME, *A Debate between Christian and Moslem Doctors,* J.R.A.S., Centenary Supplement, 1924.

HARTMANN, RICHARD, *Die Wahhábiten,* ZDNG., lxxviii, 1924.

ZWEMER, S. M., *The Moslem Christ,* London, 1912.

BELL, RICHARD, *The Origin of Islam in its Christian Environment,* London, 1926.

ALTER, S. NEALE, *Studies in Bahaism,* Beirut, 1923.

MILLER, WM. MCE., *Bahaism, its Origin, History, Teachings,* New York, 1931.

MOORE, GEORGE FOOTE, *History of Religions,* 2 vols., New York, 1926.

ANDRAE, T., *Mohammed. Sein Leben u. s. Glaube,* 1932.

WENSINCK, A. J., *The Muslim Creed,* Cambridge, 1932.

INDEX